Love, Reason, and Will

Love, Reason, and Will

Kierkegaard After Frankfurt

Edited by
Anthony Rudd and John Davenport

Bloomsbury Academic
An imprint of Bloomsbury Publishing Inc

B L O O M S B U R Y
NEW YORK • LONDON • OXFORD • NEW DELHI • SYDNEY

Bloomsbury Academic

An imprint of Bloomsbury Publishing Inc

1385 Broadway	50 Bedford Square
New York	London
NY 10018	WC1B 3DP
USA	UK

www.bloomsbury.com

BLOOMSBURY and the Diana logo are trademarks of Bloomsbury Publishing Plc

First published 2015

ISBN: HB: 978-1-6289-2732-0
PB: 978-1-6289-2731-3
ePub: 978-1-6289-2734-4
ePDF: 978-1-6289-2735-1

Library of Congress Cataloging-in-Publication Data
Love, reason, and will : Kierkegaard after Frankfurt /
edited by John Davenport and Anthony Rudd.
pages cm
Includes bibliographical references and index.
ISBN 978-1-62892-732-0 (hardback : alk. paper) – ISBN 978-1-62892-731-3
(pbk. : alk. paper) 1. Love. 2. Kierkegaard, Søren, 1813-1855. 3. Frankfurt,
Harry G., 1929- I. Davenport, John J., 1966- joint editor.
BD436.L73 2015
198'.9–dc23
2015007121

Typeset by Integra Software Services Pvt. Ltd.
Printed and bound in the United States of America

For Jeanine and Robin, again.

Contents

Preface

This volume had its origin in a conference on Kierkegaard and Frankfurt on love hosted by the Hong Kierkegaard Library at St. Olaf College in the summer of 2007. This conference was organized by Myron Penner and Søren Landkildhaus, who went on to assemble a collection of essays developed from some of the conference presentations, with further additions from other scholars. The result was the first version of the present collection in 2010, which benefited enormously from Søren's and Myron's editorial efforts to help contributors to hone and refine their essays. When life circumstances, including ministry and civic work, compelled Myron and Søren to focus on other projects, we agreed to take over editing this volume in 2013, and have worked to develop it further. But this book would not exist without Søren's and Myron's inspiration; they correctly perceived how fruitful a dialogue between Frankfurtian and Kierkegaardian themes could be on topics related to love and caring, and we have sought to stay true to their vision. Moreover, we would like to emphasize that we developed the Introduction to this book from Myron's initial draft. There is much of their loving efforts in this work, and we are all indebted to them.

This collection also follows, and to some extent builds on, provocative recent works on love in Kierkegaard and contemporary thinkers by Jamie Ferreira, Sharon Krishek, Sylvia Walsh, John Lippitt, and others. Literature on Kierkegaard and love continues to flourish, and we hope this collection will prompt further work on agapic love and other forms of interpersonal love. While many of the chapters in this book offer clear reasons for favoring Kierkegaard's conception of love, we have striven to give Frankfurt his full due, in the interests of provoking a helpful conversation; and we are certain that more scholarship informed both by Kierkegaard and Frankfurt on types of love will be forthcoming in the near future. May the conversation continue!

Acknowledgments

This volume consists almost entirely of new work. However, we gratefully acknowledge permission from Cambridge University Press to reprint small portions of John Lippitt's *Kierkegaard and the Problem of Self-Love* (2013), mainly from Chapter 6, in his chapter for the present book. We also thank Oxford University Press for permission to reprint small portions of Anthony Rudd's *Self, Value and Narrative: a Kierkegaardian Account* (2012) in his chapter for the present book. And we thank the editors of *Essays in Philosophy* for allowing Alan Soble to reprint small portions of his review of Frankfurt's *Reasons of Love* in his chapter herein. We would like to thank other contributors to this book for their encouragement in helping us complete the work begun by Myron and Søren (as described in the Preface), and for their patience with the many stages the project has gone through. We are indebted to anonymous referees from two presses who helped us all refine our work and ensure balance in the collection, to Haaris Naqvi, our editor at Bloomsbury, and to Rajakumari Ganessin, project manager. Fordham University generously provided a graduate assistant, John Gregor MacDougall, to help with the notes, bibliography, and indexing; he has rendered invaluable assistance.

Abbreviations for Parenthetical Citations

Harry G. Frankfurt

Two collections by Frankfurt (IWCA and NVL) contain most of Frankfurt's separate essays, but parenthetical citations will use sigla for the individual essays. Unless specifically noted, and with the *exception* of "On Bullshit" (which does appear in IWCA), all references to Frankfurt's essays are to the widely cited versions appearing in these two collections, rather than to the original versions appearing in journals or other edited collections. The sigla for the entire volumes of Frankfurt's essay collections are used only to refer to their prefaces or to these collections as a whole.

ANL   "Autonomy, Necessity, and Love," in *Necessity, Volition, and Love*: 129–41.

DL   "Duty and Love," *Philosophical Explorations* 1, no. 1 (1998), 4–9.

EIZ   "Een intellectueel zelfportret" [An intellectual self-portrait]. In *Vrijheid, noodzaak en liefde*, edited by Katrien Schaubroek and Thomas Nys, Kapellen: Pelckmans, 2011, 17–30.

FP   "The Faintest Passion," in *Necessity, Volition, and Love*: 95–107.

FW   "Freedom of the Will and the Concept of a Person," in *The Importance of What We Care About*: 11–25.

IE   "Identification and Externality," in *The Importance of What We Care About*: 58–68.

IWC   "The Importance of What We Care About," in *The Importance of What We Care About*: 80–94.

IW   "Identification and Wholeheartedness," in *The Importance of What We Care About*: 159–76.

IWCA *The Importance of What We Care About*, New York: Cambridge University Press, 1988.

OB   *On Bullshit*, Princeton: Princeton University Press, 2005.

OC   "On Caring," in *Necessity, Volition, and Love*: 155–80.

OT   *On Truth*, New York: Alfred A. Knopf, 2006.

NI   "The Necessity of Ideals," in *Necessity, Volition, and Love*: 108–16.

NVL   *Necessity, Volition, and Love*, New York: Cambridge University Press, 1999.

RL   *The Reasons of Love*, Princeton: Princeton University Press, 2004.

RU   "Rationality and the Unthinkable," in *The Importance of What We Care About*: 177–90.

TOS   *Taking Ourselves Seriously—Getting It Right*, Stanford: Stanford University Press, 2006.

Kierkegaard in English Translation

This book will use sigla designed for the *International Kierkegaard Commentary* by Robert L. Perkins, which are now the scholarly standard. Robert Perkins has very kindly allowed us to reproduce them for this book. Citations to other translations will be given in chapter endnotes.

AN   "Armed Neutrality." See *Point of View*.

BA   *The Book on Adler*, trans. Howard V. Hong and Edna H. Hong. Princeton: Princeton University Press, 1995.

C   *The Crisis and a Crisis in the Life of an Actress*. See *Christian Discourses*.

CA   *The Concept of Anxiety*, trans. Reidar Thomte in collaboration with Albert B. Anderson. Princeton: Princeton University Press, 1980.

CD   *Christian Discourses* and *The Crisis and a Crisis in the Life of an Actress*, trans. Howard V. Hong and Edna H. Hong. Princeton, NJ: Princeton University Press, 1997.

CI   *The Concept of Irony* together with "Notes on Schelling's Berlin Lectures," trans. Howard V. Hong and Edna H. Hong. Princeton: Princeton University Press, 1989.

COR   *The Corsair Affair*, trans. Howard V. Hong and Edna H. Hong. Princeton: Princeton University Press, 1982.

CUP   *Concluding Unscientific Postscript to "Philosophical Fragments,"* two vols. trans. Howard V. Hong and Edna H. Hong. Princeton: Princeton University Press, 1992.

EO, 1   *Either/Or*, volume I, trans. Howard V. Hong and Edna H. Hong. Princeton: Princeton University Press, 1987.

EO, 2   *Either/Or*, volume II, trans. Howard V. Hong and Edna H. Hong. Princeton: Princeton University Press, 1987.

EPW   *Early Polemical Writings*, trans. Julia Watkin. Princeton: Princeton University Press, 1990.

EUD   *Eighteen Upbuilding Discourses*, trans. Howard V. Hong and Edna H. Hong. Princeton: Princeton University Press, 1990.

FPOSL   *From the Papers of One Still Living*. See *Early Polemical Writings*.

FSE   *For Self-Examination* [and] *Judge for Yourself!*, trans. Howard V. Hong and Edna H Hong. Princeton: Princeton University Press, 1990.

FT   *Fear and Trembling* and *Repetition*, trans. Howard V. Hong and Edna H. Hong.

R   Princeton: Princeton University Press, 1983.

JC   *Johannes Climacus* or *"De omnibus dubitandum est,"* See *Philosophical Fragments*.

JFY   *Judge for Yourself!* See *For Self-Examination*.

JP   *Søren Kierkegaard's Journals and Papers*, ed. and trans. Howard V. Hong and Edna H. Hong, assisted by Gregor Malantschuk. Bloomington and London: Indiana University Press, Vol.1, 1967; Vol.2, 1970; Vols.3 and 4, 1975; Vols.5–7, 1978.

LD   *Letters and Documents*, trans. Hendrik Rosenmeier. Princeton: Princeton University Press, 1978.

NA   "Newspaper Articles, 1854–1855." See *The Moment*.

NSBL   "Notes on Schelling's Berlin Lectures." See *The Concept of Irony*.

OMWA   *On My Work as an Author*. See *The Point of View*.

P   *Prefaces* and "Writing Sampler," trans. Todd W. Nichol. Princeton: Princeton University Press, 1998.

PC   *Practice in Christianity*, trans. Howard V. Hong and Edna H. Hong. Princeton: Princeton University Press, 1991.

PF   *Philosophical Fragments* and "Johannes Climacus," trans. Howard V. Hong and Edna H. Hong. Princeton: Princeton University Press, 1985.

PV   "*The Point of View for My Work as an Author,*" including "The
          Single Individual," *On My Work as an Author* and "Armed
          Neutrality," trans. Howard V. Hong and Edna H. Hong.
          Princeton: Princeton University Press, 1998.

R   *Repetition.* See *Fear and Trembling.*

SLW   *Stages on Life's Way*, trans. Howard V. Hong and Edna H. Hong.
          Princeton: Princeton University Press, 1988.

SUD   *The Sickness unto Death*, trans. Howard V. Hong and Edna Hong.
          Princeton: Princeton University Press, 1980.

TA   *Two Ages: the Age of Revolution and the Present Age. A Literary
          Review*, trans. Howard V. Hong and Edna H. Hong. Princeton:
          Princeton University Press, 1978.

TDIO   *Three Discourses on Imagined Occasions*, trans. Howard V. Hong
          and Edna H. Hong. Princeton: Princeton University Press,
          1993.

TM   "*The Moment*" *and Late Writings*, trans. Howard V. Hong
          and Edna H. Hong. Princeton: Princeton University Press,
          1998.

TSI   "The Single Individual," see *The Point of View.*

UDVS   *Upbuilding Discourses in Various Spirits*, trans. Howard V. Hong
          and Edna H. Hong. Princeton: Princeton University Press,
          1993.

WA   *Without Authority*, trans. Howard V. Hong and Edna H. Hong.
          Princeton: Princeton University Press, 1997.

WL   *Works of Love*, trans. Howard V. Hong and Edna H. Hong.
          Princeton: Princeton University Press, 1995.

WS   "Writing Sampler." See *Prefaces.*

Kierkegaard in Danish

SKP   *Søren Kierkegaards Papirer*, second enlarged edition by Niels
          Thulstrup, with index vols. 14–16 by Niels Jørgen Cappelørn.
          Copenhagen: Gyldendal, 1968–78.

The following abbreviations are used for the *Søren Kierkegaards Skrifter* (Copenhagen: Gads) series:

SKS 1   *Af en endnu Levendes Papirer, Om Begrebet Ironi*, edited by Niels Jørgen Cappelørn, Joakim Garff, Johnny Kondrup and Finn Hauberg Mortensen, 1997.

SKS 2   *Enten-Eller, Første del*, edited by Niels Jørgen Cappelørn, Joakim Garff, Johnny Kondrup and Finn Hauberg Mortensen, 1997.

SKS 3   *Enten-Eller, Første del*, edited by Niels Jørgen Cappelørn, Joakim Garff, Johnny Kondrup and Finn Hauberg Mortensen, 1997.

SKS 4   *Gjentagelsen, Frygt og Bæven, Philosophiske Smuler, Begrebet Angest, Forord*, edited by Niels Jørgen Cappelørn, Joakim Garff, Johnny Kondrup and Finn Hauberg Mortensen, 1997.

SKS K4   *Kommentar til Søren Kierkegaards Skrifter Bind 4*, edited by Niels Jørgen Cappelørn, Joakim Garff, Johnny Kondrup and Finn Hauberg Mortensen, 1997.

SKS 5   *Opbyggelige taler, 1843–44, Tre Taler ved tænkte Leiligheder* edited by Niels Jørgen Cappelørn, Joakim Garff, Jette Knudsen, Johnny Kondrup and Finn Hauberg Mortensen, 1998.

SKS 6   *Stadier paa Livets Vei* edited by Niels Jørgen Cappelørn, Joakim Garff, Jette Knudsen, Johnny Kondrup and Finn Hauberg Mortensen, 1999.

SKS 7   *Afsluttende uvidenskabelig Efterskrift* edited by Niels Jørgen Cappelørn, Joakim Garff, Jette Knudsen and Johnny Kondrup, 2002.

SKS 8   *En literair Anmeldelse og Opbyggelige Taler i forskjellig Aand* edited by Niels Jørgen Cappelørn, Joakim Garff and Johnny Kondrup, 2004.

SKS 9   *Kjærlighedens Gjerninger* edited by Niels Jørgen Cappelørn, Joakim Garff and Johnny Kondrup, 2004.

SKS 10   *Christlige Taler* edited by Niels Jørgen Cappelørn, Joakim Garff and Johnny Kondrup, 2004.

SKS 11   *Lilien paa Marken og Fuglen under Himlen, Tvende ethisk religieuse Smaa Afhandlinger, Sygdommen til Døden og "Ypperstepræsten"—"Tolderen"—"Synderinden"* edited by Niels Jørgen Cappelørn, Joakim Garff, Anne Mette Hansen and Johnny Kondrup, 2006.

SKS 12   *Indøvelse i Christendom, En opbyggelig Tale og To Taler ved
Altergangen om Fredagen,* edited by Niels Jørgen Cappelørn,
Joakim Garff, Anne Mette Hansen and Johnny Kondrup, 2008.

SKS 13   *Dagbladsartikler 1834–48; Om min Forfatter-Virksomhed; Til
Selvprøvelse,* edited by Niels Jørgen Cappelørn, Joakim Garff,
Johnny Kondrup, Tonny Aagaard Olesen and Steen Tullberg,
2009.

Introduction

John Davenport and Anthony Rudd, with Myron Penner

This is an integrated set of philosophical essays about love: they address ways in which our identities are shaped by what we love; the extent to which our loves are or are not under our control; how love relates to reason and to volition; and whether love is a response to the value of its objects or whether it is love that endows its objects with value (or both). The collection is also an attempt to bring two philosophers—Søren Kierkegaard and Harry Frankfurt—into conversation. Some may find these two unlikely conversation partners. But Frankfurt himself has said, "Philosophers need to pay more attention to issues belonging to a domain that is partially occupied by certain types of religious thought – issues having to do with what people are to care about, with their commitments to ideals, and with the protean role in our lives of the various modes of love" (NVL, x).[1] Kierkegaard is certainly one of the modern religious writers who has thought most deeply and insightfully about these questions concerning love. We are convinced that to compare and contrast his ideas on love, caring, values, and identity with Frankfurt's more secular approach will not only shed light on both of these philosophers but also enable us to think better ourselves about these fundamental issues.

Love was, for much of the twentieth century, a topic that was ignored or marginalized in mainstream Anglo-American philosophy—or treated in rather shallow ways that were then taken for granted or not critically examined.[2] Over the past few decades, this has changed dramatically. Frankfurt played a central role in turning philosophy back to the examination of the nature of love, along with others such as Iris Murdoch, Stanley Cavell, Charles Taylor, Jeffrey Blustein, Gabrielle Taylor, Martha Nussbaum, Alan Soble, Irving Singer, and Jonathan Lear (most of whom refer directly to Frankfurt's work).[3] We are in the midst of a new era of productive scholarship on forms of human love and the importance of love-relationships in ethics, in which Frankfurt's recent work is the most widely known contribution.

Frankfurt's papers since his seminal "Freedom of the Will and the Concept of a Person" have developed an influential line of thought connecting the themes of personhood, responsibility, autonomy, practical identity, the importance and limitations of volition, and the centrality of love and care to our lives. Frankfurt elegantly synthesized the conclusions of these developments in his book *The Reasons of Love*, which argues that our most autonomous motives are wholehearted states of caring about persons, ideals, or causes for their own sake, especially when these cares are so central to our identity that they become volitionally necessary to us. Frankfurt also famously argues that such cares need not be based on (and normally are not responsive to) judgments of objective value, merit, or worthiness in the person or other object of one's devoted attention or commitment. Instead, in his considered view, caring *bestows* personal value on what we care about, giving it significance for us. Similarly, two people can see value in the same traits or qualities of another person without both loving him or her for these traits.

While Frankfurt was developing these ideas, Søren Kierkegaard's multifaceted thoughts about the nature of persons, freedom, and the efforts necessary to become an authentic self were being interpreted and reconstructed in a wave of new scholarship since the 1980s, bringing his pseudonymous and signed works out of merely historical scholarship into wide and lively consideration across several domains in the humanities today. This is not a coincidence. As our present outlook alters, so our understanding of past ideas and themes changes; the emergence of new ideas and proposals allows us to see aspects of past thinkers that had previously been occluded. (As J.L. Borges once noted, "every writer creates his own precursors"[4]; to use Borges' own example, once Kafka had written, we could see "Kafkaesque" themes in previous writers, enabling us to understand those earlier writers in a different and richer way.) Kierkegaard has often been, and occasionally still is, read as an irrationalist, a fideist, a proto-Sartrean existentialist, someone who urged "leaps of faith" made by sheer willpower in defiance of reason and morality alike. This was always a caricature, but the recent philosophical work of Frankfurt and others has helped us—and others like us, educated in the mainstream Anglophone tradition—to see just how central the themes of love and its relation to value, reason, and self are in Kierkegaard's work, and how rich, careful, and subtle his treatment of them is. In particular, Kierkegaard's thoughts on love and personal devotion have much to offer contemporary debates about the relations between love and intrinsic value.

Beyond its recognized contributions to continental philosophy, this renaissance in Kierkegaard studies has often brought to light significant points of contact with recent work in analytic moral psychology and ethics, to which Frankfurt's thought remains central. So, there is much to be gained by bringing Kierkegaard and Frankfurt more directly into conversation.

For Kierkegaard anticipated many of the insights of the recent philosophers mentioned above—and especially some of Frankfurt's central ideas—about the importance of self-choice, the need to balance active choosing or self-shaping with self-acceptance and practical limits, and the central role of volition and love in our lives. For this reason, several recent interpreters of Kierkegaard, starting with Edward Mooney, have sought to bring themes in his work back into contemporary debates by comparing them with ideas in Frankfurt and other analytic thinkers such as Alasdair MacIntyre.[5] But Kierkegaard also develops his ideas about love, care, and identity in the context of a strong moral realism, which Frankfurt explicitly rejects, and within an ultimately religious outlook, while religion is a marginal (though not entirely absent) theme in Frankfurt's writings.[6]

Thus, a conversation between Kierkegaard and Frankfurt promises to be fruitful, for it offers an opportunity to explore, analyze, and re-evaluate critical Kierkegaardian ideas about agency, identity, and love in relation to the most influential and widely discussed contemporary account. Our hope is that to put Kierkegaard in a Frankfurtian context will bring into clearer focus several central themes in his thought and demonstrate their ongoing relevance to our lives. Likewise, to put Frankfurt into a Kierkegaardian context will bring a challenging new perspective to bear on some of his claims about love and identity—and more widely, on central conceptual problems about autonomy and agency being debated anew in contemporary moral psychology.

The primary purpose of the essays in this book is, therefore, not exegetical but substantively philosophical, though we hope they will enliven both Kierkegaard and Frankfurt scholarship as well. Each essay addresses some facet of Kierkegaard's and/or Frankfurt's accounts of how love and reason enable us to live well and forge a meaningful life. Some defend Frankfurt's approach to love by drawing on Kierkegaard's Pascalian view that "reasons of the heart" may be truer or more important from the practical standpoint of engaged agency than objective reasons as they appear from a speculative standpoint detached from loving interest or passionate commitment. But other essays argue that Frankfurt's conception of volitional love, and self-love in particular, needs to be revised to take proper account of Kierkegaard's view that the "subjective appropriation" of possible goals as personal ends must respond to the value or worth that is already present in persons and goods outside the agent in order to acquire the authority that is lacking in merely wanton or aesthetic motives. Indeed, in some of these analyses, Frankfurt's own concept of personally authoritative motives provides a basis for defending more Kierkegaardian conclusions.

The essays are grouped into three thematic sections, the first of which explores the problem of whether love is responsive to values as grounds for love or not. The second section considers whether or how some forms of self-love may play a positive role in a good life. The third focuses on how we constitute our identities through relating to both ourselves and to others—and on how love, will, and reason are involved in these relations. Many of the themes in the first section reappear in the third, but we think the sequence chosen here will provide clear lines of development through the discussions of self-love in the second section.

While this collection is not a dichotomous debate between partisans of Kierkegaard on the one side and of Frankfurt on the other, some essays are more explicitly Kierkegaardian in their approach and conclusions while others are more Frankfurtian; some essays engage with epistemological and/or metaphysical issues in the works of Frankfurt and Kierkegaard, while others focus on ethical issues and practical identity. Some compare the different overall projects of the two thinkers while others deal with major specific themes related to love, such as their accounts of "wholeheartedness," "volitional necessity," "double-mindedness," or "aestheticism." But despite these differences, all the essays address key questions about the nature of love and related conditions of authentic caring. Many of them, in different ways, argue that Frankfurt's approach to love could be significantly enriched and deepened by incorporating Kierkegaardian ideas about the good as the *telos* of volition, while others argue that perhaps Kierkegaard's conception of neighbor-love could be further nuanced by linking it with Frankfurt's analysis of loving devotion to particular others (such as children or friends).

I. Overview of the Essays and Main Themes

The essays in the first section of this collection take up the question of the ground of volitional love in Frankfurt and Kierkegaard. While the analyses of Kierkegaard and Frankfurt in this section differ in their philosophical methods and perspectives, they all explore the question of whether Kierkegaard's concern for religious transcendence offers a necessary supplement to Frankfurt's thought—especially when it comes to agapic or neighbor-love.

Charles Taliaferro opens the conversation by arguing against Frankfurt that love does not create reasons for valuing in the various cases that Frankfurt addresses. Taliaferro draws on a broadly Christian Platonist construal of love—influenced not only by Kierkegaard but also by the seventeenth-century Cambridge Platonists—to show that on a Christian view, a person has reasons to love others because others have value or are precious, even if the person has no prior desire or inclination to love them.

In the following essay, Alan Soble notes that for Frankfurt love is the ground of our value judgments, rather than being one of the possible and appropriate responses to values that are grounded in some other way. However, and in sharp contrast to Taliaferro, Soble also maintains (following Nygren) that Kierkegaard too portrayed love as the bestower of value rather than as a response to it. But despite what he sees as this substantive agreement between Kierkegaard and Frankfurt, Soble also sees sharp differences between other aspects of their respective accounts of love. He argues that Frankfurt does not adequately defend the four main necessary conditions that he proposes for love, which are also in tension with one another and probably inconsistent with the evolutionary biology that Frankfurt employs in his latest work to support his account of love. Soble also examines the development of Frankfurt's account of caring and love, arguing that the problems inherent in his initial conception in "The Importance of What We Care About" are not solved in *The Reasons of Love*. In particular, Soble points out that Frankfurt's idea that we should love what we are "able to love" (given the value of loving-as-such) conflicts with agapic duties because it will effectively mean loving those objects or potential beloveds that are easier to love. As a result, Frankfurt ends up granting Plato's view that *loving* does not determine what we love: for what makes some X an X that we are able to love (love-able) is something distinct from the fact of our loving it.

Troy Jollimore takes up a position somewhat between Kierkegaard and Frankfurt on the relation of love to values. Further developing the critique of Frankfurt's "extreme will" view of caring and love, he argues for a moderate view according to which personal loves respond to inherent values in human persons, though they also depend on willed cares and emotional responses that distinguish some potential objects of our love from others. Although Frankfurt holds that any love that responds to valuable properties in its formal object makes the beloved fungible, Jollimore argues that loving someone as a distinct individual involves openness to his or her concerns and affects, and a willingness to seek out his or her particular valuable and lovable qualities. Following Velleman, he notes that the sustained attention to a loved person such as one's child enables one to perceive values in his or her activities that would not be accessible to strangers. Like several defenders of Kierkegaard in this book, he argues that loves could not be as central as they are to life-meaning if we thought that they were arbitrary, responding to no objective values in the beloved.

Concluding this section, John Davenport argues for conclusions similar to Jollimore's but from a different direction, based on some of Frankfurt's older work. After outlining several aspects of existential authenticity, he considers Frankfurt's best-selling essay on the phenomenon of "bullshit,"

comparing it with Frankfurt's own earlier analysis of wantonness and with
Kierkegaard's accounts of aestheticism and other aspects of inauthentic
living. He supports claims made by some recent commentators, beginning
with Edward Mooney, that Frankfurt's concept of "caring" resembles the
process of self-articulation in which an "ethical" self is formed according
to Kierkegaard's pseudonymous author Judge William in *Either/Or* vol.
II, except that Kierkegaard's Judge conceives cares as responding to goods
with eternal validity. Moreover, the deficiencies that Frankfurt finds in
"bs" are anticipated in Kierkegaard's critique of "the present age" for its
lack of heroic passion, and Heidegger's related critique of "idle talk." Thus,
Davenport attempts to show that Frankfurt's and Kierkegaard's analyses of
inauthenticity are similar in key respects; but this comparison reinforces the
need to recognize objective values worth caring about in a plausible account
of existential authenticity and authentic love. Contrary to Soble, then,
Davenport argues that for Kierkegaard, earnest caring must first respond to
value that it discovers rather than bestows on the "object" of love.

The essays in the second section deal with questions about self-love,
including its legitimacy and its relation to other-oriented forms of loving.
In her essay (Chapter 5), Sylvia Walsh looks back to Kant's view of self-love
in *Foundations of the Metaphysics of Morals*, interpreting both Kierkegaard
and Frankfurt as responding to Kant. Walsh uses Kierkegaard's account of
self-love, redoubling, and self-denial in *Works of Love* to defend Kant against
Frankfurt's naturalistic view of self-love. She argues that it is not Kant's
conception of self-love that is "out of focus" but Frankfurt's, inasmuch as (1)
he does not take the problem of selfishness in self-love seriously enough; (2)
the sort of naturalistic redoubling or identification of the self with the other
that he advocates is analogous to the "intoxicated self-esteem" of erotic love
and friendship that Kierkegaard contrasts with a Christian redoubling of the
self in the neighbor; and (3) that Frankfurt lacks a concept of self-denial,
however "disinterested" and "selfless" his view of love may seem to be.

John Lippitt's essay emphasizes the importance of Kierkegaard's
distinction between true or genuine self-love and deficient (selfish) forms of
self-concern, a distinction we also find in Frankfurt. Lippitt's essay is, in part,
a critical response to Walsh's paper and argues for a more positive assessment
of Frankfurt's account of self-love. Although he agrees that Frankfurt's
account of love deserves some criticisms, Lippitt argues that Frankfurt does
bring to light some key points that can help us to understand Kierkegaard's
view of what proper self-love involves. Some key themes that emerge from
this discussion are that love entails commitment, which in turn entails some
kind of appropriate self-relation; that proper self-love necessarily points
outside the self; and that love can involve self-interest without being based

upon it in a "merely selfish" way. Lippitt criticizes accounts such as Walsh's for overstressing the theme of self-denial. While recognizing that this is important for Kierkegaard, Lippitt calls attention to texts by Kierkegaard that significantly qualify the emphasis on self-denial. He points out the relevance of Kierkegaard's discussions of trust and hope for understanding how one may lovingly hope for and trust in oneself; and he notes Kierkegaard's insistence on the importance of accepting that one's sins are forgiven, and the self-forgiveness consequent upon this. In this light, proper self-love must include appropriately qualified self-forgiveness (sometimes even when the other whom we offended has not forgiven us).

Marilyn G. Piety also seeks to bring Kant into the conversation between Kierkegaard and Frankfurt. She notes that Frankfurt and Kierkegaard each argue that there is a genuine and proper form of self-love, but that it is relatively rare. Examining Frankfurt's claim that "[w]e are moved more naturally to love ourselves ... than we are moved to love other things" (RL, 81), Piety suggests that Kierkegaard's use of theological categories, such as sin and faith, enables him to explain the rarity of genuine self-love without the latent contradictions in Frankfurt's naturalistic account. She argues further that Kierkegaard's account offers a solution to the problem posed by Kant in *Religion within the Limits of Reason Alone* of how we should motivate ourselves to conform our wills to the demands of the moral law, given our obvious inability to achieve the perfection that the law demands.

The essays in the final section are concerned with the nature of the self: how we are shaped by what we love, and the extent to which this process of self-shaping is one over which we either do or should exercise a volitional control. Annemarie van Stee's chapter considers how our selves are constituted by the relations in which we stand to what we care about and love. She compares Kierkegaard's and Frankfurt's views on the self, looking first at how they characterize the self-constituting relations that the self enters into; and second at how they describe the objects of love to which we should self-constitutingly relate. Third, she examines the overall aims that Frankfurt and Kierkegaard have with their views of the self which account for the differences between them. Drawing mainly on *Sickness unto Death*, Van Stee argues that Kierkegaard does not sufficiently value self-constituting relations to people and pursuits in their concrete particularity; he is too worried that loving other human persons can lead to spiritual despair. We should look to Frankfurt on the value of personal loves in self-constitution. On the other hand, she argues against Frankfurt's strong view of self-constituting relations as volitionally necessary identifications. Against this conception of volitional necessity, Kierkegaard offers a better perspective on the interplay between affect, volition, and consciousness. His ideas provide a basis for conceptualizing selves as constituted by, yet retaining a measure of independence from, their beloved people and pursuits.

M. Jamie Ferreira is similarly concerned with the relation between love and the will; she argues that the idiom of "volition" so prevalent in Frankfurt's *The Reasons of Love* sits uncomfortably with some of Frankfurt's own best insights about love. After briefly touching on the notion of integrity of will found in *The Reasons of Love*, the remainder of her essay deals with Frankfurt's claim there that love is "volitional." Ferreira argues that this claim is unclear, and that it is important to disambiguate it. She goes on to argue that a comparative analysis of Frankfurt and Kierkegaard on the role of the will can illuminate aspects of both their thinking.

Rick Furtak draws on Kierkegaard in order to defend and expand upon Frankfurt's claim that love is "the ultimate ground of practical rationality." Examining the moral psychology of a human being's dedication to his or her final ends, Furtak seeks to explain why it is that unconditional love is a necessary condition of leading a fully meaningful life, as both Kierkegaard and Frankfurt maintain. In opposition to several other contributors, Furtak claims that on a charitable reading of his notion of "volitional rationality," Frankfurt is *not* obviously committed to a Humean-projectivist theory of value and that there are important commonalities between his work and that of phenomenologists such as Scheler and Marion. Most important for Furtak is his claim that Frankfurt's discussion of love echoes Kierkegaard's account of why it is that love must not be predicated on any prior assurance about what is "worth loving", since love is precisely what allows us to see whatever good is there to be seen. If God is love, and if love is the ground of our being, then Kierkegaard and Frankfurt have uncovered a deep insight about the meaning of existence.

Anthony Rudd, while agreeing with Furtak that values are perceived by love, also argues against Frankfurt that love must be seen as a response to the real values of things or potential objects of love—that is, values that are not themselves created by loving. According to Rudd, Frankfurt is importantly right about a range of issues: that we need to be able to reflectively consider and endorse our desires, that we are formed by what we love and care about, and that we need to be wholehearted in our loves. But Frankfurt's account is threatened with incoherence by his own insistence (especially in his latest work) that what we care about is ultimately a brute, biologically determined given. Drawing on previous criticisms of Frankfurt by Watson and Wolf, and on central themes in Kierkegaard's writings, Rudd argues for a transformation of Frankfurt's view along Platonic lines, in which our loves are understood as ultimately directed to and by an objective Good. Thus, in his conclusion to the volume, Rudd returns to themes found in the opening essay by Taliaferro.

In sum then, beyond relating and clarifying key themes in both Frankfurt and Kierkegaard, these essays advance contemporary debates about the nature of love and the complex relations between the lover and beloved. Together, they constitute the most robust response to Frankfurt's influential account published to date. They provide a way into these debates for new readers and challenge us all to reconsider the relation of love and selfhood.

Notes

1 This view is closely related to his earlier point that "volitional" phenomena are more central to personhood than rationalist accounts have suggested (IWCA, viii). Echoing Kierkegaard's own call for a kind of philosophy that is relevant to everyday human struggles, Frankfurt adds that he has "tried to stay closely in touch with problems and with lines of thought" that he can appreciate "as a human being trying to cope in a moderately systematic manner with the ordinary difficulties of a thoughtful life"—something that does not require especially arcane analytic methods (NVL, x).

2 It is probably fair to say that love fared little better in mainstream *Continental* philosophy during this period—despite a few exceptions among personalists, such as Martin Buber, Max Scheler, and Gabriel Marcel.

3 Indeed, there is now a serious literature on different forms of love in analytic philosophy, much of which responds not only to Frankfurt and classical sources going back to Plato and Aristotle but also to Kierkegaard and later personalist thinkers who Kierkegaard influenced such as Martin Buber: for example, see work by Robert Solomon, Richard White, Robert Ehman, Alan Soble, Raja Halwani, Robert C. Roberts, Troy Jollimore, and others.

4 J.L. Borges, "Kafka and His Precursors," in his *Labyrinths*, 236.

5 See Edward F. Mooney, *Selves in Discord and Resolve*, 66–67.

6 For example, see Frankfurt's essays on Descartes, Spinoza, time, and the biblical commentary with a Spinozistic-existential interpretation of the divine nature in "On God's Creation," all found in *Necessity, Volition, and Love*. Also note his reference to divine love at IWC 94.

Section I

Love and the Ground of Love

1

The Sources and Resources of Love: A Platonic Response to Frankfurt

Charles Taliaferro

Sometimes philosophers adopt such radically different concepts and terms that arguments between them seem fruitless. An old-fashioned, committed logical behaviorist might well profess simply to not understand when a phenomenologist, committed to a first-person point of view, complains that behaviorism does not account for her feeling pain. In response to the behaviorist, the phenomenologist pleads, "Do we not feel pain? Do we not perceive colors? Do we not hear sounds? No argument is offered because the only appeal that can properly be made is to our own experience of what it is like to be sentient or conscious in some further way."[1]

Would this impress a logical behaviorist? In my view, *it should*, but it is almost guaranteed only to evince the following response: "You are simply begging the question." Fortunately, Harry Frankfurt's work—whether he is offering a conceptual analysis of "bullshit" or of voluntary action—is rich with examples that appeal to ordinary language, reflection, and common sense. The clarity and elegance of his writing, and his reluctance to use highly technical terms, make him an ideal interlocutor.

In this chapter, the focus is on whether Frankfurt's work on love, care, and values does justice to our shared, ordinary, commonsense understanding of what love, care, and values are. For all I know, there may not be a crystal clear, single, ordinary, commonsense understanding of these things, but my proposal is that while Frankfurt's account has intuitive support and an enviable simplicity, it is nonetheless wide of the mark concerning what at least many of us mean and do when we love, care for, and value one another. I propose that we need a larger, comparatively more complex view of values to do justice to the matters at hand.

In this chapter, I will argue that ordinary reflection and commonsense examples lend more support to a Platonic account of love and values than they do to Frankfurt's more economic account. It might be easier to simply juxtapose a general form of moral realism vis-à-vis Frankfurt, but I will use the term "Platonic" in the broad fashion outlined below, giving an overview of the Platonic (with only minimal references to the views of the historical Plato), before going on to Frankfurt's fascinating work.

I. A Platonic preface

From a broadly Platonic perspective—my preferred version of Platonism is the Cambridge Platonist school of thought in seventeenth-century England—love is a response to value.[2] When you love another person, you love her for the value or worth she has intrinsically or for her own sake. As Fritz Wenisch puts it: "Love for another human is a response motivated by the other's intrinsic preciousness, by regarding her as what she is in herself rather than viewing her from the perspective of personal gain."[3] In the Platonic tradition, we recognize the distinction between recognizing the good of the other (beneficent love or *intentio benevolentiae*) and the desire to be united with the other (unitive love or the *intentio unionis*). When these conflict, the Platonic tradition (at least in its Christian form) invariably gives primacy to beneficent love. In this framework, my love for my wife, Jil, is not what gives her value—either for herself or for me—and my love for my son, Tiepolo, is not what gives Tiepolo value or makes him interesting. Now if lust for another person eclipsed my love for Jil, then (in the Platonic Christian tradition) I will have failed in an important office of love: fidelity. Likewise, if I falter in my love for Tiepolo because my narcissism has eclipsed my concern for the well-being of creatures who are not me, I have failed to be a loving father. In a Christian Platonic world, a person has reasons to love others because others have value or are precious, even if that person has no desire or inclination to love them.

One further feature of this tradition before turning to Frankfurt: in a healthy relationship, the Platonic Christian tradition *sees the beloved herself or himself* as the principal object of love rather than the love itself, whether this takes the form of (to put things awkwardly) loving being loved or simply loving to love. In other words, in a healthy relationship, you do not love the beloved—principally *because she loves you, or because you enjoy being a loving person*. Rather, the beloved herself is the source and reason for your love. If what you really love in a relationship is the other person's love, then when or if she stops loving you, the object of your love is no longer there. Surely it is natural and good to love being loved (*ceterus peribus*), but I suggest that the more enduring and deeper love is directed upon the beloved *whether or not the love is returned*.[4] And now, on to Frankfurt!

II. Love á la Frankfurt

Frankfurt's position is at odds with Platonism and some other forms of moral realism, but not so different that arguments and objections are impossible. The heart of the matter in terms of values is that Frankfurt locates the source of values in terms of what persons care about:

> It is by caring about things that we infuse the world with importance. This provides us with stable ambitions and concerns; it marks our interests and goals. The importance that our caring creates for us defines the framework of standards and aims in terms of which we endeavor to conduct our lives. A person who cares about something is guided, as his attitudes and his actions are shaped, by his continuing interest in it. Insofar as he does care about certain things, this determines how he thinks it important for him to conduct his life. The totality of the various things that a person cares about – together with his ordering of how important to him they are – effectively specifies his answer to the question of how to live. (RL, 23)

Unlike a Platonist who responds to a value that has an independent claim on her affection and allegiance, Frankfurt sees persons as the ones who infuse or bring about the world as important (or at least important for those of us doing the caring).

I have two questions at the outset before offering a further overview of Professor Frankfurt's position. First, I question the extent to which an appeal to care is truly explanatory. Arguably, Frankfurt's position seems to come close to a tautology. He proposes that our standards, aims, attitudes, actions, and conduct are the results of our caring and what we care about, but in a sense isn't the reference to our standards, and so on, simply a reference to different ways of caring? Imagine this exchange:

Jane: "I am looking for a way to get my son to France that meets the highest standards of safety I can afford."

John: "Why do you care about spending the most you can afford to get your son to France?"

Jane: "Because I care about my son."

I suppose there might be more reasons that are in the offing. Frankfurt allows that there may be reasons (or causes) for our caring that have a biological, evolutionary background, and Jane may have reasons for pouring more money into her son's transport than into getting him a good haircut. But once care is in place ("I care for my son") and we forego appealing to the value of the son, it seems as though caring itself is basic and not further explained in terms of justification. (So, I suggest, evolutionary biology may partially account for why I love Tiepolo, but I do not think that amounts to an account of why my love is *justified* or *warranted* or *good*.) I will continue to press home the importance of having reasons for caring, but let me put the matter in terms of a related question: casting aside whether Frankfurt's position amounts to an explanatory tautology (I care because I care), let us consider the extent to which Frankfurt's appeal to care matches our pre-philosophical (everyday or intuitive) understanding of care and value.

What seems to be missing in Frankfurt's account is concern with what a person *should* care about. In the passage cited above, Frankfurt refers to "his answer to the question of how to live." Evidently, the answer to the question "how should you live?" for any individual will lie in what the individual cares about. If an individual has no cares (consider the central character in Graham Greene's *A Burnt Out Case*), presumably there is no answer for that individual. In effect, Frankfurt defends this position by contending that an appeal to some kind of independent standard about how to live is problematic.

Frankfurt thinks that appeal to how we should live faces a problem of circularity. I cite this objection at length:

> In order to carry out a rational evaluation of some way of living, a person must first know what evaluative criteria to employ and how to employ them. He needs to know what considerations count in favor of choosing to live in one way rather than in another, what considerations count against, and the relative weights of each. For instance, it must be clear to him how to evaluate the fact that a certain way of living leads more than others (or less than others) to personal satisfaction, to pleasure, to power, to glory, to creativity, to spiritual depth, to a harmonious relationship with the precepts of religion, to conformity with the requirements of morality, and so on.
>
> The trouble here is a rather obvious sort of circularity. In order for a person to be able even to conceive and to initiate an inquiry into how to live, he must already have settled upon the judgments at which the inquiry aims. Identifying the question of how one should live – that is, understanding just what question it is and just how to go about answering it – requires that one specify the criteria that are to be employed in evaluating various ways of living. Identifying the question is, indeed, tantamount to specifying those criteria: what the question asks is, precisely, what way of living best satisfies them. But identifying

the criteria to be employed in evaluating various ways of living is also tantamount to providing an answer to the question of how to live, for the answer to this question is simply that one should live in the way that best satisfies whatever criteria are to be employed for evaluating lives. (RL, 24–25)

Just as I suggested earlier that Frankfurt's position seems close to a tautology in the wake of the question "why care?" ("I care because I care"), perhaps those of us who wish to have justificatory reasons as to why we should care about this or that do not have access to the relevant free-standing or independent criteria. After all, what are the differences between "I care about that criterion about how we should live because I care about it" and "I care about that criterion because the criterion seems right to me"? If Frankfurt is correct, then it seems that I would not be able to conceive of such criteria unless I were already working with a prior understanding of what kind of living is satisfying.

To some extent, I think Frankfurt is correct about one difficulty of appealing to criteria, but I suggest that the use of criteria in assessing ways of living does not involve any vicious circularity. The reply I propose is similar to the reply that some philosophers make to the problem of the criterion in epistemology. Let us consider the latter and then return to the terrain of values.

In epistemology, it has been charged that one cannot know anything (X) without knowing some criterion in virtue of which X is known. But how do you know that *that* criterion is correct? Perhaps you need an additional criterion by which to know whether the first-order criterion is correct. But then yet another criterion is needed, *ad infinitum*. Roderick Chisholm broke the regress by embracing what he called *particularism*: he held that you can know and grasp certain truths antecedent to possessing a criterion of how you know them.[5] Chisholm's preference for particularism rather than "methodism" (the view that knowledge of particulars is only possible if you know the method you are employing is accurate) was part of his "common sense" approach to philosophical problems. Chisholm was very much of the same mind as Thomas Reid and G.E. Moore; each philosopher claimed to be more certain of such ordinary beliefs as "I have hands" than they were of skeptical arguments that would defeat or undermine such claims. I suggest that the problem of the criterion in values should not usher in skepticism about the reality and role of values (in accounting for why we love this or that) any more than the problem of the criterion in epistemology should usher in skepticism about the reality and role of epistemic norms (in accounting for why we should believe this or that based on evidence). So, I propose that a common sense, intuitive value that most of us can grasp is that *it is good for parents to care for their children* or, putting the point more poignantly, *parents should care for their children (whether or not they actually care)*. Obviously, all sorts of caveats may need to be introduced to take care of deviant cases, but surely something like such a principle is a decent starting point.

With any invocation of values that are not reducible to statements about "natural facts," naturalists will be most unhappy, but two points may be offered on behalf of Platonists and other moral realists.

First, as a number of philosophers from G.E.M. Anscombe to Derek Parfit have argued, without an appeal to irreducible moral truths or principles, persons who care about doing great harm (e.g. genocide) or care about doing what seems utterly bizarre have reasons for doing the harm and the bizarre. Anscombe introduced the following case in which she claimed that for the agent to reply that he did the act "for no particular reason" is inappropriate. If someone hunted out all the green books in his house and spread them out carefully on the roof, and gave one of these answers ("for no particular reason," "I just felt like doing it") to the question "Why?," his words would be unintelligible unless they are taken as joking or mystification.[6] Arguably, there are cases when reported desires and motives seem so far afield ("I am placing my watch by a tree in case the tree wants to know the time") that they simply fail to make any sense.

Second, on behalf of accepting irreducible moral principles, it can be argued that this is no worse than accepting irreducible epistemic principles. The latter concern matters of evidence and justification about ordinary beliefs.[7] Arguably, if a naturalistic account of rationality and belief is not problematic, why should we think that a naturalistic account of values is problematic?[8]

Consider another objection to the kind of realism I am defending here. After advancing his objection about criteria, Frankfurt raises another worry for moral realists like Platonists:

> Here is another way to bring out the difficulty. Something is important to a person only in virtue of a difference that it makes. If everything would be exactly the same with that thing as without it, then it makes no sense for anyone to care about it. It cannot really be of any importance. Of course, it cannot be enough for it merely to make *some* difference. After all, everything does make some difference; but not everything is important. (RL, 25)

This is a difficult position for someone to assess who is not already committed to moral realism or its denial. I shall press forward the appeal of Platonic moral realism by an appeal to one's ordinary, commonsense understanding of values.

Imagine that the parents of a child are under conditions in which they and their culture have surplus goods, and so are not in poverty, and that they have the economic ability and capacity either to raise the child themselves or put the child up for adoption. Imagine that they do not see to it that the child is raised in some other loving family, but raise the child themselves with minimal care and without any affective support. They care more for parties with their peers, adult recreation, and doing crossword puzzles. Imagine the child does not realize that she is neglected, but she grows up living a stunted life, filled with a sense that she is unworthy of love and, as a consequence, undertakes high-risk activity and dies in her twenties (though she was healthy physically and, under different circumstances, would have lived till ninety). When the child is dying, she does not care whether she might live. She has never really cared, nor have her parents.

Let us consider this scenario through the lens of a Platonist. Were the parents good parents? No. They failed to live up to what it means to be a good parent. It does not matter how much the parents cared about crossword puzzles, nor does it matter whether the child was manipulated into thinking her life had little importance. This judgment seems as reasonable as any that challenges reckless private opinions and commitments. Imagine that someone suspects that every time he disbelieves in fairies, a fairy dies. He thinks he has killed twenty fairies. Is that person a killer? Maybe in his mind, but no, he is no more of a killer than the parents are good parents in the above thought-experiment.

Frankfurt makes one other point that might be interpreted as creating a difficulty for the Platonist:

> What is *not* possible is for a person who does not already care at least about *something* to discover reasons for caring about anything. Nobody can pull himself up by his own bootstraps. (RL, 26)

This may not be a source of deep tension between Platonists and Frankfurt. Platonists simply hold that it is a rare case when persons do not recognize the intrinsic goodness of at least something that merits, justifies, or calls for our love and care. When we fail to respond to such real goods, we fail to respond to reality itself and instead live a life of fantasy or denial. It may be that, from the standpoint of an external, noncommitted observer, a despondent rogue who is not a good father looks the same to someone quite independent of a commitment to Platonism or Frankfurt's position. But in a Platonist perspective, there is, I think, more of a sense that there is something of a failure to live up to what the father should be doing (regardless of what he cares about) than with Frankfurt's alternative; for, given that the person does not care about being a good father, he has no reason to be a good father.

Let us now consider the key point of conflict between Frankfurt and Christian Platonism. It is essential to consider Frankfurt's view at length:

> Love is often understood as being, most basically, a response to the perceived worth of the beloved. We are moved to love something, on this account, by an appreciation of what we take to be its exceptional inherent value. The appeal of that value is what captivates us and turns us into lovers. We begin loving the things that we love because we are struck by their value, and we continue to love them for the sake of their value. If we did not find the beloved valuable, we should not love it.
>
> This may well fit certain cases of what would commonly be identified as love. However, the sort of phenomenon that I have in mind when referring here to love is essentially something else. As I am construing it, love is not necessarily a response grounded in awareness of the inherent value of its object. It may sometimes arise like that, but it need not do so ....
>
> It is not necessarily as a *result* of recognizing their value and of being captivated by it that we love things. Rather, what we love necessarily *acquires* value for us *because* we love it. The lover does invariably and necessarily perceive the beloved as valuable, but the value he sees it to possess is a value that derives from and that depends upon his love.
>
> Consider the love of parents for their children. I can declare with unequivocal confidence that I do not love my children because I am aware of some value that inheres in them independent of my love for them. The fact is that I loved them even before they were born – before I had any especially relevant information about their personal characteristics or their particular merits and virtues. Furthermore, I do not believe that the valuable qualities they do happen to possess strictly in their own rights, would really provide me with a very compelling basis for regarding them as having greater worth than many other possible objects of love that in fact I love much less. It is quite clear to me that I do not love them more than other children because I believe they are better. (RL, 38–39)

Frankfurt offers an extensive further point about the parent–child relationship:

> It is not because I have noticed their value, then, that I love my children as I do. Of course I do perceive them to have value; so far as I am concerned, indeed, their value is beyond measure. That, however, is not

the basis of my love. It is really the other way around. The particular value that I attribute to my children is not inherent in them but depends upon my love for them. The reason they are so precious to me is simply that I love them so much. As for why it is that human beings do tend generally to love their children, the explanation presumably lies in the evolutionary pressure of natural selection. In any case, it is plainly *on account of* my love for them that they have acquired in my eyes a value that otherwise they would not certainly possess. (RL, 40)

I believe this to be a false reading of what it is to love another person, to love one's child in particular, and to be loved by a parent.

If Frankfurt is right, then when I love Tiepolo and congratulate him (for example) on his volunteer work tutoring students, the reason such work has value is because I love Tiepolo and his work. This would mean (philosophically and from my point of view) that Tiepolo would lose value when or if I stopped loving him. It also seems to imply that Tiepolo's value would fluctuate in line with my degree and depth of care. On one morning, Tiepolo's value may be the highest yet, because I am fully awake and caring, whereas by the afternoon I may be exhausted with caring and Tiepolo's value begins to diminish. This seems profoundly counterintuitive. Frankfurt's view also implies that I would cease having value should my parents, myself, and others cease caring about me.

I suggest that Frankfurt is misinterpreting the basic, natural good (value, importance) of the parent–child relationship. He assumes that if he values his children more than strangers and not due to their meriting his love through successful action or superior traits, then *he*, Frankfurt, is the source of their value. But this completely puts to one side the apparent *basic good of the parent–child relationship*. The recognition of such a basic good explains why we think that when Frankfurt loves his child he is doing something good and it also explains why we do not think a child's value becomes diminished or fluctuates depending on a parent's love.

Frankfurt does acknowledge that, in our experience, something like the basic account seems right. In a passage cited earlier, Frankfurt claims:

> The lover does invariably and necessarily perceive the beloved as valuable, but the value he sees it to possess is a value that derives from and that depends upon his love.

But I am not sure that this perception of value is possible if one fully believes that the value is completely derived from the lover. If I fully accept Frankfurt's account and have no doubt of its truth, how can I simultaneously perceive

Tiepolo as having independent value? Imagine that the *only* reason you value
a house is because you think that Brad Pitt spent the night there. And you
know that your sense of the worth of the house is *wholly derived* from a visit
by that handsome celebrity and not due to the house's intrinsic value. How
can you perceive and know this and yet simultaneously perceive the house
as possessing intrinsic value? Insofar as perceiving a house or a child as
possessing intrinsic value involves believing that they are of intrinsic value, it
seems that Frankfurt leaves us with a case in which a person must believe his
child is intrinsically valuable while believing that the child is not intrinsically
valuable.

I conclude on a conciliatory note, however, with a Kierkegaardian
suggestion that may help bring some concord between Frankfurt and
Christian Platonism. This, of course, goes well beyond the limits that
Frankfurt entertains in the vast majority of his philosophical work. And yet,
one of Frankfurt's early publications was in philosophy of religion. It was a
paper that received considerable attention in the literature on theistic divine
attributes. Frankfurt defended a unique, provocative treatment of God's
omnipotence.[9]

III. A Kierkegaardian postscript

If we suppose Christian theism is true, some of the above ostensible
problems with Frankfurt's position may be vitiated. In a Frankfurt-theism
framework, perhaps creation has value because God cares for it (as per
Frankfurt's parent–child relationship). In such a universe, in which we are
made via evolution to naturally care for each other and for our children, the
case of an individual who is utterly shorn of the desire to care for others is
an anomaly at odds teleologically with the whole point of creation. If we
assume as a backdrop a constantly loving God, there is no occasion when
persons would not have value. Moreover, even when we fluctuated in our
love for our children or one another, there would be a stable reference point
in divine love. Kierkegaard puts this beautifully in *Works of Love*:

> When we say 'Love saves from death,' there is straightway a reduplication
> in thought: the lover saves another human being from death, and in
> entirely the same or yet in a different sense he saves himself from death.
> This he does at the same time; it is one and the same; he does not save
> the other at one moment and at another save himself, but in the moment
> he saves the other he saves himself from death. Only love never thinks
> about the latter, about saving oneself, about acquiring confidence itself;

the lover in love thinks only about giving confidence and saving another from death. But the lover is not thereby forgotten. No, he who in love forgets himself, forgets his sufferings in order to think of another's, forgets what he himself loves in order lovingly to consider another's loss, forgets his advantage in order lovingly to look after another's advantage: truly, such a person is not forgotten. There is one who thinks of him, God in heaven; or love thinks of him. God is love, and when a human being because of love forgets himself, how then should God forget him? No, while the lover forgets himself and thinks of the other person, God thinks of the lover. The self-lover is busy; he shouts and complains and insists on his rights in order to make sure he is not forgotten – and yet he is forgotten. But the lover, who forges himself, is remembered by love. There is one who thinks of him, and in this way it comes about that the lover gets what he gives. (WL, 262)

In this sublime portrait of love, there is an overarching divine care that sustains the loving relations within the creation and the promise that, in the end, our best loves will not be forgotten.

In closing, I commend a Platonist philosophy of values as providing a better account of our understanding of love and the way we perceive the ones we love, but if you adopt Frankfurt's position *plus a Kierkegaardian framework* you will attain some of the stability that we Platonists love.

Acknowledgments

I am deeply grateful to Thomas Churchill and Alexander "Z" Quanbeck for their editorial work on this chapter. Thank you also to Anthony Rudd, John Davenport, and others for conversations on all the central claims of this chapter.

Notes

1 H.D. Lewis, *The Elusive Self*, 5–6.
2 For an overview of Cambridge Platonism, see *Evidence and Faith; Philosophy and Religion since the Seventeenth Century* and *Cambridge Platonist Spirituality*, ed. by C. Taliaferro and A. Tepley.
3 Fritz Wenisch, review of Dietrich von Hildebrand's *The Nature of Love, Faith and Philosophy*, Vol. 29, no. 1 (January 2012): 118–122.
4 For further exposition of love in the Platonic tradition, see *The Nature of Love* by Dietrich von Hildebrand, translated by John F. Crosby.

5   For a treatment of the problem of the criterion, see Roderick Chisholm's *Theory of Knowledge*, third edition.

6   G.E.M. Anscombe, *Intention*, 2nd edition, 26–27.

7   See Derek Parfit, *On What Matters*, ed. Samuel Scheffler, Vol. 1.

8   I have defended the ideal observer theory in various places: Charles Taliaferro, "Relativizing the Ideal Observer Theory," 123–38, and Taliaferro, "A God's Eye View," in *Faith and Analysis*, ed. H.A. Harris and C.I. Insole.

9   Harry Frankfurt, "The Logic of Omnipotence," *The Philosophical Review* 73 no. 2 (April 1964): 262–63.

2

Love and Value, Yet *Again*

Alan Soble

I. Saint Augustine on love and beauty

In his *Confessions* (ca. 397), Saint Augustine raises the issue of the relationship between love and beauty:

> I used to ask my friends "Do we love anything unless it is beautiful? What, then, is beauty and in what does it consist? What is it that attracts us and wins us over to the things we love? Unless there were beauty and grace in them, they would be powerless to win our hearts."[1]

Augustine is here entertaining the idea that something must be beautiful to be loved, that being beautiful is a necessary condition, an idea that Socrates and Diotima had asserted about *eros* in Plato's *Symposium*[2] and proposed also by Aristotle in the *Nicomachean Ethics*: "No one falls in love who has not first derived pleasure from the looks of the beloved."[3]

Will Augustine stick to this thought, although refining it by distinguishing (Diotima's strategy)[4] between "lower beauty" (e.g., bodily beauty that incites sexual desire, in particular his own sexual yearnings, which "dragged him down" and instigated the self-critical passages in the second and third books of the *Confessions*) and a "higher beauty" that would "pull him up"? Or will he break free of Plato's *eros* altogether and affirm that love for the ugly and bad is possible (*contra* Aristotle)[5] and even obligatory, joining sides with the proponents of longsuffering *agape*, which had been described and applauded by his greatly admired Saint Paul (1 Corinthians 13)?

Augustine sometimes takes the first route. He often praises God for His infinite goodness and beauty, a beauty that "drew me to you." He also alleges that God is what he had been seeking all along in his lesser sexual loves for lesser beauties ("my real need was for you, my God"),[6] a theme reminiscent of Diotima on our search for "Absolute Beauty."[7] Note that Augustine fails to distinguish beauty *qua* the object of love (that which is itself loved) and beauty *qua* the basis or ground of love (the reason that the beloved person or thing is loved, or beauty as the cause of the love). When Augustine writes, "I was in love with beauty of a lower order," he is asserting that beauty is the object of love (as it was, arguably, for Plato: "we ... love in persons ... the 'Image' of the Idea in them").[8] Augustine's central question ("Do we love anything unless it is beautiful?") is compatible with beauty being the object of love *or* its being the basis of love. This confusion, which has occurred now-and-then throughout the history of the philosophy of love, should of course be avoided. As we shall see, it occurs in Harry Frankfurt's *The Reasons of Love*.

II. Love and value

From the ancients through the twentieth century, whether the beauty or goodness of the beloved is the basis (and/or the object) of love, or has little or nothing to do with love, has been thoroughly discussed. Although some secular philosophers (Frankfurt, for one) have denied that beauty (or other value) is the basis of love, the denial is more commonly found in accounts of love inspired by Christianity. For example, Søren Kierkegaard, in *Works of Love* (1847), counters the *eros*-Platonic tradition and defends the *agape*-Christian tradition: "the task is not: to find—the lovable object; but the task is: to find the object already given or chosen—lovable, and to be able to continue finding him lovable, no matter how he becomes changed."[9] (Contrast Aristotle, who regardless of the lofty extent to which he extols the constancy of *philia*, is nonetheless willing, under extreme pressure, to jettison a radically changed beloved.)[10] Whereas Socrates made jokes about loving the ugly, that is, having sexual desires for them, a sober Kierkegaard announced that we should love "the ugly" (WL, 342). He does not mean that *X* should love *Y* in virtue of *Y*'s ugliness if *X* has a passionate preference for ugliness; nor that *X* can be expected to love *Y* if in *X*'s subjective and idiosyncratic perception of *Y*, *Y* is a hottie. Rather, we should love those who are unlovable in the worldly sense, or by the worldly criterion, of "lovable" *because* they are unlovable and we recognize that fact, not because they are *per accidens* lovable in our odd perceptions of them.

The philosophical question concerns the relationship between love and value, or between loving something and valuing it. Anders Nygren's *Agape and Eros* is a well-known theological treatment of the issue. More recently, Irving Singer provided a sustained philosophical and historical examination of the topic from Plato to the twentieth century in his monumental trilogy, *The Nature of Love*, in which he distinguishes between the "appraisal" dimension or concept of love, that is, love as a response to antecedent, independent value, and love as "bestowal," that is, love as essentially the attribution or creation of value.[11] Nygren had less comprehensively explored the two aspects or types in the 1930s.[12] Emil Brunner, following Nygren's lead, made the distinction in 1945,[13] and many other scholars have discussed it in illuminating ways.[14] The distinction presents us with a type of *Euthyphro* problem: Do I love Melinda because she is (or I judge or perceive her to be) beautiful or good, or do I think Melinda is beautiful or good because I love her? The problem remains if "beautiful" and "good" are replaced by any other valuable property (or set of properties), such as wit, charm, intelligence, and kind-heartedness.

Getting ahead of our story a little, here is Frankfurt weighing in on the Christian *agape*-bestowal side:

> It is true that the beloved invariably is, indeed, valuable to the lover. However, perceiving that value is not at all an indispensable *formative* or *grounding* condition of the love. It need not be a perception of value in what he loves that moves the lover to love it. The truly essential relationship between love and the value of the beloved goes in the opposite direction. It is not necessarily as a *result* of recognizing their value and of being captivated by it that we love things [and people]. Rather, what we love necessarily *acquires* value for us *because* we love it. The lover does invariably and necessarily perceive the beloved as valuable, but the value he sees it to possess is a value that derives from and that depends upon his love. (RL, 38–39, Frankfurt's emphasis)

Frankfurt observes that love and the beloved's value *invariably* go together. We must figure out the relationship between them, just as about the correlation between God's commanding act *A* and act *A*'s being right we must decide whether God commands *A* because it is right or *A* is right because God commands it.[15] Frankfurt's solution to the *Euthyphro* love dilemma is analogous to saying that *A* is right because God commands it. Of course, we ask: if *A* is right because God commands it and not because *A* is right, then why does God command it? Similarly, if I evaluate Melinda as beautiful and good because I love her and not because she *is* beautiful and good (and maybe I love her despite her being bad and ugly; "such things happen," says Frankfurt (RL, 38)),[16] then why do I love her *at all*? The title of Frankfurt's book is *Reasons of Love*, not *Reasons for Love*. He emphasizes how love provides us with reasons for doing things, especially for the sake of the beloved ("Love is itself, for the lover, a source of reasons" (RL, 37)), and he rejects a Platonic or Aristotelian view about loving something only if or because it is good or beautiful. Indeed, for Frankfurt, there may be no reasons at all for loving someone. Further, we can love *anything*.

But—I wonder—we do love, and we love *Y* instead of *Z*. Why? As an exercise, apply all this to hate. "I disvalue you because I hate you. Why do I hate you? I have no idea. It has nothing to do with you. It is not that you are antecedently hate-worthy, as if you did something nasty and cruel to me. I might even hate you were you especially nice to me." *Agapic* hate is pathological, and we would help someone experiencing it to get over it. Not so for *agapic* love, according to its proponents.

III. David Hume on love

In "Of the amorous passion, or love betwixt the sexes," a small section of the *Treatise*,[17] Hume offers an account of love:

> in its most natural state, [love] is deriv'd from the conjunction of three different impressions or passions[:] The pleasing sensation arising from beauty; the bodily appetite for generation; and a generous kindness or good-will.

Hume is in effect raising the *Euthyphro* love problem. Love and beauty are constantly conjoined, in his view. Because he thinks that "the most common species of love is that which first arises from beauty, and afterwards diffuses itself into kindness and into the bodily appetite," he sides with Plato. He observed what Frankfurt does: "Love is often understood as being, most basically, a response to the perceived worth of the beloved" (RL, 38). In Frankfurt's view, however, this means that those multitudes who understand love this way are mistaken and that many cases of love described this way are not genuine.

Hume's claim that sexual desire and kindness or benevolence become inseparable in the "amorous passion" is remarkable. Given Hume's view of sexual desire, which he calls the soul's "most gross and vulgar" passion, his thesis that sexual desire and kindness become inseparable is dubious. In contrast to sexual desire, benevolence is "the most refin'd passion of the soul." If benevolence and sexual desire are so different, how could they be joined together—inseparably? (Indeed, for Immanuel Kant, "benevolence … deter[s] one from carnal enjoyment.")[18] Hume acknowledges the problem: "Kindness or esteem, and the appetite to generation, are too remote to unite easily." Something powerful and exceptional must be called upon to unite such disparate passions. For Hume, this magical ingredient is the "pleasing sensation arising from beauty." His solution, though, is perplexing: "The love of beauty is plac'd in a just medium betwixt them, and partakes of both their natures: From whence it proceeds, that 'tis so singularly fitted to produce both." Oh? Really?

Maybe Hume's problem can be solved by invoking customary elements of evolutionary psychology: the adaptive significance of *responses* to beauty in instigating procreation, kindness, and pair-bonding, and the adaptive significance of *possessing* beauty (that which evokes sexual arousal) as the mark of fertility. I mention this possibility primarily because Frankfurt shores up his account of love by appealing to an inchoate mixture of evolution and biology. Because, for example, he has denied that love is a response to the perceived value of its object, Frankfurt has the task of silencing our worries about why X loves Y either at all or instead of Z. He nearly brushes off the question: "Love may be brought about—in ways that are poorly understood—by a disparate variety of natural causes" (RL, 38). His point is that *no matter* how love is caused— by the beauty of the beloved, by her ugliness, by the fact that her body odor reminds me of pizza, by a biological mechanism that triggers the release of dopamine—if it is the genuine article, the lover will still behave in loving ways, toward the things and persons he loves, as a result of that love. Singer, back in the 1960s, had already urged this point: the causal antecedents of love are irrelevant to the nature of love. Love, for Singer (and another idea duplicated by Frankfurt), is the ungrounded bestowal of value on the things and persons loved; as long as this love-bestowal of value occurs, it matters not how it comes about.[19]

Frankfurt, however, is not discussing Hume's "amorous passion." On Frankfurt's view, "relationships that are primarily romantic or sexual do not provide very authentic or illuminating paradigms of love as I am construing it" (RL, 43). This repeats a claim he made in "On Caring," a 1997 lecture: "it is not a good idea to suppose that romantic relationships provide especially authentic paradigms of love" (NVL, 155–80, at 166). Although the Christian (and Kierkegaard) agrees, many ordinary people do not. Will Frankfurt convince us?

IV. Frankfurt's "The Importance of What We Care About"

Frankfurt began his study of love indirectly in 1982 with "The Importance of What We Care About." One claim he made in that paper was that a "person who cares about something is ... invested in it. He *identifies* himself with what he cares about in the sense that he makes himself vulnerable to losses and susceptible to benefits depending upon whether what he cares about is diminished or enhanced" (IWC, 83; compare OC, 168). In *The Reasons of Love*, Frankfurt similarly writes about love (which is "an especially notable variant of caring" (RL, 11); so, how *does* love differ from caring, if the former is a "variant" of the latter?) that the lover "takes the interests of his beloved as his own. Consequently, he benefits or suffers depending upon whether those interests are or are not adequately served" (RL, 80). For Frankfurt, this union-of-interests is a "conceptually necessary" feature of love. It is an idea with a long history, going back at least to Montaigne's essay on friendship, Kant on marriage, and Hegel's remarks on love.[20] In 1980, J. F. M. Hunter defined love in part as involving "the wish to unite one's interests with those of another person." When two people love each other, they satisfy this wish together by each person's "treat[ing] the loved one's interests as if they were [his/her] own."[21] Not long afterwards, Robert Nozick also used the notion in his account of love. The intention in love is "to identify one's fortunes in large part with [the] fortunes" of a joint "we." Thus "your own well-being is tied up with [the well-being] of someone you love"; "when something bad happens to one you love, ... something bad also happens *to you*," and "as the other [person] fares, so (to some extent) do you."[22] Kierkegaard, I think, had two related objections to this view. First, this love is *l'egoîsme à deux*: "The lover's desire presumably is not selfish in relation to the beloved's, but the desire of both together is absolutely selfish insofar as they in union and in love form one self."[23] Hence, "The more securely the two I's come together to become one I," the more in loving each other the lovers love only themselves. "The beloved [is] therefore called, ... significantly enough, the *other-self*, the *other-I*" (WL, 68, 66). Second, the "nearness" of the partners to each other prevents them from focusing on God. But God is required by the dyad to hold it together. He must be invited in, to form a stable triad. Indeed, the partners "first and foremost absolutely belong to God," who should be "the only loved object" (WL, 118, 124).[24]

In "The Importance of What We Care About," Frankfurt addresses the *Euthyphro* love dilemma, although here he speaks about caring about something instead of loving it. The dilemma concerns the relationship between a person's caring about something and that thing's being important to the person. Frankfurt asserts that "The person does not care about the object because its worthiness commands that he do so" (IWC, 94), but "caring about something makes that thing important to the person who cares about it" (IWC, 92). This is analogous to saying that in loving something we create value in or bestow value on it. That which we care about is important to us because we care about it, so that which we love has value for us because we love it. Now, just as we asked why we do or should love what we love, given that our love is not a response to our beloved's value but, instead, creates it, we can ask why we do or should care about what we care about, if our caring about it is not a response to its antecedent, independent importance but, instead, makes it important. Frankfurt acknowledges, "When the importance of a certain thing to a person is due to the very fact that he cares about it, ... that fact cannot provide a useful measure of the extent to which his caring about the thing is justified" (IWC, 93). If the value that my beloved has is due to my loving her, I can hardly rely on that value to justify (or explain) my love—on pain of circularity. Recall that, according to Frankfurt, when we care about something, we *invest* in it. Hence, we must deliberate seriously about what to care about, what to make so important to us that we invest in it. Frankfurt expresses this point in a convoluted way: "the question of what to care about [i.e., of what to make important to us] ... is one which must necessarily be important to" us.

What will "justify" caring about something or "justif[y] ... making the thing important ... by caring about it"? Frankfurt approaches a solution by claiming that "the only way to justify doing this is in terms of the importance of the activity of caring as such." This notion is also part of his answer to the *Euthyphro* love dilemma in *The Reasons of Love* (RL, 51): love or loving is itself important to us. But this move generates its own tangles. Suppose we inquire about the source of the importance of caring-as-such. Either caring-as-such is important because we care about caring-as-such and so make it important for us, or the importance of caring-as-such is logically antecedent to our caring about caring-as-such. If the latter, care-independent importance underlies caring after all, as it does in the other horn of the dilemma: we judge caring-as-such important because caring-as-such has value antecedent to and independently of its being cared about. If the former, however, we must wonder about the origin of our caring about caring-as-such, that is, why we have made caring-as-such important by caring about it. How is it that *that* thing, caring-as-such, was selected as being the recipient of our caring about it when we cannot appeal to its care-independent value or worthiness to be judged important?

The importance of caring-as-such justifies, if it justifies anything, only caring *simpliciter* about things and making them, whatever they turn out to be, important. It does not justify caring about any particular thing or making any particular thing important to us. Frankfurt knows this and continues with the rest of his solution:

> What makes it more suitable ... for a person to make one object rather than another important to himself? It seems that it must be the fact that it is *possible* for him to care about the one and not about the other, or to care about the one in a way which is more important to him than the way in which it is possible for him to care about the other. (IWC, 94)

I'm struck, first, by Frankfurt's cagey and unexplained equivocation, the change from his own appropriate word "justified" to the quite different and *prima facie* irrelevant "suitable," whatever that is supposed to mean. This horn of the *Euthyphro* dilemma collapses, because we do not get the justification we were seeking. I am also struck by "possible," which Frankfurt repeats: "the worthiness of the activity of caring commands that he choose an object which he will be able to care about." Frankfurt tells us that "the choice of the object[s]" to care about is *not* "arbitrary." But that we are *able* to care about something is not a sharp or helpful test to employ in deciding exactly what we should make important to us by caring about it. It leaves the field wide open. (Perhaps so widely open as to warrant "arbitrary.") Frankfurt's test rules out only objects that we *cannot* care about (logically cannot? in virtue of natural laws? psychologically cannot?), which is useless advice: if we cannot care about something, we cannot choose to care about it. Does this looseness also apply to choosing to care about caring-as-such? If our caring about something in particular depends on our being able to care about it and so make it important to us, then our caring about caring-as-such depends on its being possible for us to care about caring-as-such. If we cannot care about caring-as-such, we have no justification for caring at all (or no way to find it "suitable").

Frankfurt's argument seems to be that it does not matter what we care about as long as we care about something, in virtue of the importance of caring-as-such. This claim is a large part of his treatment of the issue in *The Reasons of Love*, as we shall see. Frankfurt does have a point. An omnipotent God *can* care about everything, and thereby bestows importance on all His created things. We humans cannot care about everything. We must choose some things (in the broad generic sense) to care about from the infinite stock of things. At the same time, there may be from our perspective, to begin with, little that is worth caring about. Given the meager pickings, we should care about whatever it is possible for us to care about; at least we can engage in some caring and reap the benefits of caring-as-such.

Frankfurt's theory of love in *The Reasons of Love* is, as I have mentioned, indebted to the Christian *agape* tradition (insofar as caring or love precedes and creates value). But Frankfurt's idea in "The Importance of What We Care About," that we should care about that which we are *able* to care about, is not Christian.[25] Listen, by contrast, to Kierkegaard: "True love is precisely ... [to find] the unlovable object to be lovable" (WL, 343). That is, Christian love includes caring about the "unlovable," that which it is ordinarily *not possible* for us to care about, or is difficult for us to care about, or we have to force ourselves to barely care about: the physically offensive (repellent, nauseating), homeless, panhandling, conniving drug addict—the Kierkegaardian unlovable ugly.

That which we are *able* to love is often, perhaps predominantly, exactly that which is *easy* to love. It takes no skill, mentoring, determination, courage, sensitivity, or moral sense to love, care about, or make important that which is lovable. Given our nature, it is no trick to love the self, let alone the beautiful, smart, charming, talented—and clean, sweet-smelling—people who surround us and with whom we have loving relationships. Frankfurt has a reply of sorts: loving the self is *difficult* and the purest form of love: "coming to love oneself is the deepest and most essential—and by no means the most readily attainable—achievement of a serious and successful life" (RL, 68). In the essay "On Caring," published five years earlier, he had already begun this argument: "love of self may even appear to be in a certain way an exceptionally pure form of love" (NVL, 168). Be that as it may, Frankfurt's claim that we should and may care about that which it is possible for us to care about means that we should and may care about that which we find lovable. This move grants everything to Plato's horn of the dilemma, according to which we love those whom we find beautiful—independently of loving them. If we are to select, as the things to care about, those things that we find lovable (i.e., that which it is possible for us to love), then love is, after all, a response to the perceived value of its object. (Singer, too, backs into this corner: "For most men it is easier to bestow value upon a beautiful rather than an ugly woman."[26] That's convenient.) Even if bestowing value as a result of love is a significant part of love, underlying this bestowal of value on the things we love, because we love them, is already a judgment that they are antecedently worthy of our caring about them, or worthy of having further value bestowed on them.

V. Between "Importance" and *The Reasons of Love*

"The Importance of What We Care About" received critical attention from Annette Baier in 1982, briefly from me in 1990, and from Susan Wolf in 2002 (the latter in a book of new essays devoted to Frankfurt's work; he replied to each essay).[27] "Importance" was published in 1982 and *The Reasons of Love* in 2004. Between them, but closer to *Reasons*, Frankfurt wrote three other substantial pieces on caring and love: "Autonomy, Necessity, and Love" (published first in 1994 in German, in English not until 1999 (NVL, 129–41)); a 1997 lecture, "On Caring," that appeared in print for the first time in *Necessity, Volition, and Love* (NVL, 155–80); and "Duty and Love," published in the first issue of a new journal early in 1998. I want to mention a few things about "On Caring" and "Duty and Love," which are a preview of (or prequel to) *The Reasons of Love.*

First, in "On Caring," Frankfurt expresses a central claim of *The Reasons of Love*, that genuine love is "disinterested," by which he means that it is "unmotivated by any instrumental concern" (NVL, 168). In "Autonomy" (NVL, 134), Frankfurt had suggested that our love for our children is disinterested in this sense. This is one consideration that leads Frankfurt to think that "the loving concern of parents for their infants or small children is the mode of caring that comes closest … to providing pure instances of what I have in mind in speaking of love" ("On Caring," NVL, 166), as opposed to, for example, romantic or sexual love (RL, 43). In "Duty and Love" (p. 6), Frankfurt invokes parental love to illustrate his thesis about the relationship between love and value: "it is not fundamentally because I recognize how important to me my children are that I love them. On the contrary, the relationship between their value to me and my love for them goes essentially the other way. My children are valuable to me in the first place just because I love them." I presume that his children would have *antecedent* importance or value for him, and he would "love" them or care about their welfare on the basis of that importance if, say, he were thinking that his children would eventually mind the farm and take care of him in his old age. In that case, his caring about them is not disinterested but instrumentally motivated. Apparently, then, over the last few centuries we, in the developed West, have made progress in the quality of our love for our children, no longer thinking of them as insurance policies. (Right? Is this a case in which evolutionary pressure to promote the welfare of our children for our own sake is offset or held in check by the social establishment of Kantian moral principles?)

Second, in "On Caring," Frankfurt begins to connect together caring, love, and that which is important to us (a connection that becomes very tight in *The Reasons of Love*). "Among the things that we care about there are some that we cannot help caring about; and among the things that we cannot help caring about are those that we love" (NVL, 165). What is interesting about this claim is not the connection it maintains between caring and love—any treatment of love will link loving something and caring about it—but rather the suggestion that there are some things that *we cannot help caring about*. Because, for Frankfurt, caring about something makes it important for us, rather than its antecedent importance making us care about it, we had wondered what we should care about, and why. Frankfurt did not provide a justification of caring about one thing instead of another; we were merely advised to care about that which we are *able* to care about. But if there are some things we cannot help caring about, then (1) we won't necessarily have to deliberate over what to care about, and (2) a kind of weak vindication (not justification) of what we care about is in the air. No complaints can be raised about our caring about things we cannot help caring about, and we should not feel that we have to explain ourselves and our preferences, just because we care about something. In *The Reasons of Love*, Frankfurt pushes this point, that by our nature we cannot help caring about some things, and ends up with an account of love that is significantly naturalistic—which is both philosophically disappointing and, as I explain later, a philosophical disaster.

Third, in "On Caring," Frankfurt introduces another theme, the "particularity" of the beloved. For Frankfurt, "it makes no sense for a person to consider accepting a substitute for his beloved" (NVL, 170), a claim that legions of writers before Frankfurt have also made (without the obfuscating "makes no sense"). Why is the claim significant? After all, if I love you in virtue of your properties, I may well have no reason, ever, for accepting a substitute; and if I do not love you for your properties, I may still have reasons for having additional beloveds who could become more important to me than you are. "Particularity" and "accepting a substitute" are not logically linked.[28] Nonetheless, the argument often goes like this: Suppose that John loves Mary and a Jill comes along who strongly resembles Mary in salient ways. If John's love for Mary is based on her (repeatable, general) properties, that is, her antecedent value, John should also love Jill—or love her instead, if her properties are better than Mary's. But John, who loves Mary, will not substitute Jill for her. Ergo, Mary's properties do not ground John's love. (Then what does?) The substitution argument is about the *ground* of love. Frankfurt does not traverse the argument in detail,[29] but hops to his conclusion, which is ambiguous between a claim about the ontology of the beloved and the ground of love: "The focus [*object? basis?*] of a person's love is not those general and hence repeatable characteristics that make his beloved *describable*. Rather, it is the specific particularity that makes his beloved *nameable*" (NVL, 170).[30] Frankfurt admits that particularity is "mysterious" and "impossible to define" (NVL, 170), which is surely a defect in his theory: if "particularity" is impossible to define yet is necessary for "love," then "love," contrary to Frankfurt's project, is impossible to define. That is, in response to the idea that X loves Y in virtue of "her whole lovable nature ... that inexplicable quality of which I cannot give an account," we might say, as Kierkegaard does, that "anyone who wants to end with the inexplicable would really do best to begin with it and say nothing else in order not to become suspect" (SLW, 35). Contemporary philosophers have struggled with the mysteries of "particularity," "non-substitutability," "irreplaceability," and "haecceity."[31] Frankfurt neither acknowledges their existence nor shows that he has learned anything from them. As a result, he has added nothing to this ongoing discussion.

Fourth, in "Duty and Love," Frankfurt claims that "I may love a woman from a distance, with no opportunity to affect her in any way; and she may have no inkling even that I exist" (6). True, unrequited and nonreciprocal "loves" abound, in which John feels something for Mary but Mary (who may know John: they work in the same firm or live in the same apartment building) does not feel a thing for John. It is, however, implausible to understand unrequited "love" as genuine love if one *also* holds that love involves "investment." For Frankfurt, a "person who cares about something is ... invested in it. He *identifies* himself with what he cares about in the sense that he makes himself vulnerable to losses and susceptible to benefits depending upon whether what he cares about is diminished or enhanced" (IWC, 83); the lover "takes the interests of his beloved as his own" (RL, 80). Let's add the defensible, if not obvious, claim that if I am vulnerable to a loss in your welfare, if my welfare is diminished when yours is, if your interests are my interests, then I will be motivated to act to protect, preserve, and advance your interests. This much is true about love on any cogent theory—that I am concerned for your welfare and will act to protect it. (I would say that this feature of love is especially important for an account of love, such as Frankfurt's, that blesses "self-love.") In unrequited or nonreciprocal "love," it is insuperably difficult for the lover to take the interests of his beloved as his own—and not merely because John might be in prison and is in that way prevented from acting to protect Mary's welfare. He has, as Frankfurt says, "no opportunity *to affect her* in any way." Unless John is deluded, he knows this, and he knows that attempting to join his interests with Mary's, or to increase her welfare, is doomed. He doesn't even have a reliable way to know what her interests *are*. I doubt that John would be happy, and truly invested, if any old Tom, Dick, or Sally protects and promotes Mary's welfare instead.

Fifth, in "Duty and Love," Frankfurt picks up his discussion from the end of "Importance" about what we should care about. He mentions again that God has no problem because God is omnipotent: He can care about everything. Humans, by contrast, "need to exercise a cautious selectivity and a defensive restraint" ("Duty and Love," 7; see RL, 63). We must take into account two factors in choosing what to care about, to love, or to bestow importance on: (1) because care and love involve investment, our well-being will vary according to the well-being of our beloved—risky business; and (2) we should care about what we are able to care about. "It is not so easy for most of us to find things that we are capable of loving," Frankfurt bemoans; "people vary in their capacity to be deeply touched" ("Duty and Love," 7). I do not want to belabor a point I made earlier, but it is essential: if we love and make important the things by which we are "deeply touched," we love them because they have antecedent, independent value.

At this place in "Duty and Love," Frankfurt again raises the question of the value of care or love as such, going beyond "Importance" and giving us some hints where he will eventually go in *The Reasons of Love*. He concedes that "it is obscure to me why" love-as-such, disinterested concern for the well-being of the beloved, "should be so precious to us." Let's not worry that in Frankfurt's account particularity is "mysterious" and our making the value of love-as-such important is "obscure." We can always say that love is, of course, mysterious, once we think about it (or even if we don't), and we have succeeded in revealing the ways love is mysterious. What Frankfurt himself says is this: "In any case, I shall simply stipulate that without loving ... our lives would be intolerably unshaped and empty" and "miserably deprived" ("Duty and Love," 7), a claim elaborated in *The Reasons of Love*. What Frankfurt needs to do, however, is not convince us that love-as-such has value, but that love *in his sense*, which includes disinterested concern (and so forth), has value, and that love in other senses doesn't have as much if any value. What Frankfurt must argue is that unless we have disinterested concern in our lives, emanating from us, our lives will be empty and miserable. *The Reasons of Love* doesn't meet this challenge. Frankfurt says, "It is by caring about things that we infuse the world with importance" and hence with purpose (RL, 23). By loving we make things important and as a result, we have aims, ambitions, and goals (RL, 52–53). Now we know why love-as-such is important, why we consider it to be precious: without these things (aims, goals, etc.) that are made possible by love "we would be dreadfully bored" (RL, 53). "Boredom is a serious matter ... [T]he avoidance of boredom is a profound and compelling human need" (RL, 53–54). So the emptiness and misery that is avoided by loving-as-such is the emptiness and misery of boredom. It is exactly here that Frankfurt's argument collapses, for there is no reason (or Frankfurt provides none) to think that it is only disinterested love that permits us to have aims and goals and thereby avoid boredom.[32]

Even if we grant, however, that love in Frankfurt's sense has value, that fact does not help us decide what to love; all we are told is that a life in which we love something or another is likely to be better than a life in which we love nothing. We have made some progress, for the prospective lover of a particular thing or person can think: "I know that by loving this thing I will be reaping the value of love-as-such; all I need to figure out now is whether I can love this item without too much difficulty, so as not to offset the value of love-as-such, and whether the risks to my well-being through investment are not too high, so as not to offset the value of love-as-such." If the value of love-as-such is *very* high, then taking on improbable and risky beloveds would be justified. Let us cheerfully hunt down that physically offensive, homeless, conniving drug addict whom we scorned a few paragraphs ago. If the value of love-as-such is not very high, however, we would do better by waiting for a more palatable specimen of humanity. Frankfurt *is* Plato. It might turn out, if we are going to calculate, that loving a high-quality specimen of humanity will offset the lesser value of love-as-such, where that love is neither disinterested nor (otherwise) non-Frankfurtian. (Maybe what underlies Kierkegaard's promotion of loving worldly unlovable people is the idea that the value of Christian love-as-such is infinite.)

Sixth, in "Duty and Love," Frankfurt argues—which he argues at greater length in *Reasons*—that if before loving X, I take into account (1) the difficulty for me of loving X, and (2) how much of a risk X poses to my well-being through investment, that does not mean my love is, after all, self-interested: "[W]hat serves the self-interest of the lover is, precisely, the fact that his love is disinterested. The benefit of loving accrues to him only if he is genuinely selfless" ("Duty and Love," 8). Let's suppose that we can make sense of the idea that one who loves disinterestedly, because doing so makes him happy, is not being selfish, self-interested, or self-centered. Notice, however, that Frankfurt's handling of this issue depends on the claim that only disinterested love-as-such has value. For if non-disinterested love-as-such has appreciable value, then love *would* be self-interested, and Frankfurt could not *object* to that. For if non-disinterested love-as-such has appreciable value, via the power to prevent our lives from being boring or miserable, Frankfurt has no way to urge that one type of love is superior to the other.

VI. Susan Wolf on Frankfurt

In "The True, the Good, and the Lovable: Frankfurt's Avoidance of Objectivity," Susan Wolf takes on "Importance" (and "Duty"). She likes neither horn of the *Euthyphro* love dilemma and eventually proposes a solution. On the one side, she finds the idea (in Plato and Aristotle) "that one should love what is [antecedently] worth loving and in proportion to its worthiness" to be "horribly wrong" ("True," 231). On the other side, she finds "problematic as well" (but not "horribly"?) the central idea underlying Frankfurt's claim that it is "suitable" to care about what it is possible to care about, viz., that "the question of whether something is *worthy* of our love … is out of place … [,] that worthiness and love have nothing to do with each other" in this way ("True," 227, 231). For Wolf, it is strange that on Frankfurt's account there is nothing amiss in saying that Hitler's love for Naziism was "suitable" because it was possible for Hitler to care about it, given its importance in his life, and to treat it as worthy of his efforts—hence her title, the "avoidance of objectivity."[33]

Wolf proposes that what is "most suitable" for a person to care about or love depends on three considerations: (1) "whether (and how much) the object in question is worth caring about" (a tip of the hat to Plato and the objectivity of value); (2) "whether (and how much) the person has an affinity for the object" (a tip of the hat to Frankfurt's "possible," though Wolf means more by "affinity," as I explain below); and (3) "whether (and how much) the relation between the person and the object has the potential to create or bring forth experiences, acts, or objects of further value" ("True," 235). The third condition expresses additional agreement with Plato and Aristotle: Plato's *eros* involves begetting *kalos* on/with the *kalos*, while Aristotle's virtuous *philia* issues in more virtue.[34] Hitler's caring about Naziism is not "suitable," for Naziism is not worthy of anyone's love *and* the relation between Hitler and Naziism did not create further value (but destroyed value). That Hitler had an "affinity" for Naziism, which made it possible for him to care about it, does not by itself make his caring for Naziism "suitable."

Frankfurt's reply to Wolf's common sense may strike us as his going off the deep end. Consider someone (say, Adrian Monk) for whom it is possible to care *only* about "avoiding cracks in the sidewalk." Frankfurt claims that "it would be better for him to care about that than to care about nothing," given the value of love-as-such.[35] Frankfurt's claim is perfectly general, so we can substitute anything for "that" in "care about that." It would be better for Hitler to care about Naziism and promote it than not to care about it, if that were the only thing he could care about; this is justified by the value of love-as-such. Right here we could raise a Wolfian moral objection, but let's wait, for we should be considering a more plausible case in which there are a few things that Monk or Hitler could care about, and they are in a position to make a choice: yet Monk goes for avoiding cracks (instead of, say, painting), and Hitler goes for Naziism (instead of, say, painting). Now we raise the Wolfian moral objection: it is not "suitable" for Hitler to choose to care about Naziism instead of painting, because the former destroys value and the latter might well create value. Frankfurt's reply is astounding: "Morality has no independent claim in determining what to care about" (or love). Frankfurt admits that Hitler's Naziism "was a dreadful evil." But "is this a reason [as Wolf would have it] for regarding it as unsuitable to be loved?" No, Frankfurt answers.

"It is possible," Frankfurt writes, "that immoral lives may be good to live." How so? Hitler's life, as evil as it was, might have brought him "contentment and fulfillment and joy." It was Hitler's *happiness* in his immoral life that made it "suitable" for him to love Naziism.[36] The evil of his life counts only against, if anything, the *moral*-suitability of Naziism, not against the distinct *love*-suitability. We wonder: Doesn't moral-suitability sometimes take precedence over love-suitability? No. Moral-suitability is only one kind of suitability, and it does not trump every other kind. Indeed, for Frankfurt, moral-suitability is greatly overrated. "Morality has no independent claim in determining what to care about." The relationship between care and love, on the one side, and morality, on the other side, is not what we have usually taken it to be. Wolf and her comrades assume that we can first identify that which is morally good and then care about it. But—Frankfurt returns to this theme in *Reasons*—moral claims can be derived only from what we care about. If anything is to have value, including moral value, it is only and exactly because we care about it: "The loving itself is fundamental."[37] As he makes the point in *Reasons* (55), "Love is the originating source of terminal value." Hence, there could be no such Wolfian thing as deciding independently that something is morally worthy and then loving it for its merit; its merit as morally worthy *comes from* its being loved. Frankfurt has taken his *agapic* love thesis, that we do not love something because we perceive its value but grant it value (or importance) because we love it, and has expanded it to include that which has moral value. All grounds for complaining about Hitler have been swept from under our feet. Bewildered, we ask: How does something as inexplicable or mysterious as ungrounded love, love not grounded in value, acquire such an immense power to determine the value of *everything* else? (In the remainder, we'll have to pretend that I haven't already demonstrated that Frankfurt is Plato.)

VII. Frankfurt's *The Reasons of Love*

In Frankfurt's account of love, there are four "conceptually necessary features" (RL, 79–80). *First*, love is "disinterested concern for the well-being or flourishing of the person who is loved." Recall that for Frankfurt "disinterested" is "unmotivated by any instrumental concern." Hence, we *consider* the objects of our love to be "valuable in themselves" and they are "important to us for their own sake" (RL, 42). Of course, the objects are not *really* valuable "in themselves," for it is our love that grants them that lofty fraudulent Kantian status. *Second*, love is "ineluctably personal." I have already discussed this mysterious element of love, its "particularity." Frankfurt elaborates: "The person who is loved is loved for himself or for himself as such, and not as an instance of a type" (RL, 79–80; see 44). This elaboration is confusing. What does being loved "for himself" mean? Its meaning is not transparent. The contrast is supposed to be with being loved "as an instance of a type," but it is unclear whether *this* claim is about the basis of love or the ontology of the object of love. Hence, this contrast does not clarify "for himself." When an ordinary person, for example my sister, says she wants to be loved "for herself," what she might mean is that she wants to be loved *just the way she is* (which is the type of love she insists on from any *mensch,* who has Billy Joel to blame for his predicament). That is, when my sister says "for herself" she might mean something about the basis of love: that he will love her in virtue of the properties she *actually* has and does not expect her to change, improve, or make herself into his ideal imaginary woman. On the other hand, maybe she means that she wants to be loved unconditionally, no matter what her properties are.[38] Again we have failed to clarify "for herself" (an expression best avoided by philosophers of love). *Third,* the lover "identifies with his beloved." *Fourth,* love "is not a matter of choice but is determined by conditions that are outside our immediate voluntary control" (RL, 80; see 44). Heterosexual men don't have a say in the matter. They "cannot help," due to evolutionary mechanisms, being attracted, as if by biological gravitation, to hot young fecund women, and loving them, as shown by disinterestedly granting them *carte blanche* access to multiple credit card accounts—all done to avoid an empty, boring life. In what reasonable sense could Hitler have not helped caring about Naziism? Only by a *Robot Chicken* round of neurosurgery not covered by any insurance policy? That he had to care about some ideology or another, *if* he did, is too weak to support Frankfurt's analysis of Hitler and hence his account of love.

Because the four conditions are individually necessary, the absence of any one entails that the phenomenon in question is not love. If I help you primarily because I see, with squinting eyes, that doing so will benefit me, and not because it is good for you, I do not love you, even if I make sure you benefit by my action. Or if I passionately move toward you as a type, say, as the tall, thin, brunette, mousey, Oxford-smart academic of my dreams, then I do not really love you. Or if part of me is "severed" and "held back" from joining with you[39] —that is, if I retain some autonomy, in which case a bad thing will sometimes happen to me without (gladly! I should think) automatically making you worse off, and thus our mutual identification of interests has leaks (and likely intentionally, if we have any brains)—then I do not really love you. Or if I chose to love you—for example, I *decide* to grant you disinterested concern—rather than being caused, determined, forced, or compelled to love you, as if by a witch's potion or spell—I do not really love you. If these four conditions are necessary, the world has known very little love.

Even if these conditions are necessary for love, they are not jointly sufficient—at least Frankfurt never explicitly claims they are. Yet, after laying out these four necessary conditions, Frankfurt launches into his argument that a kind of love, "self-love," satisfies all four conditions. To be brief and mechanical: loving the self can be disinterested; it particularizes the beloved; it identifies with the beloved; and it is not chosen but determined. I cannot attend here to whether Frankfurt's arguments, that loving the self satisfies the four conditions, are trivial or profound.[40] I do want to protest that having shown, to his own satisfaction, that loving the self satisfies all the conditions, Frankfurt proceeds to speak as if satisfying these four conditions is *sufficient* for self-love being a case of love. Indeed, throughout the book, when Frankfurt talks about *X*'s loving *Y* he assumes that what he is talking about is really love, even though the cases in question have only satisfied (some of) the four conditions. We are entitled to ask: In virtue of *what else* is loving the self genuine love. In virtue of *what else* is *X*'s loving *Y* love?

Wolf suggests that "affinity" figures into love, but in a broader sense than Frankfurt's "possibility." What she means is that there is an *affective* component to love. An intriguing idea is that if we add an affective component (the *what else*) to Frankfurt's list of four conditions, we end up with a candidate set of five jointly sufficient conditions for love. Not only is my concern for you disinterested; not only are you an ineffable particular; not only are my interests always tied to yours; not only is my relationship with you beyond my control; but, on top of all this, I truly like you, I feel affection for you, I want to hold your hand. It would seem that Frankfurt should be open to this suggestion (despite the fact that he plays down, even dismisses, romantic or erotic types of love), for two reasons. First, Frankfurt claims that "Among relationships between humans, the love of parents for their infants or small children is the species of caring that comes closest to offering recognizably pure instances of love" (RL, 43; see 82). I suggest that it is parental affection for their children that makes this claim true. The *what else* that turns mere, albeit competent, parental attention into parental love is the fondness parents feel for their children, the joy of having your kiddies jump jubilantly in your lap and playfully pull at your beard. Second, "I love myself but I do not like myself," "I love my baby but I do not like her," and "I love my girl friend but I do not like her" are peculiar. Yet Frankfurt is (unnecessarily) committed to those locutions: he denies that "liking" and "attraction" are essential to love. "As in other modes of caring, the heart of the matter is neither affective nor cognitive" (RL, 42), and we can (on occasion) love things or people we find revolting (RL, 38). But if Frankfurt is right that the affective is not essential to love, his problem remains of uncovering the *what else* that allows him to speak with confidence about *love* throughout the book.

Why does Frankfurt reject affection? Is he afraid that an argument lurks showing that if the affective was added as a fifth condition, the result would be inconsistent propositions? Or would adding "affection" as a necessary condition imply, in his mind, that self-love is not a case of love after all, because "affection for the self" makes little sense? I don't know. Nevertheless, Frankfurt's naturalism, to which I have alluded, provides us with a good reason for including the affective within an account of love.

In "Importance" Frankfurt raised the question, "What should we care about?" and provided an answer: What it is possible for us to care about. In *Reasons*, he is more extreme, even nihilist: "No attempt to deal with the problem of what we have good reason to care about ... can possibly succeed" (RL, 24). I do not wish to repeat all Frankfurt's arguments for this conclusion; we need only a hint of his thinking. We would have to rely on evaluative criteria to weigh and compare the things we might care about, and we would first have to choose those evaluative criteria. On the basis of what? By referring to what we care about! So choosing the evaluative criteria involves us in a "circularity" that is "both inescapable and fatal." "[T]he question of what one should care about must already be answered ... before a rationally conducted inquiry aimed at answering it can even get underway" (RL, 26). The upshot is that the normative question "what to care about" (or "how to live") is replaced by a factual question, "what *do* we care about?" All we can do is determine what in fact we care about. Thus, when Frankfurt writes, "Nobody can pull himself up by his own bootstraps" (RL, 26), I am reminded of John Stuart Mill's (in)famous naturalism that "the sole evidence it is possible to produce that anything is desirable is that people do actually desire it."[41]

Frankfurt's naturalism invokes evolutionary biology in figuring out what it is that we do in fact care about. The answer to the question "what should we care about?" is already answered for us by our evolutionary history that has determined for us what we "cannot help" and *must*, not merely do, care about (RL, 27, 47–48). This answer to the original question, posed 20 years ago in "Importance," is disappointing. We had wondered, philosophically: what grounds love, if it is not based on independent value? And how does free-floating (ungrounded) love acquire the power to determine the value of everything else? *Human biology.* Detecting himself at the end of his rope in trying to answer the original question (pestered there by Baier and then Wolf), perhaps Frankfurt grabbed in desperation for anything that might help. He came up with evolutionary biology, which is all the rage nowadays, even among some philosophers. Whatever. Frankfurt is serious about pulling evolutionary biology into his account of love. But, ironically, what is disastrous for Frankfurt's account of love is not that he invokes evolutionary biology but that he doesn't take it seriously enough or underestimates and misunderstands its implications.

About these innocuous biological claims I have no complaints: "We are moved more naturally to love ourselves ... than we are moved to love other things." "Our dispositions to be loving parents and to love ourselves are innate" (RL, 81). We generally do love our children, "the explanation presumably [lying] in the evolutionary pressures of natural selection" (RL, 40).

And "thanks to natural selection, we are innately constituted to love living" (RL, 41). None of these applications of evolutionary biology is likely to raise eyebrows; evolutionary pressures favor the genetically based traits of those people who take care of themselves, their mates, and their children.

But how would a hardcore, thoroughgoing (not superficial) evolutionary theory judge Frankfurt's four-conditions account of love? The news is bad. (1) Would natural selection favor disinterested concern over instrumental concern? Hardly, for exactly the reason that evolutionary pressure makes us cling to survival, that is, to love living. Jesus' ideal disinterested and selfless concern was linked with his crucifixion. (2) Would natural selection favor the lover's seeing the beloved as an ineffable particular instead of a type? Hardly. Evolution adores types, especially types that are easily recognizable as erotically arousing and potentially procreative. (3) Does love involve joint interests? Only in part: women try to hoard the resources of the men that father their children, while men try to spread their resources around as widely as possible, wherever they successfully leave their fertilizing sperm. Or men try to have their cake and to eat it, leaving sperm but no resources. Or women try to have their cake and to eat it, convincing gullible non-fathers to share their resources. Finally, (4) would natural selection favor identification, that is, people who so strongly identified with their mates that they would routinely be willing to suffer just because their mates suffered? I don't think so. For one thing, that tendency would jeopardize the welfare of their children.

Ah, but what about Susan Wolf's "affinity" or my *affection*? Yes, natural selection would favor parents who felt affection for their children (but that affection would also help the parents, so it is not fully disinterested), as it would also favor mates who felt lasting affection for each other, benefiting themselves and their children for as long as they remained together. For these kinds of reasons, I have never quite understood why natural selection made bedroom death inevitable and thereby demolished the lifelong monogamy that was (according to Aquinas) "natural" to the human species.[42]

Notes

1   Augustine, *Confessions*, bk. 4, sect. 13.
2   Plato, *Symposium*, 201a, 202d, 203c, 204d, 205e, 209b.
3   Aristotle, *Nicomachean Ethics*, 1167a3–a8.
4   Plato, *Symposium*, 210a–d.
5   Aristotle, *Nicomachean Ethics*, 1155b15–20, 1156b5–15, 1157a15–20, 1165b12–15.

6   Augustine, *Confessions*, 7.17 and 3.1, respectively.
7   Plato, *Symposium*, 210e–211a.
8   See Gregory Vlastos, "The Individual as an Object of Love in Plato," at 110. Contrast Martha Nussbaum, "The Speech of Alcibiades."
9   WL, 158 (italics omitted); for a sarcastic version, see FT, 91.
10 Aristotle, *Nicomachean Ethics*, 1165b3–35. For discussion, see Alan Soble, *Eros, Agape, and Philia*, 43–44; Soble, *The Structure of Love*, 220–24.
11 See Irving Singer, *The Nature of Love*, vol. *1*, 3–22.
12 See Anders Nygren, *Den kristna kärlekstanken genom tiderna*, 210; Nygren, *Agape and Eros*, 94.
13 Gene Outka, *Agape*, 81–83, 157–58.
14 For example, John Brentlinger, "The Nature of Love." Almost the whole of Soble, *The Structure of Love*, is devoted to this distinction.
15 Plato, *Euthyphro*, 10d–11b.
16 Frankfurt makes the same point in replying to Susan Wolf, "The True, the Good, and the Lovable," 249.
17 David Hume, *A Treatise of Human Nature*, 2.2.11 (all passages are in this section). For an overview, see J. Martin Stafford, "Hume, David."
18 Immanuel Kant, *The Metaphysics of Morals*, 180.
19 Singer, *The Nature of Love*, vol. *1*, 13. We've now seen two examples of a major defect of Frankfurt's book. Much of what he writes in *The Reasons of Love* had been written before the book was published in 2004, and written well enough or better, by other philosophers—both in the long history of the philosophy of love and among his contemporaries. Frankfurt came onto the "philosophy of love" scene rather late and fails to acknowledge almost every philosopher who had already advanced his theses or had discussed them in detail.
20 Michel Montaigne, "On Affectionate Relationships"; Kant, *Lectures on Ethics*, Ak 27:388 158–59; G.W.F. Hegel, "On Love."
21 J.F.M. Hunter, *Thinking about Sex and Love*, 75–76.
22 Robert Nozick, "Love's Bond", 78, 70, 68, 69. For a critique of the union-of-interests view, see Soble, "Irreplaceability.".
23 Spoken by the Young Man in "The Banquet" (SLW, 42–43; VI 44).
24 See Soble, *The Structure of Love*, 233–35.
25 Frankfurt's account of love contains other non-Christian elements. For example, there is no turning of the other cheek (RL, 31): "Why should we not be happy to fight for what we wholeheartedly love, even when there are no good arguments to show that it is correct for us to love it?" This snappy rhetorical question is frightening in an age of religious terrorism.
26 Singer, *The Nature of Love*, vol. *1*, 23.
27 Annette Baier, "Caring about Caring"; Soble, *The Structure of Love*, 129–30; Wolf, "The True, the Good, and the Lovable."
28 Montaigne's much-praised essay on love/friendship contains a related confusion. He says, famously, that "If you press me to tell why I loved him,

I feel that this cannot be expressed, except by answering: Because it was he, because it was I," which may be taken as asserting the "particularity" of love. Yet Montaigne also writes, "We sought each other before we met because of the reports we heard of each other," which admits that properties played a large role in their love. The translation is Frame's "On Affectionate Relationships," 299.

29 For the details, see Mark Bernstein, "Love, Particularity, and Selfhood."
30 Does Frankfurt mean that love is *de re*, not *de dicto*? See Robert Kraut, "Love *De Re*."
31 Neera Badhwar, "Friends as Ends in Themselves"; Robert Brown, *Analyzing Love*; Mark Fisher, *Personal Love*; Roger Lamb, "Love and Rationality"; Amélie Rorty, "The Historicity of Psychological Attitudes"; Roger Scruton, *Sexual Desire*; A.W. Price, *Love and Friendship in Plato and Aristotle*, 13; Soble, "Irreplaceability."
32 For a sophisticated critique of Frankfurt on the relationship between having goals and boredom, see Elijah Millgram, "On Being Bored out of Your Mind."
33 See Baier, "Caring about Caring," 277.
34 Plato, *Symposium*. 206b, 209a–c; Aristotle, *Nicomachean Ethics*, 1172a10.
35 Harry Frankfurt, "Reply to Wolf," in *Contours of Agency: Essays on Themes from Harry Frankfurt*, eds. Sarah Buss and Lee Overton (Cambridge, MA: MIT Press, 2002).
36 Such a claim does not *bother us* if made about Monk and his avoiding cracks. It *does* bother us about Hitler. Frankfurt obliterates this difference.
37 The lines quoted in this paragraph are from Frankfurt's "Reply to Wolf" (Buss and Overton, 248, 249, 252n4).
38 Only God can love her that way, according to William Butler Yeats, "For Anne Gregory," 293.
39 Hegel, "On Love," 306.
40 I carried out this task in Soble, "Concerning Self-Love."
41 J.S. Mill, *Utilitarianism*, 37.
42 This essay is a much revised and polished version of my essay review of *The Reasons of Love*, which appeared in *Essays in Philosophy* 6:1 (January, 2005). That paper can be accessed at http://commons.pacificu.edu/eip/vol6/iss1/30. The revision is printed here with the permission of the journal's founding editor, Michael Goodman, and the current editor, David Boersema.

3

The Importance of Whom We Care About

Troy Jollimore

We love the things we love for what they are.

—Robert Frost

I

"We love the things we love for what they are." Or do we? It sounds like a nice sentiment. Who, after all, would want to be loved for something she was not? But perhaps what we really want is to be loved for no reason, or for reasons having nothing to do with what we are. For what if I am not worthy of love? Or what if I am loved for what I am, and then I cease to be what I am and become something else instead? People change. If it is true, as some say, that what we want is to be loved unconditionally, then we may have to reject the idea that we want to be loved for what we are.

"It is a duty to love the people we see," says Kierkegaard in *Works of Love* (WL, 161). The idea that one ought to love the person one sees might sound close to the idea that one ought to love that person for what he is; for what do I see when I see a person, if not that person's good and bad qualities, the particular characteristics that make her who she is? But Kierkegaard also warns us not to pay attention to those qualities; they can, he says, distract our attention from the person himself, and focusing on the qualities seems to make one's love conditional, and hence unreliable:

> The Christian point of view, however, is that to love is to love precisely the person one sees. The emphasis is not on loving the perfections one sees in a person, but the emphasis is on loving the person one sees; whether one sees perfections or imperfections in this person, yes, however distressingly this person has changed, inasmuch as he has not ceased to be the same person. He who loves the perfections he sees in a person does not see the person and therefore ceases to love if the perfections

cease […] Christian love grants the beloved all his imperfections and weaknesses and in all his changes remains with him, loving the person it sees. (WL, 173)

At least most of the time Kierkegaard seems to see a person's qualities as something separate from the person herself, so that paying attention to the former necessarily distracts us from the latter. Every person, Kierkegaard writes, "is something particular, represents something particular, but essentially he is something else [which] we do not get to see here in life" (WL, 86). This applies not only to one's surface properties—physical attractiveness, manners, health (in its more visible aspects), wealth—but to moral qualities as well. Citing Peter's love for Jesus as an example, he claims that you ought to continue to love your friend even when he disappoints you by betraying or abandoning you:

Therefore if you want to be perfect in love, strive to fulfill this duty, in loving to love the person one sees, to love him just as you see him, with all his imperfections and weaknesses, to love him as you see him when he has changed completely, when he no longer loves you but perhaps turns away indifferent or turns away to love another, to love him as you see him when he betrays and denies you. (WL, 174)

Here we find two related ideas. The first is that you ought to continue to love your beloved no matter what you see when you open your eyes to her. The second is that love should have nothing to do with your beloved's attractive qualities, that it is in no way a response to her "perfections."

When Kierkegaard speaks of seeing the beloved clearly and accurately, then, he does not seem to have in mind the kind of attention to detail and careful, discerning perception that Iris Murdoch connects with love, but rather a kind of vision that allows us to see *past* particular details and to view—well, whatever it is, precisely, that we "essentially" are.[1] Far from being a part of love or a help to love, the kind of clear and robust attention to particular details that Murdoch praises seems to be a kind of hindrance to love, even, perhaps, an insurmountable obstacle to love:

Love is commonly thought of as admiration's wide-open eye that is searching for excellences and perfections. It is then that one complains that the search is futile. We shall not decide to what extent the individual is or is not justified in this, whether what he is seeking, the lovable excellences and perfections, is not to be found, whether he is not confusing seeking with fastidiousness. No, we do not wish to dispute in this manner, we do not wish to carry on a dispute within this conception of love, because *this whole conception is an error*, since love is rather the closed eye of forbearance and leniency that does not see defects and imperfections.[2]

Consider the sort of "fastidious" person Kierkegaard has in mind here: the person who claims she can find no one to love, because no one is worthy of love. Suppose she makes her complaint out in terms of *qualities*: she simply cannot find anyone whose qualities are good enough to render them worthy of love. One might say that she is simply not looking hard enough, that everyone has some good qualities, though they are sometimes hard to see. But this is not Kierkegaard's complaint. According to him, the fastidious person's error is more fundamental: "this whole conception is a delusion." Either we should not be thinking about people's worthiness to be loved at all, or else we should not think of worthiness in terms of qualities, of "perfections."

It is difficult to determine which of these Kierkegaard means. (It is entirely possible, too, that he simply does not have a consistent position about this.) But we may at least say this with confidence: for Kierkegaard, love is not a response to the beloved's positive qualities, and a common and serious error is to pay too much attention those qualities, to the question of what the beloved is like. "It is a sad but altogether too common inversion to go on talking continually about how the object of love must be so it can be loveworthy, instead of talking about how love must be so it can be love" (WL, 159). This passage, like many others in *Works of Love*, suggests that when we (properly) love the people we love, it is not because their good qualities give us reason to do so. Indeed, our reasons for loving people have nothing to do with what they are. Either we love them for no reason at all or, if there is a reason, it is a reason having to do with the nature of love, and not with the nature of what we love.

II

According to Kierkegaard, when a person judges someone to be unworthy of love, and so refuses to love him, we should not agree with his assessment and take it that he has correctly responded to some flaw in the object. Rather, it is the person who fails to love that is flawed. This may suggest that Kierkegaard is committed to some version of the following:

The Brute Love Account: Love is not, and should not be, a reflection of or a response to its object's inherent value or worthiness. So love need not be supported by reasons having to do with the worth of the beloved, and the fact that a given love is directed toward a valueless object does not render it unjustified or inappropriate.

But as I suggested above, the matter is not entirely clear. What we have seen up to this point seems to suggest that for Kierkegaard, judgments of worth have no place in love. But it is also consistent with a different interpretation, that for Kierkegaard the people we love *are* worthy of love, but that they are not rendered worthy by their good qualities; rather, what makes people worthy and appropriate objects of love is some deeper fact about them, something that transcends or lies beneath their surface "perfections" and "imperfections." If what justifies love is some abstract and ineffable thing that all persons, regardless of their particular qualities, possess, then to hold *anyone* unworthy of love would have to be a kind of mistake.

Other philosophers have more decisively closed the door on the notion that what justifies love, when it is justified, is the fact that the beloved is valuable in some way. Among contemporaries we find Harry Frankfurt, who commits himself to a version of the Brute Love Account:

> [L]ove does not require a response by the lover to any real or imagined value in what he loves. Parents do not ordinarily love their children so much, for example, because they perceive that their children possess exceptional value. In fact, it is the other way around: the children seem to the parents to be valuable, and they are valuable to the parents, only because the parents love them. Parents have been known to love—quite genuinely—children that they themselves recognize as lacking any particular inherent merit.
>
> As I understand the nature of love, the lover does not depend for this loving upon reasons of any kind. Love is not a conclusion. It is not an outcome of reasoning, or a consequence of reasons. It *creates* reasons. What it means to love is, in part, to take the fact that a certain action would serve the good of the beloved as an especially compelling reason for performing that action. (TOS, 25)

The Brute Love Account, which holds that a person's valuable qualities—the sorts of things that we often tend to cite when asked questions like "what do you love about her?"—in fact do not function as reasons to love her, and indeed that there are no reasons for love at all, occupies one pole of a range of conceptual possibilities. At the other pole we find what I will refer to as the *Reason-Determined Love Account*:

The Reason-Determined Love Account: Reasons for loving A are directly proportional to the value of A, and questions of whom I love, how much I love them, and how I should treat them, are determined entirely by my reasoned judgments as to their objective value. (They are thus entirely independent of my preferences or will.) Thus, loving someone a great deal involves judging that that particular person is objectively more valuable than other people, and that I ought to treat her, accordingly, as an object more precious than the things around her.

Both accounts have their attractions. There is something validating and affirming about Reason-Determined Love: on this account, the people who love me have judged me to be worth loving, and in loving me (if they are getting it right) they are appreciating things about me that ought to be appreciated—perhaps, indeed, the things about me that I myself value.[3] On the other hand, Reason-Determined Love may also inspire anxiety as to whether I really am worthy of such love, whether I will continue to be worthy, and whether an even worthier object of love might come along (in which case, it would seem, my lovers, at least if they are to be rational, would be obligated to transfer their love from me to my competitor). If we think that love should be more stable than this—if we think that a love that was fickle in this way would be flawed, and that we owe those whom we love something better than that—we may be moved to reject the idea of Reason-determined Love. Indeed, this way of thinking about love may seem to some to make love into a grasping, needy, selfish emotion. It is at odds, or so it will be claimed, with the selflessness of love, the idea that true generosity of spirit is shown by the willingness to love whether the object deserves to be loved or not.

It is not surprising, given this way of approaching the issue, that parent–child love, especially love for very young children, should prove to be an especially significant source of the intuitions that support the Brute Love Account. One might love one's friend or romantic partner because he is witty, kind, physically attractive, fun, or for any number of other reasons, but infants possess none of these properties, and such attractive properties as they do possess (cuteness, perhaps) tend to be shared by most infants, so can hardly justify a parent's disproportionate love. Moreover, parents are *expected*, and in the view of many morally obligated, to love their children disproportionately, and to do so without connecting that love to any form of evaluation: love is not, here, an optional response, nor something that may be withdrawn should one's child turn out to be disappointing. Finally, as Frankfurt indicates, parents may claim to love their children even before they are born, at a stage when we might think they would know nothing whatsoever about the good qualities of the children-to-be, or about their worth in any sense:

> I can declare with unequivocal confidence that I do not love my children because I am aware of some value that inheres in them independent of my love for them. The fact is that I loved them even before they were born—before I had any especially relevant information about their personal characteristics or their particular merits and virtues. (RL, 39)

The case of parent–child love, then, is one in which we are especially likely to be persuaded by Kierkegaard's claim that with respect to love, "the task is not to find the lovable object, but the task is to find the once given or chosen object—lovable, and to be able to continue to find him lovable no matter how he is changed" (WL, 159, italics removed).

III

I take it that the most plausible claim in the first passage from Frankfurt I quoted above is the following:

> (A) "Parents do not ordinarily love their children so much ... because they perceive that their children possess exceptional value."

Of course, we are interested not only in how love ordinarily works, but also, and indeed more significantly, in how love should and must work. In addition to (A), then, we should also consider (B) (a claim that Frankfurt would also accept):

> (B) Loving someone, even loving him a great deal, need not imply judging him to possess exceptional value; and the fact that it is not accompanied by this judgment does not render it inappropriate.

The idea that a person possessing "exceptional value," in this context, is the idea that she possesses an unusually high degree of value as compared with other persons. It is only this, on the Reason-Determined Love Account, that could justify someone, her parent for example, in loving her more than others. Given this understanding of "exceptional value," I agree with Frankfurt (and, we can assume, Kierkegaard) that (A) and (B) are true, and that they need to be recognized by any adequate account of love. Most parents, after all, are not so deluded as to believe that their children are vastly more valuable than other parents' children. Some parents may think that their children are *a bit* better than *many* other children, but surely most do not literally believe that they happen to be the parents of children who would be judged by impartial and objective observers to be the very best children in the world. Moreover, as we have noted, parents may say that they love their children from the moment they are born, if not before; yet one could not know, that early on, whether or not one's children were going to have any especially significant value (and they certainly don't possess any such value yet). (A), then, seems to be true. On the assumption that there is nothing incoherent or conceptually wrong about the love these ordinary parents have for their children, (B) must presumably be true as well.

Frankfurt thinks these claims weigh heavily against the view that we love people for reasons, and that my loving someone involves the judgment that she possesses significant inherent value. He moves quickly, then, from the rejection of the Reason-Determined Love Account to a version of the Brute Love Account, one that involves what I will call Willed Love:

> *The Willed Love Account:* Questions of whom I love, and how much I love them, are entirely determined by commitments of my will. They have nothing to do with my assessments of the beloved's (independent) value.[4]

That Willed Love is a type of Brute Love is clear: if love is willed in this sense then we cannot and do not need to give reasons for loving the people we love, for it is the configurations of our will, and not our responsiveness to value or reasons, that determine and ought to determine whom we love and how much we love them.

Suppose that we agree, as I think we should, that the Reason-Determined Love Account ought to be rejected. Must our next move then be to adopt some version of the Brute Love Account? I do not think so. These two positions, as I have said, occupy two poles of a continuum, and both are too extreme. We would do better, in this case, to look for something in the middle. The Brute Love Position commits us to more than we should be willing to commit to.

To see this, let's consider three further claims. All of these claims are associated with the Reason-Determined Love Account, at least to the extent that they are all true if that account is correct; all of them, moreover, are quite explicitly rejected by Frankfurt. But each of them possesses significant independent plausibility—they seem to reflect important facts about our experiences of love—and I will suggest that we can hold on to all of them even if we reject the less plausible elements of the Reason-Determined Love Account:

(C) Loving someone involves judging her to possess significant inherent value, i.e., value that is independent of my desires or other facts about my conative nature.

(D) If P loves Q, and P's love for Q is not unjustified, then, as a minimal condition, Q must possess significant inherent value.

(E) (At least some of) our reasons for action are ultimately grounded in the inherent values of things that are affected by our actions, and that we have such reasons is a matter of objective fact, independent of an agent's motivations, preferences, etc.[5]

Frankfurt, as I have said, rejects all three of these:

(NOT-C): Loving a person, according to Frankfurt, need not involve judging her to possess any degree whatever of inherent value. As we have seen, he holds that "love does not require a response by the lover to any real or imagined value in what he loves. [...] Parents have been known to love—quite genuinely—children that they themselves recognize as lacking any particular inherent merit." (Compare OC, 172–73)

(NOT-D): That one loves a person who does not possess inherent value does not, says Frankfurt, render the love unjustified; such facts are irrelevant to love. Indeed, since love is properly grounded in brute commitments of the will, it is not the sort of thing that needs to be, or even could be, justified. "[I]f I ask myself whether my children are worthy of my love, my quite emphatic inclination is simply to reject the question as inappropriate and misguided. This is not because it goes without saying that they *are* worthy. It is because my love for them is in no way a response to or based upon any evaluation."[6]

(NOT-E): An agent's reasons for action are, on Frankfurt's view, ultimately grounded in an agent's desires, urges, brute commitments, and other configurations of his own will. Frankfurt: "[T]he most basic and essential question for a person to raise concerning the conduct of his life cannot be the *normative* question of how he *should* live. That question can sensibly be asked only on the basis of a prior answer to the *factual* question of what he actually *does* care about." (RL, 25)

The Willed Love Account adheres to Hume's statement in *A Treatise of Human Nature* that reason is nothing but "the slave of the passions." Given the way in which one's will is formed (one's preferences and affinities, etc.), reason's function is to determine, within the limits set by the will, the things one *ought* to care about. Reason can help an agent keep her carings consistent, avoid caring about things that do not cohere with the larger set of things she cares about, and so forth; but there is no question of its being able to address the issue of whether a given person or thing is, in and of itself, worthy of care. All value is brought about by acts of valuing. Acts of valuing may not be completely random, since they are shaped and constrained both by human nature and by value created by other acts of valuing; still they are, at the fundamental level, arbitrary.

This position will seem appealing to those who, like Frankfurt, are skeptical about the existence of a realm of objective values to which practical reason might be responsive. There isn't nearly enough room here to get into the complex meta-ethical issues that surround this question, beyond simply noting my view that the most frequently cited arguments for skepticism about objective value are not nearly as convincing as many skeptics tend to assume.[7] At any rate, regardless of their metaphysical underpinnings, our experiences of love and the practices that express those experiences outline a context in which practical reason does not *seem* to work the way the Brute Love Account would have it. We feel as if we love people for reasons, that our love is a response to valuable qualities that would exist and bear value whether we or anyone else were around to respond to their value. We feel, that is to say, that we love the people we love for what they are, and that this is intimately bound up with the question of why these people matter so much to us. The Brute Love Account does not fit well with our actual experiences of love. Still, that account does get some things right; it recommends, correctly, that we reject claims like (A) and (B). The question, then, is whether we can reject (A) and (B) without committing ourselves to the entirety of the Brute Love Account—and if so, how?

IV

What we are looking for is a position that supports (C), (D), and (E)—and so avoids collapsing into the Willed Love Account or any other account that sees love as merely Brute—but that can also accommodate (A) and (B). Such a position will capture what is plausible about the Brute Love Account, while avoiding the unattractive view that love is simply a brute and fundamentally arbitrary matter of the will that is in no way a response to the value of the beloved or that of her qualities. Such a position, which I will refer to as the Moderate Position, is readily available:

> *The Moderate Position:* Love is a response to the inherent value of the beloved—and in particular, to the beloved's valuable qualities—and is thus largely a matter of reason. (Reason tells us, among other things,

that it is inappropriate to love an inanimate object—one's Porsche 911, let us suppose—in the way that it is appropriate to love one's spouse or child.) Love is unjustified when directed toward an unworthy object. However, there are many persons who might reasonably be loved, depending on one's personal preferences and the circumstances of one's life. Indeed, it is entirely consistent with the Moderate Position to hold that *everyone* is sufficiently inherently valuable to be worthy of love, although different people are worthy of being loved for somewhat different reasons.

The question of which particular persons one comes to love and to form love-relationships with is answered by a combination of many factors: it is partly a matter of circumstance (whom one is related to, whom one gets to know, who finds *you* attractive, etc.), partly a matter of reason (of the various people one gets to know, one can judge that some rate more highly than others in certain respects) and partly a matter of the will and other conative factors (one has certain preferences, finds oneself drawn to some individuals rather than others, and may sometimes, as Frankfurt suggests, find that one has no choice but to love certain individual persons). It is *not*, at any rate, answered simply by our judgments about which persons happen to possess the most valuable qualities, as the Reason-Determined Account would have it.

The Moderate Position, like the Reason-Determined Love Account, asserts or implies (C), (D), and (E). Can it accommodate (A) and (B)? It seems that it can. Frankfurt writes:

> I do not believe that the valuable qualities [my children] do happen to possess, strictly in their own rights, would really provide me with a very compelling basis for regarding them as having greater worth than many other possible objects of love that in fact I love much less. It is quite clear to me that I do not love them more than other children because I believe they are better. (RL, 39)

The second sentence in this passage is surely correct. (The first is likely also true, though it depends on just how we interpret such phrases as "strictly in their own rights" and "compelling basis.") This is just another way of expressing the plausibility of (A) and (B):

> (A) "Parents do not ordinarily love their children so much … because they perceive that their children possess exceptional value."

(B) Loving someone, even loving him a great deal, need not imply judging him to possess exceptional value; and the fact that it is not accompanied by this judgment does not render it inappropriate.

But we should be able to see now that (A) and (B) raise no deep problem for the Moderate Position. For that position, as we have seen, allows both reason and the will to play substantial roles in determining whom we love. In particular, unlike the Reason-Determined Love Account, the Moderate Position allows that, while a certain degree of value is necessary to render an object an eligible target of love (i.e., the sort of love we direct toward persons, and which would be inappropriate if directed toward any object that was *not* a person), the degree of the lover's love need not vary directly with the degree of assessed value. Love, in this way, resembles such emotions as anger and resentment, which vary not only with one's assessment of the badness of the action that has provoked the response, but also with other factors, including both one's personal connection with the offender, and also one's particular sensitivities and tendencies to feel hurt or outraged by one type of insult or offense as opposed to another.

This is to say that there is plenty of room, even within a broadly shared framework of value assessments that are taken to be matters of reason and objective judgment, for personal differences and idiosyncrasies to play a role. With respect to potential partners' attractive qualities, for instance, it is not unreasonable to feel either that a well-developed sense of humor is more important in a partner than strong political commitments, or that the reverse is true; it depends on the sort of person you are, what tends to attract, please, and fulfill you, what makes you anxious, what fits with your own plans, preferences, and history, and so forth. There is much room for disagreement, here—and, outside of disagreement, plenty of room for sheer difference, in taste, preference, and attitude—yet this should not be taken to show that our judgments in these areas are not judgments at all, but instead fundamentally arbitrary matters of brute psychology. After all, although it is not unreasonable to prefer a sense of humor to political commitment, or vice versa, there are values and preferences here that would be unreasonable. A person who could not see *any* value in a good sense of humor or in political commitment, for instance, let alone one who somehow thought these things were positively *bad*, would surely be missing something important. A different but no less serious error would be committed by a person who placed a great deal of significance on something that was, in fact, completely trivial—the fact that a person had been born during the month of October, for example.

What is crucial is that a parent need not judge her child to possess "exceptional value" or "any *particular* inherent merit" (i.e., a level of merit that raises him above other children) in order to justify her love for him in terms of his value. Any ordinary human child, even a child who is less than average in many respects, is nonetheless a suitable object of love. A child's particular value, in and of itself, does not answer the question, why does her parent love her in particular, as opposed to other children? That question is answered by other facts: in this case, facts about the relationship and the shared history. But that question is distinct from the more fundamental question, why is love an appropriate and fitting response to this (or any) child? The fact that the child's value, in and of itself, cannot fully answer the first question does not show that it is completely irrelevant to either. Nor does it commit us to saying that the parent would still love the child, and *should* love the child, even if—whatever precisely this might mean—the child somehow possessed no value at all.

The upshot is that a parent need not judge her child to possess "exceptional value" in order to justify her love for him. Against the general background of things that might be valued—most of which have little inherent value of any sort—*any* child is exceptional, as is any human being. Similarly, the Moderate Position can happily acknowledge Frankfurt's observation that "Parents have been known to love—quite genuinely—children that they themselves recognize as lacking any particular inherent merit," so long as we understand that a person can lack *particular* inherent merit without possessing no merit whatsoever. Thus, the Moderate Position can happily accommodate (A) and (B); the plausibility of (A) and (B), then, does not in any way obligate us to accept the Willed Love Account, nor any other version of the Brute Love Account.

V

Much depends, it seems, on how we decide to read the word *particular* in the phrase "particular merits and virtues." What is necessary is to see that a child can possess *considerable* inherent worth without possessing *particular* worth, if by "particular worth" we mean a level of worth that sets the child apart from, and indeed above, other children. And this means that we can agree with Frankfurt (and Kierkegaard) that a parent can love her children without believing them to be more valuable than other children, without committing ourselves to the implausible idea that a parent can love her children while believing them to possess no value at all, or while not caring whether they possess value or not.

But there is, it will be urged, another relevant meaning of "particular" here, and it is one that the Moderate Position must take seriously: a person's particular merits are surely those that distinguish him from other people, those that make him the unique individual he is. (As I have said, on the reading of Kierkegaard according to which people are loved because they are worthy, he must still deny this; whatever "worth" is, it is something abstract that has nothing to do with a person's particular characteristics, and so is possessed by all persons equally.) Surely this, it will be said, is what we mean when we say that we love the people we love "for what they are." But the case of children was thought to create problems for this, for children, at least in the very early stages of their lives, are not yet unique individuals, and have not yet developed the features for which, as adults, they may be appreciated and loved.

The solution, I think, is to acknowledge that we do not love children in precisely the way that we love adults (and after all, we do not love all adults in precisely the same way, either), but that the proper understanding of how we *do* love children does not require us to detach this love from the notion of value, or even from *particular*—that is, highly concrete and specific—values.

Consider the following passage from David Velleman, in which he describes the experience of raising his children:

> [O]nce my children adopted some directions—and there have been many different directions over the years—I found myself caring about their progress in those directions, no matter how little intrinsic value I might have been inclined to see there in advance. In a quick succession of years I became deeply interested in lacrosse and Morris dancing, poetry slams and photography, and specifically in the accomplishments of a particular midfielder, Morris dancer, poet, or photographer, because these were the directions that my children had set for themselves. Of course, I eventually learned to appreciate some of these accomplishments intrinsically: I would realize with amazement that I was cheering as my son walloped a schoolmate with a metal stick or that I was applauding choreography that previously would have struck me as no more than quaint. But I learned to appreciate these accomplishments, to begin with, because they were the ones that my children had chosen to cultivate. In other words, I learned to appreciate them out of love for my children.[8]

A casual reading of this passage might take it to support either the Brute Account—at least where love for children is concerned—or something close to it. We might think that it shows that Velleman was committed to valuing the activities his children engaged in, *whatever* they turned out to be like, and that this must show that such valuing must therefore take no notice whatever of the activities' particular value. And it would only be natural to assume that what goes for the children's activities and interests also goes for the children themselves, so that it must either be the case that Velleman's love for his children is in no way a response to their value, or else that the value that matters here cannot be attached to anything particular about these specific children, but must instead be instantiated in something abstract, ineffable, and equally possessed by all. Such love, it seems, is not a *response* to any valuable thing external to itself (whether it be the children or the activities in which they are engaged), but rather a creation of the lover that is then projected onto its objects.

But Velleman does not say that he was simply projecting value onto activities that possess no value in and of themselves. Rather, what he says is only that he was, with respect to many of these activities, unable to see any value *at first*. He went on to *find* (and not *create*) value in them, in large part because he was, as a result of his relationship and love for his children, motivated to make the effort to do so. But the value he found was value that existed in the activities, independently of his perception of it. That value takes some effort to perceive or appreciate does not imply that it is a mere projection, or in any other way unreal. Moreover, even prior to the attempt to discover value in his children's activities—prior, even, to their deciding what those activities would be—he had reason to be quite confident that his attempt would, in the end, be successful. This is so for the simple reason that even in their quite early stages of development human persons, while quite various in their interest and attractions, do not tend to become attracted to and deeply involved in activities that literally possess *no* value whatsoever. They may sometimes engage in activities whose positive values are outweighed by negative values—all of us do at times, we're only human—but while that may pose difficult parenting questions, it poses no difficult philosophical problem for the view I am advancing here. (Still, it is worth saying that it is not the case that Velleman would have been able to see value in *any* interest his children might conceivably have developed. If their only desire had been to count blades of grass, my guess is he would not have found himself happily driving them to the Grass-Counting Regionals; rather, he would have been stymied in his attempt to share their experiences and values. The kind of objectivism about values that fits most naturally with the Moderate Position is happily pluralist about values, but there are still limits: some things just are not, objectively speaking, valuable.)

A parent like Velleman, then, does not have to wait and see what his children are going to become interested in in order to know, with a very high degree of confidence, whether he will be able to find value in those interests; like any parent, he can be reasonably confident, even at the beginning of the process, that *whatever* interests his children will develop, he too will be able to see value in them—a value that is not created by his interests, but which exists in its own right. (Note that if we undermine the confidence, we also undermine the love. If a prospective parent learned that it was not a fetus she carried inside her, but rather a tumor, she would surely not claim to love it in anything like the way that people claim to love their children-to-be.[9]) And the same goes for persons themselves. A sufficiently open, sympathetic, and committed eye can find something to love, to feel for, to identify with, in pretty much anyone—anyone, at least, who has achieved personhood or is on the road to doing so. And this, as we have noted, is perfectly consistent with the Moderate Position.

This is not to say that particular merits and virtues are entirely irrelevant. In fact they are essential. The point, though, is that at this stage of this sort of relationship a prior and precise knowledge of them is not necessary; it is sufficient to be confident that one's children, as they develop genuine personalities and become full-fledged persons, will acquire characteristics *of some specific sort or other* that will ground and justify one's love.[10] The love of an unborn child or an infant is not yet, for the most part, the appreciation of specific value-bearing properties; it consists, largely, in a commitment to finding and appreciating those properties that will come into existence, when they do. In fact, love always involves this sort of commitment, and is always in part a process of watching the beloved develop and change over time, a process of learning to value and appreciate the new forms she takes as extensions of and elaborations on the previous forms to which one's love was already attached. (That this is a commitment of the will is something the Moderate Position need not deny; but the Moderate Position will remind us that it is no *brute* commitment, but one grounded in reasonable beliefs and expectations about how a human life exists through time—and, in cases other than that of infants, in the value of the particular characteristics the beloved has already developed and exhibited.)

In *this* sense of "particular," then—the sense in which a particular value is one that is specific and concrete, and thus helps to define the identity of the person whose activities or character display it—loving a child, or any other person, does indeed involve appreciating their particular values, and thus believing them to possess such values. The word "involve," admittedly, is usefully loose. In many cases, such as the love of a person for a romantic lover, a friend, or even an adult relative, the relationship is straightforward: loving a person is a way of valuing him that is largely constituted by one's valuing of the particular values he instantiates and displays. In other cases, such as that of love for fetuses or infants who have not yet developed real personhood, such love as one may feel is largely anticipatory, and consists largely of a commitment to find value in that particular individual, and her interests and activities, once she has developed into a person. But what love aims at, ultimately—and what it is and must be in its complete and most flourishing form—is, precisely, an appreciation of the valuable aspects of the loved person, in all of her individual distinctiveness. We love the people we love for who they are.

VI

It would be absurd to hold that love had nothing whatever to do with the lover's desires, preferences, and commitments. Indeed, it is surely true, in some sense, that love is largely a matter of the will. But if we focus too much on the will, and on a certain conception of the will, we begin to lose sight of precisely what love itself tries always to keep in sight: the beloved, the person who means so much to the lover. It is true that loving, as an activity, adds value and meaning to our lives. But the lover will not conclude from this that the loving is more important than the person who is loved. And we should not, without a very compelling reason, accept a theory of the value of love and the beloved that would prioritize the former over the latter.

One of the things we want from our lovers is simply that they pay attention to us. Indeed, it is plausible to think that one of the great values and benefits of being in a love-relationship is that it allows one to be seen, and thus prevents one from being invisible; one feels *known*, and so one feels that one *matters*, at least to one other person. Of course there are complications: sometimes too much attention can be paid, or attention can be paid in the wrong way, and one can end up feeling surveilled, objectified, or over-scrutinized. This tends to happen, though, only when the attention is not paid in a loving manner. Truly loving attention, including criticism, is affirming even when it is painful, as when Mr. Knightley chastises Emma for her rude behavior toward Miss Bates in Jane Austen's novel *Emma*. It hurts Emma to hear Mr. Knightley's critique, but it also helps us (and eventually her) know that he loves her, that he has been paying attention, that he cares, and that he thinks well enough of her to hold her to a high moral standard.

Seeing a person, then—even, at times, seeing a person's limitations and imperfections—is both fully compatible with and a requirement for loving that person, and it is part of what we want from our lovers. These observations, though, fit poorly into the framework provided by Frankfurt. If my lover pays attention to me—if she sees me—she is going to notice me, and she is going to notice what I am like, what kind of person I am, what features I have. Indeed, I think part of what I want from love is to be appreciated for who I am, to have my qualities seen and valued. But on Frankfurt's account none of this can really matter, at least at the fundamental level. It does not matter whether my lover sees me as I am, or whether she projects a false image onto me and then cares for me under the guise of that image. The tightest allowable connection between my qualities and the love my lover feels for me is a causal connection, that the qualities *provoke* the love; and if this is so, then it does not matter whether she is seeing qualities I actually possess or qualities she merely wishes I possessed. Someone who loves me is presumably going to find most of my qualities valuable no matter what they are, or what she thinks them to be, because it is precisely her act of valuing that creates value. It is valuing (in the projective sense) and not appreciating (which is a responsive act) that does the work on Frankfurt's view:

> It is not because I have noticed their value that I love my children as I do. It is really the other way around. The reason they are so precious to me is simply that I love them so much. It is as a *consequence* of my love for them that they have acquired, in my eyes, a value that otherwise they would quite certainly not possess.[11]

Such a view entirely neglects the importance of the loved person. Most of us desire that our valuable features be noticed. We want our lovers to see what we take to be good about ourselves, and think it good. We might also want them to see, and perhaps help us to see, good things about ourselves that we might have missed. Moreover, the idea that my value, in my lover's eyes, is a mere consequence of her act of loving seems objectionable. I would be disappointed and probably insulted if she indicated that, in her view, I was only valuable because she saw me as valuable, and would not retain my value if she were to stop loving me. What kind of love is that?

We cannot really come to grips with a person's particularity, her individuality, without talking about the highly specific individual she is. My girlfriend, for instance, has a very particular sense of humor, one that helps identify her as a person; and I don't think that a person who did not notice and appreciate that sense of humor could be said to fully love her, no matter how much he might enjoy being with her or how committed he might be to her well-being, etc. In fact, I know many people, particularly in the context of parent–child relationships, who suffer from this; I have friends, that is, whose parents care for them very much and are very devoted to their well-being, but who cannot really *see* their children at all, for one reason or another. As a result, despite the parents' dedication and unwavering concern, the children do not feel seen, and often do not feel well-loved. We might say that they are loved only under the description "my parents' child," and that description is not sufficiently personal: it could have applied to all sorts of very different individuals, and does not even begin to capture what is distinctive about *them*.

Wanting to be seen in a love relationship means wanting my lover to see what is special about me; not what makes me better than other people, and not even what necessarily makes me different from other people—again, the type of value here is deeply noncomparative[12]— but rather what makes me, in and of myself, worthy of attention. That is, we want what we are like to make a difference to those who love us; we want them to be glad that we are one way and not another. In order to avoid feeling like empty placeholders of obligatory valuing, we need to feel that those who love us feel that their lives are as they are largely because of how we are, and that their lives would be different, and importantly different, if we were different. And on the whole, we want our lovers to feel that those are differences, and ways of making a difference, that they can endorse, and perhaps even celebrate.

VII

To fully grasp Frankfurt's view, it is essential to understand that he holds that the sort of love that parents feel for their children, especially their very young children, is the purest and most authentic species of love, and should be taken as a model for love in general. He states as much in *The Reasons of Love*:

> It is important to avoid confusing love [...] with infatuation, lust, obsession, possessiveness, and dependency in their various forms. In particular, relationships that are primarily romantic or sexual do not provide very authentic or illuminating paradigms of love as I am construing it. Relationships of those kinds typically include a number of vividly distracting elements which do not belong to the essential nature of love as a mode of disinterested concern, but that are so confusing that they make it nearly impossible for anyone to be clear about just what is going on. Among relationships between humans, the love of parents for their infants or small children is the species that comes closest to offering recognizably pure instances of love. (RL, 43)

It is not surprising that love for very young children, who have not yet developed into persons, should strike Frankfurt this way, given his view that love is not in any way a response to value, and in particular to the sorts of values that persons tend to possess. This choice of model, though, simply begs the question in favor of a view of love "as a mode of disinterested concern"—particularly given the apparent assumption that any form of value-responsiveness must represent an "interest" in the relevant sense. Choosing to privilege a certain type of love because it is "recognizably pure" or "less confusing" than others may in fact impede our efforts to arrive at an adequate account of love, for it is not clear that love in its essence must be pure in this sense, or that it cannot be complex and therefore confusing. It should also be said that it is not clear that the "vividly distracting elements" Frankfurt complains about in romantic love are any less present in love for children: many parents become infatuated with their newborn babies, become obsessed with them, and feel possessive toward them; and it is obvious that dependency, in several senses, is inevitably present. Moreover, outside of the constraining context of various relationships, adult human beings are relatively free to love or not to love any particular individual, at least as compared with parents, whose love for their own children is rendered very nearly nonoptional and indeed mandatory both by biological programming and by their cultural training.

I think it is a mistake, then, to assume that parent–child love must constitute a better model for love in general than the love that obtains between friends or lovers. Indeed, as should be clear by now, I suspect that the love parents feel for their infants, and which some claim to feel for their unborn fetuses, is far more complex, and far less "pure," than it might appear to be; and I have my doubts as to whether such love, *qua* love, is justifiable in the relatively straightforward manner in which friends' and lovers' love for one another is justifiable. (Perhaps with respect to *this* sort of love Frankfurt is correct to suggest that the issue of justification simply does not arise. But if this is so, it is not because justification is in general irrelevant to love; it is due, rather, to the special nature of love for children, which has a way of subverting or circumventing human reason.)

I suggested in Section V that a parent, even one who claimed that she loved the fetus she was carrying, would not continue to love that fetus once it had been determined that what she was carrying was not, in fact, a fetus at all, but rather a tumorous growth. (Let's suppose that the tumor poses no greater health risk to her than an ordinary fetus would—*that*, after all, isn't supposed to be what makes her love go away.) The explanation of this, I think, is that where love for a fetus is felt, or seems to be, it attaches to and is grounded in the expectation that that fetus will not forever remain a fetus: the love, or love-like feeling, is an anticipatory feeling, and is dependent on this organism's developing into a person and thus coming to bear some particular values that will render it a distinctive individual. A woman's love for the man before her may presuppose and thus be dependent on the belief that he is her husband and that they share a certain past history; if it turns out she is massively deceived about who he is, or about the nature of that history, the grounds of her love might be undermined or removed. (This is compatible with the view that love is, prior to anything else, a response to the beloved's values, since that view need not claim that relationships are entirely irrelevant; indeed, it is precisely through the lens of a shared history with someone that we come to perceive and appreciate their particular values.) In much the same way, a parent's love for a child may presuppose and thus be dependent on beliefs about the child's *future*: both the belief that the child will come to possess valuable properties of the sort that make persons valuable and attractive, and the belief that the parent and the child will come to share a history in the context of which those values can be meaningfully explored and recognized.

It might be suggested, however, that what the tumor lacks, and what explains why its carrier would not love it in the way she might claim to love a fetus, is not the potential for personhood but rather the status of being human. Let us put aside the tumor case, then, and ask this: what could we reasonably feel about a human fetus, or newborn infant, that had no potential whatsoever for personhood—a fetus that we knew, with complete certainty, would never progress past infancy (let us suppose, indeed, that it will never attain consciousness) and thus has no potential of becoming a person?

My view, which is that the sort of love we feel for persons would be inappropriate in such a situation, will not surprise anyone in light of what I have argued thus far. I am not, to be sure, claiming that no parent in that situation would sincerely claim to love the no-potential fetus. Some parents probably would believe themselves to feel love, and it is not clear that they must be mistaken. But such love, I think—if, at any rate, it is taken to be anything like the love we feel for persons—must be unjustified and unreasonable. In saying this, I am not saying that it would be a reasonable thing, let alone a kind thing, to tell the parents that their love was unreasonable. Presumably they are in a hard enough spot already, and this is the last sort of thing they would need to hear. It is not clear, at any rate, that any damage is being done to anyone by their feeling this unreasonable love. The question is not whether the love is harmful—that must depend on the details of the individual case— but simply whether it is reasonable; and my position is that it is not. Love for persons is grounded in either their valuable individual qualities they possess now or in the future positive qualities they will come to have; and the no-potential fetus has and will have no such qualities.

At what point, it might be asked, do we draw the line—the line, that is, between love's being unjustified and its being a reasonable response— on the continuum that runs between the no-potential fetus and the fully developed person? This is an important question, not least in the context of our feelings about and obligations toward nonhuman animals, which possess some person-like properties (many animals have a considerable degree of intelligence and can be quite good company, for instance) but cannot be said to have achieved full personhood. The question is important; it is also very difficult and complex, and I have no developed answer to offer. It is clear, I claim, that it is reasonable to love a fully developed person, and that it is unreasonable to love a no-potential fetus; this entails, presumably, that there is some line (perhaps a hard one, perhaps a very fuzzy one) such that those on one side possess either enough qualities or enough potential qualities that it is reasonable to love them, and those on the other side do not. It is not at all clear to me, however, where that line is, and past experience—reading and hearing about people's encounters with sufferers of severe dementia, for instance—has made me somewhat skeptical regarding our pre-reflective intuitions about just what it takes to be related to as a person.

I will not, then, attempt to define a precise dividing line between beings it is reasonable to love and those it is not. I do, though, want to say that it is important that we see that the issue of love for unborn children is complicated in ways we have not yet mentioned, and that the claim to love such a child—a kind of love which, as we have noted, cannot yet attach to any of the child's particular values, virtues, or characteristics—is not at all straightforward.

Suppose that in 2007, Vanessa and Alan have a child, but due to an administrative error at the hospital they are given, and go on to raise, someone else's child. (Let's suppose the parents who raise Vanessa and Alan's biological offspring name him *Tim*, and that Vanessa and Alan name the child they raise *Grant*.) Some years down the road—in 2014, let's say—the mix-up is discovered and revealed to all; but by this point, of course, Vanessa and Alan have already come to love Grant—a love that would surely not simply disappear or be annulled by the discovery that he is not, as they had believed, their biological child.

In 2014, then, Vanessa and Alan love Grant. Before the births of Tim and Grant, let's suppose, they claimed to love their unborn child. How are we to make sense of this, given that Tim was the unborn child in question? Is the love they felt in 2007 for Tim the same love as the love they feel in 2014 for Grant? At what point did the love switch over from one child to the other? Or is the love that Vanessa feels for Grant a new and distinct entity—and if so, did it leave their love for Tim intact, or somehow extinguish it? Did they continue to love Tim during all these years during which they had no contact with him at all, so that they thought they were only loving one child but were in fact loving two? If they had never discovered the switch, would they have continued loving Tim forever, without knowing it, or would it have ended at some point, and if so, when?

I have no idea how to answer these questions. Some of them might perhaps be nonsensical questions, but I am not sure about that, either. The degree of uncertainty here suggests, I think, that we are not really clear on how to describe what goes on *before* the switch, not only in this case but in ordinary cases where there is no switch, and that such matters may not be as amenable to description using the same straightforward love-based vocabulary we apply under other circumstances as we might have assumed. It is, at any rate, evidence for the claim I made above, that the love that parents claim to feel for their children in the very early stages of their lives is highly dependent on beliefs and expectations about what normally happens, and what is likely to happen, in later stages, and it is not clear that attributions of love are straightforwardly appropriate in cases in which those expectations are frustrated by unforeseen events.

VIII

I have been arguing that we should take seriously the idea that we love the people we love for what they are; that taking this idea seriously means recognizing that individuals' valuable properties play a role of a sort that is ruled out by the views of love we find in Kierkegaard and Frankfurt; and that thinking about parents' love for their very young children, and the way such love must work, does not undermine the claim that such properties play this sort of role. Since, on Frankfurt's view, there are no reasons for love at all, it can hardly be the case that the beloved's valuable qualities give her lover reasons to love her. Kierkegaard, on the other hand, might or might not accept that people are worthy of love, and that this worthiness gives us reason to love them. If we interpret him so that he does, we could even say that in a very rough and abstract sense he accepts that we ought to love people for what they are. But this "what they are" has nothing to do with their particular qualities and virtues as individuals; it is, rather, an ineffable *something* that *all* human persons possess. The young people I mentioned in Section VI, who feel that their parents do not truly love them because they do not really know them, will not be mollified by such love; indeed, this is precisely the sort of love they feel they already have, and find insufficient and unsatisfying.

What about love for things other than persons? I think that the conclusions I have drawn are true of other forms of love as well. Putting aside the case of other human individuals, we might consider for a moment the other great love of our lives: the love of life itself. I will leave Kierkegaard aside here since, at least in *Works of Love*, he is concerned specifically with love for persons.

But Frankfurt considers this case explicitly, and the conclusions he draws resemble those he draws with respect to love for persons:

> Many people claim to believe that every human life is intrinsically valuable, regardless of how it is lived. Some individuals profess that what they are doing with their lives, or what they are likely to do with them, gives their lives a special importance. However, even when people have ideas like these about the value or importance of human life, that is ordinarily not the sole or even the primary explanation of why they are determined to go on living. It is not what really accounts for the fact that, in making decisions concerning what to do, they regard preserving their lives as a significant, justifying consideration. Someone who acts in self-defense is universally conceded to have a pertinent reason for doing what he does, regardless of how he or others may evaluate his life. (TOS, 35–36)

Thus, he concludes, "What ordinarily moves us to go on living, and also to accept our desires to continue living as a legitimate reason for acting, is not that we think we have reasons of any kind for wanting to survive" (TOS, 37).

The argument by which Frankfurt reaches this conclusion involves the same reasoning about "special"-ness that we examined earlier, with respect to parent–child love. There we noticed that, in order to justify my loving a person—my child, say—I need not claim that my child is *especially* valuable; I need only claim that she possesses some value that is sufficient to make her an appropriate object of my love. Since any human child that is not prevented from developing into a person will come to be sufficiently valuable in *some* way or other, I need not worry, as a prospective parent, that my progeny will fail in this regard and that I will therefore find myself in the unpleasant position of having to choose either to love my child without justification or to not love her at all.[13]

The same goes for the argument as applied to one's life. I need not think that my life is objectively special *among lives* in order to justify my loving my life. I might regard myself as a perfectly ordinary individual and still regard my life as well worth living, simply because I think that the perfectly ordinary human life is well worth living. Indeed, there is no contradiction in holding that a perfectly ordinary human life is a quite extraordinary thing—considerably more than enough, I would tend to say, to justify its being lived and loved.

I do not think that Frankfurt's argument, then, gives us any reason whatever for thinking that we do not have reasons for wanting our lives to continue. The average person, I believe, has a great many such reasons—too many, in all likelihood, to comprehensively catalog. In Woody Allen's *Manhattan*, the character Allen plays, Isaac Davis, makes a start:

> Well, all right, why is life worth living? That's a very good question. Um. Well, there are certain things, I guess, that make it worthwhile. Uh, like what? Okay. Um. For me ... oh, I would say ... what, Groucho Marx, to name one thing ... and Willie Mays, and, um, the second movement of the Jupiter Symphony, and ... Louie Armstrong's recording of "Potato Head Blues" ... Swedish movies, naturally ... *Sentimental Education* by Flaubert ... Marlon Brando, Frank Sinatra ... um, those incredible apples and pears by Cezanne ... the crabs at Sam Wo's ... Tracy's face ... [14]

In endorsing Isaac Davis's way of answering the question of why (his) life is worth living, we are not implying that this list encompasses every reason that might be given; nor are we in any way suggesting that if these reasons were to fail, Davis would be left without a reason for continuing to live. Suppose that Davis became disenchanted with Sinatra and Swedish movies, every copy of *Sentimental Education* and the Jupiter Symphony were destroyed in an unlikely series of freak accidents, Sam Wo's stopped serving crabs, and some similar misfortune removed every other item on the list above. Would Davis be left without reason to live? The answer is no, not only because there are surely other reasons that Davis does not get around to enumerating in this particular scene, but more importantly because it would still be possible for him to find *other* reasons to live. That a certain set of considerations constitutes the reasons I (currently) have to value my life, and to want to keep living, does not imply or even suggest that if those reasons were to fail, other considerations, under other circumstances, might not do the same job.

Suppose, on the other hand, that *every* movie worth seeing, *every* piece of music worth hearing, *every* restaurant worth patronizing, and *every* person worth spending time with vanished from the face of the planet. Suppose, indeed, that all sources of pleasure and joy in human life were annihilated. In that circumstance, it is not obvious that we would have reason to value life, or to live. At any rate, I take it—and I hope you will agree—that our set of such reasons would be very seriously diminished. The question of why human life was worth living would no longer admit, under such circumstances, of an obvious answer.

But in the world as we know it there is an obvious answer—or rather, a great many obvious answers—just as there are typically many obvious answers to questions like, "Why do you love her?" (Because she is funny; because she is kind; because she is a talented and insightful philosopher;

because she rubs my feet at the end of a hard day; etc.) Perhaps it is the fact that the answers are so obvious that has led Frankfurt astray. Philosophers sometimes assume that the answer to a profound question must be something difficult to find, something that will take a great deal of effort and cleverness to discern or devise. Having been convinced, by Plato and others, that things are sometimes not as they appear, we are all too often inclined to assume that in this world *nothing* is as it appears. We tend to forget, as Iris Murdoch tried to remind us, that philosophy is very often "a matter of finding occasions on which to say the obvious."[15]

I have come to think that love works more or less in just the way it seems to work, and that the answers we should give to love's questions are the obvious answers, the answers ordinary people are generally inclined to give when asked "Why do you love your children?" or "Why do you think your life is worth living?" This is not to say that there aren't a great many details to be worked out. Love, like life, is complicated. But the place to begin, when theorizing about love, is precisely where love itself begins, with the importance and value of the things and people we love, in all their glorious specificity and individual particularity.

Acknowledgments

I have received very helpful comments on earlier versions of this paper from audiences at Cardiff University, University of Sheffield, and Queens University, Belfast, and from the editors of this volume.

Notes

1   See Iris Murdoch, *The Sovereignty of Good*, 17 ff.
2   WL 162, emphasis added. See also: "And this is the duty, to find actuality in this way with closed eyes (because in love you do indeed close them to weakness and frailty and imperfection), instead of failing to see actuality with wide-open eyes (yes, wide-open or staring like a sleep-walker's)" (WL 163). As Ferreira writes, "It is quite natural to wonder, on hearing these comments, whether Kierkegaard's ethic allows us to really see the actual other person. It is also natural to wonder whether this ethic recommends a morally culpable blindness, whether it proposes that we ignore moral failings in the other person" (M. Jamie Ferreira, *Love's Grateful Striving*, 108). (It should be noted that she goes on to argue that Kierkegaard's position does not have these unattractive implications. I do not find her reading entirely persuasive on this matter, but I will not pursue this issue here.)

3   On this see Neil Delaney, "Romantic Love and Loving Commitment."
4   We must include the qualification "independent" since on Frankfurt's
    view, there is a tie between loving and value: by loving someone I make her
    valuable.
5   This is on the assumption that it is reason that is responsible for our
    assessments of inherent value. Since I accept this assumption, and I take it
    that Frankfurt does too, I will not defend this assumption here.
6   Harry Frankfurt, "Some Mysteries of Love," University of Kansas: The
    Lindley Lecture Series, 2001, 4. See also RL, Chapter 2, especially 38–41.
7   Fairly persuasive criticisms of these arguments can be found in David
    Enoch, *Taking Morality Seriously: A Defense of Robust Realism*, Michael
    Huemer, *Ethical Intuitionism*, and Russ Shafer-Landau, *Moral Realism: A
    Defense*.
8   David Velleman, "Beyond Price," 205.
9   The more difficult question, presumably, is: what should we feel about
    a human fetus, or newborn infant, that we knew would never progress
    past infancy, and thus never become a person? I return to this question in
    Section VII.
10 This point—that the properties a person *will* possess can justify one's love
    for her in the present—is the concomitant to a point I make in *Love's Vision*,
    where I argue that properties a person *used to* possess can justify love in
    the present, and that this helps answer the common objection that love
    grounded in a person's value will be unreliable and inconstant. See Troy
    Jollimore, *Love's Vision*, 139–41.
11 Frankfurt, "Some Mysteries of Love," 4.
12 After all, there could, in principle, be an exact replica of me somewhere in
    the universe, though in practice each individual person is unique.
13 If, on the other hand, my child *is* prevented from developing into a person,
    then I *will* find myself in that unpleasant position. But this fact simply helps
    to explain why such situations are deeply tragic.
14 *Manhattan*, written by Woody Allen and Marshall Brickman (Rollins and
    Joffe, 1979).
15 Admittedly, the remark may be apocryphal. An internet search turns up a
    number of pages that quote this line, but I have not been able to locate an
    authoritative source.

4

Frankfurt and Kierkegaard on BS, Wantonness, and Aestheticism: A Phenomenology of Inauthenticity

John Davenport

I. Introduction: Kierkegaard, Frankfurt, Love, and Authenticity

In this essay, I will consider Frankfurt's conception of love in the context of his wider claims about "caring" in order to show that (a) his conception of love depends on his contrasting account of inauthenticity, and yet (b) he clearly needs the richer account of the authentic/inauthentic distinction offered by Kierkegaard. Several of the connections between Frankfurt and Kierkegaard traced in this volume were first broached in Edward Mooney's insight that Frankfurtian "caring" resembles the process of self-articulation in which an "ethical" self is formed according to Kierkegaard's pseudonym Judge William in *Either/Or* vol. II.[1] Following Mooney, I have referred to Frankfurt's distinction between 1st-order desires and "higher-order volitions" to help explain the Judge's cryptic "choice to choose" in ethical terms,[2] and the related notion of volitional "earnestness" found in several of Kierkegaard's works (both pseudonymous and signed).[3] I have also argued that Frankfurt's distinction between "ambiguity" (or division in the higher-order will) and "wholeheartedness" sheds light on different types of spiritual division and "sinfulness" in *The Concept of Anxiety*, though Kierkegaard's conception of volitional unity is superior to Frankfurt's.[4] The connections I explore below support these prior comparisons by showing that Frankfurt's and Kierkegaard's analyses of inauthenticity are similar in key respects.

Frankfurt's Problem and Forms of Love

There are also several important differences between Kierkegaard and Frankfurt, especially concerning the status of values worth caring about, or "ethics" in its widest sense. Frankfurt's mature view is that caring cannot be based on the inherent importance of anything prior to caring about it: instead, life-goals, ideals, and particular others only *become* important to us because we care about them, and we care about them for their own sake either because we can or because it is our "personal essence" to care about this kind of end or person.[5] Thus, "it is only in virtue of what we actually care about that anything is important to us" (TOS, 20). On this view, it is useless to ask what we *should* care about independently of our existing cares; even moral norms provide no autonomous motive unless we care about morality.[6] I reject this type of "existential subjectivism," and have critiqued Frankfurt's arguments for it in detail.[7] It forces Frankfurt to conclude in *Taking Ourselves Seriously and Getting It Right* that the virtually universal human instinct of self-preservation generates a "love of life" that needs no further reasons (TOS, 35–38). This directly undermines his earlier distinctions between passive desires and authoritative motives or between mere *strength* of desire and *authority* for the agent (see ANL), which was central to his project. In particular, Frankfurt's effort to resist Bernard Williams's argument that we require "ground projects" in order to have *reasons* (beyond instinctive fear of death) to go on living (TOS, 36) and his insistence that loves are generally grounded in no prior reasons beyond their own self-affirmation (TOS, 40) force Frankfurt back to the claim that a wanton desire to continue living is authoritative for us.[8] Such an implication that conflates wanting something with caring about it has to count as a *reductio* for Frankfurt, because it conflicts with his main claims about volitional identification.

In my view, Kierkegaard offers the solution that Frankfurt needs: while objective judgment about value is not sufficient for "love" in the sense of an autonomous motive, because such valuations must be taken up "subjectively" through the agent's own commitment, such personal "appropriation" must also be a response to the perceived reality of others and the world.[9] Kierkegaard is not always read this way; for there are some passages in Kierkegaard's signed *Works of Love* that may give the impression that he also holds that a psychic state of love makes its own reasons for loving devotion (an idea that also has roots in Pascal's "reasons of the heart"). For Kierkegaard says that agapic love (kjærlighed) shares the "perfection of eternity" in transcending other kinds of love that can only love "the extraordinary" or great (WL, 65). "Thus, the perfection of the object is not the perfection of the love" when it is like God's love, which extends to grace beyond merit. By contrast, "Erotic love [Elskov] is defined by the object; friendship is defined by the object; only love for the neighbor is defined by love [Kjerlighed]" (WL, 66). These passages, in which Kierkegaard is stressing that interhuman agapic love exceeds what could be deserved on the basis of contingent differences between human persons, may have inspired Anders Nygren's famous thesis that whereas loves with an eros-structure of lack-seeking fulfillment are "property-based," agapic loves are gratuitous in relation to their object, or not property-based (in Alan Soble's helpful terminology). For the need to express agapic love is a pure generosity "so great that it seems as if it itself might almost be able to produce its object" (WL, 67; compare WL, 158)—much like divine generosity in freely creating *ex nihilo*. This has also been called the thesis that love "bestows" the value it sees in its beloved, rather than discovering it; and Frankfurt was clearly inspired by this idea in developing his own conceptions of caring and love: "When a person makes something important to himself, accordingly the situation resembles an instance of divine agape at least in certain respects" (IWCA, 94)—and he footnotes Nygren's *Eros and Agape* as his source for this point.

Yet, the contrast that Nygren and Soble draw between erosic and agapic structures of motivation is different than Kierkegaard's contrast between "preferential" loves and agapic love, which still responds to something objectively valuable and essential (not a varying basis of merit) in each person: namely, the image of God that Kierkegaard calls the "watermark" (WL, 89). This shared capacity that Kierkegaard also calls "spirit" includes each person's potential for freely willed love, no matter how fallen they are—a potential "built up" or encouraged when they are loved (WL, 217). What first looks like bestowing value for Kierkegaard actually refers to taking people back to that original God-given potential in them by way of believing in them, hoping for their return, enduring their hatred in trust that they can eventually rediscover their highest gift (WL, 219–24; compare WL, 253, on "the possibility of the good for the other person"). One could not rightly love a pet rock or a bird in this way, but only a person.

Despite this central contrast, there remain other deep continuities between Kierkegaard and Frankfurt: for example, in their agreement that there is a kind of love that is distinctively volitional (WL, 81), and which is directed to the good of (other) persons as unique individuals (WL, 69)—though for Kierkegaard, these potential objects of volitional love are also *equally* all persons with a distinctiveness that does not reduce to the physical or social respects in which they are manifestly unequal (WL, 68). Yet Frankfurt's paradigms of willed essentially particularistic loves are cases that Kierkegaard would call "preferential," for example, love of one's child or spouse (thus Frankfurt effectively challenges Kierkegaard's apparent view that these loves must be based on contingent properties of their object that make that object fungible; although Frankfurt does not consider whether love of child and spouse could also express neighbor-love).

These preliminary observations show how complex the links are between Kierkegaard's and Frankfurt's accounts of love. Frankfurt and Kierkegaard both hold that volitional love focuses on the other as an irreplaceable individual, and aims purely at the other's good for its own sake rather than at the lover's happiness. But, unlike Kierkegaard, Frankfurt (following Nygren) takes this to imply that volitional love is not a response to the value of the beloved (partly because he assumes that any such value will be a universal that could be instantiated just as well in others), whereas Kierkegaard does not.[10] Like Rudd, Walsh, and Jollimore in this volume, I will critique Frankfurt's subjectivist account of the relation between love and values, but from an indirect angle. I will focus on Frankfurt's and Kierkegaard's related conceptions of authenticity—and their suggestively similar portrayals of inauthenticity—in works that do not focus so directly on love. In particular, I will consider Kierkegaard's famous essay on "The Present Age" and Frankfurt's popular essay "On Bullshit" (a term hereafter abbreviated as "BS" except when quoting). These comparisons will show that aspects of Frankfurt's own diagnoses of wantonness and "BS" should lead him to Kierkegaard's conception of authentic selfhood as requiring cares and loves to be sufficiently in touch with (and guided by) values that are *real* or objectively irreducible to the self's psychic states and natural facts of biology: as Anthony Rudd has recently argued in detail, "Our loves need to be understood … …as responses to the experienced value of things," a value they have independent of our contingent desires and *prior* to being loved, even if we miss it.[11] This thesis is compatible with the caveat that serious devotion may make more of the beloved person's qualities stand out for us, or make normally hidden aspects clearer and more salient to us than they are to strangers—so we save a legitimate nonsubjectivist sense in which "only love sees true."

Five Aspects of Existential Authenticity

My method, then, will be to compare Frankfurt's and Kierkegaard's *phenomenologies of inauthenticity*, which in turn shed light on conditions of authenticity and thereby clarify love as central to authentic identity. But authenticity is a complex and multidimensional concept, and we need to pin down a basic sense of it to ensure that we are comparing rival conceptions of the same concept. This is why, as Charles Larmore notes in his valuable discussion, "Few philosophers still consider giving authenticity a philosophical articulation;"[12] most assume that the concept is confused and lacking in unity. While an adequate account requires more space than I have here, a few suggestions about positive conditions for authenticity will suffice for my later arguments. While the term is now used loosely in many ways, we should distinguish an *existential* concept of "authenticity" coming down from the romantic tradition(s) that refers to an agreement between the identities one shows in social relations and a deep or "true" identities that may easily be hidden from others, or covered over for the agent himself. We can say this much about phenomena of authenticity in its core existential sense without prejudging among rival *conceptions* of that concept. For its original sense from Greek meant that you are the author of something, and so it bears your authority within it: you stand behind it. In the related legal sense, an authentic document or act is truly derived from a genuine authority: it is not fake. Thus in the original sense, our authentic identity must derive from our inner authority, whatever that may be, which licenses us to express our commitments and values openly to others. This is the core sense Kierkegaard has in mind when he complains in "The Present Age" that during his time, authors not only write anonymously—some even "write anonymously over their own signature," because they have not put "their whole soul" into their work; it lacks a sense of conviction, any expression of a deeper life-view (TA, 103). This implies that a genuine author must stand for some convictions that could unify a life.

This outline clarifies why the idea of authenticity has seemed so closely related to autonomous motivation, sincerity in our relations with others, integrity in the conduct of our life, or genuine emotional response to the values in our situations:[13] being authentic connotes *being true* to something authoritative, something that can even obligate categorically. It is often said to consist in being true to *yourself* in the sense of "following your own heart," or not selling out your deepest interests for temporary advantages, or remaining loyal to your principles: this is what Kierkegaard calls "faithfulness to oneself" (TA, 7; compare 13). Here authenticity is understood as primarily a mode of self-relation: for example, the hero in the movie *Cinderella Story* gives up football for poetry and writing. Since such loyalty to a deeper calling often requires acting contrary to social expectations or the demands of preexisting roles into which one has been cast, authenticity becomes associated with transcending conformism and cultivating originality: these capacities may be necessary means to finding that calling. Thus in the film *Billy Elliot*, a young boy growing up in a Welsh mining community with macho ideals of manhood has to resist social pressures in order to discover and take up his nascent love of dance. This influential idea was popularized by John Stuart Mill after Rousseau: "Where, not the person's own character, but the traditions or customs of other people are the rule of conduct, there is wanting one of the principal ingredients of human happiness" because "the free development of *individuality*" is stifled.[14]

The core concept of existential authenticity "implies being fully or purely oneself" or acting "in such a way that the self one is appears without deformation and in keeping with its intrinsic character," as Larmore suggests.[15] But it is simplistic to assume that this intrinsic character lies there hidden within us, like a pearl in an oyster, just waiting to be found once we cast off conventional assumptions and traditional roles. Yet this is clearly the root of Frankfurt's idea that discovering what we simply have to care about, our "volitionally necessary" loves, makes us authentic—though he follows Mill in calling this "individuality" (NI, 110). As Larmore explains, this romantic view has been subject to withering critique. Paul Valéry, for example, argues that Stendhal's "*Natural-Self* to which culture, civilization, and custom are enemies" depends on the false view that we can identify "natural" loves that are unaffected by social learning.[16] And Larmore agrees that naturalness is measured by communal paradigms: "… behavior and sentiments seen as 'spontaneous' always carry the stamp of cultural codes deep within them."[17] In this, he follows Pierre Bourdieu's and René Girard's arguments that "imitation enters into the very heart of our being" because reason itself is intersubjective, "rooted in belonging."[18] There is no "deep self" that is unaffected by convention, no desire pure of a mimetic element, nor any sense of identity without an implicit sensitivity to how others interpret us.[19] Thus authenticity cannot mean realizing a "true self" not influenced by "forms of thought we have made our own by modeling ourselves on others."[20]

Yet we should not take this rejection of a private, self-justifying "inner core" self waiting to be found within the psyche[21] as a reason to exclude all senses of originality from counting as conditions for authenticity. What Mill means by "individuality" has more to do with originality and critical reason. He argues that "originality is a valuable element in human affairs" because it prevents rote repetition of past practices, prompts us to reconsider the grounds of our socially shared beliefs, and saves people from falling or being forced into pre-scripted identities (many will not fit well into "the small number of moulds which society provides in order to save them from the trouble of forming their own character").[22] In other words, originality is a mark of autonomy, understood as the freedom to be responsible for one's character. But Mill does not conceive this as an origination of identity *ex nihilo* without any socially shared bases; rather, he means that people should not act like "automatons in human form," mindlessly following custom; nobody concerned for aretê and social progress recommends that "people should do absolutely nothing but copy one another." For excellence requires that people use "their own judgment" in deciding their own "plan of life."[23] This does not entail that there are no objective grounds for such decisions, or that past exemplars can do nothing to help us discern them.

These points associate authenticity with the idea of *enlightenment* or thinking for oneself by drawing on innate resources of reason and one's life-experiences to form critical judgment with practical relevance for one's historically conditioned situation. An authentic person is one who does not take custom or convention at face value, but who looks for a more authoritative basis in critical reasoning (which may respond to insights from emotional experience). This helps answer Larmore's worry that the "cult of authenticity" may also lead to "contempt for the expectations of others" and thus to "social anomie;"[24] for a person who reasons critically about such expectations is not barred from solidarity.

So we have found a fourth aspect: if the "self" to which an authentic person remains true involves commitment to moral principles or ideals of excellence articulated in an enlightened way, then authenticity can mean something very close to *integrity* in the sense of loyalty to principles and ideals that one has articulated for oneself (one's individual variation of shared norms). Wyatt Earp and Thomas More are alike in this one respect: neither can be bought and both stay true to their sense of justice—a sense which is indebted to the Platonic tradition, but also imbued with their personal style. Given that interpersonal relations are often central to the commitments and ideals to which the authentic person remains loyal in the face of external pressures— and some debts to interpersonal sources for value-concepts are inevitable if Girard, Taylor, and Larmore are correct—the integrity aspect easily blends into norm-based or noble friendship. Integrity and genuine devotion to friends are in turn associated with a fifth aspect, namely "sincerity," in the sense of presenting one's true emotions, devotions, and values honestly to others (or at least to intimate companions). Sincerity in this sense, like Kierkegaard's concept of earnestness, does not demand "total lucidity with regard to who we are," or what our cares, values, and emotions are (pace Larmore and Sartre[25]). The authentic person simply does the best he can to understand what he cares about, and on this basis, expresses his cares openly.

Two levels of Authenticity in relation to Autonomy

To put these five aspects together, we also have to distinguish two "levels" of personality or practical identity. The initial idea of an inner-core self suggests that an identity not immediately on the surface of our life, or not solely determined by our culturally prescribed station and customary habits, must either be found or fashioned by our effort, or both.[26] This is the aspect of authenticity evident in the development of heroes in familiar epic quest narratives; for example, in the *Lord of the Rings*, Aragorn has to find his inner potential to be the returned king. The central message of epic literature as a genre is that our *social identity*, including our interpersonally recognizable roles, habits, and personality traits that others would use to describe us, should have at its core an *existential identity* that is to a significant extent a result of our effort to define it. Thus the close association between authenticity and existential autonomy understood as the control and powers needed to be responsible for our inward identity. Authenticity, then, is an enhanced version of personal autonomy in two ways: first, social authenticity requires that an autonomous character already be formed (at least to some extent) and then be expressed throughout varying social contexts. Second, existential authenticity makes further normative demands about the sources of inspiration for one's inner existential identity beyond those source-conditions (whatever they are) that must be met to be morally responsible for that identity. We can be deeply responsible for an autonomous character that is still not existentially authentic because the sources on which we base it are too uncritically conventional.

The aspects of originality and enlightenment operate on this inner or intrasubjective level, dictating that one should find inspiration for one's inward identity in critical reasoning, one's sense of unique potentials, or even private vision. Interested critical deliberation refers to a *process* by which existential identity is shaped, or its discovered elements are honed—an active way of arriving at purposes, relationships, and values that define us in the practical sense (as more than a reflective subject of consciousness). By contrast, originality requires some distinctiveness in the *content* of one's existential identity; while we might not aim directly at such distinctiveness, it should accompany the outcome if we took self-shaping seriously. This aspect thus involves a substantive claim that the received and discovered ingredients of a person's practical identity will *naturally* lend themselves to a relative type of uniqueness in relation to others (above mere numerical individuality): such individual difference is part of our *telos*. For example, individual "style" is important because two people can have similar goals and values but pursue them in different ways in their concrete historical situations.[27]

Yet "style" in the needed sense cannot refer merely to flair or panache, or any artificial set of behavior-devices selected merely to make one's name have "brand" appeal; for that would be a clear sign of *affectation*. In tracing the influence of this concept as Kierkegaard received it from his mentors, Bruce Kirmmse explains Poul Møller's sense of "permanent affectation" in which, for ulterior reasons, a person wishes to acquire a personality that is out of sync with his "real self."[28] By contrast, an authentic "style" expresses an effort to make something positive of one's historically particular temperament, traits, proclivities, affinities, interests, learning styles, etc., which may be assets or defects depending on how they are deployed. "Style" in this sense acknowledges that one must work from the materials one is given; one cannot live a whole life as a square peg in a round hole. It also trusts that there is something unique in the identity that best fits each of us.

By contrast, the "proto-virtues"[29] of loyalty to the heart, integrity, and sincerity are instead found in the *relation between* our existential identity and our more outwardly accessible social identity. Thus Mooney can say that authenticity is relational and evaluative: I can either live by, or betray, "the values I ... overtly affirm or tacitly endorse."[30] A person can ask "whether she is in line with the self she most deeply, most truly, takes herself to be."[31] Such social authenticity has a reflexive aspect: when Peter denied Jesus out of fear of arrest, he was being inauthentic not only to his friends and his proclaimed savior, but more immediately to his 'true self'; thus his intense remorse. But this simply shows that the social sense of authenticity depends on the existential sense: our diagnosis of Peter requires that he has an authentic inner identity as a disciple of Jesus at least partly in place. This is the inner identity to which he can be true or false; social authenticity respects its authority. If inner identity is not developed, then as Mooney says, the human being is in "indifferent oblivion regarding the options of being true or false to oneself."[32] Such a person lacks enough existential authenticity to make social inauthenticity even a possibility for him.

This does not entail that an agent could be completely authentic at the existential level yet utterly false in social relations. The division of labor between the two levels is compatible with personal authenticity remaining a unified kind of phenomenon, because failing to stand up for our central commitments or falsifying our autonomous purposes to others tends to erode our own sense of this inner identity or loosen our grip on its ultimate bases. This view is most plausible if a person's existential identity itself must respect or be guided by authoritative sources, such as norms and values, with bases in reality outside the self to which our access is (partly) mediated by our social world—as the aspect of enlightenment suggests. An authentic existential identity consists in part of projects and ideals that are central to our sense of what our life is *for*, which finds its ultimate touchstone in the contours of what is worth our devotion or love. So examining the concept of authenticity yields the solution to "Frankfurt's problem" proposed above.

Personal Meaning and Projective Motivation

This solution is further supported by the common association between authenticity and the agent's sense that her life is rich in first-personal meaning *to her* as the person living it is. A fully meaningful life is not the same as a happy life (consider Abraham Lincoln's many causes for sadness); nor is it the same as a virtuous or morally righteous life. But we suspect a deep connection between authentic devotion to worthwhile ends and ideals, authentic appreciation of values worth caring about, and a sense of robust significance in one's activities. For an authentic life cannot seem utterly pointless to its agent; such "absurdity" in the existential sense is a bar to full authenticity.[33] A moderate originality condition also makes more sense in this light: an authentic identity cannot be formed simply by copying others' identities because that indicates too little concern to discover what is really valuable in the world and what our most distinctive capacities for response to reality may be.

Frankfurt conceives the first-personal meaning of one's life as a result of caring about people, projects, ideals, and ambitions that motivate productive work (RL, 23, 51–52, 58). Bernard Williams similarly conceives a rich or fulfilling life as one in which commitments to family, friends, "intellectual" and "creative" goals, and to political causes play a central role.[34] He defines "ground projects" as final ends for which one would sacrifice one's life, although he also recognizes other character-shaping commitments that are not this absolute.[35] This idea of "identity-defining commitments,"[36] cares, or higher-order volitions as central to one's "practical identity" has become widespread;[37] yet no twentieth-century account adequately explains how such cares, commitments, or personal projects are formed or what they consist in. If they are simply interests and emotional dispositions that result from our contingent history and the social forces that shape us, or desires that are instinctive in our kind, then they seem less than fully autonomous. But if they are simply the result of arbitrary choices, then again it is hard to see them as manifestations of self-governance or self-rule.

Here Kierkegaard's widespread remarks on will and passion inspire a possible answer: forming new final ends, reinforcing our determination to pursue goals already set, and altering projects central to our identity when necessary, are *active processes* of our agency, not merely changes that happen to us. Although they are distinct from making decisions in the familiar sense (e.g., deciding on opera rather than a movie tonight), the processes of setting, sustaining, and reshaping central life-goals involve kinds of "willing" that control our deep character. "Willing" in this sense is related to the older notions of "strength of will" and heroic striving or persistence in the face of adversity. I call this "projective willing" to indicate that it projects ends beyond those suggested by passive desires, forming projects and generating new motives that do not derive (entirely) from prior needs or attractions, including even the general desire for happiness (*pace* the eudaimonist tradition). But I do not mean that the agent's emotions or cares project the perceived values to which they respond; on the contrary, our projective striving is grounded in perceptions or judgments of objective value. In projecting new aims or renewing commitment to standing projects, the agent can express values that need not passively move her by way of "erosiac" attraction. On this view, the operative motives that Frankfurt calls "cares" and "loves" are established and altered by the agent's projective efforts over time.[38] This explains why Frankfurt finds them to be "active" or "volitional," having an inherent "authority" that (unlike passive desires) needs no endorsement by separate higher-order attitudes (ANL, 133, 137). The projective theory also avoids the problems of reification and essentialism inherent in Frankfurt's alternative hypothesis that our loves originate from "volitional necessities" of our individual practical identity (ANL, 138; NI, 108–16; RL, 46).[39]

I believe the projective conception also provides a better way to understand Frankfurt's notion of "higher-order volitions" through which we "identify" with certain 1st-order motives and alienate others,[40] and to make sense of his argument that cares and loves are distinct from passive desires (see ANL).[41] As I noted earlier, his aim in developing these concepts was to explain how we can be active or autonomous in our identity-defining commitments and thus deeply responsible for an inward character that is distinct from contingencies of temperament and personality traits that we might be actively resisting. It is because Kierkegaard shares this aim that his contrasts between "aesthetic" and "ethical" life-views or volitional orientations shed light on Frankfurt's themes. For both Kierkegaard and Frankfurt, ongoing failure to care or to will deeply prevents human beings from becoming authentic personal agents with distinct inward identity. Yet Kierkegaard offers a more convincing and consistent account of the relation between caring and values. In what follows, I work toward this conclusion starting from Frankfurt's criticism of "BS" and its implicit relation to his account of "wanton" lack of care. The underlying existential dangers in both these phenomena can be explained by recognizing their similarity to forms of aestheticism that Kierkegaard explains in *Either/ Or* and in *Two Ages*. Several important *phenomena of inauthenticity* shed light on each other and should be understood together.

II. Frankfurt on "BS" and Volitional Wantonness

In the last decade, Harry Frankfurt's essay *On Bullshit* became very popular[42] after it was reprinted as a book.[43] We might compare its unusual success to the sensation that Kierkegaard produced with his pseudonymous "Seducer's Diary" (EO I, 301–444). Yet the serious intent of both works was missed by many of their readers. Frankfurt's critique of "BS" continues a line of thought beginning with Socrates's critique of the Sophists and culminating with existential critiques of neutrality, insincerity, and superficial mass consciousness. But even philosophical discussions of the essay's significance have largely overlooked its (conscious or unconscious) debts to the existential tradition. Yet this connection will require us to rethink several related themes in Frankfurt's work.

Frankfurt's thesis and Cohen's two criticisms

As many reviewers have remarked, in his essay on "BS", Frankfurt's key thesis is that a BSer is different and potentially worse than a liar. He describes the intentional state of a liar L as one who tries to bring about that his interlocutor believes something X, and believes that L believes X, and that L has communicated this belief, when in fact L thinks X is false. Frankfurt distinguishes this from another act (called "bullshit") in which the agent does not care whether X is true *or* false, though he conveys the sense that he does care and believes X. As Frankfurt puts it, this "lack of connection to a concern with truth" in one's speech is the distinguishing feature of "BS" (OB, 33). Unlike the liar, the BSer is not trying to get others to believe that something false is true. Frankfurt is surely right about the importance of this distinction (whether or not he is correct about common usages of "bullshit"). For, like the liar, the BSer also falsely represents himself as "endeavoring to communicate the truth"; yet what he intentionally conceals is not his belief but rather that "the truth-value of his statements are of no central interest to him" (OB, 54–55). For example, in Frankfurt's sense, you could "BS" person A by telling A something P that you think is probably true, but without any concern about P's truth in choosing to communicate it.

However, in an insightful response nicely titled "Deeper into Bullshit,"[44] G.A. Cohen argues that Frankfurt confuses the BSer's *own* indifference to the truth-value of his communications (explicit or implied) with "the bullshitter's not caring whether his audience is caused to believe something true or false."[45] Cohen's point is that these can come apart: someone who is herself concerned about the truth or falsehood of some claim X might want her audience to believe X, but for reasons *other* than wanting them to know a truth or to believe a falsehood. For it might just be materially advantageous for her in some way if the audience believes X, whether it is true or false; for example, consider exaggeration in advertising. But this kind of "BS" does not seem obviously worse for human society than outright lying.

Cohen also objects that "while Frankfurt identifies the liar by his goal, which is to mislead with respect to reality, he assigns no distinctive goal to the bullshitter" but only a standard "tactic." Although "Frankfurt's bullshitter asserts statements whose truth-values are of no interest to him, and he conceals *that* fact," he acts this way for "a variety of goals."[46] This point reveals a problem in Frankfurt's analysis, though Cohen misdiagnoses it. Cohen acknowledges that the "standard" goal by which he and Frankfurt define the liar need not be the liar's "ultimate or final goal;"[47] it rarely is, since it is perverse simply to intend that someone else be mistaken just for the heck of it. Similarly, we should define Frankfurtian "BS" by a standard *proximate* goal, and the kind of communicative act so defined could still be done for a variety of final ends: for example, getting paid, amusing an audience, staving off boredom, creating a diversion, taking revenge, or even exposing fashionable intellectual nonsense by parody.[48] So it is consistent with Frankfurt's approach that BSing be used as a means to many different final ends. The problem in Frankfurt's account is that it does not offer a standard proximate goal: as Cohen says, the BSer "lacks any goal such as that by which the liar is defined."[49]

Frankfurt responds to Cohen that "The defining feature of the sort of bullshit that I considered is a lack of concern with truth, or an indifference to how things really are."[50] This could be construed as a *negative* proximate goal that guides the communicative acts in question: if the communicative act has a declarative (as opposed to interrogative or imperative) illocutionary mode, yet the agent is *not* trying to produce true or false belief through her communication, then her act is an instance of "BS". But this negative condition is too wide: for it would count as "BS" all cases in which a person says whatever comes to mind without concern about truth or falsity, even if merely to entertain a small child, or to comfort an ailing elderly friend, or for other benign purposes in contexts where "small talk" is appropriate enough. Instead, Frankfurt means to isolate a problematic phenomenon in human life: he affirms that "Characterizing something as bullshit is naturally construed as a serious pejorative."[51] What we are really interested in isolating is the underlying intentional attitude that deserves such disapproval or rebuke.[52] To accomplish this, we need to find a more positive description of its definitive proximate end.

"BS," Wantonness, and the Categorical-Evaluative Distinction

The problem we have found in Frankfurt's negative condition for "BS" is interestingly similar to a problem with his closely related notion of the "wanton," who is defined as lacking 2nd-order volitions concerning her own 1st-order motives (in contrast to "persons" who take an active stand with respect to their own 1st-order motives, *identifying with* some and *alienating* others) (FW, 16). While this conception of identification with 1st-order desire has been the topic of intense debate in the literature on personal autonomy ever since Frankfurt introduced it in 1971, there is an obvious analogy between the wanton who has no higher-order will and the BSer:[53] just as the BSer remains unconcerned about the truth-value of what he is saying, and thus does not care whether the beliefs or attitudes that his listeners acquire from him are true or false (or probable/improbable, warranted/unwarranted, etc.), the wanton is unconcerned about which 1st-order desires move her to action. We might express this relation by saying that Frankfurt's BSer has a "wanton" attitude to the truth: he identifies neither with a project of honesty nor with a project of lying. Thus the attitude that disposes to BSing is wanton in at least one important respect. In both cases, what interests Frankfurt is the absence of a *categorical condition* for other contrastive states, as Table 4.1 illustrates:

Table 4.1

	Attitudes toward motives		Attitudes toward truth-value	
Lacking the categorical condition		Wanton		BSer
Meeting the categorical condition	Identifying w. motive M$_1$	Alienating motive M$_1$	Aiming at true belief	Aiming at false belief

A "categorical condition," as Ronald de Sousa explains, is a teleological orientation toward some type of value V that is intrinsic to an intentional state of some natural kind K (which de Sousa calls K's "formal object").[54] In this schema, standards implied by V only apply when the categorical conditions for being an instance of K are met: when they are, then such an instance has fulfilling V as its natural goal, but may fail by this standard (an evaluative distinction). For example, beliefs are about the world and should try to correspond with reality; they fail if they are false. Thus trying and failing to attain V is distinct from not even being in the V-game; for example, merely imagining *what it would be like if P* does not fail if P is false. The contrastive standard of truth or falsehood evaluates only propositions aiming at truth.

De Sousa broadens this schema from intentional states to the kind of beings for whom these states are natural. For example, Aristotle's claim that "man is a rational animal" must be taken in the categorical sense: it is natural for us to form beliefs, but our beliefs are often irrational or unwarranted: "The evaluative sense presupposes the categorical sense: to be either rational or irrational (evaluatively) is to be rational (categorically)."[55] He also applies this to emotions, which naturally aim at a kind of "appropriateness" relative to the agent's situation. Thus an inappropriate emotion still meets the categorical conditions of emotional intentionality, whereas non-emotional states are neither emotionally rational nor irrational because they lack the categorical precondition for such evaluative contrasts.[56] So there is kind of "intrinsic rationality" (or cognitive function) in all emotions because it is constitutive of them to aim at a type of axiological correctness, even when they are inappropriate.

This two-level pattern is repeated for several other kinds of intentional states. A tradition from Socrates to Habermas holds that communicative action is naturally oriented toward truth (or belief warranted by evidence alone) as its ideal. The liar who aims at deception is categorically communicative in this sense since she participates in social practices to which this truth-standard is intrinsic; but she exploits them by violating their natural requirement for her strategic advantage. In other words, she plays the game, which involves at least implicit acceptance of the rules, but she cheats. Her deficient case of communicative action is parasitic on the norm, as Kant famously argued.[57] This is distinct from ignoring or rejecting the standard that defines the practice altogether, as a BSer does on Frankfurt's analysis. Similarly, a small child who says something that he believes is false only because he wants to copy an older sibling is not lying, for he does not yet know how to play that game. Yet we would not count him as BSing because that label implies that the agent *ought* to meet the categorical condition of communicative action. It is important that there are different ways to fail to meet a categorical condition.

Suppose we applied de Sousa's model to higher-order volitions in Frankfurt's sense. Like the BSer who is not really engaged in the communicative game (on the robust Habermasian understanding of it), beings that Frankfurt calls "wanton" lack a categorical condition of "personhood." He specifies this only as forming higher-order volitions, but de Sousa's analysis suggests a teleological standard that we might call *worthiness* in one's own 1st-order motives (which, notably, are the motives that are most accessible to interpretation by others, which therefore figure most saliently in one's social identity). Then higher-order volitions would be constituted in part by the standard implied in their natural function, namely to govern the 1st-order motives on which we act and the social persona these give us. Frankfurt has constantly resisted the idea that there is any rational standard implicit in the function of superintending one's 1st-order motives,[58] but de Sousa's analysis implies that there should be. And this analysis explains Frankfurt's distinctions: the analogy evident in Table 4.1 between two ways of leaving the categorically inferior state (the pairs of arrows) suggests that the options in both cases involve an *evaluative* distinction resting on a categorical one.

Frankfurt first illustrated the idea of wantonness with his famous "wanton addict" who "cannot or does not care which of his conflicting first-order desires wins out"; this is due either to "his lack of capacity for reflection or to his mindless indifference to the enterprise of evaluating his own desires and motives" (FW, 18–19). The ambiguity here arises because, as with "BS," Frankfurt defines wantonness negatively: so he does not distinguish between *essentially* wanton beings (such as "nonhuman animals ... and very young children"—FW, 16) who cannot form higher-order volitions and *contingently* wanton older humans who have (or could develop) the power to identify with certain motives and alienate opposing desires, but who do not. For the first class, it is psychologically impossible to form a higher-order will; for the second, the absence of higher-order volitions demands another explanation. Frankfurt focuses on the second class in contrasting a wanton addict both with an "unwilling" addict who alienates his addictive craving and with a "willing" addict who identifies with his compulsive desire (FW, 17–18; 24–25). For this contrast suggests a wanton who *could* become either willing or unwilling to be an addict. But this second class of wantons who could overcome wantonness must be subdivided into those who simply fail to care about their 1st-order motives (call them "unawakened" or "accidental" wantons) and those who *intentionally refrain* from forming commitments involving higher-order volitions ("voluntary wantons"). For example, Pippin and Merry start off in the *Lord of the Rings* as accidental wantons interested primarily in fun-loving tomfoolery, and then grow into more caring agents; whereas Stendhal famously aimed at spontaneity and immediacy. We can expand this taxonomy as follows:

1. Essentially wanton animals (psychologically unable to form higher-order volitions):
   (A) Nonhuman animals.
   (B) Human beings who are too young or mentally incapacitated to form higher-order volitions.
2. Contingently wanton animals (with the requisite mental capacities for higher-order will):
   (A) Accidentally wanton human beings to whom it has not yet occurred to form higher-order attitudes toward their own 1st-order motives.
   (B) Voluntarily wanton human beings who voluntarily omit to form higher-order volitions
       (i) through tacit or unacknowledged refusal to engage this capacity when it is called for, or
       (ii) through explicit and reflectively acknowledged refusal according to plan (fully *intentional* wantons).

This further subdivision of class 2B recognizes that 2nd-order volitions may be voluntarily avoided either through more or less self-deceptive inattention or in more explicit awareness of this stance (which constitutes a minimal 3rd-order volition not to permit any 2nd-order volitions).

Such voluntary wantons (2B) are more disturbing than both accidental and essential wantons, for they play some positive role in their wantonness; intentional wantons (type 2Bii) even try to remain wanton. Similarly, some statements that would count as "BS" under Frankfurt's overly wide negative condition are simply made in ignorance of communicative norms, whereas others are distinguished by the agent's positive intention *not* to concern herself with the truth-value of her claims or consequent beliefs in her listeners—that is, her intention is to *omit* caring about the warrant that her claims have or lack. Such a person, we might say, practices *detachment* from the primary concerns to which communicative action normally commits us.[59] In her communicative action, she intentionally avoids aiming at the normal proximate goal of conveying truth (and thus may avoid free-riding on this normal expectation in the way liars do).[60]

This could be for several reasons: (1) Perhaps, like Eddie Murphy in the film *Beverly Hills Cop*, the agent is merely using "BS" as a means to some material advantage; call such an agent an instrumental BSer. As Cohen noted, such agents "BS" intentionally, though they would not "BS" if they believed other means would be more effective in securing their further ends. (2) Things are worse if the agent is in the grip of an ideology that values spontaneity in communication without the "narrow shackles" of concern for truth or better-warranted beliefs. (3) Worse still, perhaps she is a skeptic who thinks that the very ideas of truth and warrant are bunk. As Jonathan Lear argues in response to Frankfurt, the "BS" that fills many public addresses in the United States today is often more brazen than Frankfurt expects since the speaker is rather open about the fact that she cares little whether the content of her claims is true or false.[61] Instead of trying to hide her unconcern about the truth-value of what she says, or lull her audience into mistaken confidence that she knows what she is talking about (like the ancient Sophists), this type of BSer corrupts society by inviting audiences to enjoy rhetorical flourish while ignoring the possible truth or falsehood of what is said. She encourages her listeners to focus on form of delivery rather than the substance. Even if what she says happens to be accurate, she seduces them to participate in her cynical refusal to care about, or even believe in, objective truth.[62] Against concern about truth-values, such a Nietzschian BSer aims not at deception, but rather at promoting the value of power or charisma. No doubt this kind of skeptical sophistry is corrosive, as Frankfurt suggests in his follow-up book *On Truth*.[63] It is especially destructive to deliberative democracy, which then disintegrates into mere tyranny of majority desires, the collective rule of blind prejudice and brute preference. This is what Kierkegaard means by the anonymous "public" that he reviles as spiritually hollow in his essay, *The Present Age* (in the volume *Two Ages*).

(4) But Kierkegaard is even more concerned about self-deceptive "BS". Consider an agent who is too dissolute to face the difficulties involved in caring about the truth-value of controversial and important ideas or beliefs—especially those that could make a deep practical difference in the conduct of her life—but who finds herself carried along by the common expectation to interact through constant speech; so she complies with vacuous talk.[64] This is the type of BSer that Kierkegaard has in mind when he describes "chatter" as "the annulment of the passionate disjunction between being silent and speaking" (TA, 97). The distinction between categorical and evaluative levels is found again here: the chatterer lacks the passion either for authentic speech *or* silence. He lacks the conviction necessary for genuine "conversation between man and man"; his talk becomes pure gossip, "garrulous confiding" about nothing that really matters to him, for his real "aim is to find something to chatter about" (TA, 99). In other words, this dissolute BSer tacitly aims at self-distraction more than any further goal. It is possible to do this in writing as well as speech. Those noted earlier who "write anonymously over their own signature" (TA, 103) say nothing they genuinely care about. So they are not "authors" in the essential sense; they lack the categorical condition to be either good or bad authors.

This comparison brings us closer to isolating a distinctive proximal goal of the communicative act-type that Frankfurt considers damaging to human society and to the agents who perform it. In forms (2), (3), and (4), "BS" involves intending distinctive ends that have to do with avoiding communicative norms. In these noninstrumental forms, "BS" resembles species of the general pattern of attitudes and motives that Kierkegaard calls "aestheticism."

III. Frankfurtian "BS", Acedia, and Kierkegaardian Aestheticism

Aestheticism and "BS"

In Kierkegaard's broad sense of the term, "aestheticism" is not (as the label might suggest) simply a way of life focused on the beautiful, but rather an encompassing attitude or practical orientation toward choices that (tacitly or more reflectively) seeks to avoid deep responsibility for serious life-choices.

More advanced aesthetes in Kierkegaard's cast put this in a positive light (via self-deception) as the task of avoiding the "boredom" they fear in conventions of ordinary social life and the repetitiveness resulting from vocational or interpersonal commitments. Instead, they seek interesting nuances in the passage of moments, cultivating what Martin Heidegger calls a "curiosity" that is an aspect of inauthentic social relations in his view. Curiosity looks

> not in order to understand what is seen … but *just* in order to see. It seeks novelty only in order to leap from it anew to another novelty … Therefore curiosity is characterized by a specific way of *not tarrying* alongside that which is closest [or most important] … In not tarrying, curiosity is concerned with the constant possibility of *distraction*.[65]

This spontaneity in "immediacy" (among naive aesthetes) and the effort to cultivate it among their more reflective cousins puts aesthetes *beneath* good and evil as states of character: unlike the resolutely evil agent who knows that she is violating moral norms but accepts this price (or even delights in it for sheer rebellion), the aesthete does not take seriously the moral appropriateness or inappropriateness of her acts or their underlying motives. She may (speculatively) recognize the authority of ethical ideals and standards, but she does not personally appropriate them or give them motive-force in her life.

We find here another range of causes from accidental failure through voluntary but tacit consent, to fully intentional action. The aesthetes presented in *Either/Or* I range from pure sensualists like Mozart's "Don Giovanni" who use others for erotic pleasure[66] and prudent "shopkeepers" who care only for material advantage, to more self-aware figures like the young man "A" who writes the morose and obsessive "Diapsalmata" and cynical treatises like "The Rotation of Crops." This typology culminates with the sentimental and complex "Johannes" who keeps his "Seducer's Diary."[67] Like the accidental wanton, the most unconscious or childish of these aesthetes may not recognize his failure to form commitments that could be deeply good or evil. Others, like "A" in his treatises, self-consciously advocate an aesthetic life while repressing awareness of its frivolity. By the time of his Preface to the "Seducer's Diary," however, "A" is clearly more disturbed; against his will, he is awakening to the hollowness and absurdity of the Seducer's way of life (EO I, 303–13, esp. 310). The Seducer himself is at the farthest extreme: he has embraced superficiality in full reflective determination to cultivate emotions and experiences that seem beautiful or full of amoral meaning; he forms the paradoxical *project* of remaining wanton.[68] While the category is named for the Seducer's attitude toward beauty, the essence of aestheticism in all these forms is the absence of commitments involving higher-order volitions taken up *as* ethically good or evil. Thus, as Harvey Ferguson has helpfully argued, aestheticism does not reduce merely to spontaneous living in the flow of experience. In Kierkegaard's critique, both the "way of reflection" as speculative detachment and "the way of immediacy" as a (false) index of one's real existential identity are rejected.[69]

If we compare this range of aesthetes to our other two taxonomies of wantons and BSers, the key analogy should be obvious: Frankfurt's BSer is to the value of Truth as Kierkegaard's aesthete is to the Good in general. These agents fail, avoid, or refuse outright to care about the value-ideal that is implicit in communication, on the one hand, and in projective willing, on the other. Extending our previous table, we can add these comparisons:

Table 4.2

	Attitudes toward ends worth caring about (or identity-defining commitments)		Attitudes toward truth-value of communicated contents	
Lacking the categorical condition		Aesthete		BSer
Meeting the categorical condition	Ethically good projects/cares	Ethically evil projects/cares	Aiming at belief	Aiming at true false belief

Of course, this analogy involves the controversial thesis that there *is* an ethical *telos* naturally connected to projective volition and higher-order will. But we have now seen that two sets of comparable phenomena fit an analogy supporting this distinctively Kierkegaardian thesis. When avoiding ethical considerations becomes a central goal of one's life, a disposition to "BS" is likely to become an ongoing defense-mechanism, and thus an *aspect* of aestheticism.

Johannes in "The Seducer's Diary" is the ultimate aesthete: his romantic attentions to his "Cordelia" are neither a simple deception nor a straightforward lie (for he really is attracted to her[70]), but rather a kind of "BS" that hides his detachment from both her emotions *and* his own. Most people are earnest emoters in this sense: they want their emotional responses to events, situations, and acts or sufferings of other persons to reflect the positive or negative values in those acts and events, because emotional expression of value is intrinsically important (much like truth). Sensitive emotional response may be beneficial to us in several ways, but accurate expression of the values we encounter in the intentional object of the emotion is inherently appropriate, as de Sousa argued. So normal agents guided by this *telos* of emotion do not view emotional expression of the salient values as a *mere means* to any further end or goal.[71] By contrast, Johannes the Seducer is an emotional BSer: his emotions toward Cordelia are not feigned or simply pretended; but he does not care whether he accurately expresses their axiological objects because he cultivates these emotions only as a means to a quasi-artistic end. He has the vice of "sentimentality" in David Pugmire's sense: one who uses emotions for ends that are insensitive to the emotion's accuracy, with "indulgent and insistent" intentional disregard for this gap between reality and his emotional construal of it.[72] Johannes is a spectator of emotional drama, aiming to take *sentimental pleasure* in contemplating Cordelia's erotic pathos *and his own* 1st-order emotional response to her feelings (both in the moment and in later refection): for these passions appear beautiful in their tension, and therefore "interesting" (EO I, 424). This serves his project of preserving "the interesting" in all things and thereby avoiding ethically significant commitment (EO I, 438). But it also means that his affects do not meet the categorical condition for real emotions; he experiences only their affected simulacra. In that sense, his method is self-defeating: for real emotions are far more meaningful.

Boredom and Acedia

Another connection between the habits of "BS" and aestheticism is suggested by their respective attitudes toward boredom. As we saw, more reflective aesthetes understand their cultivation of "the interesting" as a way of avoiding "boredom" through keeping a series of novel experiences going. However, there is more than one form of boredom. Ordinary boredom is just a state of disappointed expectation of aesthetic or intellectual goods: when kids are hoping for some entertainment or thrill and the ride is closed, they say that are bored. Similarly, adults may be bored with a class, lecture, movie, or novel that was not as enlightening or moving or informative as they expected. In these cases, an ordinary human desire for interesting activity is frustrated. This differs from boredom as a *mood* without the absence of any particular expected good as its intentional object. The empty listlessness of a hot summer day when we cannot pin down why everything seems dull differs from the tedium a child may experience on a long car ride. Mood-boredom in turn can be due to external circumstances that block intrinsically worthwhile activity (such as prison) or due to an internal lassitude of the will. The latter type, which I call *existential boredom*, is what Frankfurt has in mind when he writes that boredom is more than an unpleasant feeling; it is a loss of psychic "vitality" due to not caring about anything going on around us (RL, 53–55). In this sense, a wanton who literally cared about nothing and therefore made no effort "to maintain any thematic unity or coherence" in her desires (RL, 16) would be bored in the existential sense. Such agents lead lives that are insignificant to them. In less extreme cases,

> ... they may be emotionally shallow; or they may lack vitality; or they may be chronically indecisive. To the extent that they do actively choose and pursue certain goals, they may devote themselves to such insipid ambitions that their experience is generally dull ... In consequence, their lives may be relentlessly banal and hollow and – whether they recognize this about themselves – they may be dreadfully bored. (RL, 6–7)[73]

Such deep existential boredom comes from lacking significant purpose; it is a symptom of *acedia*—the vice of sloth—as Gabrielle Taylor interprets it. In Taylor's sense, "acedia" is not simple laziness, idleness, or complacency (as it was classically understood),[74] but rather a voluntary failure to form cares or commitments that could define a meaningful life. Thus as Taylor describes him, Goncharov's character Oblomov sees

> that there are worthwhile things to achieve in life, which he will not achieve because he will not make the effort, because he cannot get himself sufficiently engaged with what he thinks worthwhile to push him into activity.[75]

Acedia so understood is very similar, Taylor rightly notes, to the attitude of "Kierkegaard's aestheticist" who sees "nothing worth engaging with."[76] This comparison supports Kierkegaard's critique of aestheticism: while "A" and the "Seducer" refuse to recognize objective values beyond aesthetic pleasure because caring about them involves true attachment, investment of self, and thus risk of suffering, this dooms them to acedia, or existential boredom, although it may appear outwardly in the guise that Taylor calls superficial "busyness."[77] Haunted by the absence of an identity based on earnest devotion to concrete final ends, both "A" and the Seducer seek to escape the negative experience of existential boredom by various kinds of distraction: for example, playing with roles and relationships without real engagement, curiosity without deep interest, seductions carried out as light-minded experiments without any commitment to love. All such distractions are forms of "BS" in the *existential* sense, since they amount to so many ways of refusing to endorse the *truth or weight* of values that we ought to care about for their own sake.

Existential "BS" and Heideggerian "Idle Talk" (Again)

We have traced the problem underlying Frankfurt's concern about "BS" to its root. Cohen's common instrumental BSer is cavalier toward truth-value occasionally or intermittently. This evinces a certain shallowness analogous to the typical hedonism or materialism of the unreflective aesthete. By contrast, existential "BS" is a deeper attitude that denies, refuses, or at least demotes the objective importance of truth (and thereby any other agent-transcending value) as a final end for human life. It is not merely a matter of *passive* "indifference to truth,"[78] but of active (even if not reflected on) opposition to caring about truth.

Thus existential "BS" is not intermittent or occasional: it is an orientation that comes to pervade one's attitudes toward anything that might matter in one's activities. It is a way of life aimed at avoiding the kinds of cares and commitments that require serious and sincere communication with others. This is the distinctive goal that gives us a positive definition of "BS". It has to be a self-effacing, self-deceptive project simply because there are so many goods worth caring about in the realms of reality outside oneself: in the practices or professions (such as the arts or sciences), in relationships with other persons, in social movements and political causes, and perhaps in religious callings—to list only some familiar ones. But caring about goods that we could pursue in these contexts comes with a high price: it requires commitment to ideals of excellence and devotion to particular others, and hence concern about both (a) the truth of what one communicates to others in these activities and relationships, and (b) about making the sincerity of one's interest clear to them. It also requires willingness to experience those emotions that are appropriate given one's cares and commitments in relation to the actual situations one confronts in the world; for that is part of caring. By contrast, existential "BS" is a shield against the ways that persons, social life, or the natural world call us to cares and thus to earnest communication with others about the values to which our projective devotions respond.[79]

Because the underlying goal that constitutes existential "BS" characterizes not only isolated speech-acts but a whole way of being that levels off the deep practical significance of goals, activities, and relationships worthy of devotion, its influence can spread, becoming a social phenomenon. In this social form, existential "BS" is comparable to what Martin Heidegger calls "idle talk" in which the anonymous "they" (*das Man*) say things without the "primary relationship-of-Being towards the entity talked about."[80] The "primary relationship" or natural attitude to which Heidegger refers is what he calls *disclosure*, i.e., letting things or others reveal their true character without distortion by our preconceptions or agendas. Although this is part of our *telos* and essential to "authenticity" or being able to "stand by oneself" as Heidegger conceives it, this kind of clarity is never easy to achieve. Heidegger borrows from Kierkegaard the idea that we may reach such clarity by grasping our own mortality, or choosing in the face of death.[81] Probably this is not the *only* way to achieve clarity about how things really are and what our possible responses may be; but there is something to the idea that facing death can help us come to terms with what should matter most to us—or that it helps us cut through the "BS" that builds up a barrier between us and the deep values that are most relevant for projective motivation.

Anticipating Frankfurt, Heidegger also notes that "idle talk" is distinct from intentionally lying; its function is to "close off" possibilities for understanding how things really stand. And "[t]o do this, one need not aim to deceive. Idle talk does not have the kind of Being which belongs to consciously passing off something as something else."[82] Rather than lying, idle talk, like gossip, passes off questionable claims as something taken for granted, or as something everybody knows, and thus it discourages serious effort to understand the reasons for (or against) such a claim. For example, consider the way that the Heritage Foundation has taught most Americans to assume that "liberal" means favoring a nebulous something called "Big Government," which is a menacing albeit vague combination of high taxes for the sake of waste and Orwell's "Big Brother." When common in a society, such catchphrases and images foster knee-jerk reactions that control average, everyday thinking: as Heidegger puts it, "[t]he dominance of the public way in which things have been interpreted"[83] intervenes between us and how things really are. In Frankfurt's terms, what this means is that the average Joe is caught in an invisible net of "BS" that undermines the deliberative processes that alone can justify democratic law-making. Ideologies are especially strong nets of this kind because people caught in them are unaware of their pervasive influence and the blinders they impose. People living in societies ruled by such ideologies are trained away from "the primordially genuine relationship-of-Being towards the world" (i.e., our natural orientation toward truth) and are kept "floating unattached" to hard facts, floating with others in the superficial camaraderie of "BS".[84]

IV. Authentic Willing clarified in Kierkegaard's attack on Aesthetic Culture

At this point we can return to our hypothesis that one condition of authenticity is achieved by our capacity to project new ends and reform old ones, to devote oneself and unify one's energies through the work of sustained commitment. "Will" in this sense refers to the kind of striving that Oblomov would not undertake. Nowhere in the existential tradition is this idea clearer than in Kierkegaard's riveting, direct, and devastating critique of "The Present Age" of his own culture. In this signed work, Kierkegaard portrays mid-nineteenth-century Europe as a period of reflective detachment, indolence, shrewd egoism, and superficiality that has lost the passionate engagement and heroic willpower of the preceding revolutionary age (TA, 69). The revolutionary age had its demons, but it was not lukewarm. In the present age, aestheticism is linked to ubiquitous "BS". Kierkegaard suggests that the irresoluteness of Europe in his time is related to its being an "age of publicity," in which announcements and committee meetings substitute for action, and bureaucracy saps decisiveness: he asks "if a whole generation could be presumed to have the diplomatic task of procrastinating and of continually frustrating any action and yet make it seem as if something were happening …." (TA, 70); it almost sounds as if he were describing the U.N. today! True political revolution, like true scholarship, has been replaced by simulacra. In this situation, even a bad decision is better than no resolve, or the mere illusion of willing: "Even if it is a rash leap, if only it is decisive, and if you have the makings of a man, the danger of life's severe judgment upon your recklessness will help you become one" (TA, 71).

This is a direct affirmation in Kierkegaard's own name of Judge William's pseudonymous claim in *Either/Or* II that "choosing oneself" in earnest commitment to a task, role, or relationship will strengthen conscience and make ethical considerations more salient, even if one's particular choices are not always for the best options at the start. In fact, the main goal of "The Present Age" sections of *Two Ages* is to develop this central thesis of *Either/Or* II that personal authenticity starts with the primordial "choice" to make serious choices or form commitments to projects, roles, and relationships in light of their ethical value (broadly understood). But in this text, Kierkegaard makes two crucial additions to the Judge's analyses. First, he develops the social dimension of aestheticism through clarifying the normative basis of willing. Second, he defends the converse of the Judge's thesis: just as volitional initiative helps clarify ethical sensibility, volitional weakness loosens our cognitive grasp on values because the importance of many contrasts can be well-appreciated only from an engaged perspective. In other words, Kierkegaard diagnoses "BS" and idle talk partly as *symptoms* of volitional shallowness. Unfortunately these symptoms in turn worsen the spiritual disease. Because willing requires conviction concerning the objective worth of goals and persons to whom we dedicate our efforts, a dulled normative sensibility makes it harder to muster the will to "stand" for anything.[85] Thus existential "BS" and aestheticism are two sides of a vicious circle. This is the true root of the connection we saw indicated by the analogy between "BS" and wantonness in Frankfurt.

These two developments of the Judge's thesis are woven together in "The Present Age." Like the aesthetes of the pseudonymous works, typical people in Kierkegaard's culture are described as "spectators" rather than "participants"; they have forgotten that "a person stands or falls on his actions" (TA, 73). They have grown incapable of the sincere admiration of greatness that heroic pathos requires (TA, 72). These problems are linked because willing (in the projective sense) is a response to what Kierkegaard calls "primitive experiences" of value (TA, 73), by which he means the sense of coming in contact with inexorable reality, being riveted with an impression of eternal validity, without which there is "no hero, no lover, no thinker, no knight of faith, no great humanitarian …" (TA, 75). The objective worth of different types of greatness derives from pursuing such eternally valid goods. This crucial point explains why it becomes harder to will earnestly when society popularizes forms of cynicism that prevent people from trusting enough to have such experiences. Sensitivity to value and passionate response, in contrast to fleeting status and wealth, constitute a kind of existential "asset" (TA, 74), following the biblical metaphor of spiritual riches. Art and literature free from indulgent artifice and haughty skepticism build up such assets by putting us in touch with values outside us: "a well-grounded ethical view" supporting an ideal of "nobility" and "unselfishness" can inspire volitional initiative (TA, 74).

The Russian novelist Solzhenitsyn recognized a similar existential function for art in its capacity to break through "the lie" on which violence depends: when opposing ideology, "One word of truth is of more weight than all the rest of the world."[86] But it is not only the lies of totalitarian violence that art must fight in order to free us from delusion: it may be even harder to cut through pervasive "BS" in popular culture. Kierkegaard describes a more subtle miasma that "lets everything remain but subtly drains the meaning out of it" by obscuring ethical contrasts in "equivocation" and vague insinuation (TA, 77). Terms that were fully meaningful only in relation to resolute devotion still remain in use, but they are robbed of the live significance they once had (TA, 81). In our time, we see this when terms like "patriot," "family values," "job creators," and even "racism" are so overused that they reduce to mere catchphrases or emotive triggers. As Heidegger says, *das Man* is an average or everyday sense of things in which the deeper meanings that could form the basis for personal appropriation or heroic striving are leveled off. The dominance of such an encompassing web of "BS" in the "ambiguity and equivocation" of polite society conceals the lassitude of the individual's will, making this illness difficult to detect and "root out" (TA, 80).

This collective state of hollow banter and self-congratulatory conceit reflects and helps maintain the volitional void of its individual members. Aesthetic amoralism is characterized for Kierkegaard by ambiguity and flux in which nothing is held absolute and no stand is taken: "Morality is character; character is something engraved, but the sea has no character, nor does sand, nor abstract common sense [*das Man*] … for character is inwardness" (TA, 77–78). By contrast, even a radically evil agent has character in her inward commitment to harm: "As energy, immorality is also character" (TA, 78). For earnest evil at least has volitional continuity.

"Character" here stands for a stable set of devotions that tend to last because they are ever-renewed in projective striving; it consists in *volitional* dispositions. As Joel Kupperman says, character involves "loyalty to commitments and projects" and a willingness to change them only for one's "own reasons."[87] Similarly, Frankfurt describes "cares" as binding past and future together for the agent because they involve "a certain consistency or steadiness" maintained by higher-order volition (IWC, 83–84): if one cares about some X, the desire for X's good "must endure through an exercise of his own volitional activity" rather than simply by its own inertia (OC, 160). For caring about X involves "identifying" with one's desire for X (OC, 161),[88] and decisive identification involves "coherence and unity of purpose over time" (IW, 175). By contrast, inauthenticity is characterized by the absence of passionate engagement and thus by narrative discontinuity. For Kierkegaard, a volitional pathos that makes inward character can have different grades of moral worth; yet without it,

> The distinction between good and evil is enervated [or blurred] by a loose, supercilious, theoretical acquaintance with evil, by an overbearing shrewdness which knows that the good is not appreciated or rewarded in the world …. No one is carried away to great exploits by the good, no one is rushed into outrageous sin by evil, the one is just as good as the other, and yet for that very reason there is all the more to gossip [or "BS"] about, for ambiguity and equivocation are titillating and stimulating …
> (TA, 78)

This passage, which anticipates much of Heidegger's remarks on "ambiguity" as part of *das Man*,[89] implies the same distinction that Judge William describes in terms of two levels of "choice" in the second letter in *Either/Or* II. The aesthete fails to appreciate the importance of moral distinctions because she avoids the kind of willing that Kierkegaard calls "pathos," "spirit," or "inwardness" (a term which implies that caring involves a relation to oneself as well as to the objects of one's care).[90] But while *Either/Or* II diagnoses this kind of failure in the individual agent, "The Present Age" emphasizes that it is sometimes partly a result of cultural pathology: prevailing social conditions can obscure the ethical distinctions that are required for projective willing to break out of aesthetic paralysis.[91] Aesthetic "BS" or idle talk that dulls all value-contrasts acts on the will like the magic harp that lulls the giant to sleep. Then even a stark encounter with genuine evil can, for all its harm, be helpful in shocking the quiescent will out of its slumber.

Like Rousseau before him, Kierkegaard sees status-oriented society as playing this soporific role by creating an atmosphere of artificial politeness or decorum in which sincerity about one's views and direct expression of one's commitments is replaced by simulacra of concern. In Rousseau's analysis, society corrupts the individual by encouraging invidious comparisons that lead to "envy" as desire for relative equality, and thence to desires for domination.[92] For Kierkegaard, the problem is instead that what we might call *existential envy* blocks earnest respect for the heroism of others, which is ennobling and can provide a basis for the agent's own resolve (TA, 82). This envy is a kind of paralysis that renders us afraid to make life-decisions or commit to a concrete identity lest others mock it: "Reflection's envy holds the will and energy in a kind of captivity" (TA, 81). Unlike the more honest envy that at least recognizes another's superiority, this is "characterless envy" that "makes sport" of any kind of excellence to which identity-defining vocations, practices, or interpersonal relationships can aspire (TA, 83–84). Such denial of excellence is what Kierkegaard means by "leveling" (TA, 84).[93] Even the passions in aestheticism that can be taken up and transformed in ethical caring are beaten down in such leveling,[94] which is the opposite of ethical equality before God (TA, 88). For the existential leveler "fears more than death … [social] reflection's judgment upon him, reflection's objection to his wanting to venture something as an individual" (TA, 85). By fear of public scorn, "Envy turns into the principle of characterlessness" (TA, 83): it teaches us to see *caring* in Frankfurt's sense (which generates volitional character) as inferior, simplistic, old-fashioned, or hopelessly out of touch with current fashion. Without strong value-contrasts between excellence and its opposites, or a keen sense of goods beyond our own material self-interest and pleasures, the agent's will is robbed of the necessary basis for projective motivation. The result is shrewd or ironic detachment in place of active participation or "belonging" through one's own free endeavor:

> the individual does not belong to God, to himself, to the beloved, to his art, to his scholarship; no, just as a serf belongs to an estate [involuntarily], so the individual realizes that in every respect he belongs to an abstraction in which reflection subordinates him. (TA, 85)

In other words, the individual is absorbed into a vaporous "aggregate" that can think and choose for him; only the collective can determine how things will go, so there seems to be no individual responsibility. In this special sense, "the public" is defined as the *opposite* of free association from earnest passion, or authentic democracy. This "public is not a *people*" (TA, 92, my italics); one cannot "belong" to it as lovers belong to each other; one can only lose oneself in it through an abdication of responsibility. In Heidegger's sense of *das Man*, "the public" is the anonymity in which people hide when they lack the courage for autonomy or self-rule (TA, 89).

This does not mean that *all* solidarity or self-definition through group membership necessarily cause inauthenticity. Being a loner is neither necessary nor sufficient for authenticity. Authentic collective action is possible, but it requires active engagement from each participant, which requires their personal appropriation of shared goods to be pursued by joint action as their own purpose. Being a (positively) "free" participant in concrete groups can "reinforce and educate the individual, yet without shaping him entirely" (TA, 92). Like authentic art, this kind of existential *bildung* requires rather than suppresses individual response and initiative: each member of the group cultivates her own interpretation of its common life and benefits from the unique interpretation of others. Likewise, in religious faith, the individual is "educated to make up his own mind instead of agreeing with the public" by default. So "strong communal life" and even action by "the people" as a whole are possible for Kierkegaard (TA, 91); like Mill and Kant before him, he even associates them with enlightened thinking for oneself. Kierkegaard contrasts such "contemporaneity with actual persons" in joint efforts to the anonymous public that suppresses individual alterity (TA, 91). Like Buber after him, Kierkegaard believes that such vital community arises from encounters in which the participants are freely present in "resolute mutual giving" (TA, 79). It requires the kind of "personal human discourse" or sincere self-revelation that is blocked by "BS" (TA, 104). Genuine communion is impossible when "chatter" replaces "essential speaking" or earnest communication (TA, 97).

Thus Kierkegaard's analysis of authenticity emphasizes the need for norms with the universal and overriding significance of ethical ideals, and more generally, for values outside the self that can inspire "excellence" (TA, 78, 89). Traditional romantic conceptions err in imagining that sources for an authentic existential identity can be found solely within the individual, and especially in the "immediacy" of affective promptings. As Ferguson says, for Kierkegaard,

the realisation of all higher forms of life … depend[s] on the suppression of immediacy through wilful identification of the self with values that have their course and justification outside of momentary states of pleasure. The self shapes itself in relation to its own commitment to these values.[95]

So it is ultimately because the culture of the "present age" blocks respect for the alterity of objective values that command us from beyond our own psyche, and undermines awe in the face of "something sacred" (TA, 64), that it closes off the option of authentic existence. Its "formlessness" prevents the primitive experience of "essential truth" that requires passion to see (TA, 100; compare TA, 61 on "form" and "passion" in the age of revolution).

V. How Existential "BS" Conflicts with Caring about Self-Transcending Ends

We have seen that Frankfurt's critiques of "BS" and wantonness can be better explained in the more fundamental terms of Kierkegaard's analysis of inauthenticity in the single aesthete and the general public. Kierkegaard's diagnosis implies a conception of authenticity in terms of projective motivation that is in deep concord with Frankfurt on two points.

First, it suggests that most of the goals, activities, or relationships (both dialogical and social) to which we devote ourselves when we "choose the ethical" lie literally outside us—in the other, or in the world, though of course we can also will our own good.[96] Frankfurt agrees, since "selflessness" is a defining feature of caring on his account: our attention is focused outward on our ideal or on the person(s) we love (IWC, 89). Indeed, the object of care is entrancing in a way that we find liberating, especially in the case of "volitionally necessary" cares from which we cannot choose "at will" to disengage (IWC, 88). In another essay, Frankfurt suggests that the difference between caring and desires that are initially passive (or wanton unless we identify with them) is found in the devotion of cares to something beyond the self as a final end. An agent's "active love" aims at goods that "are altogether distinct from and independent of his own" (ANL, 134). Later he recognizes that this kind of pure motive that distinguishes care-love can also be directed at the agent's own good (OC, 168).[97] But "aesthetic, cultural, and religious ideals" to which people may be devoted are not egoistic, even if they are not based on moral duties (RL, 8); in these cares, and in love of family members, the agent focuses on something beyond herself. Although discovering and articulating our loves is "inherently important" to us because it gives our lives shape and meaning, this existential benefit depends on our outward focus on what or who we care about: "The value of loving to the lover derives from his dedication to his beloved," or his taking her well-being as his final end (RL, 59).

Second, the cares that constitute the center of an authentic identity have a reflexive side. Kierkegaard's emphasis on "inwardness" agrees with Frankfurt's stress on the higher-order volitions involved in caring: both suggest that authenticity requires certain self-directed attitudes and efforts. These must be distinct from the sort of morose obsession with self that we typically find in various sentimental and narcissistic states, which are instead symptoms of aestheticism. Some forms of self-reflection are *authenticity-reducing*, and these include reflexive attitudes in existential "BS". In 1991, Frankfurt argued that the weakest human passion is not "love of truth," as Housman wrote, but specifically "our love of the truth about ourselves" (FP, 95).[98] The many varieties of self-deception in human experience all indicate the difficulty of commitment to self-disclosure, or caring to know how we really are.

But as Kierkegaard helped us recognize, the self-deception involved in existential "BS" as a way of life, or as a way of stalling in matters that call for caring about truth, is especially damaging to prospects for knowing oneself. For the person who wishes to hide from the importance of truth in general has a project that works against honest appraisal of all his other significant motives as well. "BS" as a way of life, or more broadly all voluntary wantonness, requires a refusal to care about the truth regarding one's *own practical identity*. In turn, this usually requires *BSing oneself* about one's identity, that is, telling oneself stories about one's roles and activities that are sometimes true, sometimes false, but chosen only with regard to aesthetic criteria such as how pleasing or flattering they are, or whether the *self-image* they paint fits in well with other expectations. Even if such an agent enters psychoanalysis, this is only to distract from recognizing his real hope, which is to flow along in life without ever being halted, sobered, or humbled by deeper values beyond his own psyche. Thus Frankfurt is surely correct in "The Faintest Passion" that it is vitally important to care about our true nature or identity, even though we may lack privileged access to it (and here friends can help us). Indeed, it seems that one could never escape a life of "BS" or wantonness without caring to some extent about one's character, who one really is, or what one stands for. This is because volitional caring about any plausible candidate X entails caring$_2$ that one has this care$_1$—which may be explained in terms of two conditions:

(a) caring to understand one's own practical identity (or to know that self-sustained commitment to X is part of one's identity), and
(b) caring about the *worthiness* of this devotion, including the value of X (and the resulting worth of the practical identity that caring about X partially constitutes).

This is a plausible interpretation of Frankfurt's 1982 claims that "it is necessarily important to people what they care about" and that "if anything is worth caring about, then it must be worth caring about what to care about" (IWC, 92). These are among several passages in which Frankfurt (perhaps inadvertently) implies that care or love *can* be based on objective evaluations of their objects.

Thus if (a) and (b) capture the 2nd-order caring that is natural to full personhood, we have to revise Frankfurt's more recent subjectivism in light of his own earlier essays: earnestly caring about anything or anyone requires honesty about one's own character, which includes caring about the truth regarding one's own projects, commitments, *including* their worth—which is at least partly a function of the *intrinsic value* of their objects. Frankfurt should embrace Kierkegaard's view that willingness to face one's "eternal significance" as an ethical chooser, or to consider one's life-goals in light of universal ethical ideals, is a transcendental condition for avoiding a life of wantonness or aestheticism: without meeting this condition, we cannot earnestly commit to anything or anyone. This explains why "BS" in its existential form as basic attitude is not only contrary to caring about truth-value in one's speech, but also undermines caring about *anything*. For if caring about X implies caring about the truths concerning X and X's worth as an object of devotion, then caring about truth is a transcendental condition for the possibility of caring about anything else.

Conclusion: Authenticity and Love

For both Frankfurt and Kierkegaard, there is no such thing as *inauthentic love* that is still love, or more than a mere semblance. Agapic love for Kierkegaard is always earnest and makes other loves earnest when it infuses them; for it responds to conscience. And all love in Frankfurt's volitional sense has something akin to an agapic structure, which Frankfurt calls its "selflessness" or independence from any desire for the agent's own satisfaction. A loving state is already affirmed as one's own in arising from one's volitional identity and its inherent limits. However, Kierkegaard recognizes that authentic devotions are impossible without the objective worth of final ends (or excellence of activities involved in their pursuit) being at least part of the reason for committing oneself to them. Authentic willing is a personal response to goods that are disclosed in experience, not arbitrarily posited by caring; in the religious stage, willed commitment is even a response to paradoxical goods that are revealed to us. This is why idle talk and vapidity are so harmful, as Frankfurt's related critiques of "BS" and wantonness implied.

Yet this requires rejecting Frankfurt's subjectivist thesis in *The Reasons of Love* that things become important to us, or worth caring about from our perspective, only because we already care about them. Frankfurt has fallen for the romantic myth of authenticity as loyalty to one's own inscrutable heart: he imagines that there are goals or persons that one simply *must* love or care about, and that our task is only to discover this volitional destiny, since without caring and loving we cannot have a life that is robustly meaningful to us. There are terrible ironies in this: at the end of *On Bullshit*, Frankfurt argued that "BS" is proliferating because of "forms of skepticism which deny that we can have any reliable access to objective reality" (OB, 64). Yet his own subjectivism about values as normative guides for caring is now another influential type of such skepticism. He warned us that the person who believes he cannot "arrive at accurate representations of a common world" shared with others may fall back on being "true to his own nature" (OB, 65); yet in later work Frankfurt did precisely this in saying that our cares can only be justified by our inscrutable volitional nature. He dismissed this notion earlier, insisting in more Sartrean fashion that our natures are indeterminate, "elusively insubstantial," and unstable (OB, 66–67); but later, he returned to the myth of a determinate inner self in his doctrine of volitional necessities.

The truth is surely somewhere between these extremes: we are not endlessly malleable or without individual tendencies that affect our interests and potentials; but we also have some control over our cares, loves, or projective motives in general—forming, sustaining, and modifying them over time in response to values we recognize in reality outside us (though our discernment itself depends often *partly* on our caring). Frankfurt could have avoided his later turn to neo-Humean subjectivism if he had developed the key implication of his essay on "BS", namely that we ought to care about the truth-value of what we communicate because on significant issues, *truth and truthfulness are among the goods objectively worth caring about*. In a *Times* interview, Frankfurt reaffirmed this point: "I had always been concerned about the importance of truth … the way in which truth is foundational to civilization and the various deformities of it that were current."[99] He also repeated that "BS" is harmful to self and society because it refuses to care about something that we all *ought* to care about:

> indifference to truth is extremely dangerous. The conduct of civilized life, and the vitality of the institutions that are indispensable to it, depend very fundamentally on respect for the distinction between the true and the false. Insofar as the authority of this distinction is undermined by the prevalence of bullshit and by the mindlessly frivolous attitude that

accepts the proliferation of bullshit as innocuous, an indispensable human treasure is lost.[100]

This is challenging stuff, worthy of juxtaposition with Kierkegaard's own critique of "idle talk" and Heidegger's remarks on "the They." But it implies that truth is *objectively* worth caring about. When we extend this to say that all our 1st-order cares, identity-defining commitments, and projects should be based on truth about their value, we accept that authenticity is not entirely reducible to self-regarding attitudes: it is impossible for the total skeptic about intrinsic values in the world outside his agency. Such a skeptic's "heart" is either empty or unstable, without any firm content to which he could be loyal. Since authenticity requires devoting ourselves to goods beyond our material interests, or even beyond our self-development and interest in a meaningful life, an authentic agent must believe that such goods exist.

This is the vital conclusion that follows from the striking analogies between "BS", wantonness, aestheticism, and idle talk: in each case, explaining these symptoms of inauthenticity requires positive conditions of authenticity involving recognition of objective goods. Frankfurt's greatest insights cannot be properly understood outside the context of the existential tradition. But when reconstructed in their deepest form by comparison with Kierkegaard, these insights turn out to be incompatible with the subjectivist thesis in Frankfurt's account of love.

Notes

1   See Edward Mooney, *Knights of Faith and Resignation*, 99, and *Selves in Discord and Resolve*, 66–67. Along with C. Stephen Evans and Robert Perkins, Mooney is also among the first to explain the errors of reading Kierkegaard as an irrationalist (see *Knights of Faith and Resignation*, 7–9).

2   See Davenport, "The Meaning of Kierkegaard's Choice Between the Aesthetic and the Ethical," in Davenport and Rudd, eds., *Kierkegaard After MacIntyre*.

3   See Davenport, "Towards an Existential Virtue Ethics: Kierkegaard and MacIntyre," in *Kierkegaard After MacIntyre*; and "Earnestness," in *Kierkegaard's Concepts*.

4   I argue in detail for the superiority of Kierkegaard's conception of wholeheartedness to Frankfurt's in Davenport, *Narrative Identity, Autonomy, and Mortality: From Frankfurt and MacIntyre to Kierkegaard*, chs. 3–4.

5   See Frankfurt, RL, 21–28. This book is a much longer version of an essay titled "On Caring" that was first published in NVL, 155–80, see esp. 172.

6   Ibid., 21–24. As Rudd points out, this has the counterintuitive implication that evil agents are not bound by practical reasons contrary to their unjust or cruel cares (see Anthony Rudd, *Self, Value, and Narrative: A Kierkegaardian Approach*, 103).

7   See Davenport, *Will as Commitment and Resolve*, ch. 14.

8   Ibid., 5. Rudd notes the same contradiction: "Frankfurt, having initially distinguished persons sharply from mere animal choosers … ends up making that distinction only a relative one (we too are determined by our biology, just in a more complex way)"—see Anthony Rudd, *Self, Value, and Narrative*, 103.

9   This is how I read the pseudonymous account of "Truth is Subjectivity" in Kierkegaard's *Concluding Unscientific Postscript*.

10 On these points, see John Crosby's very helpful comparison in his essay, "Personal Individuality: Dietrich von Hildebrand in Debate with Harry Frankfurt," in *Personality Papers*. Kierkegaard's view is like von Hildebrand's in holding that volitional love is a response to the unique value of persons, but von Hildebrand may have a clearer account of this value.

11 Anthony Rudd, *Self, Value, and Narrative*, 89.

12 Charles Larmore, *The Practices of the Self*, 4. Larmore notes that Charles Taylor and Allessandro Ferreira are key exceptions in recognizing the importance of authenticity in its existential sense. This must be contrasted with the narrower use of "authenticity" in some recent analytic literature following Frankfurt as simply a label for acting on motives with which one identifies. In this artificial sense, "authenticity" is a term of art for a procedural condition of "autonomy."

13 On this aspect of existential authenticity, see Rick Anthony Furtak, "The Virtues of Authenticity: A Kierkegaardian Essay in Moral Psychology," *International Philosophical Quarterly* 43, no.4 (December 2003): 423–38.

14 J.S. Mill, *On Liberty and Other Writings*, ed. Stefan Collini. See ch.3: "Of Individuality as one of the elements of well-being," 57 [my italics].

15 Charles Larmore, *The Practices of the Self*, 7.

16 Ibid., 2, quoting from Paul Valéry's essay on Stendhal in *Oeuvres complètes* (Gallimard, 1957): I, 570.

17 Ibid., 2.

18 Ibid., 34.

19 Ibid., 37–39.

20 Ibid., xiii.

21 Ibid., 17.

22 J.S. Mill, *On Liberty*, 64–65.

23 Ibid., 58–59.

24 Charles Larmore, *The Practices of the Self*, 5. This risk of anti-social egotism also seems to be the reason for Poul Martin Møller's view that some "affectation" or modeling oneself on others is needed if one not to become close-minded and "encapsulate himself solely within the sphere of his

own thoughts," as discussed in Bruce Kirmmse's insightful essay on the nineteenth-century history of the concept of affectation: "Affectation, or the Invention of the Self," in *Ethics, Love, and Faith in Kierkegaard*, ed. Edward Mooney, 28 [quoting Møller's "Preparations for an Essay on Affectation," in *Posthumous Papers of Poul M. Møller*, 3rd ed. by F.C. Olsen, in 6 vols., vol. 3, 169–70].

25 Ibid., 21. Larmore thinks that Sartre and Valery are correct that it is willing sincerity that is incoherent, as if somehow the very conscious awareness of this goal is self-defeating (20–21). I do not agree that sincerity or authenticity can only be nontargetable ends, as the final section of this paper partly explains.

26 Thus Anthony Rudd argues in *Self, Value, and Narrative* that in Kierkegaard's view, our core identity is partly received (as passive or given facticity) and partly self-shaped by efforts that both discover the given elements and work on them. This agrees with my interpretation of *Sickness unto Death* in my essay in the *Oxford Handbook of Kierkegaard*, ed. John Lippitt and George Pattison.

27 See Joel Kupperman, *Character*, 13, 43, 47: "character is our style of thought and action in matters of importance." This work is influenced by both Frankfurt and Kierkegaard.

28 See Bruce Kirmmse, "Affectation, or the Invention of the Self," op. cit, 28–29, citing Møller.

29 I use this term to indicate that these traits are not sufficient by themselves for some positive level of moral worth in character; rather, proto-virtues are ethically significant as essential *preconditions of both good and evil* in volitional character. See my "Towards an Existential Virtue Ethics," 294, 296, and note 99. Authenticity is something like a master proto-virtue in this sense, connecting all the others.

30 Edward F. Mooney, "On Authenticity," in *Excursions with Kierkegaard*, 163–64.

31 Ibid., 154–55.

32 Ibid., 152.

33 See Thaddeus Metz, "Recent Work on the Meaning of Life," 776–77, citing Susan Wolf, "Happiness and Meaning." This meaningfulness condition is also the one I stressed in some past remarks on authenticity in contrast to autonomy (see Davenport, *Narrative Identity, Autonomy, and Mortality*, 99).

34 Bernard Williams, "A Critique of Utilitarianism," 77–150, pp. 110–16. Like Frankfurt on "cares," Williams suggests that agents are "identified" in a distinctive way with their "commitments," which involve something more than mere desires or "tastes." Yet the Humeanism that emerges in his later essays leaves Williams no adequate way to explain their volitional "seriousness" or "depth" in one's life.

35 Williams, "Persons, Character, and Morality," 20–39, pp. 11–13. He also refers to such motives as "categorical desires."

36 See Jeffrey Blustein, *Care and Commitment*.

37 See Korsgaard, *Sources of Normativity*, 100–02.

38 See Davenport, *Will as Commitment and Resolve*, ch.13.

39 I critique Frankfurt's arguments for volitionally necessary cares in Davenport, "Norm-Guided Formation of Cares without Volitional Necessities."

40 Frankfurt offers different explanations of the phenomenon of volitional "identification" with motives in "Freedom of the will and the concept of a person," "Identification and externality," and "Identification and wholeheartedness," and later in his Presidential Address to the APA titled "The Faintest Passion."

41 I borrow the term "erosic" from Alan Soble's work on love; see the full explanation in Davenport, *Will as Commitment and Resolve*, ch.4.

42 According to Bob Thompson, *Washington Post*, July 28, 2005 (p.C01), the book had sold 250,000 copies then; see online story. Princeton University Press confirmed that as of June 2006 the book had sold 400,000 copies.

43 Harry Frankfurt's essay "On Bullshit" was originally published in *Raritan* 6 (1986), abridged in *Harpers* (February 1987), and then reprinted in his collection, *The Importance of What We Care About*, 117–33. It was reprinted virtually unchanged as a small book, *On Bullshit*. I cite the book.

44 G.A. Cohen, "Deeper into Bullshit," 321–39.

45 Ibid., 330.

46 Ibid., 329.

47 Ibid., 328.

48 For example, consider Alan Sokal's famous and invaluable hoax article, "Transgressing the Boundaries: Towards a Transformative Hermeneutics of Quantum Gravity," 217–52.

49 Frankfurt, "Reply to G.A. Cohen," in *Contours of Agency*, 340–44, p. 341.

50 Frankfurt, "Reply to G.A. Cohen," 340.

51 Ibid., 343.

52 When the agent does not intend to communicate truth or falsehood as an essential part of her goal in communicating, this is usually either (i) because the context does not call for such concern, or allows for benign chatter; or (ii) because the agent *herself* does not care about the truth-status of the ideas she is expressing. For a person who cares about the truth-value of the ideas that she is communicating normally also cares about the truth-value of the beliefs that her interlocutors acquire from her communication.

53 This link has not, to my knowledge, received attention in the large secondary literature on Frankfurt's ideas concerning personal autonomy, although connections have now been made in some recent popular collections: for example, Gary Hardcastle and George Reisch (ed.), *Bullshit and Philosophy*.

54 Ronald de Sousa, "The Rationality of Emotions," 128–30. Also see the later version in de Sousa, *The Rationality of Emotions*, 158–61.

55 Ibid., 130, and de Sousa, *The Rationality of Emotions*, 160.

56 Ibid., 132–34, and de Sousa, *The Rationality of Emotions*, 159–62.

57 Immanuel Kant, *Groundwork of the Metaphysics of Morals*, Part I, 402–3 (Academy pages).

58 Frankfurt first describes 2nd-order volitions as expressions of "reflective self-evaluation" (FW, 12) and says that such critical awareness involves rational capacities (FW, 17); but he then adds that 2nd-order volitions need not express any practical evaluation of 1st-order desires and may be mere preferences (FW, 19, note 6). This anticipates his later claims that cares need not be at all responsive to rational evaluation of their objects.

59 Most of the so-called "informal fallacies" are dialectical errors precisely because they violate dialectical expectations that are implicit in the shared assumption that the communicative *exchange aims at truth or better-warranted belief as its primary final end.*

60 More precisely, where the context and illocutionary mode of her speech-act involves an apparent validity-claim, and thus ordinarily requires some good-faith effort to communicate what she believes, this BSer deliberately *refuses* to care about whether the content of what she says tracks (directly or inversely) what she regards as the truth of the matter at hand.

61 Jonathan Lear, "Whatever," 23–25.

62 In *On Bullshit*, Frankfurt notes the connection between the rise of "BS" and skepticism about the possibility of "any reliable access to objective reality" (OB, 64).

63 Yet this sequel is disappointing because it lacks the critical edge of *On Bullshit*. For it focuses almost entirely on the *instrumental* values of truth-telling or honesty and so emphasizes the social harms that result from "BS" when widely used as a mere means to all sorts of other ends (OT, 4, 6, 15–17). As if having realized his earlier inconsistency, Frankfurt here says very little about the intrinsic value of truth. Though he clearly does think that we need truth to "understand how to live well" (OT, 36), his own subjectivism blocks him from challenging postmodernist suspicions that normative or evaluative judgments have no objective truth-value (OT, 28–29). He is limited to asserting that *non-normative* factual knowledge is important for forming commitments and for "validating the purposes and goals that we choose and that we set ourselves to pursue" as instrumentally rational (OT, 31). For he agrees with those who think that choice of *final* ends cannot "be justified rationally at all" (OT, 31).

64 For a harrowing example of such a character taken to an extreme, see Charles Williams's description of Evelyn in *All Hallows Eve*.

65 Martin Heidegger, *Being and Time*, I.5 ¶36, H172, p. 216.

66 See "The Immediate Stages of the Erotic" in EO I, 45–135, esp. 85, where Don Giovanni/Don Juan is described as an ideal type of the sensual without even the psychic components of the erotic; he represents maximal immediacy, the "spirit of flesh" incarnate (EO I, 88).

67 These aesthetes are all BSers of different sorts: those who live only for pleasure or material reward are like the Greek sophists who seek to persuade their audience by any rhetorical device as a means to monetary or political ends. The reflective aesthetes, by contrast, are not merely instrumental BSers; they lose themselves in reflection in order to avoid the moral seriousness of weighty life-choices and commitments. I now also recognize a further kind of "heroic" aesthete (in EO II) who does form positive cares for nonmoral ends (e.g., various kinds of greatness) but who avoids recognizing the ethical norms that regulate such cares: see the full taxonomy of aesthetes in Chapter 3 of my Davenport, *Narrative Identity, Autonomy, and Mortality*.

68 See Davenport, "The Meaning of Kierkegaard's Choice," op. cit., and Davenport, "Entangled Freedom."

69 Harvey Ferguson, "Modulation: A Typology of the Present Age," 129.

70 For example, Johannes says, "Plainly and simply to deceive a girl, for that I would not have the stamina" (EO I, 437).

71 The thesis that emotions are naturally for their own sake, or for the sake of *appropriateness* in response to the world and others in it, deserves a detailed defense. I have begun this task in Davenport "The Binding Value of Earnest Emotional Valuation."

72 David Pugmire, *Sound Sentiments: Integrity in the Emotions*, 127. As Pugmire explains, because the sentimentalist uses an emotion as a mere "means to an emotional experience," she betrays her real "indifference" to the theme of the emotion, that is, what it is about (134). Note the similarity to the BSer's indifference to truth.

73 However, I would not grant Frankfurt's additional claim that "persons who are scrupulously moral" could be this hollow (RL, 6); for moral motivation requires cares that are incompatible with wantonness. The truth in his observation comes from the fact that there is a rich array of nonmoral ends worth caring about.

74 Gabrielle Taylor, "Deadly Vices?," 161.

75 Ibid., 163.

76 Ibid., 165–66.

77 Ibid., 168. As Taylor says, in this state, "since her commitment to whatever she is doing is merely a shallow one, it will not generate reasons for embarking on a coherent, life-guiding plan of action" (ibid., 169).

78 Frankfurt, "Reply to G.A. Cohen," 343.

79 As described here, existential "BS" obviously has important similarities to Jean-Paul Sartre's conception of "bad faith." I hope to explain Sartrean bad faith using Frankfurt's concepts in a later essay.

80 Martin Heidegger, *Being and Time*, I.5 ¶35, H168, 212.

81 See my essay in Stokes and Buben, *Kierkegaard and Death*.

82 Martin Heidegger, *Being and Time*, H169, 213. Heidegger scooped Frankfurt on this point, but his analysis of "idle talk" is directly indebted to

Kierkegaard's account of "chatter" in *The Present Age*, and to Kierkegaard's critique of speculative philosophy that attempts to replace religious faith (especially in the *Postscript*).

83   Ibid.

84   Ibid., H170, 214.

85   In Cheshire Calhoun's sense: see "Standing for Something," 92, no.5: 235–60.

86   Alexander Solzhenitsyn, *Nobel Prize Lecture*, 55.

87   Joel Kupperman, *Character*, 14.

88   In at least ten passages, Frankfurt either directly links caring and volitional identification or describes them in parallel terms. Yet after returning to a weaker structural or synchronic conception of identification in terms of "satisfaction" in "The Faintest Passion," he concluded that caring did not require identification or the converse: see his "Reply to Gary Watson" in *Contours of Agency*, 161. In personal conversation with me, he recanted that claim and returned to his more consistent earlier position.

89   In *Being and Time*, Heidegger describes "an intent, ambiguous watching of one another, a secret and reciprocal listening in," in which each hopes to maintain his status as one of the "in-crowd" who of course knows what is going; and yet the basis for being accepted by others is only smug distain for any genuine commitment, along with readiness to denounce anyone who defects from this false camaraderie (H174, 218–19). With its presentiments totalitarian society, this Kafkaesque description is even more unsettling than Kierkegaard's account of conscience-killing ambiguity in the "anonymous public" (to which it is obviously indebted).

90   As Kierkegaard says in discussing four examples, the agent "does not relate [to] himself in the relation but is a spectator" (TA, 79).

91   On this feedback relation, see the last section of my "Towards an Existential Virtue Ethics."

92   See Rousseau, "Discourse on Origin and Foundations of Inequality Among Men," in *The Basic Political Writings*, 25–82, Part Two, pp. 64–68.

93   Thus what Kierkegaard means by "leveling" is not redistribution for material equality, but rather *existential leveling* in which strong evaluative judgment in Charles Taylor's sense is undermined or short-circuited. Also see TA 96 on the contrast with religious equality.

94   As Norman Lillegaard argues, some of Kierkegaard's aesthetes do have passions that provide some constancy in their lives, which could become the basis for their ethical transformation. For example, "Claudine" in the novel *Two Ages* is faithful in erotic love, although her passion remains immediate or unchosen; she does not make the (projective) "effort" to integrate the desires given to her by "nature and history" in a rational "self-concept"; see Lillegaard, "Thinking with Kierkegaard and MacIntyre about Virtue," 213–14.

95 Harvey Ferguson, "Modulation: a Typology of the Present Age," 129.
    Compare Kierkegaard's claim that satire "must have the resource of a
    consistent and well-grounded ethical view, a sacrificial unselfishness, and a
    high-born nobility that renounce the moment" (TA, 74).
96 See the discussion of proper self-love in Kierkegaard's *Works of Love*.
97 Yet the distinction between caring and mere desires or inclinations drawn
    in "Autonomy, Necessity, and Love" does not really *explain* the inherent
    authority or activeness of care-motives. I instead explain this distinction
    by referring to the structural contrast between projective and erosiac
    motives.
98 That this talk is connected with the essay on "BS" is evident from the
    detailed discussion of lying near its beginning (FP, 96–97).
99 Peter Edidin, *The New York Times*, February 14, 2005; www.nytimes.
    com/2005/02/14/books/14bull.html.
100 Frankfurt, "Reply to G.A. Cohen," 343.

Section II

Love and Self-Love

5

The Dear Self: Self-Love, Redoubling, and Self-Denial

Sylvia Walsh

Frankfurt's naturalistic view of self-love in *The Reasons of Love*, presented as an alternative to Kant's characterization of self-love in *Groundwork of the Metaphysics of Morals*, may be fruitfully clarified and critiqued by comparing it to a third perspective, namely Kierkegaard's Christian understanding of self-love, redoubling, and self-denial in *Works of Love*. In this essay, I shall argue by way of Kierkegaard that it is not Kant's conception of self-love that is "out of focus," as claimed by Frankfurt (RL, 76), but Frankfurt's, inasmuch as (1) he does not take the problem of selfishness and self-deception in self-love seriously enough; (2) the sort of identification of the self with the other envisioned by Frankfurt does not constitute a proper self-love, which according to Kierkegaard requires an unselfish redoubling of the self in the other regarded first and foremost as a neighbor or separate, independent self; and (3) Frankfurt lacks a concept of self-denial, no matter how "disinterested" or "selfless" his view of self-love may appear to be. This is not to claim that Kierkegaard entirely agrees with Kant on these issues, as there remain major differences between them as well concerning the duty to love and God as the source and object of love that will also be briefly discussed.

I. "The Dear Self" in Frankfurt's view

The main philosophical problem under deliberation in *The Reasons of Love* is the question of how a person should live. In Frankfurt's estimation, this question is best answered by considering what we care about or what we regard as important to ourselves, inasmuch as it is the "totality of the various things that a person cares about" that "effectively specifies his answer to the question of how to live" (RL, 23). In thinking about how to live, therefore, it is incumbent upon us first of all to examine the notion of caring. Frankfurt points out that caring about something or someone is not the same as wanting that thing or person, as we may want many things without really caring about them. Neither does caring entail attributing intrinsic value to an object of care since we may recognize the intrinsic value of something or someone without being attracted to that thing or person. Rather, according to Frankfurt, caring is first and foremost to be understood as "an activity that connects and binds us to ourselves," inasmuch as it is what gives meaning and character to our lives (RL, 17). If we cared about nothing, he hypothesizes, we would be unable to sustain any interests or aims in life and our lives would lack unity, purpose, and coherence. Caring, then, is essential to being human or having the kind of psychic complexity that is peculiar to the human species, which includes the ability to think or reflect.[1]

Now if as thinking beings we wonder whether we are right to care about the things we actually do care about, or to state it more philosophically, whether we are rationally justified in caring and living the way we do, Frankfurt maintains that our deliberations will inevitably fail because rational inquiries of this sort are inescapably circular, presupposing what they set out to prove. From his standpoint, then, "the most basic and essential question for a person to raise concerning the conduct of life cannot be the *normative* question of how he *should* live" but "the *factual* question of what he actually *does* care about" (RL, 26). Since most of us do in fact care about something or someone, including ourselves, and in our common humanity care about many of the same things, Frankfurt concludes that what we need to do in moral reflection is to get clear about what we really do care about and then to become "decisively and robustly confident" in caring about them (RL, 28). Such clarity and confidence, however, are to be gained not by attending to the commands of rationality but those of a particular mode of caring, namely the commands of love, which in Frankfurt's view are innately grounded in human nature. The particular mode of caring that Frankfurt is concerned to elucidate in this text, then, is love.

Although Frankfurt does not claim to give a comprehensive account of love, he nevertheless offers a general description of its essential or distinctive features: (1) it cares for the object of love as an end, not merely as a means (shades of Kant here); (2) it is volitional in nature yet "not under our direct and immediate voluntary control"; (3) it is "ineluctably particular" rather than general in character; and (4) "most centrally," it constitutes a disinterested concern for the existence and good of the object of love (RL, 42–44). The forms of love that most nearly exemplify these characteristics, in Frankfurt's estimation, are self-love and parental love, both of which involve the identification of one's own interests with those of the beloved—the latter being, in the case of self-love, oneself, consequently involving an identification of one's own interests with one's own interests, i.e., a tautology.[2] That would immediately seem to call into question the so-called disinterestedness of self-love—a problem Frankfurt strives mightily to resolve in the interest of demonstrating that self-love does not represent a character flaw or sign of weakness in ourselves but rather "the deepest and most essential … achievement of a serious and successful life" (RL, 68).

It is in this context that Frankfurt addresses Kant's skepticism concerning self-love in *Groundwork of the Metaphysics of Morals*, charging that what Kant says about the self and our attitudes toward ourselves in this work is "significantly out of focus" (RL, 76). What Frankfurt finds objectionable in Kant's account is the claim that we can never be certain that any of our actions possess moral worth because we can never know with certainty whether they are performed solely out of a sense of duty, which alone determines the moral worth of an action for Kant, or out of "a secret impulse of self-love," as there is an "intractably inimical relationship between the requirements of morality and the demands of personal desire" (RL, 76). Rather, it is Kant's attitude toward self-love itself that is at issue, namely whether the propensity to self-love in human beings is regrettable, embarrassing, unfortunate, or distasteful and constitutes an impediment to the attainment of a morally good life (RL, 77). Over against Kant's negative view of self-love, which is (mis)construed by Frankfurt as being more like self-indulgence in its association of self-love with the gratification of one's own inclinations and desires (RL, 78–79),[3] Frankfurt proposes a positive understanding and attitude toward self-love that seeks to protect and advance the self's true interests in the expression of a genuine self-love that should be affirmed rather than denigrated.

In line with his characterization of love in general, Frankfurt identifies four features that are conceptually necessary to self-love: (1) it consists in "a disinterested concern for the well-being and flourishing" of the self; (2) it is "ineluctably personal;" (3) it identifies with the beloved; and (4) it entails constraints upon the will (RL, 79–80). With regard to the first feature, Frankfurt claims that self-love may be regarded as disinterested, if not selfless, inasmuch as it is "motivated by no interests other than those of the beloved" (RL, 82). While such a definition may be appropriate when the object of love is another person, it hardly conforms to the standard definition of this term as "not influenced by considerations of personal advantage."[4] For even if one is concerned to protect and pursue one's "true interests" rather than to indulge one's momentary desires and inclinations, one is still motivated by self-interest or considerations of personal advantage, namely one's own personal flourishing and well-being.

Although Frankfurt claims that self-love, like parental love, is innate, he maintains that it is "never primary," inasmuch as self-love is "necessarily derivative from, or constructed out of, the love that people have for things that are not identical with themselves" (RL, 85). But he quickly qualifies this claim, stating that "room must be made for the possibility that a person may in fact love himself even though he actually does not love anything else" (RL, 87). If so, then self-love can hardly be *necessarily* derivative from love for other things (or persons). Frankfurt further qualifies self-love by reducing it to its most elementary form, which in his view is simply the innate desire to love: "we are constituted to love loving" (RL, 90). For that reason, he thinks, love is not only innately important to us but also what gives meaning and purpose to our lives.

The second feature of self-love identified by Frankfurt, namely that it is "ineluctably personal," is self-evident in that self-love is always directed to one's own person. What Frankfurt is concerned to point out here, however, is that one loves oneself as this particular individual and not impersonally as an instance of a type or class. Like love in general, which is always directed to a particular individual and must be distinguished from impersonal acts of charity for which any person in need would qualify, there is no substitute for the object of love in self-love. In this instance, therefore, the third feature of self-love, namely the identification of oneself with the beloved and one's own interests with those of the beloved, is tautological, as pointed out earlier.

Less self-evident is the fourth feature of self-love, which involves constraints upon the will. Although, according to Frankfurt, self-love, like all forms of love, is volitional rather than affective or rational in character, it is not under "our direct and immediate voluntary control" (RL, 44, 81). It may thus be described in oxymoronic fashion as "a volitional necessity" inasmuch as we cannot help loving ourselves and are more naturally inclined to love ourselves than to love other persons or things (RL, 46, 81). But only by wholeheartedly loving ourselves with an undivided will do we truly love ourselves. Identifying Kierkegaard's notion of "purity of heart" with wholeheartedness or having an undivided or unified will, Frankfurt claims that being wholehearted "*is* to love oneself" inasmuch as self-love consists in "the purity of a wholehearted will" (RL, 95–96). Finally, self-love is desirable and important to Frankfurt because, in his view, it is equivalent to being satisfied with oneself—not in the "smugly complacent" sense of having accomplished something valuable or having fulfilled one's ambitions, but in the sense of being content with what one is, whether that be good or evil (RL, 96–97, 100). For as Frankfurt sees it, "the function of love is not to make people good" but rather "to make their lives meaningful, and thus to help make their lives in that way good for them to live" (RL, 99). In the event that one is unable to love oneself wholeheartedly and experience such self-contentment, Frankfurt's parting advice to the reader is not to take oneself too seriously or "at least be sure to hang on to your sense of humor" (RL, 100).

II. Self-love, Redoubling, and Self-denial in Kierkegaard's *Works of Love*

In this essay, I shall confine my analysis to Kierkegaard's understanding of self-love, redoubling, and self-denial in *Works of Love*, using it as a counter-position by which to critique Frankfurt's view of self-love and his charge against Kant.[5] Taking the biblical commandment in Mt. 22:39, "You shall love your neighbor as yourself," as the starting point for a series of Christian deliberations on love (or more accurately, the *works* of love, since for Kierkegaard Christian love is "sheer action"), Kierkegaard acknowledges that self-love is presupposed by Christianity— not as a prescriptive right, however, but as something to be wrested away from human beings (WL, 17, 98–99). In his view, however, Christianity does not propose to do away with self-love per se but only to teach us to love ourselves in the right way or as we ought to love ourselves. This is done by driving out selfishness or sensuousness[6] within us through the transformation of self-love by the biblical command to love the neighbor as oneself. Kierkegaard states: "To love yourself in the right way and to love the neighbor correspond perfectly to one another; fundamentally they are one and the same thing .... The Law is therefore: You shall love yourself in the same way as you love your neighbour when you love him as yourself" (WL, 22–23, 44, 52–53, 55). But who is our neighbor and how does love of the neighbor constitute a proper self-love?

Kierkegaard explicates this equation by first noting that the word "neighbor" in Danish (*Næste*) is etymologically derived from the word "nearest" (*Nærmeste*), which means that the neighbor is or should be "the person who is nearer to you than anyone else" (WL, 21). Indeed, the neighbor is so close to us that he/she may be regarded as a *redoubling* (*Fordoblelse*) of ourselves in the other.[7] By redoubling, however, Kierkegaard does not mean that the neighbor is to be regarded as an "other I" or "other self" as in preferential forms of love for others such as erotic love and friendship, which in his view seek to form "a new selfish self" in union or identification with the other that constitutes the very peak of selfishness in intoxicated self-esteem, self-deification, and idol worship (WL, 53–57). From Kierkegaard's viewpoint, all preferential love in its natural forms and expressions is simply another form of selfish self-love in which the other is regarded merely as an extension of ourselves, not a redoubling, which requires a duplication of the self in the other in such a way as to be two rather than one (WL, 21, 53–54).[8] Redoubling thus occurs only when the other person is regarded as an "other you," that is, as a spiritual being who is a separate and independent self like oneself: "Love for the neighbor is love between two beings eternally and independently determined as spirit" (WL, 56). As defined by Anti-Climacus, the Christian pseudonymous "author" of Kierkegaard's *The Sickness unto Death*, to be spirit is to be a self that relates itself to itself as a synthesis of the finite and the infinite, the temporal and the eternal, freedom and necessity, and to that power, namely God, who establishes it as a self (SUD, 13). Since for Kierkegaard "two spirits are never able to become one self in a selfish sense," it follows that love for the neighbor "cannot make me one with the neighbor in a united self" (WL, 56). Unlike erotic love and friendship, which contain a sensate and/or psychical component, "the neighbor is a purely spiritual specification," which means that only in love for the other as a neighbor is the self defined purely spiritually (WL, 57). Neighbor love, then, is not based upon a spontaneous natural determinant such as a drive or inclination but on the *duty to love*, which in Kierkegaard's view "did not arise in any human being's heart" but is commanded by divine authority (WL, 24–25, 27).

In becoming a duty, human love in all its forms, including erotic love and friendship, undergoes a fundamental transformation or "the change of eternity" so as to become a matter of conscience or consciously grounded upon a relation to God, who is the source and true object of love (WL, 3, 9–10, 18, 32, 38, 142–43, 147). The Christian commandment is first and foremost to love God, who is to be loved above all, and then the neighbor (WL, 57–58). To love God is to be like God, who is love itself (WL, 62–63, 190, 264–65, 281). We can only be like God, therefore, by loving like God, who loves all human beings without preference or distinction. Unlike preferential love, in which one or more persons are loved above or in contrast to all others, the Christian doctrine of love is to exist essentially equally for everyone and to love everyone without exception—including one's own self, spouse, children, friends, and enemies—on the basis of the equality of all persons before God (WL, 19, 49, 55, 58, 67–69, 84–85). Christianly understood, then, the neighbor is not just one other person but all people, although in Kierkegaard's view it only takes one other person to test whether one loves the neighbor; for "if there is one other person whom you in the Christian sense love *as yourself* or in whom you love *the neighbor*, then you love all people" (WL, 21).[9]

As Kierkegaard sees it, Christianity seeks to make God "the middle term" or "third party" in every love-relationship, thereby going beyond mutuality in human relations to require "threeness" in the form of the lover, the beloved, and love or God as that which binds them and constitutes the "sole object of love" in the relation (WL, 58, 67, 107, 120–21, 301). According to "the divine conception of love" introduced by Christianity, which is infinitely different from worldly wisdom or "the merely human conception of what love is," the true idea of what it means to love oneself, to love others, and to be loved in return is to love God: *"To love God is to love oneself truly; to help another person to love God is to love another person; to be helped by another person to love God is to be loved"* (WL, 107–8, 109–10, 113–14, 130). Since God is love, this means that the goal of every love-relation between two persons is to help each other learn to love rather than seek to be loved in and through their relation to one another (WL, 62, 130). If God is left out of a love-relationship or both parties are not led to God in and through the relation, in Kierkegaard's estimation it is not genuine love but "a mutually enchanting defraudation of love" (WL, 107, 120). Stating this conviction even more forcefully, he declares:

> Every person is God's bond servant; therefore he dare not belong to anyone in love unless in the same love he belongs to God and dare not possess anyone in love unless the other and he himself belong to God in this love—a person dare not belong to another as if that other person were everything to him; a person dare not allow another to belong to him as if he were everything to that other. (WL, 107–08)

Another way of describing Christian love is to say that it is "self-denial's love" (WL, 52, 55, 369). As Kierkegaard sees it, self-denial constitutes "Christianity's essential form" and is "the very transformation by which a person becomes sober in the sense of eternity" (WL, 56). In self-denial's love the neighbor functions as a middle term, stepping in between self-love's "*I* and *I*" and preferential love's "*I* and the *other I*" as a means of testing and driving out selfishness in them by placing every demand upon oneself rather than on the other, and by desiring for the other what one would have desired for oneself (WL, 21, 54, 90, 100, 142). Proper self-love, then, is to love oneself in the same way one loves one's neighbor when one loves that person as oneself, that is, unselfishly. Most simply defined, love is a giving of oneself; but Christianly understood, it is a giving of oneself in such a way as *not to seek one's own* in a selfish manner (WL, 264). Seeking or demanding reciprocity, reward, or repayment in love, even giving oneself in unlimited devotion to an "*other I*" or "*other self*" as one's sole object of love, is not true love or true devotion but false and self-deceptive inasmuch as it has the effect of turning back "in a selfish way into the *I* who loves" (WL, 39, 54–55, 90, 100, 120, 130–31, 236–37, 241, 269, 349–51).[10] For Kierkegaard, "*the distinctive characteristic of love*" is that "*the one who loves by giving, infinitely, runs into infinite debt*," which can never be repaid "since to give is continually to run into debt" as expressed by the Apostle Paul in Rom. 13:8: "Owe no one anything, except to love one another" (WL, 176–77). Moreover, "When a human being seeks another human being's love, seeks to be loved himself, this is not a giving of oneself," Kierkegaard contends, because "To be able to seek love and oneself to become the object of love, yet without seeking one's own, is reserved for God alone" (WL, 264). The prototype of Christian love or unselfish self-giving is Christ, who seeks his own in an entirely different sense from a selfish seeking of one's own, namely through the sacrificial giving of himself for all human beings so that they may be like him and/or God in seeking His own, which is love. In Christian love, therefore, there is no "mine" and "yours," not even in a communal sense of "ours," inasmuch as the truly loving or self-giving person is totally self-denying in all things, yet in such a way that, at the same time, all things wondrously become his or hers by having won God in self-denial (WL, 265–68).

This notion of receiving a return without seeking one's own introduces a further dimension of the concept of redoubling in Kierkegaard's understanding of Christian love, which involves not only a redoubling of oneself in the neighbor but also a redoubling in love itself by infinitely becoming its own object (WL, 182). Unlike a temporal object, which never has a redoubling in itself because it exists only in its various characteristics and vanishes in time, when the eternal is present in a person it "redoubles in him in such a way that every moment it is in him, it is in him in a double mode: in an outward direction and in an inward direction back into itself, but in such a way that this is one and the same, since otherwise it is not redoubling" (WL, 280). In like manner, Christian love goes out of itself in performing the works of love and then returns to itself in such a way as to be "simultaneously one and the same," so that "what love does, that it is," and vice versa, "what it is, that it does—at one and the same moment" (WL, 280). Christian love is thus a redoubling in which "the one who loves receives what he gives" (WL, 281). Kierkegaard provides several examples of such redoubling: in giving bold confidence to others, we have or acquire it in ourselves without seeking it; in saving another from death, we save ourselves without thinking of being saved; and in forgetting our own suffering in order to think of someone else's, we are not forgotten by God (WL, 280–81).

Redoubling is thus equivalent to what Kierkegaard at the end of *Works of Love* calls the Christian "like for like," that "God will do unto you exactly as you do unto others," in contrast to the Jewish "like for like," i.e. "as others do unto you ... do likewise unto them," in conformity with the Old Testament law of "an eye for an eye and a tooth for a tooth" (Exod. 21:24; WL, 383). In the Christian "like for like," God's love is understood as being "the greatest leniency" and "the greatest rigorousness" at the same time, as expressed in

Jesus' declaration, "Be it done for you as you have believed" (Mt. 8:13), and in his teaching, "Forgive, then you will also be forgiven" (Mt. 6:14) (WL, 376–80). Seeking to guard against a possible misinterpretation of the latter example, Kierkegaard offers the following clarification: "Christianity's view is: forgiveness is forgiveness; your forgiveness is your forgiveness; your forgiveness of another is your own forgiveness; the forgiveness you give is the forgiveness you receive, not the reverse, that the forgiveness you receive is the forgiveness you give" (WL, 380). However, he is careful to point out that "We truly do not say this as if it were our view that when all is said and done a person deserves grace. Ah, the first thing you learn when you relate yourself to God in everything is that you have no merit whatever" (WL, 385). Just as Christian love does not demand reciprocity or repayment, then, it does not merit God's grace, but it does receive a return that corresponds to the gift of love.

Another way Christian love "seeks not its own" is by making it appear that the gift of love belongs to the recipient as his/her own property (WL, 274–75). Interestingly, the model of this unselfish but deceptive work of love for Kierkegaard is not Christ but that "noble rogue" of ancient times, Socrates, who magnanimously, unselfishly, and "with every self-sacrifice" helped others to become independent and stand on their own by annihilating himself, making himself anonymous or hidden to the persons being helped by playing the maieutic role of a midwife who merely assisted them in giving birth to themselves or acquiring self-knowledge (WL, 276). Nevertheless, "however noble and magnanimous and unselfish that rogue was," Kierkegaard contends, "he still did not in the sense of concern love the one he wanted to help" (WL, 277). The person who loves not only understands that to help a person to stand by him/herself and to become a free, independent self is "the greatest, the only beneficence one human being can do for another" but also understands the danger, suffering, and terrible responsibility that comes with this work of love (WL, 277–78). Whereas Socrates enjoyed the reward of "proud self-consciousness" or the self-satisfaction of knowing that it was through his help that others stood alone, the one who loves works without reward in the understanding that, essentially, every human being stands alone only through God's help and that one's own self-annihilation "is really only in order not to hinder the other person's God-relationship" (WL, 278).

To those who object that a person's life is wasted in self-sacrifice for others, Kierkegaard agrees that "In a certain sense his life is completely squandered on existence, on the existence of others. Unwilling to waste any time or energy on asserting himself, on being something for himself, in his self-sacrifice he is willing to perish, that is, he is completely and wholly transformed into simply being an active power in the hands of

God" (WL, 279; cf. WA, 155).[11] Only in self-denial is it possible to hold fast to God and become an instrument of God's love (WL, 363–65). Like the redoubling of Christian love, self-denial is present in a human being in both an inward and outward direction, assuming the inward form of making oneself nothing before God and then giving it outward expression in self-sacrificing unselfishness, which is one and the same as self-denial (WL, 362–66, 374). To become "nothing" before God, then, as Kierkegaard understands it, is to renounce becoming self-important in the world in the recognition that one is able *to do nothing* on one's own but *everything* as God's coworker in love (WL, 362, 365; cf. WA, 140, 155).

If one ventures to become God's instrument in love, however, the outward expression of Christian love in self-sacrificing unselfishness will inevitably encounter opposition from the world or what Kierkegaard calls *double danger* (WL, 72–73, 76, 81–82, 192–94). As a result of one's willingness to make every sacrifice for the truth, "the truly Christian struggle always involves a double danger because there is struggle in two places, first in the person's inner being, where he must struggle with himself, and then, when he makes progress in this struggle, outside the person with the world" (WL, 366, 192). "What Christianity calls self-denial specifically and essentially involves a *double danger*," Kierkegaard contends, for "otherwise the self-denial is not Christian self-denial" (WL, 194). Whereas the worldly or merely human idea of self-denial is "to give up your self-loving desires, cravings, and plans— then you will be esteemed and honored and loved as righteous and wise," the "Christian idea of self-denial is: give up your self-loving desires and cravings, give up your self-seeking plans and purposes so that you truly work unselfishly for the good—and then, for that very reason, put up with being abominated almost as a criminal, insulted and ridiculed" (WL, 194; see also 119–20). In Kierkegaard's estimation, only Christian self-denial constitutes true self-denial. Merely human self-denial is a "counterfeit self-denial" that "can make a good show ... of denying oneself for the sake of God" but does it in such a way as to receive esteem and honor rather than opposition from the world (WL, 195).

III. Kierkegaard as (implicit) critic of Frankfurt

Having reviewed Kierkegaard's Christian understanding of self-love, redoubling, and self-denial, we are now in a position to consider how his views on these concepts provide a critical counterpoint to Frankfurt's perspective on "The Dear Self." The first thing to be noted is that Frankfurt and Kierkegaard start from fundamentally different standpoints, the former from a naturalistic position that views human love as innate and biologically determined (although still a matter of volition), the latter from a divine command ethic that seeks to transform and inform natural forms of love with love of the other first and foremost as a neighbor.[12] To the extent that Frankfurt takes account of the biblical command to love the neighbor as oneself, he interprets it in a self-affirming fashion as encouraging us "to love others with the same intensity, or with the same relentless dedication, that we are disposed to lavish upon ourselves" (RL, 78). Kierkegaard, by contrast, sees it as requiring a total self-giving or self-denial that does not seek its own in loving the other. Frankfurt narrowly focuses on natural self-love and parental love, which he regards as pure forms of disinterested love, while Kierkegaard takes a critical stance toward natural self-love and preferential love—particularly erotic love and friendship—regarding them in their natural or immediate expressions as disguised forms of self-love that need to be purged of selfishness. For Frankfurt, human love is selective and exclusive in nature, justifiably extended only to those we actually care about, while for Kierkegaard, Christianity makes it a duty to love everyone equally and without exception as one's neighbor or spiritual equal before God. The object of love for Frankfurt can be a person, thing, country, tradition, or abstract ideal such as social justice or scientific truth, whereas the object of love for Kierkegaard is God or love itself rather than either party in the relation. Moreover, for Frankfurt love is not based on the perceived worth or inherent value of an object of love but simply on love itself, which is "the generator of value" (RL, 41), while Kierkegaard affirms the inherent value and worthiness to be loved in every human being based on the fundamental equality of all persons before God.

Such differences do not appear to be very promising for much if any substantive dialogue between Frankfurt and Kierkegaard on the subject of love, but there are some agreements between them that would seem to provide a basis for bringing them together in the present volume. First of all, both thinkers agree with Kant that love is an end, not merely a means, and that it consists in disinterested concern for the object of love. Second, neither thinker rejects self-love per se, as both identify a proper self-love that should be affirmed and nurtured for the sake of the true flourishing or good of the self. Third, they agree that true love is free and volitional in nature, that is, not a matter of believing or self-willful feeling but, as Frankfurt expresses it, "a configuration of the will that consists in a practical concern for the good of the beloved" (although the volitional character of love is seemingly compromised in Frankfurt's account by the parallel claim that it is "not under our direct and immediate voluntary control" but a matter of necessity), while for Kierkegaard Christian love is an emotion or passion that has been transformed into a matter of conscience (RL, 43, 45, 64; WL, 112, 139). Fourth, while reciprocity in love may be hoped for, they agree that it is not required, although for both thinkers there is a sort of return that comes in loving others. Fifth, they agree that, as Frankfurt puts it, love is "ineluctably particular" in character, inasmuch as Kierkegaard holds that we are to love the persons we see, regardless of their perfections or imperfections, and that all persons are to be loved individually in their particularity or within their dissimilarities, even though we must, as it were, close our eyes to or look away from their differences in order to see the "eternal equality" of all persons before God (RL, 44; WL, 66–68, 86–89, 141, 173). Sixth, they concur that love is what gives meaning and purpose to life. Kierkegaard concludes that "to love people is the only thing worth living for, and without this love you are not really living," while Frankfurt sees the function of love as to make life meaningful (WL, 375; RL, 99).

When the surface similarities between these two philosophers are probed more deeply, however, it becomes clear that, even on his own terms, Frankfurt's viewpoint falls short of legitimizing self-love, especially when subjected to critical analysis from a Kierkegaardian perspective. This is particularly true with regard to Frankfurt's understanding of self-love as a disinterested concern for the well-being or flourishing of one's own self. In addition to the reservations already expressed concerning this claim, Kierkegaard's analysis of preferential forms of love exposes the hidden selfishness and self-deception that underlie both self-love and parental love as Frankfurt sees them. Although Frankfurt views self-love as advancing what he takes to be the true interests of the self as opposed to merely self-indulgent or momentary desires, from a Kierkegaardian perspective this is still a selfish form of self-love because it is devoted to serving one's own interests rather than those of others (RL, 85). Frankfurt contends that "[a] person cannot love himself except insofar as he loves other things" (tellingly, he frequently lapses into speaking of loving other "things" rather than persons), yet he admits that we are more naturally inclined to love ourselves than to love other things (and presumably other persons) and that it is possible for a person to love only him/herself (RL, 81, 85–87).

With regard to love of other persons, Frankfurt suggests that the disinterestedness or selflessness of self-love is comparable to that of parental love, which in his view has only the best interests of one's children at heart: "It is only when the beloved is the lover's child that love is likely to be as free of … calculated or implicit expectations as it is almost invariably free of them in the case of a person's love of himself" (RL, 83). Kierkegaard's exposé of natural or preferential forms of love as selfish forms of love focuses primarily on erotic love and friendship, but parental love is also branded as a selfish form of love inasmuch as it seeks reciprocity or repayment of love—even though, in one respect, it resembles what for Kierkegaard is the most unselfish love, namely the recollection of one who is dead:

> In this regard there is a similarity between lovingly recollecting one who is dead and parents' love for their children. Parents love the children almost before they come into existence and long before they become conscious beings, therefore as nonbeings. But a dead person is also a nonbeing, and the two greatest good works are these: to give a human being life and to recollect one who is dead; yet the first work of love has a repayment. If parents had no hope whatever, no prospect at all, of ever receiving joy from their children and reward for their love—well, there would indeed still be many a father and mother who still would lovingly do everything for the children—ah, but there certainly would also be many a father and mother whose love would grow cold. By this it is not our intention to declare outright that such a father and mother are unloving; no, but the love in them would still be so weak, or self-love so strong, that this joyous hope, this prospect, would be *needed*. (WL, 349–50)[13]

As perceptively observed by Louise Carroll Keeley, "In attributing self-love to parental love Kierkegaard does not mean to denigrate it—after all, he has just identified parental love as the closest correlate to the work of love in recollecting one dead. Instead, his point seems to be that even here—where *selflessness* might be most likely to be found—*selfishness* persists."[14]

Frankfurt is apparently also unaware of dominating parents who seek to project and realize their own dreams in and through their children, which brings us to another feature of his view of self-love that is subject to critique from a Kierkegaardian point of view, namely the identification of the lover with the beloved. We have seen that one of the chief characteristics of self-love as defined by Frankfurt is that it identifies with the beloved by taking the interests of the beloved as its own, which in the case of self-love is tautological since one's own interests and those of the beloved are identical (RL, 80–81). With respect to love for others, however, Frankfurt maintains that the interests of self-love and those of the beloved are also identical, inasmuch as one's own life is "enhanced" and "profits" when the beloved's interests prevail (RL, 61). At the same time, however, such identification is said to be an act of selflessness on the part of the lover, inasmuch as "the benefit of love accrues to a person only to the extent that he cares about his beloved disinterestedly, and not for the sake of any benefit that he may derive either from the beloved or from loving it [sic]. He cannot hope to fulfil his own interest in loving unless he puts aside his personal needs and ambitions and dedicates himself to the interests of another" (RL, 61). From a Kierkegaardian perspective, this is a classic example of the kind of self-deception and hidden selfishness that characterizes all preferential love, which may appear to be unselfish in its unlimited devotion to the other but is really not because the other is loved on the basis of personal preference rather than first and foremost as a neighbor or fellow human being.

That this is so is made evident in Frankfurt's account by the "cautiousness" with which persons are enjoined to enter into a love-relation, which in his view is always "risky" (RL, 62). Frankfurt admits that the lover's interests and those of his/her beloved "can never be entirely the same," that "it is improbable that they will even be wholly compatible," and that the beloved "is unlikely to be the only thing [sic] that is important to him," thereby creating "a strong possibility that disruptive conflict may arise between the lover's devotion to the well-being of something [sic] that he loves and his concern for his other interests" (RL, 62). Consequently, lovers are cautioned to be "careful" and "to avoid being caused to love what it would be undesirable for them to love" (RL, 62). (How they can avoid doing that which is not under their immediate voluntary control, however, is not explained.) According to Frankfurt, God can afford to love "everything" (sic) because he is an infinite and omnipotent being and thus runs no risks, but "our readiness to love needs to be more mindful and more restrained," because "finite creatures like ourselves ... cannot afford to be so heedless in our loving" (RL, 62–63). Since we "incur substantial vulnerabilities when we love ... we need to maintain a defensive selectivity and restraint. It is important that we be careful to whom and to what we give our love," Frankfurt advises (RL, 63). Moreover, because of "our lack of immediate voluntary control over our loving," it "may engage us in volitional commitments from which we are unable to withdraw and through which our interests may be severely harmed" (RL, 63). And because we love "some things" (sic) more than others, we "may love something [sic] and yet be willing to harm it, in order to protect something [sic] else for which our love is greater" (RL, 46). Frankfurt further observes that "what a person loves reveals something significant about him. It reflects upon his taste and his character; or it may be taken to be so. People are often judged and evaluated on the basis of what they care about. Therefore pride and a concern for reputation encourage them to see to it, insofar as they can, that what they love is something that they and others regard as valuable" (RL, 67).

These statements utterly belie Frankfurt's claim that natural love of oneself and others is disinterested or selfless. Still less do they support the notion that natural love of others is self-sacrificing or self-denying. In fact, in spite of stating that a person "cannot hope to fulfil his own interest in loving unless he puts aside his personal needs and ambitions and dedicates himself to the interests of another," Frankfurt admits: "Any suspicion that this would require an implausibly high-minded readiness for self-sacrifice can be allayed by the recognition that, in the very nature of the case, a lover *identifies himself* with what he loves" (RL, 61). Moreover, according to the statements quoted above, we should identify ourselves only with those things or persons which/who will serve our own (selfish) interests, and we should love them only so long as they do not interfere with our other (selfish) commitments and interests.

Over against Kierkegaard's lofty ideal of Christian neighbor-love, therefore, Frankfurt may be judged to have advanced a rather shallow conception of human love that, far from making a case for the affirmation of natural self-love, merely underscores the need for the transformation of selfish self-love by attending to the biblical command to love the other first and foremost as a neighbor or fellow human being in the recognition that God or divine love is not only the source of all human love but also its infinite measure and goal.

IV. Kierkegaard versus Kant

Although Kierkegaard supports and amplifies Kant's view of the ubiquity of "The Dear Self" or the "covert impulse of self-love" as the secret incentive or determining cause of the will in many of its actions, including those performed in conformity with the commands of duty, there remain some major differences between the Dane and his rationalist predecessor concerning the duty to love and the role of God in their respective accounts of the Christian imperative to love the neighbor as oneself.[15] In the short space left in the present essay, I shall focus on only two. In the *Groundwork of the Metaphysics of Morals* (1785), Kant interprets the biblical command to love the neighbor as requiring a distinction between *pathological love*, or love in the form of an inclination, which cannot be commanded, and *practical love*, or beneficence from duty, which resides in the will, not in the propensities of feeling, and in principles of action, not in sympathy, and which alone can be commanded.[16] This distinction is reaffirmed in the *Critique of Practical Reason* (1788), with the added provisos that to love God means to do His commandments "gladly" and that to love the neighbor means "to practice all duties toward him gladly"—although "[t]he command which makes this a rule cannot require that we have this disposition but only that we endeavour after it," since "[t]o command that one do something gladly is self-contradictory."[17] In *The Metaphysics of Morals* (1797), he further points out that "Love is a matter of *feeling*, not of *willing*, and I cannot love because I *will* to, still less because I *ought* to (I cannot be constrained to love); so a *duty to love* is an absurdity. But *benevolence* (*amor benevolentiae*), as conduct, can be subject to a law of duty. However, unselfish benevolence to human beings is often (though very inappropriately) also called *love* ... ."[18]

From these statements it is apparent that Kant gradually moves from an equation of neighbor-love or practical love with beneficence from duty to the recognition that it is absurd and inappropriate to identify the latter as a form of love, especially since "To *do good* to other human beings insofar as we can is a duty, whether one loves them or not."[19] Nevertheless, he maintains that if we practice helping others and succeed in it, we will eventually come to feel love for those we have helped: "So the saying 'you ought to *love* your neighbor as yourself' does not mean that you ought immediately (first) to love him and (afterwards) by means of this love do good to him. It means, rather, *do good* to your fellow human beings, and your beneficence will produce love of them in you (as an aptitude [*Fertigkeit*] of the inclination to beneficence in general)."[20] Here we see a major difference between Kierkegaard and Kant, inasmuch as Kierkegaard does not equate neighbor-love with an external act of benevolence as such but understands it to be a form of love, namely spiritual love, which can and should lie at the base of and inform every expression of love as a result of the transformation of love that takes place through the commandment to love the other as a neighbor. Thus, as C. Stephen Evans has correctly pointed out, "we misunderstand Kierkegaard's account if we conflate it with Kant's understanding of neighbour-love as a purely practical 'love' that consists solely of actions."[21] Evans further suggests that "what seems missing from Kant is the notion that the moral worth of an action might be related to an emotion that is the basis for the action."[22] In *The Metaphysics of Morals*, however, Kant does begin to make that connection, although he gets it backward from Kierkegaard, who maintains that Christian love is simultaneously a passion or emotion that is what it does and does what it is, not a consequence of moral actions.

A second major difference between Kierkegaard and Kant has to do with the role of God and human autonomy in their respective moral philosophies. We have seen that a relation to God is absolutely central in Kierkegaard's understanding of the second commandment to love the neighbor as oneself. Kant, by contrast, finds no need of the idea of God in order to be able to recognize and perform our duties to ourselves and others—although in his view morality does extend, through its inevitable connection to religion, to the idea of God, derived *a priori* by practical reason from the idea of moral perfection and conceived as the moral originator of the world and its moral lawgiver, benevolent ruler, just judge, and highest good.[23] Religion, for Kant, is simply "the recognition of all our duties as divine commands," whether it be *revealed religion*, in which one must first know that something is a divine command in order to recognize it as one's duty, or *natural religion*, in which one must first know that something is one's duty in order to acknowledge it as a divine command.[24] Philosophically, Kant is wholly committed to the moral autonomy of human beings, finding a place for God only as a rational support for the idea of moral perfection, and for divine grace only as a supplement to the deficiency of our moral capacity to achieve moral perfection. In contrast to Kierkegaard's claim that we can "do nothing" to merit salvation or to do the good, but "everything" as God's instrument of love, Kant requires that "to become a better human being, everyone must do as much as it is in his powers to do; and only then … can he hope that what does not lie in his power will be made good by cooperation from above."[25] In order to qualify for such supernatural cooperation, however, one must make oneself "antecedently worthy of receiving it."[26]

It is this ambiguity or incoherence at the heart of Kant's position on moral autonomy that has led some commentators to be critical of him, in one case claiming that Kierkegaard (in *Philosophical Fragments*) calls his bluff, challenging him (among others we might add) to cast the human predicament of sin or radical evil in Socratic rather than Augustinian (Christian) terms if he really wants to avoid dependence upon God and affirm human free will as the source of moral action.[27] In *Works of Love*, Kierkegaard is again critical of Kant without naming him, likening "the merely human determination of what constitutes the Law's requirement" to "a mutiny against God" (WL, 116–17).

Another ambiguity in Kant's autonomous ethics can be seen in his rejection of drives and inclinations as expressions of self-love while affirming our sovereignty as moral agents. From a Kierkegaardian perspective, such self-sovereignty itself may be seen as "a disguised form of self-love" inasmuch as the self is the sole ground and middle term of its relation to the other in Kantian ethics.[28] Ironically, then, Kant, like Frankfurt, ends up affirming selfish self-love while Kierkegaard seeks to do away with it through the transformation of self-love into a proper self-love in the redoubling of the self in the other so as to become an instrument of divine love by loving the neighbor as oneself.

Notes

1   While Frankfurt recognizes that animals of lesser species have desires, attitudes, and perhaps (in some) thoughts as well, they are not self-critical and are "moved into action by impulse or by inclination … without the mediation of any reflective consideration or criticism of their own motives" (RL, 17–18).

2   Romantic or sexual love-relations are explicitly excluded as "authentic or
    illuminating paradigms of love" in Frankfurt's account because they are
    (presumably) characterized by "infatuation, lust, obsession, possessiveness,
    and dependency" (RL, 43).
3   While self-love does include indulgence in pleasure and a propensity
    to amusement or enjoyment in Kant's account, it is not limited to that
    inasmuch as sympathy, suicide, acts done for personal advantage, neglect
    of natural gifts, refusal to help others, and other expressions of self-interest
    are included under that category. See Immanuel Kant, *Groundwork of the
    Metaphysics of Morals*, 11–12, 32–33, 49*.
4   Arnold B. Come, *Compact Oxford English Dictionary of Current English*,
    3rd ed.
5   For more extensive treatments of *Works of Love*, see Sylvia Walsh,
    Kierkegaard: Thinking Christianly in an Existential Mode, 162–72, and
    Walsh, *Living Christianly: Kierkegaard's Dialectic of Christian Existence*,
    91–112; C. Stephen Evans, *Kierkegaard's Ethic of Love: Divine Commands
    & Moral Obligations*, 112–222; M. Jamie Ferreira, *Love's Grateful Striving:
    A Commentary on Kierkegaard's "Works of Love"*; Robert L. Perkins, ed.,
    International Kierkegaard Commentary: Works of Love, Vol. 16; Niels
    Jørgen Cappelørn and Hermann Deuser, eds. *Kierkegaard Studies Yearbook
    1998*; Sharon Krishek, *Kierkegaard on Faith and Love*; and John Lippitt,
    Kierkegaard and the Problem of Self-Love.
6   It is important to note that Kierkegaard distinguishes between *sensuousness*,
    which he equates with selfishness or the flesh in rebellious conflict with
    spirit, and *the sensuous nature* in the form of a natural drive which "human
    beings have … not given to themselves" and thus is no more forbidden by
    Christianity than "it has wanted to forbid people to eat and drink" (WL,
    52). Selfish self-love is also associated with arbitrary self-willfulness in
    giving oneself to "one and only object" (WL, 55).
7   On redoubling, see also Martin Andic, "Love's Redoubling and the
    Eternal Like for Like," 9–38; Andrew Burgess, "Kierkegaard's Concept of
    Redoubling and Luther's *Simul Justus*" in the same volume, 39–55; and
    Ferreira, *Love's Grateful Striving*, 62, 170–72.
8   On the moral value of preferential love, see M. Jamie Ferreira, "The
    Problematic Agapeistic Ideal—Again," and the response by Alastair Hannay,
    "Kierkegaard on Natural and Commanded Love" in the same volume,
    111–18.
9   In a passage deleted from the final copy of *Works of Love*, Kierkegaard
    explains further that "the neighbor is *the other person*, and it makes no
    difference if there are thousands or only one if that one is *the other person*"
    (JP, 4:4447; SKP, VIII² B 71:10).
10 On reciprocity or repayment in love, also see Ferreira, *Love's Grateful
    Striving*, 209–27, and Louise Carroll Keeley, "Loving 'No One,' Loving
    Everyone: The Work of Love in Recollecting One Dead in Kierkegaard's
    Works of Love," 233–34.

11 John Lippitt has raised related criticisms: he suggests in his *Kierkegaard and the Problem of Self-Love* that Kierkegaard places an excessive focus on and valorization of self-denial that is unlimited (112, 125, 127, 128, 135), self-centered (125), neurotic (126), morally objectionable (131), and servile (132), though he goes on to argue that Kierkegaard does recognize a positive sense of self-love in other places. I think we agree that Kierkegaard explicitly rejects excessive self-sacrifice in the form of a false, unlimited devotion or passionate giving of oneself to another as one's sole object of love, which in his view is idol worship (WL, 54–55, 125). Kierkegaard also condemns the "desire to exist for the powerful person" in self-abasement and abject servility by vulnerable and powerless persons (usually women) (WL, 125–26). Neither should one comply with a demand or request from someone that one considers harmful or damaging to that person (WL, 19–20, 273). However, while Lippitt thinks that these views stand in tension with some of what Kierkegaard says in praise of self-denial, I see them as forming a consistent whole.

12 On Kierkegaard as (a kind of) divine command ethicist, see Evans, *Kierkegaard's Ethic of Love*, 1–33, 117–39.

13 In a journal entry from 1849, Kierkegaard makes the following statement about maternal love: "Much that is said praising a mother's love for her child is, of course, rooted in a misunderstanding, since maternal love as such is simply self-love raised to a higher power … That this kind of love in its initial state is self-love is apparent also in other analogous relationships where the fatuousness of this kind of praise is obvious to everyone" (JP, 3:2423; SKP, X¹ A 489). On the egotism of parental love, both maternal and paternal, see also JP, 3:2441 (SKP, X⁵ A 34) and JP, 4:4998 (SKP, XI¹ A 141).

14 Keeley, "Loving 'No One', Loving Everyone," 235.

15 Kant, *Groundwork of the Metaphysics of Morals*, 19–20. For more extensive treatments of Kierkegaard's relation to Kant, see Ronald M. Green, *Kierkegaard and Kant*; Paul Martens, "You Shall Love: Kant, Kierkegaard, and the Interpretation of Matthew 22:39"; D. Z. Phillips and Timothy Tessin, eds. *Kant and Kierkegaard on Religion*; Ulrich Knappe, *Theory and Practice in Kant and Kierkegaard*.

16 Kant, *Groundwork of the Metaphysics of Morals*, 12–13. See also Ronald M. Green, "Kant on Christian Love," 261–80.

17 Kant, *Critique of Practical Reason*, 3rd edition, trans. Lewis White Beck, 86–87.

18 Kant, *The Metaphysics of Morals*, 161.

19 Ibid.

20 Ibid., 162.

21 Evans, *Kierkegaard's Ethic of Love*, 190–91.

22 Ibid., 191; see also 194–95 and WL, 112.

23 Kant, *Religion within the Boundaries of Mere Reason*, ed. and trans. Allen Wood and George di Giovanni, 33, 35, 90, 141–42; and Kant, *Groundwork of the Metaphysics of Morals*, 21.

24   Kant, *Religion within the Boundaries of Mere Reason*, 153.
25   Ibid., 71; see also 167, 169.
26   Ibid., 65.
27   Gordon E. Michalson, Jr., *Fallen Freedom: Kant on Radical Evil and Moral Regeneration*, 130. See also Martens, "'You Shall Love'" 70–71; John E. Hare, *The Moral Gap: Kantian Ethics, Human Limits, and God's Assistance*, 26–27, 60–68; Chris L. Firestone and Nathan Jacobs, *In Defense of Kant's "Religion*," 46–100.
28   Merold Westphal, "Commanded Love and Moral Autonomy," 5.

6

Giving "The Dear Self" Its Due: Kierkegaard, Frankfurt, and Self-Love

John Lippitt

Casual readers of Kierkegaard's *Works of Love* have sometimes got the impression that Kierkegaard holds an unequivocally negative view of self-love. They effectively place Kierkegaard in the camp of those who, in Harry Frankfurt's words, "believe that this headlong tendency of most of us to love ourselves is a grievously injurious defect of human nature" (RL, 71). Yet as much recent commentary on *Works of Love* has shown, it is in fact important to Kierkegaard's analysis that a distinction be drawn between genuine, true or "proper" self-love, on the one hand, and improper (sometimes labeled "selfish") forms of it, on the other.[1] Self-love is also a vitally important concept in Frankfurt's *The Reasons of Love*, and Frankfurt's analysis likewise aims to draw a distinction between proper and improper forms of self-love. In her highly critical account of Frankfurt in this volume, Sylvia Walsh presents Kierkegaard's Christian view as a corrective to Frankfurt's naturalistic account. Walsh criticizes Frankfurt for lacking a concept of self-denial, and this notion is central to the view of self-love she finds in Kierkegaard. In this chapter, I argue that while Frankfurt's account of self-love certainly warrants criticism, it does bring to light some key points that can be brought to bear on how we may best understand Kierkegaard's view of proper self-love. First, we can see from Frankfurt's account how love—not just of oneself, but also of others—entails commitment, and that such commitment requires an appropriate relation *to oneself*. Further, Frankfurt shows clearly how self-love necessarily points outside the self and how love can *involve* self-interest without being *based* upon it in a "merely selfish" way. For Frankfurt, love involves caring about the good of the person or thing loved for their own sake. So in self-love, I care about the good of *myself* for my own sake. This reminder—phrased in more Christian terminology, that I am a "neighbor" too—gives an important standard against which accounts of Kierkegaardian self-love should be measured. It is, I argue, a problem for accounts that would have us put too much emphasis on self-denial. There is, on these matters, a more moderate—more loving?—Kierkegaard, and his voice should be heard. While it is true that Kierkegaard describes self-denial as "Christianity's essential form" (WL, 56/SKS 9, 62), there are other things he says that qualify this. In the final section, I'll point out the relevance for oneself of his focus on trust and hope, and his insistence on the importance of accepting that one's sins are forgiven, and the self-forgiveness consequent upon this.

I. Kierkegaardian self-love, selfishness, and self-denial

Walsh has given a detailed exegesis of Kierkegaard on self-denial in earlier work,[2] on which I have commented elsewhere. I shall not repeat that critique here, except insofar as it is necessary to address her position in this chapter.[3]

As Walsh rightly notes, for Kierkegaard Christianity is concerned not with getting rid of all self-love, but rather with teaching us to love ourselves in the right way. This she characterizes as driving out *selfishness*, through self-love being transformed by the commandment to love the neighbor as oneself.[4] Certainly Kierkegaard is troubled by regarding the other simply as an "other I" or "other self," and when the problem is reducing the other simply to their role in one's own life and projects, that is surely a reasonable objection. But this does not itself warrant the view that "*all* preferential love in its natural forms and expressions is simply another form of selfish self-love in which the other is regarded merely as an extension of ourselves."[5] That sounds like an error akin to conflating treating someone as a means to an end with treating them as *merely* a means to an end—a very important distinction.[6] I have argued elsewhere that the best accounts of friendship in the "pagan" world can easily avoid Kierkegaard's charge against "the poet," namely that for the latter friendship (and erotic love) "contain no moral task" (WL, 50–51/SKS 9, 57).[7] While neighbor-love, based on duty, is clearly vital to Kierkegaard's account, neither Kierkegaard nor Walsh offers us a compelling argument for the claim that *only* neighbor-love can provide us with a sense of the other's genuine alterity.

A second respect in which I think my reading differs from Walsh's concerns how we are to understand the passage in which Kierkegaard *appears* to reduce proper self-love to love of God: "*To love God is to love oneself truly; to help another person to love God is to love another person; to be helped by another person to love God is to be loved*" (WL, 107/SKS 9, 111, emphasis in original). But can Kierkegaard really be saying that there is *nothing* more to proper self-love than love of God?

I think this is so only in the sense that ultimately, for Kierkegaard, all genuine love has its roots in God (WL, 9–10/SKS 9, 17–18). But we need to be clear that it does not follow from this that there is nothing more to be said to the person struggling with how to love himself properly than "Love God!". I shall suggest below that Kierkegaard gives us—in *Works of Love* and elsewhere—some valuable concrete suggestions for *how* we might love ourselves properly, in terms of what it would mean properly to trust; hope for; and forgive, ourselves. I also think it is important to avoid giving the impression—which equating proper self-love with love of God can easily do—that Kierkegaard's repeated claim that God is the "middle term" in love commits him to the implausible view that God is constantly the explicit object of the loving believer's thought. As Patrick Stokes has suggested in his work on *interesse* in Kierkegaard, the Dane often talks of "interest" in ways similar to Sartre's talk of "non-thetic" consciousness: a "self-awareness implicit in or attendant upon each moment of consciousness without forming part of its intentional, thetic content."[8] Kierkegaard's claims about God as the "middle term"—and the passage at issue here—become more plausible if we understand them in this light. God is, for Kierkegaard, at the heart of all loving action, but we do not necessarily consciously reflect upon God as we perform our "works of love." If we did, in loving the neighbor or the self, there is a serious risk that we would be merely *using* the neighbor or the self in order to love God.

Probably the major difference between Walsh and myself concerns what we make of Kierkegaard's focus on "self-denial." As noted, it is true that Kierkegaard describes this as "Christianity's essential form." Walsh highlights Kierkegaard's more strident demands under this aspect, under the heading of "unselfishness." She also offers us, on Kierkegaard's behalf, a model of Christian love whereby "the truly loving or self-giving person is *totally self-denying in all things*."[9] Some vital questions arise here. First, what is the scope of what counts as "selfishness"? Does it include even the kind of basic self-respect that the recognition of oneself as also a neighbor, as a creature of God, demands? I don't think so—and I think Kierkegaard would agree. His commitment to such basic self-respect is implicit in the examples he gives of those who do not love themselves properly: such as those "bustlers" who waste their lives pursuing trivialities; "light-minded" followers of fads; depressed would-be suicides; and those who succumb to despair (WL, 23/SKS 9, 30–31). It is important therefore to ask what limits are placed on "self-denial" by recognizing the importance of such self-respect as part of proper self-love. Second, is "self-denial in all things" really either an ethically commendable or coherent aim? On the former point, it surely cannot be the case that self-denial—for its own sake?—is to be valorized even to the point of accepting manifest injustice. Here the passivity that has historically been often recommended, especially to women under the guise of self-sacrifice as a "feminine" virtue, is a real problem.[10] The danger in talking of "self-denial in all things" is that we might fail to pay sufficient attention to Kierkegaard's countervailing warnings against taking this to excess. For instance, Kierkegaard is clear that when self-denial becomes self-torment, then a line has been crossed: "When someone self-tormentingly thinks to do God a service by torturing himself, what is his sin expect not willing to love himself in the right way?" (WL, 23/SKS 9, 31) As to the coherence of "self-denial in all things," consider Paul Ricoeur's stress—in his critique of Levinas—on "self-esteem" and "self-attestation": "if the injunction coming from the other is not part and parcel of self-attestation, it *loses its character of injunction, for lack of the existence of a being-enjoined standing before it as its respondent.*"[11] In other words, without a self I am able and willing to affirm, the call of the other cannot be responsibly recognized. In opposition to Levinas' insistence on self-emptying obedience in the face of the summons of the other, Ricoeur insists on the need to maintain self-love and love of others in creative tension. Otherwise, we end up in a position close to that of Anders Nygren, whose unlovable self knows *agape* as God's love for all, but is paradoxically excluded from offering this love to itself.[12] What we might call the "Levinasian" element in Kierkegaard—which is undeniably there—needs to be resisted. But, as we have already started to see, and as I shall further argue in the final section, other aspects of what Kierkegaard says can be used in the service of this end.

II. Defending Kierkegaard against Kierkegaard: A possible use of Frankfurt?

As will become clear, I agree with Walsh that there are problems with Frankfurt's view of self-love, and that Kierkegaard offers one vantage point from which to judge it. Yet in this section, I want to draw on Frankfurt in a somewhat more positive light than does Walsh, before advancing some criticisms of Frankfurt of my own. To begin with, for reasons sketched above, I think there is merit to Frankfurt's concern that worries about self-interest are sometimes exaggerated. Relatedly, need we disagree with Frankfurt's claim that proper self-love is shown by a person "protecting and advancing what he takes to be his own true interests, even when doing so frustrates desires by which he is so powerfully moved but that threaten to divert him from that goal" (RL, 79)? Is this focus on one's "own true interests" simply to be dismissed as a case of "selfishness"? It is worth noting that such a view of proper self-love as being inextricable from one's "own true interests" has a long heritage within the Christian tradition. Augustine, for instance, claims that "you did not love yourself when you did not love the God who made you."[13] In other words, loving God *is* in our own true interests. Kierkegaard's association of true self-love with love of God seems to fit within this tradition. The question of what the opposition to "selfishness" and the valorization of "self-denial" amount to, therefore, needs to reckon with this fact: if we are to use such terms, we must recognize—as Frankfurt recognizes[14]—their possible compatibility with a kind of higher self-interest.[15]

Relatedly, in many cases, self-interest and the interests of others may be impossible to tease apart, both in practice and in principle. We can draw on some of John Davenport's work on Frankfurt to see why. First, to love someone involves a *commitment* to them. Davenport suggests, drawing on what he calls the "existential tradition," a sense of commitment according to which "committing is an *act* with the same intentional content as promising or contracting: the agent *binds* himself to do, say, or deliver something."[16] This entails a "backward-looking consideration" for my future actions and decisions: I have a *prima facie* duty to keep my promise to you *because* I promised. Crucially, Davenport notes, "Commitments of this most primordial kind are volitional in nature; although they are commitments *to* something or someone outside the self, they also involve a reflexive or intrasubjective relation-to-self. The agent binds herself not to others ... but, rather, to *herself*, forming the sort of higher-order volitional disposition that proves central to caring, on Frankfurt's account."[17] (The reference to a higher-order volitional disposition is to my desires or cares *about* my desires or cares, as in Frankfurt's much discussed example of the unwilling drug addict who wants his next fix, but desperately does not *want* to want his next fix.[18]) Given that love entails commitment, then, some kind of appropriate *self*-relation—which goes beyond raw "self-denial"—is necessary in *any* kind of love. Now Frankfurt himself recognizes this point when he notes:

> love is in a certain way reflexive. Insofar as a person loves something, the fact that he cares about it as he does requires that he must care similarly about how he acts in matters that concern it. Because love entails that the lover has certain volitional attitudes toward the object of his love, it also entails that he has the corresponding volitional attitudes towards himself. In the very nature of the case, he cannot be indifferent to how what he does affects his beloved. To the extent that he cares about the object of his love, therefore, he necessarily cares about his own conduct as well.
>
> Caring about his beloved is tantamount, then, to caring about himself. In being devoted to the well-being of his beloved as an ideal goal, the lover is thereby devoted to an effort to realize a corresponding

ideal in himself – namely the ideal of living a life that is devoted to the interests and ends of his beloved. (NVL, 138–39)

But would we be right to read this as meaning devoted *only* to her interests and ends (and to his own only insofar as they are hers)? An earlier passage suggests so:

> to leave the dear self behind it is not necessary, as [Kant] supposes, to renounce all interests. We need not render ourselves volitionally pure. We can keep our interests, as long as they are disinterested. What is essential for leaving the dear self behind is not that the will be pure or impersonal, but only that it be selfless. (NVL, 134–35)

But this line is problematic. First, I think the term "selfless" is best avoided— as does Frankfurt himself, according to what he says elsewhere. In his essay "On Caring," one of Frankfurt's reasons to prefer the term "disinterested" to "selfless" is that the scope of the latter is "insufficiently inclusive. What is essential to the lover's concern for his beloved is not only that it must be free of any *self*-regarding motive but that it must have no ulterior aim whatsoever" (NVL, 167; cf. also RL, 82). But whatever term we choose, there is a problem here. In claiming that "we can keep our interests, as long as they are disinterested," Frankfurt is claiming that we can avoid egregious selfishness if we take an entirely "disinterested interest" in the well-being of the beloved. But is this coherent? Here I share Walsh's skepticism. Frankfurt attempts to make sense of this (albeit by obscuring the distinction he attempted to draw above) as follows: "The appearance of conflict between pursuing one's own interests and being selflessly devoted to the interests of another is dispelled once we appreciate that what serves the self-interest of the lover is nothing other than his selflessness," which in turn depends upon "caring selflessly about the well-being of a beloved …. Accordingly, the benefit of loving accrues to a person only to the extent that he cares about his beloved disinterestedly, and not for the sake of any benefit that he may derive either from the beloved or from loving it" (RL, 61).

But how in practice may these be teased apart? As Walsh suggests, the danger is self-deception, and there is at the very least an epistemological worry about how we could ever know that our motives were so "pure." But there is also a perhaps deeper point. Frankfurt attempts to make a distinction between "active" and "passive" love. Volitional love is "active," and in active love, "the lover values this activity for its own sake, instead of for the advantages that he himself may ultimately derive from it" (NVL, 133). Love is passive when "the lover is motivated by an expectation that obtaining or continuing to possess the object of his love will be beneficial to him … his love is conditional upon his attribution to his beloved of a capacity to improve the condition of his life" (NVL, 133). This might remind us of the distinction, central to C.S. Lewis's *The Four Loves*, between need-love and gift-love.[19] Lewis describes the typical examples of each as follows. Gift-love is "that love which moves a man to work and plan and save for the future well-being of his family which he will die without sharing or seeing"; need-love "that which sends a lonely or frightened child to its mother's arms."[20] But Lewis expands the latter idea to incorporate any need for nurture, attention, company or "completion." While these can clearly have odious manifestations, such as a selfish craving for attention, Lewis insists that he "cannot deny the name *love* to Need-love."[21] Crucially, he says that not to feel need-love "is in general the mark of the cold egoist."[22] His concern here seems to be an unwarranted sense of independence from others.[23]

Like Lewis with need-love, Frankfurt does not deny the word "love" to passive love, but it certainly has a secondary place in his hierarchy. He is clearly committed to some version of the gift-love/need-love distinction. Caring, and thus love, in his preferred sense is not instrumental, nor is it focused on any part of one's own good.[24] But this means that Frankfurt does not seriously entertain the possibility that a failure to recognize our requirement for "need-love" or passive love might be *a failure to recognize the kind of creatures that we are*.[25] And if this is indeed true of us, then what becomes of the distinction Frankfurt is trying to draw? Lewis says that he started off aiming to disparage need-love and praise gift-love, before he realized that matters are more complicated than he originally envisaged. And if we follow this shift in Lewis's thinking, we may well end up with the view that need-love, as well as being a genuine form of love, *aims at what is truly good for us*—our higher interests. Man's love for God, especially, says Lewis, is "largely" and often "entirely" need-love. Indeed, "our whole being by its very nature is one vast need" for God.[26] Kierkegaard expresses a similar view in the very first deliberation of *Works of Love*. Observing one's reluctance to be described as a "needy person," he responds:

> Yet we are saying the utmost when we say of the poet, "He has a need to write"; of the orator, "He has a need to speak"; and of the young woman, "She has a need to love." Ah, how rich was even the neediest person who has ever lived, but who still has had love, compared with him, the only real pauper, who went through life and never felt a need for anything! This is precisely the young woman's greatest riches, that she needs the beloved; and this is the devout man's greatest and his true riches, that he needs God. (WL, 11/SKS 9, 18–19)

Similarly, in one of his discourses on "The woman who was a sinner" from Luke's gospel, a passage much discussed by Kierkegaard, he observes:

> If someone were to say: Yet there was something self-loving in this woman's love; after all, in her need she still basically still loved herself. If someone were to talk that way, I would answer: Naturally, and then add, God help us, there is no other way, and then add, God forbid that I would ever presume to want to love my God or my Savior in any other way, because if there were literally no self-love in my love, then I would no doubt be only imagining that I could love them without standing in need of them – and from this blasphemy may God preserve me! (WA, 142/SKS 11, 278)

My point here is twofold. First, I agree with Walsh that talk of "disinterested interest" is typically self-deception.[27] But second, it is at least as important to recognize that love—not just self-love, but love for another—can properly *involve* self-interest (and not only in Frankfurt's "disinterested" sense) without being *based* upon it in a "merely selfish" way. It is on this second point that I think Walsh's account of these matters is insufficiently nuanced.

So if proper self-love requires recognition of what is in our "higher self-interest," and if there is a kind of need-love that is not just objectionable "neediness," what features might such proper self-love incorporate? What is the more positive view of self-love that we can find in Kierkegaard? I propose that the beginnings of an answer may be found by applying to oneself three key ideas discussed in *Works of Love*: trust, hope, and forgiveness.

III. A more loving Kierkegaard? Trust, hope, and forgiveness[28]

I take the three discourses "Love builds up," "Love believes all things," and "Love hopes all things" to be crucial for our purposes here. Taken together, these discourses suggest that one should never lose belief or hope in one's ability (through God's grace[29]) to will and act in the light of, and for, the good.

The theme of love's relation to trust is implicitly sounded as early as the first sentence of *Works of Love's* very first deliberation:

> If it were so, as conceited sagacity, proud of not being deceived, thinks, that we should believe nothing that we cannot see with our physical eyes, then we first and foremost ought to give up believing in love. (WL, 5/SKS 9, 13)

The contrast between love's attitude of trust and one of mistrust is central to "Love believes all things," which builds on "Love builds up." As Kierkegaard argues, trust and mistrust are often alternative responses to the same evidence: which way we go is an existential choice that reveals something important about us. To "believe all things" means "to presuppose that love, even though it is not seen – indeed, even though the opposite is seen – is still present in the ground, even in the misguided, even in the corrupted, even in the most hateful." By contrast, "Mistrust [*Mistroiskhed*] takes away the very foundation by presupposing that love is not present – therefore mistrust cannot build up" (WL, 221/SKS 9, 223).

Albert Hirschman has argued that trust is a moral resource "whose supply may well increase rather than decrease through use"; and that such moral resources "like the ability to speak a foreign language … are likely to become depleted and to atrophy if *not* used."[30] This line of thinking goes some way toward defending the default attitude of trust Kierkegaard seems to commend. But we should also note how Kierkegaard's comments about how love presupposes love in the one loved can be applied specifically to trust. As Annette Baier points out, only when trust is to some extent already present can its foundations be built upon:

> Only if trust is already there in some form can we increase it by using what is there to contrive conditions in which it can spread to new areas. Good parents do this when they use the trust that the child already has in them, and in their eyes and gestures, to teach trusting and trustworthy habits of speech, which then become involved in so many other cooperative practices where trust is present.[31]

Note the similarity of this reasoning—using trust in order to cultivate its growth—to Kierkegaard's thinking in claiming that love presupposes love in the person loved.

But what does this mean as regards trusting oneself? The point here is that despite many of Kierkegaard's claims about self-love being "natural," and what we need to get beyond through "self-denial," an inability to trust themselves is a huge problem for some people (and for most of us in some contexts). Some of Kierkegaard's comments on trust as a manifestation of love invite comparison with Iris Murdoch's famous example of the mother-in-law who, having prejudged her son's choice of wife as a "silly, vulgar girl," has the honesty to recognize her own prejudices, and make the effort to "look again" at her daughter-in-law with greater generosity of spirit.[32] Consider, for instance, Kierkegaard's observation in one of his 1843 discourses on "Love will hide a multitude of sins": "It does not depend, then, merely upon what one sees, but what one sees depends upon how one sees; all observation is not just a receiving, a discovering, but also a bringing forth, and insofar as it is that, how the observer himself is constituted is indeed decisive" (EUD, 59/SKS 5, 69). But some people have a view of *themselves* at least as uncharitable as the initial view of the mother of her daughter-in-law. This is perhaps particularly true of those prone to a profound and debilitating sense of shame, a topic recently discussed with great insight by the theologian Stephen Pattison.[33] For such people, an attitude of greater trust toward the self is precisely what is needed. A mother may enable a child to become trustworthy by trusting him—rather than wrapping him in cotton-wool. In this way, offering trust *in advance* may increase the objective trustworthiness of the recipient. But this can be so for oneself as well as for others: by trusting myself, I may become more worthy of that trust. Of course there are circumstances in which we cut ourselves too much slack, but an important implication of applying these *Works of Love* discourses to oneself is that we should not beg the question in favor of mistrust: an account of what it means truly to love oneself should make room for the idea of self-trust.

Yet as Baier also argues, I typically cannot make myself trust by a sheer act of will: trust involves both active and passive elements. It is for precisely this reason, I suggest, that Kierkegaard stresses that it is only *love*—understood as a kind of God-given force within us—that is able to trust. Applied to myself, part of what this means might be to encourage me away from my tendency to need to prove to myself, beyond doubt, that I am indeed trustworthy. As Baier puts it, "Trust is a fragile plant, which may not endure inspection of its roots, even when they were, before the inspection, quite healthy."[34] And as a result of not doing so, the plant may again—"slowly and imperceptibly"— start to flourish again. How to bring this about? That sounds like a job precisely for the love that believes all things. For the overly self-critical, more of the attitude of trust Kierkegaard commends is a key part of what it would mean to love oneself properly.

This connects with hope. Like trust and mistrust, Kierkegaard tells us, hope and despair have access to the same knowledge, and which way we go is an existential choice. Kierkegaard is quite clear that the kind of hope he commends includes hope for oneself: "in the very same degree to which [the hoper] hopes for others, he hopes for himself, because this is ... the eternal like for like that is in everything eternal" (WL, 255/SKS 9, 255). One parallel between hope and trust is that, just as trusting someone (including oneself) can have a beneficial causal effect on one's trustworthiness, so can hoping have such an enabling function. Hope is not mere wishful thinking: as Luc Bovens puts it, "A hopeful rather than a defeatist attitude may at least be partly responsible for bringing some task to a successful end. It arouses a certain zeal and helps me explore alternative means to realize my goals."[35] The literature on such hope includes compelling accounts of the value of hope in palliative care,[36] and Viktor Frankl's profound reflections on the vital importance of hope in the concentration camps, as part of the "will to meaning" that was central to his later mode of psychotherapy.[37]

For Kierkegaard, hope is "a formed disposition of the person of faith."[38] His primary focus is on "eternal" hope—the Christian eschatological promise— and he claims that the self is such that it needs this eternally valid goal and criterion (EUD, 263/SKS 5, 259). But too hard and fast a distinction between eternal and "earthly" hope would be misleading: Kierkegaard himself notes that they "grow up and play together in childhood as peers [*Ligebørn*]" (UDVS, 113/SKS 8, 215). So what links them? A key part of the answer concerns hope's ability to engender new constitutive hopes. For example, in light of our eschatological hope, we typically radically revalue our temporal hopes. Yet something similar can take place with respect to the ordering of those temporal hopes themselves. Bovens argues that hope can engender self-knowledge: "Through hoping we spend a certain amount of mental energy on the projected states of the world and we may come to realize that what we were originally hoping for is not worth hoping for after all."[39] A growing knowledge can affect *that for which we hope*: "As I come to have such insights, I will set new constitutive hopes that I am more likely to realize because they are more in line with what I truly stand for, with my skills or with the limitations of my surroundings."[40] Bovens' example is of an academic who desires to win a certain prize in order to advance his career, but who comes over time to see this as relatively unimportant. The fact that hope is not abandoned but replaced by alternative, more appropriate hopes, is crucial to another dimension of hope: its role as part of self-worth, the foundation for self-respect. Here we see how trust, hope, and forgiveness interconnect. In a discussion of why it is important that wrongdoers avoid self-hatred, Linda Radzik argues that such a person "must also make it the case that he can view himself as someone who can be trusted to perform morally acceptable actions in the future, which helps explain why personal reformation—'a change of heart'—is usually seen as so important to atonement."[41] Note that such personal reformation requires both trust in and hope for oneself. Here is where self-contempt and self-hatred are so dangerous: "A person who feels self-contempt is hampered from seeing himself as capable of improvement. He instead regards his alienation from other people and himself as the proper order of things rather than as a problem that he can and must fix."[42]

How might we aid such a person? Try encouraging them to heed Kierkegaard's advice: "Even if the one who loves was unable to do the slightest additional thing for others … he still brings the best gift, he brings hope"

(WL, 258/SKS 9, 258). Trust in and hope for oneself is key to proper self-love. Once again, it matters that it is *love* that brings this message to the sufferer: "If there is no love, hope would not exist either; it would just remain lying there like a letter waiting to be picked up" (WL, 259/SKS 9, 258).[43]

This counterbalance to a tendency Kierkegaard has, in places, to encouraging extreme harshness with the self, connects with our third major aspect of proper self-love: accepting the forgiveness of one's sins, and the implications of this for self-forgiveness.

Forgiveness is a central yet surprisingly underexplored topic in Kierkegaard's thought. "The woman who was a sinner" in Luke's gospel teaches us that finding forgiveness is what is "unconditionally important."[44] Yet worries are often expressed about self-forgiveness: does this not amount to letting oneself off the moral hook too easily? Any adequate account of self-forgiveness must reckon with the crucial distinction between genuine forgiving—a key part of which involves recognizing myself as being or having been in the wrong—and condoning or excusing. But as with the self-trust case, it is important to see that some find self-forgiveness difficult verging on impossible. What might need to be overcome in such cases is a dubious kind of pride in "never buckling under the weight of one's humanity."[45]

For Kierkegaard, strictly speaking only God can forgive sins, but importantly, he does speak of self-forgiveness. *The Sickness unto Death* gives short shrift to the use of the phrase "I will never forgive myself." Far from this showing the speaker's "deep nature," Anti-Climacus suggests that "if God would forgive him this, well, he certainly could have the goodness to forgive himself. No, his despair over the sin is a far cry from being a qualification of the good, is a more intensive qualification of sin, the intensity of which is absorption in sin" (SUD, 111/SKS 11, 223). The assertion that "I will never forgive myself" is "exactly the opposite of the broken hearted contrition that prays to God to forgive" (SUD, 111/SKS 11, 223). And in an 1850 journal entry on someone convinced that he had committed the unforgivable sin against the Holy Spirit and was thus beyond the reach of divine mercy, Kierkegaard observes: "Perhaps the sin against the Holy Spirit was rather the pride with which he *would not forgive himself.* There is also a severity in condemning oneself and not wanting to hear about grace which is nothing but sin" (JP, 4, 4029/SKS 23, NB15 94; my emphasis). So for Kierkegaard, precisely *because* we have been forgiven, we should *accept* this forgiveness, difficult though this will be for many of us.[46] Indeed, to fail to recognize and accept this forgiveness is a form of despair. And as in the cases of trust and hope, *love* is once again the soil in which forgiveness, of both self and others, is nourished: "only love has sufficient dexterity to take away the sin by means of forgiveness" (WL, 295/SKS 9, 293).

However, it is important to note that by "taking away" the sin Kierkegaard does not mean what some have meant: his model of forgiveness is not one of "wiping the slate clean," as "the consequences of sin remain." As an 1846 journal entry puts it,

> Forgiveness of sins cannot be such that God by a single stroke, as it were, erases all guilt [Skyld], abrogates all its consequences. Such a craving is only a worldly desire which does not really know what guilt is. It is only the guilt which is *forgiven*; more than this the forgiveness of sins is not. It does not mean to become another person in more fortunate circumstances, but it does mean to become another person in the reassuring consciousness that the guilt is forgiven *even if the consequences of guilt remain.* (JP, 2, 1205/SKS 27, 355, my emphasis)

It is this fact—that the consequences remain even though God has forgiven us—that is at the heart of Kierkegaard's recognition of the sheer difficulty of self-forgiveness. He remarks that although a loving person can "lovingly shut *his* eyes to your sins ... he cannot shut *your* eyes to them" (WA, 184/SKS 12, 298, my emphasis). The self-accusing gaze we encountered in our discussion of trust reappears here and poses a threat to genuine self-forgiveness.

Yet one of the strengths of Kierkegaardian self-forgiveness is that it steers a middle course between two extremes: the excessive ease of a "cheaply therapeutic" self-forgiveness,[47] and the prideful despair of refusing God's forgiveness. Crucially, such self-forgiveness faces up to its wrongs in such a way as to leave room for continued remorse or self-reproach, but does *not* let that self-reproach become debilitating. Here Kierkegaard comes close to accounts of forgiveness found in the writings of contemporary Kantians on this topic. As Robin Dillon puts it,

> being hard on oneself, ... and not just one's actions, isn't pathological or egocentric. Rather, it enacts broad features of the human psyche, including the dispositions to express one's values and to take matters of character very seriously. The power and persistence of negative self-assessments manifest the value one places both on the things one has harmed and on being a certain kind of person. One cannot have a normative self conception without a disposition to assess one's self and not just one's actions in light of it, and without being liable, unless one is a saint, to self-reproach.[48]

The key is that this self-reproach is not debilitating. As Dillon adds, "Forgiving oneself means not that one no longer experiences self-reproach but that one is no longer in bondage to it, no longer controlled or crippled by a negative conception of oneself and the debilitating pain of it, no longer alienated from oneself, so that one can now live well enough. This is possible even if one retains a measure of clear-sighted self-reproach, overcoming it without eliminating it."[49]

But Kierkegaard's account differs from prominent secular accounts. His Christian position enables him to resist the insistence, prevalent in much secular literature on forgiveness, that the "victim's prerogative" entails that one cannot forgive oneself either before, or independently of, forgiveness from one's victim.[50] The case for the victim's prerogative, recently argued for by Radzik, is much weaker when judged from a Christian standpoint. Radzik is right to stress the importance of apology, atonement, making amends to and seeking reconciliation with those one has wronged. But when push comes to shove, if God forgives me, then is not the importance of being forgiven by the wronged party less crucial than Radzik suggests?[51] From a Kierkegaardian perspective, one cannot share Radzik's view that:

> The victim has the role of ratifying the wrongdoer's atonement and determining whether her standing as a trustworthy member of the moral community (with regard to the moral issues in question) is to be restored. The victim deserves this role because of his epistemic and other forms of authority ... The conciliatory or nonconciliatory reactions of community members should also guide the wrongdoer's self-regarding attitudes in some cases in virtue of the fact that they are either indirect victims or have epistemic authority in judging the wrongdoer's trustworthiness.[52]

From a Kierkegaardian point of view, all this gives to the victim and the community a role that is ultimately God's. This is certainly not to deny the importance of apologizing and attempting to atone for one's wrongs, making amends and seeking reconciliation. But the ultimate point is that if God forgives me, the refusal of my victims to do so—while it should certainly be taken seriously and may continue to occasion profound sorrow and regret on my part—should not *ipso facto* prevent me from accepting divine forgiveness and extending to myself the self-forgiveness that this acceptance makes possible. Though importantly, such self-forgiveness is of a kind that still has room for appropriate self-reproach.

In conclusion, although Kierkegaard's comments about self-love cast it as a largely negative phenomenon, he clearly takes the second love commandment to signal the need for proper self-love. Commentators such as Ferreira and Krishek have done valuable work in aiming to tease apart proper and improper forms of self-love in Kierkegaard. Yet I think we can go further than their accounts, and also further than placing too much emphasis on self-denial, as Walsh tends to. Central to a more fully fleshed-out account of what Kierkegaardian proper self-love would be, I have argued, is the application to oneself of proper forms of trust, hope, and forgiveness. The present chapter has offered a brief sketch of what this might amount to.

Notes

1   See, for instance, M. Jamie Ferreira, *Love's Grateful Striving: A Commentary on Kierkegaard's Works of Love*; Sharon Krishek, *Kierkegaard on Faith and Love*; and John Lippitt, *Kierkegaard and the Problem of Self-Love*.

2   Sylvia Walsh, *Living Christianly: Kierkegaard's Dialectic of Christian Existence*.

3   For my critique of the "truly Christian" element of self-denial that Walsh discusses elsewhere, see Lippitt, *Kierkegaard and the Problem of Self-Love*, 122–27. The present chapter was written in response to a slightly earlier version of Walsh's paper than the one that appears in this volume.

4   Sylvia Walsh, "The Dear Self: Self-Love, Redoubling, and Self-Denial," 121.

5   Ibid., my emphasis.

6   Nor is it clear that the reading Kierkegaard here seems to be giving to the phrase "another self" is the only option available. As Lorraine Smith Pangle puts it, in a discussion of Aristotle's use of this phrase, "As *another* self, is the friend loved mainly as a reflection or extension of oneself, or as a *separate* being with *different* qualities? Again, as another *self*, is he loved as belonging to oneself, or as true, independent end?" (Lorraine Smith Pangle, *Aristotle and the Philosophy of Friendship*, 152).

7   Lippitt, *Kierkegaard and the Problem of Self-Love*, 33–38.

8   Patrick Stokes, *Kierkegaard's Mirrors: Interest, Self and Moral Vision*, 56.

9   Walsh, "The Dear Self," 124, my emphasis.

10 Interestingly, Walsh elsewhere recognizes precisely this point: commenting on both Kierkegaard and Levinas, she remarks that "neither of them adequately recognizes that some kinds of human suffering require the concerted effort of public policy change rather than individual response" (Walsh, review of M. Jamie Ferreira, *Love's Grateful Striving*, 117). For a nuanced account of self-sacrifice in feminist Christian thought, see Ruth Groenhout, "Kenosis and feminist theory," 291–312.

11 Paul Ricoeur, *Oneself as Another*, 355, my emphasis.

12 See Erin Lothes Biviano, *The Paradox of Christian Sacrifice*, 138.

13 Cited in Oliver O'Donovan, *The Problem of Self-love in St. Augustine*, 1.

14 See especially RL, 78–79.

15 Relatedly, we should not place too heavy a burden on the term "selfishness."
    For more on the distinction between selfishness and other vices of self-
    focus such as self-centeredness, see John Lippitt, *Kierkegaard and the
    Problem of Self-Love*, 115–16.
16 John J. Davenport, *Will as Commitment and Resolve*, 473.
17 Ibid.
18 For Frankfurt, having "second order volitions" is essential to being a
    person. See FW (IWCA, 11–25).
19 C. S. Lewis, *The Four Loves*. This distinction is also, of course, vital to
    Anders Nygren in *Agape and Eros*, and Lewis's book was in significant part
    a response to Nygren's theology of love.
20 Lewis, *The Four Loves*, 1.
21 Ibid., 2.
22 Ibid., 3.
23 Gabriele Taylor notes this as a feature of the "arrogantly proud" (Gabriele
    Taylor, *Deadly Vices*, 74–82).
24 See the discussion of selflessness in IWC, as well as the discussion of active
    and passive love in ANL, esp. 133. I am grateful to John Davenport for
    discussion of this point.
25 I think that Kierkegaard would argue that what has led Frankfurt to this
    position is an excessive concern with autonomy. Again, see especially ANL,
    129–41.
26 Lewis, *The Four Loves*, 3.
27 See also Davenport's argument against Frankfurt on this point (Davenport,
    Will as Commitment and Resolve, especially 446–47).
28 For a more detailed account of the material in this section, see Lippitt,
    Kierkegaard and the Problem of Self-Love, chapters 7 and 8.
29 This qualifier is crucial, in light for instance of Kierkegaard's assertion in the
    Conclusion that "the first thing you learn when you relate yourself to God
    in everything is that you have no merit whatsoever" (WL, 385/SKS 9, 378).
30 A. O. Hirschman, "Against Parsimony: Three Easy Ways of Complicating
    Some Categories of Economic Discourse," 88–96, cited in Annette
    Baier, "Trust," *Tanner Lectures on Human Values* 13 (1992): 168n59, my
    emphasis.
31 Baier, "Trust," 169.
32 Iris Murdoch, *The Sovereignty of Good*, 17–18.
33 For a profound and thought-provoking account of shame as identity-
    shaping, see Stephen Pattison, *Shame: Theory, Therapy, Theology*. Such
    shame is understood thus: "Shame is an inner sense of being completely
    diminished or insufficient as a person. It is the self judging the self … A
    pervasive sense of shame is the ongoing premise that one is fundamentally
    bad, inadequate, defective, unworthy, or not fully valid as a human being"
    (Merle A. Fossum and Marilyn J. Mason, *Facing Shame*, 5; cited in Pattison,
    Shame, 71). On the link with trust, Pattison suggests that such shame

emerges "when trust in other people and the self is shattered" (ibid., 74), though in a vicious circle, he also suggests that a pervasive sense of shame can also *cause* the erosion of trust in self and others (ibid., 202, 219). Pattison also notes Donald Capps' suggestion that Christianity's focus on guilt and the avoidance of "selfishness" tends to obscure from its view the prevalence of shame (ibid., 204; see Donald Capps, *The Depleted Self*).

34   Annette Baier, "Trust and Anti-trust," 231–60 at p. 260.

35   Luc Bovens, "The Value of Hope," 667–81 at p. 671.

36   See, for instance, Stan van Hooft, *Hope*, 66–80.

37   Viktor E. Frankl, *Man's Search for Meaning*.

38   Robert C. Roberts, "The virtue of hope in *Eighteen Upbuilding Discourses*," 181–203 at 189. This highlights the importance of the difference between what van Hooft calls merely "episodic" hope and hopefulness as "a character trait that marks a person's way of being for significant lengths of time, if not their whole life" (van Hooft, *Hope*, 50).

39   Luc Bovens, "The Value of Hope," 673.

40   Ibid.

41   Linda Radzik, *Making Amends: Atonement in Morality, Law and Politics*, 83.

42   Ibid., 90. Fix through the grace of God, Kierkegaard would again insist. But we should not overlook that the "striving born of gratitude" (JP, 1, 993) in response to this grace is indeed a striving.

43   For more on hope in Kierkegaard, and its connection with what Jonathan Lear has labeled "radical hope," see John Lippitt, "Learning to Hope: The Role of Hope in *Fear and Trembling*," 122–41.

44   Lk. 7:37ff.; WA, 150/SKS 12, 264.

45   Charles Griswold, *Forgiveness*, 122. In *The Sickness unto Death*, this theme is connected to the rejection of hope: "Hope in the possibility of help, especially by virtue of the absurd, that for God everything is possible – no, that he does not want ... he prefers, if necessary, to be himself with all the agonies of hell" (SUD, 71/SKS 11, 185).

46   As Kierkegaard puts it in a journal entry: "A man rests in the forgiveness of sins when the thought of God does not remind him of the sin but that it is forgiven, when the past is not a memory of how much he trespassed but of how much he has been forgiven" (JP, 2, 1209/SKS 20/KJN 4, NB2:116).

47   I borrow the term from Eve Garrard and David McNaughton, *Forgiveness*, 3–6.

48   Robin S. Dillon, "Self-forgiveness and Self-respect," 53–83 at p. 69. Strictly speaking, I think Dillon should say "isn't *necessarily* pathological or egocentric."

49   Ibid., 83, my emphasis.

50   Cf. Trudy Govier and Wilhelm Verwoerd, "Forgiveness: The Victim's Prerogative," 97–111. For more on an important dispute between Radzik and Margaret R. Holmgren on this, and the relevance of Dillon thereto, see Lippitt, *Kierkegaard and the Problem of Self-Love*, chapter 8.

51 As Hugh Pyper notes, "The New Testament's model is consistently contrary to the common view that forgiveness has to be a transaction between one who asks forgiveness and the offended party" (Hugh S. Pyper, "Forgiving the Unforgivable: Kierkegaard, Derrida and the Scandal of Forgiveness," 7–23 at p. 12).

52 Linda Radzik, *Making Amends*, 149.

7

The Fullness of Faith: Frankfurt and Kierkegaard on Self-Love and Human Flourishing

Marilyn G. Piety

I. Introduction

Frankfurt asserts, in *The Reasons of Love*, that "[w]e are moved more naturally to love ourselves ... than we are moved to love other things" (RL, 81), yet he observes at the end of the book that genuine self-love is relatively rare. Is it possible that self-love could be both a powerful and natural impulse and also rare? This appears to be a contradiction, a contradiction that Frankfurt's beautiful and otherwise illuminating book never resolves. I will endeavor to show that Kierkegaard provides us with a resolution to this contradiction. The problem appears to be one of motivation in that, as many contemporary psychologists would argue, we are moved naturally not only to love ourselves but also to hate ourselves. Kierkegaard agrees with Frankfurt that we are moved to love ourselves, but he assumes, as well, that we are often moved to hate ourselves, because we feel that we are less than we should be. Hence, rather than consistently willing our own flourishing, we regularly succumb to an inclination to punish ourselves for being less than we should be.

The reason, Kierkegaard would argue, that genuine self-love is both natural and yet rare is that while man was made by God to love himself, this capacity is impaired by sin. I will argue that, according to Kierkegaard, it is only when we feel loved by God that we can feel good enough about ourselves to love ourselves properly. That is, I will argue that it is only through faith, according to Kierkegaard, that we are able to love ourselves properly, and thus to love others properly.

II. Self-love

Frankfurt's examination of self-love begins with the observation that it is very often considered antithetical to morality, or to a genuine love of others. He cites Kant as one of the best-known philosophical proponents of this view. In order, however, to understand Kant's position on the apparent opposition between self-love and morality, we must look briefly at Kant's views on the nature of morality. Frankfurt explains that what concerns Kant about morality

> does not arise from doubts as to our ability to identify which action, in the pertinent circumstances, the laws of morality prescribe. For Kant, that is the easy part. The serious problem in arriving at judicious moral evaluations of what people do lies, as he sees it, in the impenetrable obscurity of human motivation. (RL, 72)

"According to his account of the matter," continues Frankfurt, "there is only one way to earn real moral credit: namely by doing the right thing *because* it is the right thing to do. No action is morally worthy, he believes, unless it is performed with a deliberate intention to meet the requirements of morality" (RL, 74). Moral action must be motivated by an unalloyed desire to conform one's will to the substance of the moral law. If there is any admixture of things such as the desire to be viewed positively by others, or even a desire to avoid the pain of a guilty conscience, then the act is not genuinely moral. Unfortunately, as Frankfurt observes, for Kant,

> [i]t is not our devotion to morality but our interests in following our own inclinations ... that uniformly enjoys the higher priority and that exerts the more conclusive influence on our conduct. We may tell ourselves – in what we suppose to be all sincerity – that our attitudes and our actions are, at least at times conscientiously designed to respond compliantly to the commands of duty. Kant suspects, however, that in fact they always respond primarily to the pressures of desire. It is our own desires that we care about most dearly. We are inextricably immersed in them, and it is invariably and most urgently by them that we are driven. Even when we do the right thing, we do it basically to satisfy our own impulses and ambitions, and not out of respect for the moral law. (RL, 76)

This fact, if it is a fact, appears to make it nearly impossible for people to be genuinely moral. It has been argued that Kant makes the demands of morality impossibly high. Kant appears, however, to be articulating what is a pervasive, if not universal, intuition concerning the nature of morality. "Even children," observes Kant, "are capable of discovering … the slightest taint of admixture of spurious incentives: for in their eyes the action then immediately loses all moral worth."[1] There is, in fact, widespread cynicism about how much of what passes for moral behavior is really concealed self-interest. There are even people who argue, like Glaucon in *The Republic*, that *all* of what passes for morality is really self-interest.[2] Yet, in defense of Kant, we seem unable to rid ourselves of the idea that there is something like a moral law that commands our respect and that is essentially distinguished from and sometimes even opposed to self-interest, at least in any straightforward sense. A study published in *Social Psychology Quarterly* showed that even self-proclaimed egoists have more respect for what they believe to be genuinely altruistic behavior than for egoistic behavior.[3]

There is some ambiguity, however, with respect to what constitutes self-interest, or self-love. "As I understand self-love," begins section five of the third and final chapter of *The Reasons of Love*, "it is quite unlike the attitude that Kant has in mind when he laments that we hold the self too dear. In speaking of those who love themselves, Kant describes people who are motivated predominantly by an interest in satisfying their own inclinations, and desires" (RL, 78). But this, he continues, is not really self-love, but only self-indulgence, and self-indulgence is not merely different from self-love, it is often opposed to it. "Genuine love for ourselves," he asserts, "like genuine love for our children, requires conscientious attention of a different kind" (RL, 79).

Love, according to Frankfurt, has four main features:

> First, it consists most basically in a disinterested concern for the well-being or flourishing of the person who is loved. It is not driven by any ulterior purpose but seeks the good of the beloved as something that is desired for its own sake. Second, love is unlike other modes of disinterested concern for people–such as charity–in that it is ineluctably personal. The lover cannot coherently consider some other individual to be an adequate substitute for his beloved, regardless of how similar that individual may be to the one he loves. The person who is loved is loved for himself or herself as such, and not as an instance of a type. Third, the lover identifies with his beloved: that is, he takes the interests of his beloved as his own. Consequently, he benefits or suffers depending upon whether those interests are or are not adequately served. Finally, loving entails constraints upon the will. It is not simply up to us what we love and what we do not love. Love is not a matter of choice but is determined by conditions that are outside our immediate voluntary control. (RL, 79–80)

Self-love, Frankfurt asserts, is actually "purer than other sorts of love because it is in cases of self-love that the love is most likely to be unequivocal and unalloyed" (RL, 80). That is, self-love appears to conform more closely "to the criteria that identify what loving essentially is" (RL, 80). Our pursuit of our own flourishing, he asserts, is almost never alloyed by any ulterior purpose. It is, in fact, difficult to conceive how it could be. To love oneself is to be devoted to a particular individual—that is, oneself—rather than to "an instance or exemplar of some general type" (RL, 81). Finally, not only can we not help but love ourselves, "[w]e are moved more naturally," Frankfurt asserts, "to love ourselves, than we are moved to love other things" (RL, 81). Such love, according to Frankfurt, "is deeply entrenched in our nature" (RL, 82).

III. The obscurity of interest

Frankfurt distinguishes between the common conception of self-love, which he argues is really just self-indulgence, and genuine self-love. Genuine self-love, he asserts, requires "conscientious attention" (RL, 79) to the true interests of the self, and these are often opposed to the immediate impulses the self is ordinarily inclined to indulge. To love oneself in the genuine sense, he asserts, is to be devoted to one's own interests and these, according to Frankfurt, are determined by what one loves. So to love oneself is simply to love what one loves. Thus it appears that "[p]eople cannot avoid loving themselves, as long as they love anything at all. If a person loves anything, he necessarily loves himself" (RL, 86).

"There are sometimes difficulties," Frankfurt observes, however,

> in determining whether a person who loves a certain object is truly devoted to it. These difficulties arise from the fact that people may be divided within themselves, in a way that makes it impossible to say unequivocally what it is that they love and what they do not love. (RL, 87)

Frankfurt observes that "love is a configuration of the will, which is constituted by various … dispositions and constraints" (RL, 87). There is no reason, he asserts, that these should always be transparent to the self. Thus, it is possible to be mistaken about what one loves. This is not a serious obstacle, according to Frankfurt, however, to genuine self-love.

> A person who does not know what he loves, and who therefore does not know what his true interests are, may nevertheless demonstrate that he loves himself by making a determined effort to understand what is

fundamentally important to him–to become clear about what he loves and what that love requires. This does not imply any deviation from the principle that love requires a concern on the part of the lover for the true interests of what he loves. Being concerned for the true interests of his beloved surely requires that the lover also be moved by a more elementary desire to identify those interests correctly. In order to obey the commands of love, one must first understand what it is that love commands. (RL, 88)

But if genuine self-love is as simple as making a determined effort to understand what is important to oneself, why is it so rare? The problem would appear to come back to the division within the self. "In order," observes Frankfurt,

for a conflict of this sort to be resolved, so that the person is freed of his ambivalence, it is not necessary that either of his conflicting impulses disappear. It is not even necessary that either of them increase or diminish in strength. Resolution requires only that the person become finally and unequivocally clear as to which side of the conflict *he* is on ... [A]s soon as he has definitively established just where he himself stands, his will is no longer divided and his ambivalence is therefore gone. He has placed himself wholeheartedly behind one of his conflicting impulses, and not at all behind the other. (RL, 91)

To the extent that Frankfurt asserts a division in the will can be eliminated through sheer force of that same divided will, his position looks very much like the position that is often attributed to Kierkegaard by scholars such as Alasdair MacIntyre. That is, MacIntyre argues in *After Virtue* that Kierkegaard's primary contribution to the history of moral philosophy is the "discovery" that one can choose something, and presumably remain committed to that choice—for no reason. Yet, as I, and others, have argued, Kierkegaard does not really believe that it is possible to resolve a division in the will through nothing more than a resolution of that same divided will.[4] There has to be a reason for choosing one thing over another.

The issue here is again identifying the true interests of the self. Frankfurt asserts that it is fundamental to genuine self-love that one be moved by an elementary desire "to identify those interests correctly" (RL, 88). He gives the example of a man who "is ambivalent with respect to loving a certain woman, part of him loves her, but part of him is opposed to loving her and he is undecided concerning which of these two inconsistent tendencies he wants to prevail" (RL, 92–93). That is, he is unsure concerning which tendencies, if given free reign, would lead to his flourishing. Should he give himself over to this love, or should he resist it?

In order to make sense of this dilemma, let us assume some sort of obstacle such as a significant difference in age, or that one or the other, or perhaps both parties are already married. In the first instance, the man in question might fear that it would be unfair to saddle his beloved with what he views as the burden of his advanced age. But then the issue is no longer his flourishing, but hers. If he truly loves her and believes in love, then he must also believe that his age, no matter how advanced, would not be a burden to her, but that she would cherish every gray hair on his head and view their love as a blessing for which she could never be sufficiently grateful. His real concern is more likely that his age, as it became even more advanced, would at some point cause her to stop loving him and turn to a younger man instead. He tells himself that giving her up is the *right* thing to do when it is really only the *fearful* thing to do.

The situation is more complicated, of course, if the man's reluctance to give in to his love for this woman stems from the fact that one or the other, or perhaps both parties are already married. It would be an oversimplification to assert without argument that partners in a "good marriage" could not find themselves falling in love with someone who was not their spouse. Let us assume, therefore, for the sake of brevity that the man in question, while he loves his wife, is not happily married in the sense that the marriage is not contributing toward his thriving and that this failure is due either to factors over which his spouse has control but chooses not to exercise it or to factors over which neither spouse has any control, such as a general incompatibility of temperament or values that emerged only after the couple had married. Let us assume as well that the man has some evidence that the woman in question may reciprocate his affection.

In this situation, the man's reluctance to give in to his love for the woman who is not his wife may stem from a fear that she is interested in him only as a diversion. Here again we have his fears and insecurities masquerading as self-sacrifice on the altar of marital fidelity. Of if he has utilitarian proclivities, he may fear that their one union could not generate so much happiness as their two albeit imperfect, but at least undisturbed, unions. Such a fear makes sense, however, only if he assumes the rejected spouses would be irrevocably emotionally damaged and never again able to find even so much happiness as they have at present. Yet this, one could argue, is unreasonably pessimistic. People often find happiness again after a divorce, even at very advanced ages, and second marriages are typically happier than first marriages. To assume that one's spouse has little chance of being part of these statistics is to betray that one views her as particularly unlovable and the choice to remain with a spouse of whom one has such an opinion cannot be an expression of a fundamental desire to correctly distinguish what is in one's own interest or what would lead to one's own flourishing.

Such considerations are, however, not normally those that create ambivalence in the heart of a prospective adulterer. Uppermost in the minds of such individuals, even ones in so unhappy a union as we are supposing here, is usually the concern that guilt over the betrayal of their spouse will be their psychological undoing. So the issue is not really one of thriving, but of simply surviving. If, on the other hand, the ambivalence stems from a fear of losing the emotional closeness to his present spouse on which he has, to a certain extent at least, come to depend, then again, this fear is nothing other than a lack of faith in love. That is, he fears his present spouse will withdraw affection permanently either because of his affection for this other woman (something over which he presumably has no control) or because of his desire to pursue this affection (which would presumably be an expression of his seeking his own flourishing). In either case, however, his present spouse emerges as singularly unloving, at least in his estimation of her. In the first instance, she condemns him for something over which he has no control and in the second instance she condemns him for pursuing his own happiness— something that if she loves him, she must be presumed to want. For him to expect such a reaction from his spouse to the revelation of his new affection is to betray that he has little faith in her love and the choice to remain with a spouse in whose love one has so little faith cannot be the expression of a fundamental desire to correctly distinguish what is in one's own best interest, or what will lead to one's flourishing.

There can be several reasons for such a lack of faith in a spouse's love. They would all appear to come down, however, to two fundamental problems— either a lack of faith that one is truly lovable (e.g., I better do whatever I can to hang onto what little affection I have now because I'm lucky to have even that and could lose all affection forever if I make a misstep) or a lack of faith in love (e.g., no one can really forgive such a betrayal; I will lose the love of my present spouse and will never again be adequate as an object of anyone else's love—not even that of the woman for whom my affection has created this dilemma).

A lack of faith in love and a lack of self-love start to look very much alike. And indeed, Kierkegaard would argue that they are inextricably linked. We cannot really understand where our true interests lie unless we are able to look at ourselves honestly, but most of us, Kierkegaard would argue, fear that we cannot withstand close scrutiny.

It is not merely erotic relationships, however, that highlight our lack of faith in love and how this manifests itself in our failure to love ourselves genuinely. This lack can be seen as well in the relationship that is often presented as the ideal of a loving relationship—that between parents and children. "[P]arental love," asserts Frankfurt, "and self-love are similar in the practically inescapable power with which they naturally grip us" (RL, 84). Yet truly selfless parental love is as rare as genuine self-love. The professions of both psychiatry and psychology have emphasized repeatedly that many of our emotional struggles are a result of our sense that the love we received from our parents was not unconditional, but came with a very specific set of conditions, most of which were not set with the objective of furthering our flourishing, but which stemmed from our parents' struggles with their own feelings of not being good enough.

Rosina Wheeler Lytton, wife of the writer Bulwer Lytton, is reputed to have said that she did not like the company of her children, and did not know what people meant when they spoke of maternal affection.[5] She is not alone. History is rife with accounts of parents who could barely tolerate the company of their children. Even parents who feel the strong instinctive affection for their children that we think of as normal and healthy often have to labor mightily to avoid letting the stresses of their own lives erode their relationships with their children and, consequently, erode their children's self-esteem. It is one of our most cherished, and yet most destructive, fictions that parental love is so instinctive as to be essentially unproblematic. People naturally love their children, we think. The real problems arise in their relationships with people to whom they do not have these parental ties. Yet, I know a woman who despite being the best mother I have ever seen liked to take her infant daughter for walks because she felt that being out in public would mean someone would stop her if she tried to hurt her baby. She suffered from postpartum depression from which she eventually enjoyed a complete recovery. Many women, however, if we are to believe the statistics concerning child abuse, never recover from an almost hysterical sense of being trapped by and chained to their offspring.

Fathers, too, struggle with such feelings. And parents almost invariably impose upon their children expectations that have nothing to do with their children's talents, abilities, drives and desires, and everything to do with the parents' own feelings of inadequacy. I do not mean to suggest, as Phillip Larkin does in "This Be The Verse," that we all suffer from wretchedly bad parenting and that we impose this curse on our children as well.[6] I think it is relatively uncontroversial to claim, however, that most of us suffer from less than ideal parenting and that good parenting, even when it is not perfect, is the result not so much of instinctive forces as of repeated moral victories that are probably more numerous in our struggles to be good parents than in our struggles to love ourselves properly, because the former struggles are more socially acceptable. Even here, though, we lose these struggles far more often than we are willing to admit.

Not only do we frequently force our children into molds better suited to our own ambitions than to theirs, the growing epidemic of childhood obesity suggests that we are as likely to confuse loving our children with indulging them as we are to confuse loving ourselves with indulging ourselves. We punish our children for failing to be the kind of people we think they should be and then try to make up for it by giving them things we know, or ought to know, are not good for them.

Such phenomena are inexplicable for Frankfurt. If parental love naturally grips us with an inescapable power, why do we so often fail to be sufficiently attentive to the genuine interests of our children? And if self-love grips us with this same inescapable power, why are we, by Frankfurt's own admission, more inclined to indulge ourselves than to love ourselves in a genuine sense?

We know there is a difference between our immediate drives and desires and what is in our long-term interests, or the long-term interests of our children, and yet we continue to be divided from moment to moment concerning which should be given priority. If we are commanded, as Frankfurt observes, to love others as ourselves, then we need to be able to distinguish genuine self-love from self-indulgence and to pursue the former wholeheartedly. There are two problems here. The first is distinguishing what is genuinely in our interest, and the second is how to discipline ourselves to consistently pursue those interests once they have been distinguished.

The former, I would argue, should not be difficult. We know, for example, that our short-term drives and desires, such as those for immediate gratification, tend to frustrate our pursuit of goals that lead to our long-term flourishing. We know we are better off exercising than sitting in front of the TV, or eating a piece of fruit rather than a hot fudge sundae. We know we are better off pursuing a hobby such as painting or poetry than spending yet another night in front of the TV. We know we are better off tackling our "to do" list than spending the afternoon at the mall or watching football. We know these things not merely abstractly, but from experience. Who has not "wasted" time in a manner that precipitated brutal self-recriminations later? Who has never hurt a friend or loved one through impatience or indifference, regretted this injury bitterly, and yet found himself repeating it later? Many people, if one is to judge from the mental health professions, even slip into the *habit* of repeating such behavior, despite the fact that the memory of the injuries it causes is a source of almost constant torment.

The Greeks were familiar with this problem. They called it *akrasia*, weakness of the will.[7] Naming it didn't make it less mysterious though. The philosophical tradition, which at least in its Western instantiation abhors mysteries as much as nature abhors a vacuum, fled from it, leaving it to psychologists and theologians to explain. Psychologists give us a reasonable explanation, which can be summarized as that the pain of low self-esteem is so acute we are driven to numb it with the opiate of immediate gratification. This actually seems plausible, yet it is not entirely satisfactory, because it engages us in an infinite regress. Where did the low self-esteem come from? From one's parents. But where did they get it? From their parents. And so on it goes without anyone ever being able to explain, in a manner that is truly satisfying, how this bad parenting first got started. One thing is clear, however, and that is that, whatever the reason, we seem constitutionally unable to consistently conform our wills to what is in our own best interest, let alone to what is in the best interests of others. To put this problem in moral terms: we seem constitutionally unable to consistently conform our wills to what is our duty to ourselves, let alone to what is our duty to others.

IV. The incentive problem

The Judeo-Christian tradition has an explanation for our inability to conform our wills to what is genuinely in our own interest, let alone the interests of those we love: sin. Kant appears to accept this explanation but seems untroubled by it. There is, for Kant, a reason for choosing to conform one's will to the substance of the moral law: respect for that law appears to be inherent in human nature. Kant is aware, however, of what one could call the incentive problem. He describes this problem in his *Religion within the Boundaries of Mere Reason*. "A human being," observes Kant,

> considers himself virtuous whenever he feels himself stable in his maxims of observance to duty–though not by virtue of the supreme ground of all maxims, namely duty, but [as when], for instance, an immoderate human being converts to moderation for the sake of health; a liar to truth for the sake of reputation; an unjust human being to civic righteousness for the sake of peace or profit, etc., all in conformity with the prized principle of happiness. However, that a human being should become not merely *legally* good, but *morally* good (pleasing to God) i.e., virtuous according to the intelligible character [of virtue] (*virtus noumenon*) and thus in need of no other incentive to recognize a duty except the representation of duty itself–that, so long as the foundation of the maxims of the human being remains impure, cannot be effected through gradual *reform* but must rather be effected through a *revolution* in the disposition of the human being (a transition to the maxim of holiness of disposition). And

so a "new man" can come about only through a kind of rebirth, as it were a new creation (John, 3:5; compare with Genesis, 1:2) and a change of heart. (Kant, 68)

"We cannot start out in the ethical training of our connatural moral predisposition to the good," Kant continues, however, "with an innocence which is natural to us but must rather begin from the presupposition of a depravity of our own power of choice in adopting maxims contrary to the original ethical predisposition; and, since the propensity to this [depravity] is inextirpable, with unremitting counteraction against it" (Kant, 70).

Of course, the Judeo-Christian tradition may be wrong in its assumption that we are fundamentally depraved in this way. We know from our own experience, however, that our motives are often mixed, and indeed that it is virtually impossible for us to become transparent to ourselves in a way that what one could call our "moral intuitions" would appear to require. So what hope is there that we could ever become truly moral? Why would we ever even try to be moral if we knew that in a certain sense, at least, we were doomed to fail? Some sort of change in our character appears to be required. But such change alone will not be enough. Kant is clearly correct in his claim that without confidence in this new disposition, "perseverance in it would hardly be possible" (Kant, 86).

Kant proposes a solution to the incentive problem that is charming in its optimism. "We can," he asserts,

find this confidence, ... by comparing our life conduct so far pursued with the resolution we once embraced. –For [take] a human being who, from the time of his adoption of the principles of the good and throughout a sufficiently long life henceforth, had perceived the efficacy of these principles on what he does, i.e., on the conduct of his life as it steadily improves, and from that has cause to infer, ... a fundamental improvement in his disposition: [he] can yet also reasonably hope that in this life he will no longer forsake his present course but will rather press in it with ever greater courage, since his advances, provided that their principle is good, will always increase his *strength* for future ones;[8] nay, if after this life another awaits him, that he will persevere in it ... and come ever closer to his goal of perfection, though it is unattainable; for on the basis of what he has perceived in himself so far, he can legitimately assume that his disposition is fundamentally improved. (Kant, 86)

So there you have it—a solution to the incentive problem. Just be a glass-half-full optimist! So what if you continue to be morally imperfect, even after you have experienced a revolution in your disposition such that you now have an unalloyed respect for the moral law. Even if you are still imperfect, you are a better person than you were before, right? And this suggests that you can expect to continue to improve morally. That's enough, isn't it, to ensure the *"moral happiness"* that, according to Kant, is equivalent to an "assurance of the reality and *constancy* of a disposition that always advances in goodness (and never falters from it)" (Kant, 85)? That is, a revolution in your moral disposition combined with subsequent moral improvement will be sufficient to motivate you to eradicate the division in your will so that only the desire for conformity with the moral law, or what it may be more helpful in this context to identify as our duties to ourselves and others, remains. A little moral improvement goes a long way for Kant.

A little improvement in our disposition is far from sufficient, according to Kierkegaard however, to encourage us to continue our efforts at moral improvement. Such improvement will not rid us of the consciousness that we are not so good as we should be. Not good enough to earn God's love, not good enough to meet the unconditional demands of the moral law. If we are so fundamentally flawed, what incentive do we have even to aspire to consistently pursue the good in the sense of what is genuinely in our interests? What incentive do we have to strive for wholeheartedness when we know we will inevitably fail to achieve it? Not only do we know we will inevitably fail, we must on some level feel that we do not even deserve to succeed. Even if we have some success in improving our behavior, or character, we will still be far from meeting the absolute demands of the moral law, far from deserving God's love. Indeed, God's love, "the forgiving love," asserts Kierkegaard, "which does not want, like justice, to make the guilt manifest but on the contrary wants to hide it by forgiving and pardoning, ... makes the guilt more frightfully manifest than justice does!" (WA, 173). Thus we sink deeper and deeper into the abyss of self-recrimination.[9]

Frankfurt asserts that our pursuit of our own flourishing is almost never alloyed by any ulterior purpose and that it is even difficult to conceive how it could be. Kierkegaard would argue, however, that this is not at all difficult to conceive. It would appear, in fact, that our pursuit of our own flourishing is almost *always* alloyed by an ulterior purpose—that is, by the purpose of obscuring from ourselves how short we fall from the moral ideal. Frankfurt acknowledges himself that most of what passes for self-love is actually self-indulgence and self-indulgence does not lead to the flourishing of the self. On the contrary, it more often than not is an obstacle to such flourishing. Yes, we have an interest in our own flourishing. Yes this is something that we will. The difficulty is that our will is divided. We will our own flourishing, but to do this effectively would involve exposing ourselves to closer self-scrutiny than we fear we can bear. We flee from the awareness of our own inadequacy into the refuge of immediate gratification of both the sensual and the psychological (or egoistical) sort. We seek pleasure. We equate being "good" to ourselves with indulging our immediate inclinations. We give ourselves permission to do things we know are not good for us. We eat more than we should, and the wrong kinds of food. We "rest" rather than exercise. We spend more money than we make. We abstain from political life and spend what free time we have on ourselves rather than on helping others. We encourage those we love, including (and often most especially) our children, to do things we think will reflect positively on ourselves rather than to actualize their specific potential for genuine happiness.

Often, however, our failure to love ourselves rightly is not obviously an expression of self-indulgence, except to the extent that it can be characterized as an indulgence of our fears. Often it is more properly viewed as an avoidance of pain than as a pursuit of pleasure. That is, self-love, in the negative sense, can also appear in the form of cowardice. We can be so afraid of social censure, or censure from those we love, that we come to care more for maintaining the appearance of propriety (our bird in the hand) than for pursuing what would genuinely make us happy (the elusive bird in the bush). We can be so afraid to lose the love of those we love that we endeavor to acquiesce in their every wish. At the same time, however, that we do these things, we are aware, according to Kierkegaard, on some level that those are precisely the things we should not be doing.[10] If we construe "self-gratification" broadly so that it involves both self-indulgence in the positive sense of the pursuit of pleasure and in the negative sense of the avoidance of pain, then we can say that the more we pursue self-gratification, the more we come to despise ourselves, the more we need the opiate of self-gratification to dull the pain of self-loathing. So while on one level we think we are being good to ourselves, on another level we know we are punishing ourselves for not being so good as we feel we should be. That is, we allow ourselves to descend into a vortex, or abyss, of self-gratification because we think we deserve no better than this kind of existence. The more we ignore our true interests in favor of our immediate sensual and egoistical desires, the harder it is for us to do anything else.[11] We find ourselves actualizing Kierkegaard's observation in "Three Upbuilding Discourses" that "the punishment of sin breeds new sin" (EUD, 68).

Thus Kierkegaard's references to "self-love" often appear to equate it with self-indulgence in the manner that Frankfurt says is so common. He observes, for example, that the reason the lower class was just as indignant with Christ as was the upper class was that "each was pursuing his own interest and wanted him to join them in self-love" (WA, 59). That is, the interests referred to here are clearly not the genuine interests of the self. They are the interests of selfishness, of the self that has sunk into the abyss of self-gratification. The association between self-love in this sense and selfishness is so close in many of Kierkegaard's works that the Danish *"Selvkjærlighed,"* which translates literally as "self-love," is sometimes translated as "selfishness," as is the case, for example in the following passage from the Hongs' translation of *Eighteen Upbuilding Discourses.* "[C]owardliness is mistaken for sagacity with a generally esteemed common sense that secretly is selfishness" (EUD, 355).

This self-love is not genuine self-love, though, according to Kierkegaard. When Christ said we were to love our neighbors as ourselves, he was not advocating that we should endeavor to indulge our neighbors' every wish, that we should make efforts to ensure that their desires were gratified just as immediately as we wish our own to be gratified. The self-love that is the foundation of Christianity, according to Kierkegaard, is very different from what people ordinarily understand by "self-love."

V. The fullness of faith

"The commandment," writes Kierkegaard in *Works of Love,* "said, 'You shall love your neighbor as yourself', but if the commandment is properly understood it also says the opposite: *You shall love yourself in the right way"* (WL, 22). "When the light-minded person," he continues

> throws himself almost like a non-entity into the folly of the moment and makes nothing of it, is this not because he does not know how to love himself rightly? When the depressed person desires to be rid of life, indeed of himself, is this not because he is unwilling to learn earnestly and rigorously to love himself? When someone surrenders to despair because the world or another person has faithlessly left him betrayed, what then is his fault (his innocent suffering is not referred to here) except not loving himself in the right way? When someone self-tormentingly thinks to do God a service by torturing himself, what is his sin except not willing to love himself in the right way? And if, alas, a person presumptuously lays violent hands upon himself, is not his sin precisely this, that he does not rightly love himself in the sense in which a person ought to love himself? (WL, 23)

Christianity, according to Kierkegaard, presupposes that no one knows how to love himself in the sense in which a person ought to love himself. We are all conscious, quite independently of Kant, of how short we fall of the moral ideal. We are too conscious of this, it would appear, for us to feel we deserve to flourish in the sense in which it would be possible for us to flourish if we loved ourselves rightly. Most of us cannot even conceive of what it would mean to love ourselves rightly because we are too preoccupied with finding ways to deaden the pain of what we take to be our unworthiness.

Frankfurt is right when he says that genuine self-love requires "conscientious attention" to the true interests of the self. The difficulty is that such attention is profoundly problematic. How can we look at ourselves honestly when it is just such a view of ourselves from which we so often want to flee? Not only is it clear that we are often, if not always, ignorant of what it would mean to love *ourselves* properly, it is similarly clear that we do not know how to love *others* properly, not even those we do, in fact, really love. "If your beloved or friend," writes Kierkegaard, "asks something of you that you, precisely because you honestly loved, had in concern considered would be harmful to him, then you must bear a responsibility if you love by obeying instead of loving by refusing a fulfillment of the desire" (WL, 20).

We fear censure from those we love, so we give them what they want, even when we know, on some level, that it is not what is best for them. To the extent that we really love them, we earnestly desire their flourishing, but fear of losing their love will often lead us to sacrifice their true interests to our immediate need for their approval. Our will is divided. We want what is best both for ourselves and for others, but we also need to feel loved. Our persistent sense of our own inadequacy makes the need to feel adequate so urgent that it often obscures our better judgment. This explains Kant's observation, paraphrased by Frankfurt that, "[i]t is not our devotion to morality but our interests in following our own inclinations ... that uniformly enjoys the higher priority and that exerts the more conclusive influence on our conduct" (RL, 76).

"Being concerned for the true interests of his beloved," asserts Frankfurt, "requires that the lover also be moved by a more elementary desire to identify those interests correctly" (RL, 88). But is the husband who sacrifices the love of his life on the altar of fidelity to a dysfunctional marriage motivated by a desire to identify anyone's true interests correctly? Is the wife who knowingly accepts such a sacrifice? Is the parent who forces a child into a profession such as law or medicine, on the grounds that art or music will not pay the rent, moved by a desire to identify anyone's true interests correctly?[12]

According to Kierkegaard's retelling of the story of the incarnation in *Philosophical Crumbs*, God, or "the god," as he is referred to throughout much of this work, resolves to become a human being in order to communicate his love for human beings, or for "the learner," the person who would receive the gift of faith. "But just as love is the reason," asserts Kierkegaard, "so must love also be the goal … The love must be for the learner and the goal must be to win him, because only in love are the different made equal, and only in equality or unity is there understanding."[13] The "understanding" that comes from faith is thus not simply that God is love, but that one is loved by God. Thus Christ says "love one another *as I have loved you*."[14] We learn what genuine love is, including genuine self-love, from the example of God in the person of Christ. That is, we come to understand love, according to Kierkegaard, when we feel loved by God.

Is it possible, asks Kierkegaard, for anyone to misunderstand the injunction that appeared originally in Lev. 19:18 that we should love our neighbor as ourselves "as if it were Christianity's intention to proclaim self-love as a prescriptive right? Indeed, on the contrary, it is Christianity's intention to wrest self-love away from human beings" (WL, 17). That is, it is Christianity's intention to wrest the tendency to self-gratification, or self-indulgence, away from human beings. To the extent, however, that the tendency is necessary in order for us to be able to live with the pain of our sense of not being worthy of genuine love, the only way to wrest the tendency away from us is to effect a radical transformation in the way we feel about ourselves. Kant was right. So long as the will is divided, moral goodness "cannot be effected through gradual *reform* but must rather be effected through a *revolution* in the disposition of the human being" (Kant, 68). This revolution is effected, according to Kierkegaard, by faith.

According to Kierkegaard, if we believe God appeared in human form, lived among us, and suffered and died for us, we cannot help but believe that he loves us. If we believe that God loves us, then we will feel loved by him and if we feel loved by God, we cannot help but feel that we are love*able*. This is Kierkegaard's insight. If we feel we are loveable, despite being morally imperfect, then and only then can we believe that we deserve to flourish, then and only then can we will to love ourselves rightly. If we feel we are lovable despite our failings, we can look those failings squarely in the face and resolve to be better people out of sheer gratitude for the love we feel, just as the child who feels genuinely loved by his parents resolves out of gratitude to be worthy of that love.

For Kant the issue is how we are to maintain faith that we can succeed in a project in which we have reason to believe we cannot help but fail. The situation for Kierkegaard is a little more complex and hence more interesting. Indeed, Kierkegaard actually anticipates insights of the later psychiatric profession in his view that not only do we fear we cannot succeed, we feel we do not deserve to succeed. We punish ourselves for what we feel is our fundamental unworthiness by systematically undermining our efforts to ensure our own flourishing.

According to Kant, what is needed is a revolution in one's disposition that amounts to what one could call a radical reordering of our priorities so that the desire to be "*morally* good (pleasing to God)" takes precedence over all other desires. For Kierkegaard, on the other hand, the new man is properly characterized not as one who desires to be pleasing to God so much as one who has faith that he *is* pleasing to God. It is, Kierkegaard would argue, only when one believes he is loved by God and thus, by inference, is inherently loveable, that he can love himself properly—that is, will his own flourishing.

Faith solves the problem posed by Kant in *Religion within the Boundaries of Mere Reason* of how one is to motivate himself to conform his will to the demands of the moral law given his obvious inability to achieve the perfection the law demands. That is, to the extent that faith enables us to love ourselves properly it encourages us to focus on our moral successes rather than on our moral failures and thus transforms us from glass-half-empty pessimists to glass-half-full optimists.

Kierkegaard would agree with Frankfurt's claim that self-love requires "conscientious attention" to the true interests of the self and that these are often opposed to immediate inclination. Kierkegaard has an explanation, however, for why self-indulgence so often passes for self-love. According to Kierkegaard, the effect of sin on human consciousness not only makes us unable to love ourselves properly, but even to understand what that would mean. Kierkegaard's is a dogmatic, Christian position, yet it coheres more closely with ordinary experience than does Frankfurt's position in that it accounts for the fact that, as Frankfurt observes himself at the end of the book, genuine self-love is rare.

There is no genuine self-love, according to Kierkegaard, without faith. Kierkegaard may be wrong, of course. It may be that the whole story of the incarnation is only that—a story. Given, however, that, according to Kierkegaard's interpretation, this story resolves the mystery of why genuine self-love is so rare, it offers a more coherent account of our experience than does Frankfurt in *The Reasons of Love*. Given that it recognizes the division in the will, which Frankfurt acknowledges so often plagues us, but does not propose the paradoxical solution that we can eliminate this division through a resolution of that same divided will, it offers a more coherent solution to the problem of eliminating that division than does Frankfurt. Perhaps it is only a story. It is a story, though, that is rich with promise, a story that holds out the hope that we can attain a kind of happiness, a kind of flourishing that we glimpse now only dimly.[15] So perhaps even if we cannot know whether it is more than a mere story, it demands our conscientious attention.

Acknowledgments

I would like to thank John Davenport for encouraging me to read Frankfurt. I would also like to thank Miriam Kotzin for encouraging me to read poetry. I would not have had the Larkin reference had she not very generously allowed me to sit in on her poetry class. I would also like to thank Deirdre McMahon for helping me to track down the Rosina Bulwer Lytton material. Finally, I would like to thank Brian J. Foley who read and commented on the manuscript.

Notes

1 Immanuel Kant, *Religion within the Boundaries of Mere Reason*, 69.
2 *Republic* 358e--359c. Such a view has often been attributed to Hobbes. See, for example, David Hume, *An Enquiry Concerning the Principles of Morals*, 296–97. I am indebted, for this latter reference, to the editors of this volume.
3 Brent Simpson and Rob Willer, "Altruism and Indirect Reciprocity," 37–52.
4 Cf., for example, M. G. Piety, "Kierkegaard on Rationality," 59–74.
5 This remark was recorded by Lady Elizabeth Stanhope (*née* Greene) in a manuscript entitled "Miss Green's Recollections" in the collection of Knebworth House, Hertfordshire. It is quoted by Leslie Mitchell in her book, *Bulwer Lytton*, 68.
6 Philip Larkin, "This Be The Verse," 2, 223.
7 Cf., for example, Aristotle's *Nicomachean Ethics*, VII.1–10.
8 It is interesting to note that Kant sounds very much like Aristotle here when the latter asserts in the *Nicomachean Ethics* that virtue is the habit of acting virtuously. That is, the more often one behaves virtuously, the easier such behavior becomes. It thus "makes no small difference," asserts Aristotle, "whether we form habits of one kind or another from our very youth; it makes a very great difference, or rather all the difference" (II.1). I do not mean to suggest that there is no difference between Kant's position and Aristotle's, but only that their positions are perhaps much closer than the philosophical tradition generally acknowledges. Cf. also Aristotle's claim in Book III that "the exercise of appetite increases its innate force" (II.12).
9 Cf., ibid.
10 Cf., for example, WA, 182, on how "a person cannot hide his sins from himself."
11 Cf., note 8.
12 It is perhaps important to acknowledge here that instances such as these can also be described as attempts at storming the walls of moral perfection rather than as instances of moral cowardice. That is, such a husband,

or parent, endures the excruciating pain of sacrificing the immediate happiness that comes with the fulfillment of erotic desire, or with the vision of a child's joy and loving gratitude, for what he often thinks to himself is the greater good of doing his duty. That is, such a husband, or parent, may fear the censure of what he takes to be his own conscience even more than the censure of society, or of those he loves. If this is, in fact, what a person takes to be his motive for such self-sacrifice, then, I would argue that his is nothing other than the case of the person who, according to Kierkegaard, "self-tormentingly thinks to do God a service by torturing himself" (WL, 23).

13 Søren Kierkegaard, *Repetition* and *Philosophical Crumbs*, tr. M.G. Piety, 101.
14 Jn. 13:34. Emphasis added.
15 Cf. 1 Cor. 13:12.

Section III

Love and Its Reasons

8

Selves, Existentially Speaking

Annemarie van Stee

"Who am I really?" When people ask themselves this question, they often find themselves in situations or dilemmas that may be labeled "existential." They may ask themselves, for example, whether to move far away for a job or stay close to family and friends and try to find something else. Their dilemma is exactly that they both love their job and love their family and friends. People may also question their identity after a loved one dies or they lose the job they love. They understood their identity as involving their relation to their loved one and in terms of the job they held; now they rethink who they are in terms of what is most important to them. Furthermore, people do not need to be in existential crisis for the existential aspect to their self to be at play in their lives. People are naturally motivated to act on behalf of what they love, and they are personally affected by what happens to what and whom they love.

This chapter addresses the self as it comes to the fore, and may be at stake, in existential situations: selves as constituted by our relations to what we love. If we want to think through the structure of existential selves, Harry Frankfurt and Søren Kierkegaard are philosophers to turn to. Harry Frankfurt has been a major instigator behind a surge of interest into existential issues in recent Anglo-American philosophy. His work contains a view of the self in terms of what we care about and love. Søren Kierkegaard is often considered to have been the first to introduce existential issues into philosophy at large. His books contain many individuals asking themselves existential questions and responding in different ways to existential situations. Kierkegaard's pseudonym Anti-Climacus developed a view of the structure of selves to account for the human ability to do so.

In dealing with dilemmas such as the one above, moral concerns are not always decisive, motivating, or even relevant at all, Frankfurt points out. Furthermore, as Kierkegaard points out, objective facts cannot decide for us. We will have to choose. Both Frankfurt and Kierkegaard emphasize that we do not deal with these situations by means of bare, universal reason. Our answers to existential situations and dilemmas are deeply personal, and our will is involved in giving them. What is more, not dealing with such questions when they arise, or answering them in ways that are not true to who we are, will not lead to situations that are objectively wrong or immoral, but instead to alienation from ourselves.

My aim in this chapter is to compare the conceptual resources that Harry Frankfurt and Søren Kierkegaard have to offer concerning the constitution of selves, existentially speaking. My point of departure is in their respective texts on self-constitution. I examine their views on our relations to what we love and how these relations are constitutive of who we are by asking several questions. First, what characterizes these relations that are constitutive of the self? Second, what may we relate to in self-constituting ways? For both questions, it becomes clear that in spite of resemblances at first sight, Frankfurt's and Kierkegaard's views diverge in interesting ways. For whereas both emphasize the importance of the will in the constitution of selves, they disagree on the role of affect and consciousness. Also, whereas Frankfurt clearly indicates the importance of what we love in the constitution of the self, Kierkegaard is much more ambiguous toward or even dismissive of the idea that selves could be constituted by relations to particular people or pursuits. The third section addresses the question why their views diverge in the ways that they do by taking into account the overarching aims Frankfurt and Kierkegaard have with their views of the self. This results in an evaluation of the strengths and weaknesses of their views in explicating the structure of selves, existentially speaking.

I. Self-constituting relations to loves: Relations

Humans have the capacity to reflect. This allows them to distance themselves from themselves, as it were, and to relate to themselves from that distance. Harry Frankfurt writes:

> What is it about human beings that makes it possible for us to take ourselves seriously? [...] It is our peculiar knack of separating from the immediate content and flow of our own consciousness and introducing a sort of division within our minds. This elementary maneuver establishes an inward-directed, monitoring oversight. It puts in place an elementary reflexive structure, which enables us to focus our attention directly upon ourselves. (TOS, 3–4)

When someone has thus distanced herself from herself, she may relate to herself in several ways. Frankfurt writes: "we may want to remain the sort of person we observe ourselves to be, or we may want to be different" (TOS, 4). Kierkegaard's pseudonym Anti-Climacus describes a wide variety of (mostly troubled) ways in which people relate to themselves. Both Kierkegaard and Frankfurt emphasize the role of the will: we may *want* to remain who we are or *will* to be someone else than we are. These volitional relations we have to what we find ourselves to be are in turn constitutive of who we are and are becoming. Despite these similarities, the actual characterizations Frankfurt and Kierkegaard give of the relations that constitute our selves, existentially speaking, are rather different from each other.

Frankfurt: Necessary volitional identification

In his early work, Frankfurt introduced the concept of second-order volitions to distinguish between what does or does not belong to the self. Second-order volitions are relations that people hold to their first-order desires that make them part of their self. Although all animals, including human beings, can desire, for example, foods, it is only human beings that may form desires of the second order about what they desire: they may not just want ice cream, but they may also want to want ice cream. Their relation to their desire for ice cream is one of appropriation in this case, thereby making their desire part of their self. Conversely, if someone wants ice cream (at the first order), but does not want to want ice cream (second order), she distances herself from her desire (FW, 16–18; OC, 159).

In later work, Frankfurt distinguishes different types of second-order volitions and thereby different types of self-constituting relations (IWC, 85–88). The second-order desire to want to want ice cream is a first general type. But not all desires that we also want to have or experience are particularly important to us. Even if someone accepts her desire for ice cream and identifies with it, she may not be particularly concerned if for some reason she had to give it up (OC, 159). Those desires that we do not just want to want, but also want to continue to want, we stand in a second type of self-constituting relation to: we care about them. Beyond identification with a desire, the relation of care thus also involves a commitment to that desire, in the sense of wanting the desire to be sustained (RL, 14–16, 20–21; OC, 160). In this way, cares form a subset of second-order volitions, and ensure a measure of continuity over time in our individual identities. A further subset of cares (TOS, 40) forms the third type of self-constituting relation: loving. Loves are those cares that we cannot help but treat as final ends (ANL, 137–38). Whereas some of the things we care about, we care about because they are instrumental toward something else, we care about our beloveds for their own sakes.

Out of the three types of self-constituting relationships, it is only the latter two that involve the self as an entity that has some continuity over time. In existential situations such as described in the introduction, it is generally people's final ends that are at stake. The latter type of relation, that is, loving, is therefore constitutive of selves, existentially speaking.

Frankfurt describes that relation of loving in terms of volition. Love is "a volitional necessity, which consists essentially in a limitation of the will" (RL, 46). As with other second-order volitions, Frankfurt conceives of loves as inherent to the will, structuring the will. In the case of love, he even speaks of love as a limitation of the will. Through loving, our will can be said to be both free and unfree. We, and our wills, are free when we form intentions and act based on what is internal to our will (FW, 20–21). As our loves are inherent to our will, our will is free when we act based on what we love. We are not free, however, in deciding what we love, that is, we are not free in *forming* our will in the case of loves. In this sense then, our will is limited by loves. Frankfurt writes: "The lover cannot help being selflessly devoted to his beloved. In this respect, he is not free. On the contrary, he is in the very nature of the case *captivated* by his beloved and by his love. The will of the lover is rigorously constrained. Love is not a matter of choice" (ANL, 135; compare IWC, 89). In contrast, Frankfurt's early work emphasized the control we have over what to identify with and what to dissociate ourselves from. This measure of freedom to choose what may structure our will does not hold for love, however. "What we love and what we fail to love is not up to us" (RL, 46).

In fact, we need not even be conscious of what we love or care about. In *On Caring*, Frankfurt writes: "This volitional activity [caring] may not be fully conscious or explicitly deliberate" (OC, 160). What is more, we may not like what we love. Frankfurt writes that "enthusiasms are not essential. Nor is it essential that a person likes what he loves. He may even find it distasteful. As in other modes of caring, the heart of the matter is neither affective nor cognitive. It is volitional" (RL, 42). In sum then, according to Frankfurt, the self-constituting relations of love are volitional relations. We identify with what we love and therefore act freely, out of our own will, when we act based upon what we love. We are not free to decide what to love and what not to love however. We thus are not free to decide who we are, existentially speaking. We do not need to be consciously aware of what we love either. That is to say, we may not be aware of what provides us with important motives to act. Lastly, we need not like what we love. Love is first and foremost volitional, sometimes even only volitional.

However, what may "volitional" mean if it need not involve affect or cognition? According to Frankfurt, it "consists in a practical concern for what is good for the beloved" (RL, 43). We have a practical concern for what we love as we identify ourselves with what we love, according to Frankfurt. He writes that

> a lover *identifies himself* with what he loves. In virtue of this identification, protecting the interests of his beloved is necessarily among the lover's own interests. The interests of his beloved are not actually *other* than his at all. They are his interests too. Far from being austerely detached from the fortunes of what he loves, he is personally affected by them. [...] The lover is *invested* in his beloved: he profits by its successes, and its failures cause him to suffer. To the extent that he invests himself in what he loves, and in that way identifies with it, its interests are identical with his own. (RL, 61–62)

Characterizing the relations that constitute our selves, existentially speaking, as necessary volitional identifications with what we love leads to a few worries. First, Frankfurt's use of "identification" leads to the worry that the self dissolves too much, that the self is being surrendered to others and their interests too much. Naturally, using the term "identification" ensures a measure of continuity between Frankfurt's early and later work: what we identify with is part of our selves and when we act upon what we identify with, we act freely. It is something rather different, however, to identify with desires arising *within us*, as per his early work, versus identifying with *what we love*, which is *outside of us*. Frankfurt does not distinguish between these cases enough. If identification entails that we accept the interests of our beloveds as our own, as Frankfurt has it, the relation of the self to the other collapses. This eliminates an important source of freedom however. For although the necessity of love seems plausible, that is to say, it seems plausible to think that it is ultimately not up to us to decide what we love or not, we may nevertheless evaluate and try to influence the way in which we relate to what we cannot help but love. Indeed, several people have criticized Frankfurt for not sufficiently taking this into account.[1]

A second worry concerns the characterization of loving as volitional first and foremost and the possible divorce of volition from affect or emotion. This seems unrealistic at best and self-alienating at worst. When Frankfurt writes that our identification with the beloved entails that we profit by its successes and suffer when it fails, it is hard to see how this could be understood without reference to affect. When he writes that we need not like what we love, the possibility of self-alienation appears. According to Frankfurt, we may end up in a situation where we cannot help but be partly constituted by volitional relations to what we find distasteful. When we act upon that love however, presumably not liking that we do so as we do not like what we love, Frankfurt would still consider us to act freely. He does not view this type of situation as problematic for his account. If we were to move for a job that we did not like, for example, but that we could not help but have a practical concern for (which, somehow, in itself need not imply any measure of liking), then we have still decided to move abroad freely for Frankfurt. However, acting upon such a volitional constraint that we do not like is surely going to lead to "a kind of nagging anxiety, or unease" (RL, 5), that is, to the type of psychic distress that Frankfurt himself views as the opposite of a person acting out of her own free will. It seems likely that deciding to move, out of a practical concern for a job we find distasteful, could "cause us to feel troubled, restless and dissatisfied with ourselves" (RL, 5). Describing the relations that constitute our selves in terms of volition only, divorced from affect, without noting the resulting ambiguities in our selves makes Frankfurt's account of relations problematic. When we turn to Kierkegaard's account of relations that constitute our selves, we find a rather different picture.

Kierkegaard: Consciousness and will

Anti-Climacus, Kierkegaard's pseudonym who wrote *The Sickness unto Death*, outlines a view of the self as constituted by relation(s). It starts as follows: "A human being is spirit. […] Spirit is the self. […] The self is a relation that relates itself to itself or is the relation's relating itself to itself in the relation; the self is not the relation but the relation's relating itself to itself" (SUD, 13). The next section analyzes this quote and its context more extensively; for now it is enough to note how Anti-Climacus describes different ways of relating, not all of which are constitutive of the self. The basic relation for example is not in itself a self. It is this relation's relating itself to itself that constitutes the self.

What characterizes self-constituting relations according to Anti-Climacus? He distinguishes between an enormous variety of ways of relating and deems virtually all of them unhealthy. That is to say, Anti-Climacus differentiates varieties of despair, that ominous yet omnipresent "sickness unto death." People relate to who they are in such a way, thereby constituting their selves in such a way, that they are not selves in the most healthy, eminent sense. As a chapter title points out, we may in despair not be conscious of having a self; we may in despair not will to be ourselves; and we may in despair will to be ourselves (SUD, 13). These three categories in turn are subdivided into many variations and gradations. Throughout, the despairing ways in which people self-constitutingly relate themselves to themselves are distinguished from each other along two dimensions: consciousness and will.

"Generally speaking," Anti-Climacus writes, "consciousness—that is, self-consciousness—is decisive with regard to the self. The more consciousness, the more self; the more consciousness, the more will; the more will, the more self. A person who has no will at all is not a self; but the more will he has, the more self-consciousness he has also" (SUD, 29). First of all then, the self-constituting relation of the self to itself is characterized by consciousness. As noted earlier, through their powers of reflection, human beings can distance themselves from themselves and relate themselves to themselves from that distance. When we become consciously aware of who we are, we gain the distance from ourselves that allows us to like what we find ourselves to be, or not; and accept who we are or try to change it, or try to forget about it, etc. The capacity that human adults have to relate to themselves in such a way brings about their freedom to try and influence who they are and are becoming. For Kierkegaard, it also entails the responsibility that human adults have to try to establish themselves as healthy instead of despairing selves. Thus, Anti-Climacus characterizes self-constituting relations first of all according to whether and to what extent people are conscious of who they are.

Consciousness of the self does not just *allow* us to willfully relate ourselves to what we find ourselves to be, it *entails* it according to Anti-Climacus. He never speaks of "self-knowledge" or "self-understanding" as if a conscious awareness of the self could exist that is toward which the self is neutral. On the contrary, "self-relation" captures the idea that whenever we become aware of part of who we are, our will is immediately involved in accepting or rejecting aspects of what we find ourselves to be. It is through becoming consciously aware of ourselves that we may will something regarding who we are. Just as Anti-Climacus wants to speak of "the self" only when we reflexively relate to who we are, he reserves the term "will" for the attitude we may have toward ourselves once we become aware of who we are. Hence also the possibility of saying, "[t]he more consciousness, the more will"; for when we become aware of a larger part of who we are, we automatically will toward ourselves to a greater extent too. Secondly then, the qualitative nature of the willing stance we take toward what we find ourselves to be characterizes the relations that constitute our selves, according to Anti-Climacus.

An accepting or rejecting will may sound rather like Frankfurt's identification versus dissociation. Yet there are many differences from Frankfurt's view of self-constituting relations however. First, whereas Frankfurt uses "will" to describe the source of our actions and intentions, irrespective of whether we are conscious of what moves us to act in the ways that we do, Anti-Climacus' "will" applies to what we have become conscious of about ourselves. Furthermore, whereas Frankfurt unpacks his view on self-constitution in binary terms—you either love or you do not, meaning that you volitionally identify with something/someone or you do not—Anti-Climacus' view admits of many different shades of gray in the self-constituting relation, such that the ambiguous nature of people's relation becomes constitutive of their selves. He writes:

> Very often the person in despair probably has a dim idea of his own state, although here again the nuances are myriad. [...(gives an example)...] Or he may try to keep himself in the dark about his state through diversions [...], through work and busyness as diversionary means, yet in such a way that he does not entirely realize why he is doing it, that is to keep himself in the dark. Or he may even realize that he is working this way in order to sink his soul in darkness [...]; but he is not, in a deeper sense, clearly conscious of what he is doing [...] There is indeed in all darkness and ignorance a dialectical interplay between knowing and willing, and in comprehending a person one may err by accentuating knowing exclusively or willing exclusively. (SUD, 48)

What is more, in Anti-Climacus, as in other pseudonyms of Kierkegaard,[2] will is not something like the pure volition unaffected by affect that Frankfurt speaks of. In another literary example, Anti-Climacus discusses a man who, despairingly, does not want to be himself, but wants to be Caesar. He introduces this man as "the ambitious man whose slogan is 'Either Caesar or nothing.'" When the ambitious man does not get to be Caesar, he despairs over it and now "cannot bear to be himself. [...] This self, which, if it had become Caesar, would have been in seventh heaven [...], this self is now utterly intolerable to him" (SUD, 19). By using the phrases "he *cannot bear* to be himself" and "utterly intolerable" as opposed to "in seventh heaven," Anti-Climacus clarifies that he discusses someone who *does not like, or even hates, what he finds himself to be*. In contrast to Frankfurt's take on the will, Anti-Climacus' conception includes an affective component. He never divorces affect from volition in thinking through the will as Frankfurt does. When he outlines example after example of people who do not *want*, or do not *wish* to be who they find themselves to be, it is always clear that this is because they do not *like* who they are and would prefer to be different.

In sum, Frankfurt characterizes the relations that constitute our selves as necessary volitional identifications with what we love. He is thus able to account for the practical nature of existential selves and the consequences on our actions. His use of "identification" removes the distance between ourselves and what we love, however, and his emphasis on the volitional nature of self-constituting relations, possible divorced from affect, also seems odd. The third section discusses why Frankfurt develops his view of self-constituting relations along these lines. Kierkegaard, through Anti-Climacus, characterizes self-constituting relations by the level of consciousness involved and the willful stance we take toward what we find ourselves to be. The will is affective-volitional in his view and he definitely does not collapse the distinction between self and other as Frankfurt does. However, Kierkegaard may seem to overintellectualize the human self by giving conscious awareness such a prominent role in describing the relations that constitute us. Again, his reasons for this focus are clarified in the third section. Before we move on to examining the contexts in which Frankfurt and Kierkegaard develop their views of selves, existentially speaking, let us first have a look at what we may relate *to* in the constitution of the self, according to these authors.

II. Self-constituting relations to loves: Loves

People occasionally have to make existential decisions such as whether to move country for a job or to stay close to friends and family. People may encounter a situation that makes them rethink their identity, for example, when a loved one among friends and family dies, or when they lose the job they care for. In situations such as these, they may reflect on who they are by wondering what is truly meaningful to them, or in other words, what really matters to them, or in yet other words, what they truly care about and love.[3] Can the relational views of the self that Kierkegaard and Frankfurt describe account for these phenomena? That is to say, are we, in their views of the self, relating to specific significant others, pursuits, values, etc., that we love? For Frankfurt, the answer is yes, definitely. For Kierkegaard, on the other hand, this is not so clear.

Kierkegaard: "… in which there is something eternal …"

When Kierkegaard, or rather Anti-Climacus, states that the self is relationally constituted, what then are we relating to? Are we relating to particular people, pursuits, ideals, and the like, that we love? Anti-Climacus gives the following succinct description of the self:

> The self is a relation that relates itself to itself or is the relation's relating itself to itself in the relation; the self is not the relation but the relation's relating itself to itself. […] Such a relation that relates itself to itself, a self, must either have established itself or have been established by another.

[...] The human self is such a derived, established relation, a relation that relates itself to itself and in relating itself to itself relates itself to another. (SUD, 13–14)

That quote from the beginning of *The Sickness unto Death* does not speak of love directly. Let us examine the basic relation, the relation of this basic relation to itself and the relation to another that established it for the object that is being related to. Do these relations include relations to what we love? Could they?

Anti-Climacus describes the basic relation that in itself is not a self also as synthesis. He discusses the synthesis' constituent pairs in terms of infinitude and finitude, and of possibility and necessity (SUD, 29). With respect to the former, Anti-Climacus states that "the self is the synthesis of which the finite is the limiting and the infinite the extending constituent" (SUD, 30). Becoming oneself consists in "an infinite moving away from [the...] self in the infinitizing of the self and an infinite coming back to itself in the finitizing process" (SUD, 30). In other words, in becoming themselves, people should use their imagination to come up with possible ways in which they might be, but should then also "return to themselves" to deal with the limiting facts about who they are and take the small, practical steps that can be taken at this very moment to move in the direction of who they would like to become. Only in this way may they become concrete selves. Likewise, possibility and necessity refer to the self having the task of becoming itself (possibility) that can only be done by taking into account what it already is and cannot help but be (necessity). These descriptions clarify that the constituents are actually movements or processes. When fleshing out the meaning of the synthesis and its poles, Anti-Climacus time and again uses verbs, not nouns, to describe the constituents. Thus, the relation that holds between these constituents, a relation that is not yet a self, holds between processes. It does not hold between loves or between a person and what she loves.

This basic relation, a synthesis, is a self if it relates itself to itself. The reflexive awareness of who we are that is necessary for selfhood always involves the will as well. It is clear from the start that this relation does not extend out to people, pursuits, or other things in the world-beyond-self. The self as a grand relation of the self to itself is nowhere more clear than here. Anti-Climacus is definitely not thinking of a self constituted by relations to loves here.

The final relation included in the grand relation that is the self is the relation to another that established us. Anti-Climacus later identifies this other as the ultimate Other, that is, as God. Mostly however, he uses the phrases "another that established us" or "the power that established us."

These formulations are in turn answers to a question Anti-Climacus poses early on: a self, he claims, "must either have established itself or have been established by another" (SUD, 13).[4] Because of the possibility of a particular type of despair, that of despairingly willing to be oneself, Anti-Climacus concludes that a self cannot have established itself (SUD, 14). The way we deal with the fact that we have not established ourselves, or, in Anti-Climacus' terminology, the way in which we relate to the power that *did* establish us, is therefore constitutive of who we are. Furthermore, as cause of our inability to establish ourselves, our relation to God also becomes the route to establishing a non-despairing self-relation. In Anti-Climacus' words: "The formula that describes the state of the self when despair is completely rooted out is this: in relating itself to itself and in willing to be itself, the self rests transparently in the power that established it" (SUD, 14). God is not described as an object of love in the text of *The Sickness unto Death*. He was in earlier drafts of the text, however, and is often discussed as someone we can and should love in other works by Kierkegaard as well.[5] Therefore, our self-constituting relations to God provide us with an instance in Kierkegaard of relations to what we love that constitute our self.

God, however, is a very peculiar object of love. Is the fact that Anti-Climacus thinks our relation to him is constitutive of who we are due to God being a category unto himself? Or can our love for particular human others be constitutive of our self along the same lines as our love of God can? Given that God in Anti-Climacus' view of selves mainly has the role of being the cause of our inability to establish ourselves, it is hard to extend his view to include particular human others. They are not responsible for establishing us in the way that God is, according to Kierkegaard. To be sure, our parents have had something to do with the fact that we were established in the first place, but not as the individual that we are, with these particular characteristics and not others. Also, our relations to human persons whom we love cannot bring us peace in the way that our relation to the one that established us can, according to Anti-Climacus. In his words: we cannot *transparently* rest in their power; this is only possible with God (SUD, 14). All in all, Anti-Climacus' description of the self does not include relations to loves that are constitutive of selves as introduced in the example, that is, of selves, existentially speaking.

Nevertheless, some commentators do argue that Kierkegaard includes relations to what we love in his view of self. They tend to refer to other works of Kierkegaard besides *The Sickness unto Death* and its rigorously systematic, somewhat abstract exposition of the structure of the self. Anthony Rudd, for example, offers an interpretation of the second part of *Either/Or*, consisting of letters of B (Judge Wilhelm) to A, to argue that Kierkegaard does view relations of commitment to concrete human others and to particular pursuits as being constitutive of selves, ethical selves in particular. Rudd explains as follows:

> The person who has ethically chosen and found himself possesses himself defined in his entire concretion. He then possesses himself as an individual who has these capacities, these passions, these inclinations, these habits, who is subject to these external influences [...]. Here he then possesses himself as a task [...] in short, to produce an evenness in the soul, a harmony, which is the fruit of the personal virtues. But although he himself is his objective, [...] the self that is the objective is not an abstract self that fits everywhere and therefore nowhere but is a concrete self in living interaction with these specific surroundings, these life conditions, this order of things. The self that is the objective is not only a personal self but a social, a civic self. (EO II, 262)[6]

In light of all this concretion, and the social nature of the self, the following statement by Rudd reflects his take on ethical selfhood in Kierkegaard: it "arises with the willingness to make long-term commitments, to accept social roles, and, by so doing, to accept the standards of evaluation that go with them."[7]

Rudd's view can be challenged however. It can be argued that Judge Wilhelm, with his German name, should be read as a character Kierkegaard developed to show the inadequacy of the position he, that is, Wilhelm, espouses. At the very least he is an exception among the pseudonyms where his emphasis on the social or even civic nature of the self is concerned. Nowhere else in Kierkegaard's oeuvre are the duties of the world, such as the duty to work and the duty to marry, treated as positively in their character as civic duties. Alastair Hannay argues that the letter by an older friend of Wilhelm that is included immediately after Wilhelm's letters already demonstrates the inadequacy of Wilhelm's position: the civic realm is opposed to true selfhood.[8]

Even Wilhelm himself states that loving another human being or a job is not what is crucial to selfhood. Sure enough, he states that *what* one chooses is one's personality in its "entire concretion," describing this concretion using nouns such as "these capacities" and "these passions" where Anti-Climacus speaks of a synthesis of processes, that he refers to by verbs. Note however that the judge does not prioritize our relations to whom and what we love over other "inclinations," "habits," and so forth. More importantly, Wilhelm *agrees* with Anti-Climacus that the most crucial thing is *that* one chooses, that is to say, that people become consciously aware of who they are and will to be themselves. "Either/Or" is the admonition Wilhelm shouts at his friend A (EO II, 157). Either/or, that is to say: choose!

> But what is it, then, that I choose—is it this or that? No, for I choose absolutely, and I choose absolutely precisely by having chosen not to choose this or that. I choose the absolute, and what is the absolute? It is myself in my eternal validity. Something other than myself I can never choose as the absolute, for if I choose something else, I choose it as something finite and consequently do not choose absolutely. (EO II, 214)[9]

Choosing is what matters most for Wilhelm and choosing should be done absolutely, he says. The only "things" we can choose *absolutely* however are things in which there is something *eternal*, to use Kierkegaard's words, just as we saw earlier that we can only relate *transparently* to God who established us. That is to say, the only objects that we may self-constitutingly relate to according to Kierkegaard are objects in which there is something eternal. As "next to God there is nothing as eternal as a self" (SUD, 53), we may relate to ourselves and to God in such a way as to constitute our selves, but not to particular, concrete human others, or pursuits that are not eternal, not even if we love them.

All in all then, Kierkegaard focuses on the relations of the self to itself and to God in his view of selves, existentially speaking. His texts do not present relations to particular human others or particular pursuits as constitutive of the self. He therefore passes by an important facet of the self as it comes to the fore and may be at stake in existential dilemmas and other existential situations. The third section provides context as to why this is so. Let us first see, however, what Frankfurt has to offer with respect to our relations to what we love and their role in the constitution of our existential selves.

Frankfurt: "Involuntary, nonutilitarian, rigidly focused and [...] self-affirming"

What may contribute to the constitution of self, existentially speaking, for Frankfurt? The answer is clear: what we care about and, most of all, what we love. Frankfurt describes what we love in three ways. First, he mentions that loves form a subset of cares (TOS, 40), that is, a subset of those things we want to want and want to continue to want. We may care about getting up early, for example, not because this is *in itself* terribly important to us, but rather as a means to the end of pursuing a particular line of work. This work is what we love then, it is an end in itself. Others may care about, though not love their work: they may pursue it as a means to the end of sustaining the family that they love, for example. Secondly, Frankfurt lists examples: "The object of love is often a concrete individual: for instance, a person or a country. It may also be something more abstract: for instance, a tradition, or some moral or nonmoral ideal" (RL, 41). Elsewhere, he declares that "[t] he object of love can be almost anything" (TOS, 40) and adds "a life" and "a quality of experience" to the list. When fleshing out his views however, he returns time and again to his favorite example: that of parents loving their children.

The third way in which Frankfurt delineates loves is by putting forward four conceptually necessary features: love is "an involuntary, nonutilitarian, rigidly focused and [...] self-affirming concern for the existence and the good of what is loved" (TOS, 40; see also RL, 41–47, 79–80; TOS, 40–43). As we have already seen in the previous section, loving is involuntary: we cannot help loving what we love. Love is "a volitional necessity, which consist essentially in a limitation of the will" (RL, 46). Furthermore, loving is nonutilitarian: we care about what we love for its own sake, rather than as a means to some other goal. Loves are final ends. Also, loving has a rigid focus: we cannot substitute what we love with someone/something of a similar type (TOS, 40). Finally, loving is self-affirming: we identify with what we love, Frankfurt states. We accept the interest of our beloved as our own. We benefit when what we love flourishes, we suffer when it is harmed (TOS, 41; RL, 80).

The three different ways of describing what we may love, and thereby, what we may relate to in such a way that it constitutes our selves, make it clear that unlike Kierkegaard, Frankfurt clearly thinks we are who we are, existentially speaking, through what we love. Kierkegaard circumscribed what we may relate to in such a way by his focus on objects in which there is something eternal. Frankfurt, on the other hand, focuses very much on concrete human others in the world, concrete pursuits in the world, ideals and traditions that may orient us in situations in which existential choices have to be made. Indeed, he focuses on what we love as what guides us and motivates us in life, regardless of whether we engage in explicit reflection on our lives or not.

This does not mean Frankfurt's account should be accepted, no questions asked. We have already considered objections to the involuntariness of love and the idea that we identify with our beloveds. Although it may be true that love is involuntary in the sense that we cannot ultimately decide by an act of our will to love this person but not the next, we do have a measure of freedom in influencing the relation in which we stand to a beloved. We evaluate and try to influence the way in which we relate to what we cannot help but love. This cannot be understood, however, if we characterize the relation to our beloveds as one of "identification," for then the relation we have to them is effectively erased from the picture. The characterization of love as "nonutilitarian" has also been criticized. Identifying with whom (and what) we love without expecting something in return seems closer to admiration or benevolence than to love. It has been proposed that a criterion of "reciprocity" be added.[10]

The "rigid focus" on an object of love in its particularity, instead of as an example of a general type, seems unproblematic.[11] It is a strong point of Frankfurt's account of the self, existentially speaking, as it contributes to the idea that we may be individuated by our relations to what we love. Where Kierkegaard focuses on the love that all of us should have for all of our neighbors, Frankfurt focuses on objects of love that are particular to an individual.

Overall, Frankfurt's view on love and on how love shapes our identities tries to account for precisely the phenomena regarding selves, existentially speaking, that were exemplified in the introduction. Although certain aspects of his views can be questioned, his ideas exactly tackle questions about how love binds our will and thus provides us with an identity and a sense of direction when it comes to dealing with existential situations. In contrast, although Kierkegaard explicitly develops a relational view of the self, he is much more hesitant to say of relations to concrete beloveds that they are constitutive of selves. In the previous section, we have also seen how Kierkegaard and Frankfurt's views diverged with respect to the question of how self-constituting relations can best be conceptualized. Why do their relational views of the existential self differ to such extent?

III. Frankfurt's and Kierkegaard's selves in context

If we want to understand why Kierkegaard's and Frankfurt's relational views of the self end up looking so different, both in terms of what characterizes self-constituting relations and what we may self-constitutingly relate to, we need to take a step back and look at the contexts in which their views of the self function. What overarching aims motivate Frankfurt and Kierkegaard to develop their relational views of selves, existentially speaking? And how do these aims influence the strengths and limitations of their views when it comes to thinking through the structure of the self as it comes to the fore in existential situations?

In a reflection on his own professional journey, Frankfurt describes his dissatisfaction with "the philosophical irrelevance of much philosophical activity."[12] According to Frankfurt, the standard focus of (Anglo-American) philosophy on matters of truth and morality leaves many urgent concerns of human life out of the picture. It is to gain a fuller view of these human concerns that Frankfurt introduced the concept of "what we care about," later extending its discussion by the concept of "what we love."

The particular context where he deems these concepts relevant is in discussions of practical reason. When we are trying to figure out how to live, what guides us? Frankfurt asks. He reacts against practical philosophers who want to locate the sources of our practical reason in an independent normative reality (TOS, 32) or in the impersonal demands of rationality (TOS, 21–22). Instead, Frankfurt argues that practical reason is not at all universal or impersonal. On the contrary, practical reason is individual and personal. It is grounded in ourselves, particularly in the structure of our will: in what we care about and love (TOS, 33). Frankfurt wants his account not only to be an account of how people act according to what they love, but also an account of why people *are justified* to act based on what they love. He does not want to build his account of practical reason on feelings, as they may be fleeting and occur coincidentally, and therefore lack normative force. Figuring out how to live and what to do is never just a cognitive exercise, nor is it ultimately based on feelings. It is volitional first and foremost.

Frankfurt's overarching aim is exactly to be able to account for situations such as those described in the introduction. In the preface to his collection *The Importance of What We Care About* (1998), he writes that he tries to understand the structure of the self in such a way that it can accommodate "our experience of ourselves and [...] the problems in our lives that concern us with the greatest urgency" (IWCA, viii). His view of the self in terms of our relations to what we care about and love is developed to account for the phenomenon that people may find themselves with existential dilemmas, as well as for the phenomenon of them drawing on what they love when making decisions regarding how to live, forming intentions and acting on them. It is thus understandable that he has an account of selves in terms of what we love.

Where Frankfurt wants to correct practical philosophy, as he thinks its main theories do not do justice to important ways in which people actually live, Kierkegaard wants not just to correct Hegelian thought for not being able to do justice to categories that belong to human existence; he also wants to correct the people of his times for not living their lives to the full potential of human existence, and Christian existence in particular. His account is therefore explicitly and heavily normative. Anti-Climacus states that he is writing in "resemblance to the way a physician speaks at the sickbed" (SUD, 5). He is addressing a readership that has forgotten what it means to exist; diagnosing all the different ways in which people can fail to exist; and presenting his diagnosis in such a way as to be upbuilding for his patients, that is to say, for all of us. The first part of *The Sickness unto Death* deals with what it means to exist humanly, as a self; the second part with what it means to exist Christianly, as a self before God. The structural view of the self he presents allows him to articulate an ideal self that people should strive toward, as well as all the ways in which people deviate from that ideal. This ideal self is one in which we consciously relate to who we are, will to be ourselves, and in doing so transparently rest in the power that established us. This is a radical ideal, practically impossible to reach. Anti-Climacus declares: "there is not one single living human being who does not despair a little" (SUD, 22). He wants to annoy his readers out of their complacency and into a conscious awareness of their own (despairing) self through the confrontation with his radical ideal.

Anti-Climacus, like other pseudonyms of Kierkegaard, does not necessarily consider a self constituted by relations to what we love as a true self, in his rich sense. It may only be "what we in our language call a self" (SUD, 56). He reserves the term "self" for what arises when we start to consciously relate to who we are, for it is this conscious relation that gives us a measure of freedom to influence who we may become. It is there that we may take upon ourselves the responsibility for who we are and are becoming. Thus, in his exposition on selves, Anti-Climacus does not refer to what people draw on when they find themselves in existential situations, questioning their identity. He does not discuss people's relations to what they love as if they may constitute their true self. He may refer to such relations in passing, as when he discusses "a young girl, [...who] despairs over the loss of her beloved" (SUD, 20), but only to deplore the misguided idea that such relations actually constitute selves. "This self of hers, which she would have been rid of or would have lost in the most blissful manner had it become 'his' beloved, this self becomes a torment to her if it has to be a self without 'him.' This self, which would have become her treasure (although, in another sense, it would have been just as despairing), has now become to her an abominable void" (SUD, 20). As Anti-Climacus finds such a take on self, that would crucially depend on others, to be despairing, he never focuses on what it would entail to have such a self.

If we want to address the self as it comes to the fore in existential situations, Frankfurt's views are more on topic. Unlike Kierkegaard, Frankfurt does point out how our relations to what we love shape who we are, existentially speaking. The plight of people who have lost a loved one, as the young girl has, is taken to be a reality of the human condition by Frankfurt, and taken to indeed involve her identity. Kierkegaard, on the other hand, deplores it as a misguided notion of what it means to be an existing self. Also, Frankfurt's view fleshes out the possibility that we may not be consciously aware of what we love, nor, therefore, of the motivations underlying our actions and intentions. Kierkegaard acknowledges this possibility, but is dismissive of it and therefore does not pay it the attention that it, given its ubiquity, deserves.

At the same time however, Frankfurt's account of the self runs the risk of alienating us from ourselves where he allows for the possibility that we volitionally identify with what we do not like; as well as the risk that our self dissolves too much into others, surrendering our independence from others to a too large an extent. Kierkegaard, on the other hand, focuses exactly on what remains independent and would dismiss the idea that our selves can be summed up by reference to our loves as despairing and as self-forgetfulness. In the context of existential selves, we can use several aspects of Anti-Climacus' thought without necessarily embracing his normative ideal or his unease with people not living up to that ideal. We can, for example, extend his notion of self-constituting relations we have to what we find ourselves to be to include self-constituting relations to what we find ourselves to love. These relations are characterized by their affective-volitional quality and by the level of conscious awareness we have of them. We can use Anti-Climacus' analysis of the freedom we gain when we become consciously aware of who we are, what we love, and how we relate to what we love, that is, the freedom to try and influence our relations to what we love and thereby how our selves are constituted.

All in all then, in elaborating relational views of the self and doing so with a particular interest in existential issues, Kierkegaard and Frankfurt nevertheless come up with very different selves, plural. Frankfurt aims to enrich discussions regarding practical rationality with concepts that do justice to people's experiences and the problems they encounter. Kierkegaard aims to correct Hegelian wrongs and to remind his readers of a normative ideal of selfhood and the ways in which they fall short with respect to it. These different aims are reflected in their different characterizations of the relations that constitute our selves, as well as in their different answers to the question whether our relations to what we love are constitutive of our selves. If our own interest is in explicating the structure of the self as it comes to the fore and may be at stake in existential situations, we can use aspects of both views to flesh out the idea that our relations to what we love constitute our selves, existentially speaking.

Acknowledgment

This work is part of the research program "What can the humanities contribute to our practical self-understanding?," which is financed by the Netherlands Organization for Scientific Research (NWO).

Notes

1   Susan Wolf, "The True, the Good and the Lovable," 227–44.

2   Likewise, though vice versa, in the *Concluding Unscientific Postscript*, another pseudonym called Johannes Climacus develops a concept of subjective truth, which is truth of appropriation, This truth needs to be passionately appropriated. Passion here, however, does not just refer to some emotional state. It has to do with volition as well, with commitment.

3   To use the words of, respectively, existential psychotherapists such as Viktor Frankl; of Charles Taylor; and, obviously, of Harry Frankfurt.

4   He does not discuss the possibility that a self may be established by impersonal, natural forces.

5   Most notably in *Works of Love*, to which other contributions to this volume testify.

6   Anthony Rudd, *Kierkegaard and the Limits of the Ethical*, 77. Rudd uses a different translation of *Either/Or* than is used here, the one by Walter Lowrie.

7   Ibid., 72. Although originally pertaining to morality in general, not just to ethical selfhood. Rudd's newest book *Self, Value and Narrative* takes up the same point, especially in chapter 2 and the Introductions to parts 2 and 3.

8   Alastair Hannay, *Kierkegaard*, 62–63.

9   Rudd quotes this passage too, on p. 75 of his book, but does not take it to have the consequences I take it to have.

10 For example, Kyla Ebels-Duggan, "Against Beneficence," 142–70. Reciprocity, however, does not sit easily with objects of love that are not people.

11 It seems a bit strange though to say of, for example, an ideal or a quality of experience that it is rigidly focused, whereas it can easily be said of people, projects, countries, and football teams.

12 Harry Frankfurt, "Een intellectueel zelfportret" [An intellectual self-portrait], in *Vrijheid, noodzaak en liefde*, eds. Katrien Schaubroek and Thomas Nys (Kapellen: Pelckmans, 2011), 17–30, my translation.

Willing and the Necessities of Love in Frankfurt and Kierkegaard

M. Jamie Ferreira

In *The Reasons of Love*, Harry G. Frankfurt mounts a provocative defense of "self-love" against the background of a somewhat popularized version of his earlier philosophical analyses of love. In the course of his defense of "self-love," Frankfurt explicitly invokes Søren Kierkegaard's insight about the importance of integrity as "willing one thing." This opens up the possibility for an interesting discussion, as does the way in which Frankfurt's bold claim that love is "volitional" implicitly engages other Kierkegaardian concerns with the role of the will.

A continuing motivation in Frankfurt's philosophical thought has been, by his own account, an exploration of "how we are to conceptualize ourselves as persons, and what defines the identities we achieve" (IWCA, vii). Accordingly, in many of his essays his "approach" to understanding "what we are" is "to consider the structure and constitution of the self," and his "emphasis" has been "mainly on the will, on "the inner organization of the will and what that implies for us" (IWCA, viii). In reacting against the way in which "reason has usually been regarded as the most distinctive feature of human nature," Frankfurt shows himself congenial to Kierkegaard's own ongoing discomfort with rationalism. However, I want to suggest that Frankfurt's formulation of his alternative—namely, that "volition pertains more closely than reason to our experience of ourselves and to the problems in our lives that concern us with the greatest urgency" (IWCA, viii)—fails to do justice to the phenomenon of concerned and practical engagement to which he and Kierkegaard both point. The idiom of "volition" so prevalent in *The Reasons of Love*, I will argue, sits uncomfortably with some of Frankfurt's own best insights about love and needs to be disambiguated. After briefly touching on the notion of integrity of will found in *The Reasons of Love*, I will spend the remainder of the essay dealing with Frankfurt's claim there that love is "volitional," and I do so for two reasons. First, I find the presentation of Frankfurt's position on volition in *The Reasons of Love* to be unclear, and this is particularly important because this small book is a popular rendering of Frankfurt's philosophical analyses of love and is likely to have a far greater audience than academic philosophers. I consider it important, therefore, to disentangle the strands of Frankfurt's claim that love is "volitional," hoping to minimize the confusion it may generate for other readers of *The Reasons of Love*. Second, engaging Frankfurt and Kierkegaard on the role of the will can be mutually illuminating.

I. Self-love as integrity

Although Kierkegaard has often been criticized for denigrating "self-love," an appreciation of Kierkegaard within a defense of self-love is unsurprising. I have elsewhere defended Kierkegaard against the charge of denigrating "self-love."[1] There is a significant commonality between Frankfurt and Kierkegaard on the question of the validity and importance of self-love, but within this general commonality, there is at least one important difference (which I will touch upon briefly)—it concerns the notion of "integrity" of will.

One could argue that Frankfurt and Kierkegaard are similar insofar as both affirm the validity and importance of self-love: both see the need to encourage self-love[2]; both posit a crucial distinction between proper self-love and improper self-love[3]; both refer to the implicit commendation of self-love found in the commandment to love the neighbor[4]; and both see proper self-love as a form of faithfulness to one's self.[5] Frankfurt suggests that "the divine command to love others as we love ourselves might even be taken to convey a positive recommendation of self-love as an especially helpful paradigm—a model or ideal, by which we ought seriously to guide ourselves in the conduct of our practical lives" (RL, 77). Moreover, there is, for Frankfurt, a proper kind of self-love and an improper kind: self-love is not "self-indulgence" (RL, 78). Kierkegaard would agree with both claims. What, then, is proper self-love? On Frankfurt's terms, "self-love consists … in the purity of a wholehearted will" (RL, 96). Self-love is "desirable and important" because being "volitionally wholehearted," "enjoying the inner harmony of an undivided will is tantamount to possessing a fundamental kind of freedom"; a person loves himself insofar as he is "free in loving what he loves" (RL, 97). Frankfurt continues: "Loving ourselves is desirable and important for us because it is the same thing, more or less, as being satisfied with ourselves"; self-love is the "condition in which we willingly accept and endorse our own volitional identity … [and] are content with the final goals and the loving by which our will is most penetratingly defined" (RL, 97). This discussion of the value of a unified will includes Frankfurt's reference to

Kierkegaard's writing, "Purity of Heart," and his conclusion that Kierkegaard "intended to convey" an affirmation of the value of "wholeheartedness," the "integrity" of the will (RL, 95–96).

If Frankfurt thinks that he and Kierkegaard share an understanding of integrity, however, he is mistaken. What is most provocative about Frankfurt's defense of self-love is that it ends up arguing that genuine self-love is compatible with loving "what is bad, or what is evil" (RL, 98), and here Kierkegaard would disagree. On Frankfurt's view, "love is not necessarily a response grounded in awareness of the inherent value of its object"; a perception of something's value is "not at all an indispensable *formative* or *grounding* condition of the love" (RL, 38). "Rather," he continues, "what we love necessarily *acquires* value for us *because* we love it" (RL, 39). You might say that Frankfurt's proposes an account of love "without why" as the medieval mystics have put it. He concludes that "love need not be grounded in any judgment or perception concerning the value of its object" (RL, 67).[6] Frankfurt explains that although such judgments or perceptions may "arouse" love, "appreciating the value of an object is not an essential condition for loving it" (RL, 67). Elsewhere Frankfurt writes that love is "not equivalent to or entailed by any judgment or appreciation of the inherent value of its object" (NVL, 129). That is, "the value of what [a person] loves is irrelevant to the question of whether he is wholehearted in loving it" and "whatever the value and importance of self-love, it does not guarantee even a minimal rectitude" because "the function of love is not to make people good" (RL, 98–99). Although Frankfurt is right in noting something valuable in Kierkegaard's thought for his defense of self-love—namely, Kierkegaard's appreciation of the importance of the "how" of willing, that is integrity and wholeheartedness in willing—there is a chasm between Frankfurt and Kierkegaard on the question of the relevance of the content and the value of the object of love.[7] Frankfurt's claim may well be true of Kierkegaard's view of God's love, since God's love gives things their value, but, for Kierkegaard, normative human love is love of the good. For this reason, it is misleading to present Kierkegaard as an ally on this matter.

II. A matter of volition

The apparent dilemma

A central element in Frankfurt's various discussions of love is his constant reference to "volition," and the claim that love is "volitional" is found in various forms in *The Reasons of Love*. It is found in his explicit insistence that "the heart of the matter is neither affective nor cognitive"—"it is volitional" (RL, 42). Here he is repeating a formulation that has long been part of his understanding of love: it is found at least ten years earlier in his essay "Autonomy, Necessity, and Love," where he discusses love as a "species of caring about things," concluding that "the heart of love … is neither affective nor cognitive. It is volitional" (NVL, 129). Elaborating this stark contrast, he writes that love has "less to do with what a person believes, or with how he feels, than with a configuration of the will" (RL, 43); love has to do with our "volitional configurations" (RL, 95).

Yet in apparent contrast to both a common sense notion and an ordinary philosophical notion of "volitional,"[8] Frankfurt goes on to say that "what we love is not up to us" (RL, 49). He insists that "it is a necessary feature of love that it is not under our direct and immediate voluntary control" (RL, 44). Frankfurt does not mean by this merely to exclude "direct and immediate" voluntary control, since he later concludes that "it is by these *nonvoluntary* tendencies and responses of our will that love is constituted and that loving moves us" (RL, 50, my emphasis). He points to cases (presumably not cases of loving) where "a person may discover that he cannot affect whether or how much he cares about [some things] merely by his own decision" for "the issue is not up to him at all" (RL, 44). In such cases, there is "no choice"; "we are subject to a necessity that forcefully constrains the will and that we cannot elude merely by choosing or deciding to do so" (RL, 45); such cases of "volitional necessity" illustrate "a limitation of the will" (RL, 46).[9] Frankfurt goes on to link loving with such "volitional necessity" when he writes that "loving is circumscribed by a necessity of that kind" in that "what we love and what we fail to love is not up to us" (RL, 46). It seems in order to ask how something that is "not up to us" is appropriately called "volitional"? What does it mean to say love is "volitional" if one then goes on to claim that love is a matter of "nonvoluntary tendencies" (RL, 50), of being "bound to final ends by more than adventitious impulse or a deliberate willful choice" (RL, 55) and that it is "impossible to exercise control over the formation of beliefs and our will" (RL, 66). In particular, what does it mean to say that love is volitional if "logic and love preempt the guidance of our cognitive and volitional activity" (RL, 66)? Thus, within *The Reasons of Love* there is an (at least apparent) contradiction between an action being "volitional" and yet "not up to us" between being "volitional" and yet "nonvoluntary," between being "volitional" and yet something we "cannot muster the will to do" (RL, 46).[10]

This (at least apparent) contradiction is found in more detail (even exacerbated) in his earlier essay, "Autonomy, Necessity, and Love." There, in defending his claim that love is "volitional" rather than cognitive or affective

(NVL, 129), Frankfurt begins with some claims about actions in general. Of actions that "we *must* perform" it can be said that there is "no choice," "no real alternatives to performing them," but at the same time we correctly say that they are "not coerced" "nor compelled"; indeed, "the actions are wholly voluntary" (NVL, 129). Yet he goes on to extend this formal possibility of "no choice" to love: "love is not a matter of choice" because "the unconditional importance to the lover of what he loves is not a voluntary matter ... In this respect, he is not free ... [the] will of the lover is rigorously constrained" (NVL, 135). Yet he has just allowed that even in cases when there is "no choice" for us, the actions can be "wholly voluntary" (NVL, 129). He later says that "since love is itself a configuration of the will, it cannot be true of a person who does genuinely love something that his love is entirely involuntary" (NVL, 137).

If we put the two discussions of love together, we end up in the peculiar position of having Frankfurt's claim that "love is volitional" mean (1) that love is "wholly voluntary" (NVL, 129) or at least *not* "entirely involuntary" (NVL, 137), yet (2) love is "nonvoluntary" (RL, 50) in that we cannot choose what we care about. In other words, Frankfurt ends up claiming that love is "volitional" but not "voluntary," *and* that love is "voluntary" yet "not up to us." He claims both that love is "volitional" *because* it "preempts the guidance of our ... volitional activity" (RL, 66) and that love is "volitional" *and yet* "love constrains the will" (NVL, 141). All of this is understandably confusing even to a sympathetic reader.

What is at stake for Frankfurt?

To determine why he calls love both "voluntary" and "nonvoluntary" requires figuring out more clearly what is meant by a "volitional necessity." What is at stake for Frankfurt? Why is he forced into these contortions? In part the answer is that his agenda (including its available contrasts) is set by Kant, even though he is criticizing Kant. In addition to Kantian hypothetical imperatives (the necessities of prudence), and the Kantian categorical imperative (the necessity of duty), Frankfurt wants to make room for the "*necessities of love*" (NVL, 129), which he considers "unconditional" "categorical" imperatives not done out of duty: "the dictates of love, like the requirements of the moral law, enjoy an unconditional authority" and there are "categorical requirements both of duty and of love" (NVL, 141). The requirements or constraints at issue are "not logically necessary" (NVL, 130),[11] and his goal is to show that the necessities commanded by love do not constitute heteronomy. His defense of love is a defense of autonomy under the conditions of love. Just as Kant emphasized that autonomy requires freedom,

Frankfurt emphasizes that freedom "requires necessity" (NVL, 131). Perhaps his project is best construed as an attempt to deconstruct Kant's opposition between heteronomy and autonomy in the light of Kant's recognition that freedom requires necessity.[12] Moreover, Frankfurt wants the necessities of love to be just as authoritative as the demands of morality.

The question is how to reconcile the freedom of love with the "necessities of love."[13] Frankfurt poses the question explicitly several times: "How could we claim convincingly to cherish freedom and at the same time welcome a condition that entails submission to necessity?" (RL, 64); "How can it be that we find ourselves to have been strengthened, and to have been made somehow less confined or limited, by being deprived of choice?" (RL, 65). What is at stake for Frankfurt is that love can be autonomous even while it binds in certain ways, that love can be both free and demanding (or commanding).

Now, I have no problem allowing that love involves both freedom and necessity, and that love can be both liberating and constraining. As I will soon show, Kierkegaard agrees. However, I find myself troubled by Frankfurt's use of the phrase "love is volitional." My first reservation is that Frankfurt's appeal to the volitional is misleading because it calls to mind a volitional position like that proposed repeatedly by Robert C. Solomon. In his attempt to dispel the "myth of the passions" as passive, Solomon was led into the equally untenable position that love was a "decision."[14] In his attempt to counter the dangers of thinking that love is something we "fall" into, Solomon stressed that loving is a "decision" or "choice" we make. Although Frankfurt rejects the view that caring is a decision or choice that we make,[15] the language of "volition" quite naturally predisposes the reader to think along those lines; that is, the language of "volition" used by Frankfurt works against his own aims. Why then does he use it? Is there a better alternative? My second reservation is that while it might seem easy to see why one would want to speak of love as "volitional" in order to address the concern that love is a matter of freedom, it is not easy to see why one would want to link "volitional" with love's "necessities." To see why he does this, we need to make some clarifications that Frankfurt himself does not make in *The Reasons of Love*.

Diagnosis of ambiguity

I propose that there is an important ambiguity in Frankfurt's presentation of his account of love—namely, that his repeated use of the phrase "the heart of the matter [of love] is volitional"[16] is used to cover two quite different things. Once they are distinguished, it becomes clearer that what is at stake for Frankfurt does not depend on calling love "volitional."

Frankfurt first sets out his position boldly as follows: "As in other modes of caring, the heart of the matter is neither affective nor cognitive. It is volitional" (RL, 42). It seems natural to read this as a claim about the source or constitution of love—that is, love arises, not affectively, not cognitively, but by volition. In fact, Frankfurt soon reinforces the notion that we are to think about the origin of love by introducing and repeating the theme that "what we love and what we fail to love is not up to us" (RL, 46), "what we love is not up to us" (RL, 49). These claims are most plausibly read as claims how love is brought (or not brought) about, and it is natural to think that the claim that love is volitional is part of this same discussion. That is, there is no indication that this is a different context of discussion and the reader is taken aback by the conjunction of the claims that love is "volitional" and that "what we love and what we fail to love is not up to us."

The problem is that it seems natural to read the claim about volition as having to do with the source of love, but this is precisely what Frankfurt denies—he insists that we do not come to love by choice or volition. Indeed, Frankfurt insightfully describes how we come to love something or someone in terms that are decidedly not volitional—on Frankfurt's own account our particular loves are a function of concern, interest, captivation, and engagement that we cannot simply choose or reject. He writes of our love being "aroused" (RL, 67) and of "being captivated by our beloved" (RL, 65).[17] In affirming captivation, arousal, and engaged concern, he is excluding the idea that love's origin is volitional in either a common sense notion or and ordinary philosophical notion of "volitional." The language of "captivation" and "arousal" that Frankfurt himself uses suggests that what is at issue is not best construed as volitional. Frankfurt's appeal to the term "volitional" even while he speaks of the source of love as nonvolitional obscures his own insight. In the context of the *source or origin of love*, love is decidedly not a matter of the volitional—indeed, it is precisely Frankfurt's message that we cannot decide what we care about or love.

Why, then, does Frankfurt use the term "volitional"; in what sense is "volitional" relevant to the phenomenon of loving? Frankfurt speaks of love in terms of a second context of discussion—namely, that love is "volitional" insofar as our love binds us or guides us our practice. This insight is found in his claims that "Loving something has less to do with what a person believes, or with how he feels, than with a configuration of the will that consists in a practical concern for what is good for the beloved," and that "This volitional configuration shapes the dispositions and conduct of the lover with respect to what he loves, by guiding him in the design and ordering of his relevant purposes and priorities" (RL, 42–43). In this context of discussion, but only in this context, does the talk of love as "volitional" make any sense: that is, love is a matter of the "practical"—a matter of doing rather than feeling or knowing; love does not constrain our feelings or our judgments, but rather our willing. In this context we are no longer talking about the source of loving (how we come to love someone or something)—but rather about the *entailments*[18] of loving or the practical expression of loving (the necessities that bind us or guide us when we love). Frankfurt's discussion, unfortunately, does not distinguish between these two different contexts.

In various passages Frankfurt commingles these two contexts of discussion—origin and entailments—without calling attention to their difference. The following claim is a good example of the way in which reference to love's origin is conflated with reference to love's entailments:

> *What we love is not up to us.* We cannot help it that the direction of our practical reasoning is in fact *governed by the specific final ends* that our love has defined for us. We cannot fairly be charged with reprehensible arbitrariness, nor with a willful or negligent lack of objectivity, since *these things are not under our immediate control at all*. (RL, 49, my emphasis)

First, the fact that "what we love is not up to us," like "the fact that we cannot help loving" (RL, 65–66), is a claim that bears on *how love arises* in us. Here the term "volitional" is misleading, at best, and inaccurate, at worst—one is forced to appeal to it simply because of the limits of an anthropological structure where the only options are feeling, knowing, and volition. Second, the fact that the "direction of our practical reasoning" is "governed by the specific final ends that our love has defined for us" bears on love's *entailments*. To end this passage with the claim that "these things are not under our immediate control at all" makes it easy to ignore *the difference* between the way in which *what* or *that* we love is not up to us and the way in which *how* we love is not up to us.

He elides the two contexts when he writes that "We are certainly not free to decide 'at our liking' *what to love* or *what love requires of us*" (NVL, 136, my emphasis). Similarly, to say that love is a "configuration of the will" (RL, 43, 87) is ambiguous as to whether it is a claim about how we come to love something or how love guides the will when we do love. This is true as well of his claim that "[finally], loving entails constraints upon the will. It is not simply up to us what we love and what we do not love. Love is not a matter of choice but is determined by conditions that are outside our immediate voluntary control" (RL, 80). In sum, when Frankfurt elaborates "volitional" in terms of both the way that caring constitutes the "more or less stable motivational structure that shapes [one's] preferences and that guides and limits his conduct" (NVL, 129) *and* the way in which what we love is "not up to us," he muddies the waters. Frankfurt's emphasis on what love "entails" constitutes his way of highlighting the "necessities of love." Although it seems counterintuitive to connect the term "volitional" with the "necessities of love" and the fact that love "constrains" our will, this is precisely Frankfurt's point. Frankfurt does not see the term "volitional" in tension with the fact of the *constraint* of the will because he is in this context more concerned with the constraint of the "will" than with the "constraint" of the will. Love is volitional *because* it involves a *practical* constraint, not just constraint as such. The context in which the use of the term "volitional" makes sense is simply the context in which love is seen as a matter of *practical* expression.

The Kierkegaardian challenge

Once we have located the precise context (of *entailments* of love) in which Frankfurt means that love is volitional, distinguishing it from the context of the *source* of love (where the attribution of volitional is misleading at best or inaccurate at worst), it is worth reconsidering how Frankfurt treats the question of the origin of loving. He has used the language of "arousal" and the language of "captivation," but his tripartite anthropology limits him to calling these either affective or cognitive or volitional. So which is it to be? Both Frankfurt and Kierkegaard agree that love is not a matter of cognition; moreover, both Frankfurt and Kierkegaard agree that love is not a matter of "feeling."

Yet Kierkegaard does not in the end appeal to the claim that love is volitional. Given their commonalities, I find their difference on this point intriguing.

I want to suggest that Kierkegaard's position on the volitional dimension of love is actually more nuanced than Frankfurt's. In part, this is because Frankfurt's rejection of the view that love is a matter of feeling leads him to reject the category of "affect" altogether; that is, Frankfurt's tripartite division limits "affect" to how someone "feels" (RL, 43). Kierkegaard has a broader view of the "affective" dimension of life and employs a category not available on Frankfurt's model—namely, the category of "passion" (*Lidenskab*).[19] Moreover, Kierkegaard does not appeal to the more restrictive notion of "volition," but rather has a broad sense of what willing is and of its relation to passion or affect.

How do they fare with respect to the two contexts (origin and entailments of love)? Kierkegaard and Frankfurt are in agreement about the origin of love insofar as they agree that what we love is not something we deliberately choose, but is a function of the things that engage and captivate us; for both, being concerned or engaged is not something we can deliberately choose or deliberately reject. Moreover, they are in agreement that love is a matter of practice (or the practical): when we love, we are bound to certain attitudes or actions; love is a matter of doing, not feeling or judging. They are in agreement that loving *guides our will*, that in loving we are *moved to will* in certain ways and not others. However, to use the term "volitional" as if it covers both of these contexts of discussion (as Frankfurt does) is misleading, and Frankfurt obscures his own best insights by its indiscriminate use.

In this respect, Kierkegaard's account of love is less confusing. That is, when he claims that loving is a matter of a decisive engagement or captivation that guides our will, he is distinguishing the *origin* from the *entailments*, while calling neither of them "volitional." He speaks of the origin of love in the idiom of "passion"—as something that is neither simply passive nor simply active; both Climacan works, *Philosophical Fragments* and the *Concluding Unscientific Postscript*, elaborate the hybrid of passionate engagement, passionate interestedness, and passionate captivation. Kierkegaard speaks in *Works of Love* and some of the upbuilding discourses of the different topic of the entailments of love in terms of the way in which it leads us to different volitional choices or "fruits."

Levels of willing

It is not enough, however, just to distinguish between the two contexts. We also need to distinguish between "will" and "volition." Frankfurt's attempt to guarantee the autonomous character of love—that love is not a heteronomous imposition because "the constraint operates from within our own will itself" (RL, 46)—depends on this crucial distinction that is not made explicit in *The Reasons of Love*. Some of his other essays provide resources for more clarification.

In "The Importance of What We Care About," for example, Frankfurt implies that there are different levels or senses of "will" at work when he explains that in the case of "volitional necessity" one does not

> accede to the constraining force because he lacks sufficient strength of will to defeat it. He accedes to it because he is *unwilling* to oppose it and because, furthermore, his unwillingness is *itself* something which he is unwilling to alter … In the case of the person constrained by volitional necessity, there is also something which he cannot do but only because *he does not really want to do it.* (IWC, 87, final emphasis is mine)

Frankfurt adds that volitional necessity is "to a certain extent self-imposed" in that "it is generated when someone requires himself to avoid being guided in what he does by any forces other than those by which he *most deeply wants to be guided*" (IWC, 87, my emphasis). It seems clear that different levels of will or wanting are being referred to in these passages. Moreover, while Frankfurt's claim that "a person's will is that by which he moves himself" (IWC, 84) is less than illuminating, he appeals to an important distinction when he suggests that what someone cares about "is far more germane to the character of his will than the decisions or choices he makes"; moreover, he refers to the "exaggerated significance … sometimes ascribed to decisions, as well as to choices and to other similar 'acts of will'" in contrast to what one's will "truly *is*" (IWC, 84).

This distinction between "the character of the will" and volitions is also found in Frankfurt's discussion in "Autonomy, Necessity, and Love." Agreeing with Kant that "a person acts autonomously only when his volitions derive from the essential character of his will," he notes that "the same relation *between volition and will* holds when a person is acting out of love" (NVL, 132, my emphasis). This "essential character of his will" is "what he himself wants his will to be"—"the essential nature of a person" (NVL, 137, 138). He insists that "changes in the will … are not under our deliberate volitional control" and that love is *not* "a matter of free choice" because "as far as what he loves is concerned, he cannot directly *affect his will* by *a mere act of will*" (NVL, 136, my emphasis). We can construe this distinction as one between "ultimate will" (the foundational character of our will) and the choices, volitions, or acts of our "proximate will."

Such a contrast between "ultimate (foundational) will" and "proximate will (choice)" is embedded in Frankfurt's agreement with Kant that autonomy is guaranteed "only when [one's] volitions derive from the essential character of [one's] will" (NVL, 132). The constraint of our essential will on our volitions does not constitute heteronomy; to be constrained in this way by "our own will itself" (RL, 46) is liberating. If the binding is to remain nonheteronomous, we need this crucial distinction between levels or senses of will, or between "will" and "volition," rather than the monolithic term "volitional."

Our "will" is not gained volitionally, not chosen by us: "the formation of a person's will is most fundamentally a matter of his coming to care about certain things, and of his coming to care about some of them more than about others" (IWC, 91), and it is this "essential will" that normatively constrains our particular decisions or choice. Frankfurt rightly notes that the paradox is that "even if volitional necessity is self-imposed there must be some respect in which it is imposed or maintained involuntarily"; that is, "it must be an essential feature of volitional necessity that it is imposed upon a person involuntarily. Otherwise it will be impossible to account for the fact that the person cannot extricate himself from it merely at will" (IWC, 88). The only way to account for this paradox is to distinguish first-order volition from "essential" will.

This distinction between "the character of [one's] will" and one's "decisions or choices" is also necessary in order to make sense of the notion of "the freedom of the will" which Frankfurt elaborates in the essay, "The Freedom of the Will." His distinction between "first-order desires" and "second-order desires" (IWC, 12)[20] is followed by a distinction between first-order and second-order volitions: when a person "wants a certain desire to be his will," we have a case of a "second-order volition" (IWC, 16). He connects freedom of the will to such second-order volitions: "it is only because a person has volitions of the second order that he is capable both of enjoying and of lacking freedom of the will" (IWC, 19).[21] Although Frankfurt initially proposes that one can "identify an agent's will" with his effective first-order desires (IWC, 14), another sense of will emerges in the notion of second-order volitions: he contrasts the will of effective first-order volitions with "freedom of the will" (the situation of an agent whose will is free). It seems clear that when Frankfurt writes that "conformity of his will to his second-order volitions" is equal to exercising "freedom of the will" (IWC, 20), he is appealing to two notions of the "will" (or contrasting "will" and "volition"). We need to add such a clarification to the discussion in *The Reasons of Love*.

The "necessities of love"

That love constrains the will means, for Frankfurt, that love involves necessities of a sort or imposes constraints of a sort (though clearly not logical necessities). It is worth noting that there are at least two different kinds of necessity at work in Frankfurt's discussion: sometimes the necessities of love are seen as contingently threatening and at other times they are seen as necessarily enriching. At times, Frankfurt warns that love entails commitments that may harm us:

> Our lack of immediate voluntary control over our loving is a particular source of danger to us. The fact that we cannot directly and freely determine what we love and what we do not love, simply by making choices and decisions of our own, means that we are often susceptible to being more or less helplessly driven by the necessities that love entails … Love may engage us in volitional commitments from which we are unable to withdraw and through which our interests may be severely harmed. (RL, 63)

At other times, he suggests that love's "commanding necessity neither entails for us any sense of impotence or restriction" (RL, 64). And even more strongly, he suggests that "the constraint itself contributes significantly to the value for us of loving" and that "the necessities with which love binds the will are themselves liberating" (RL, 64).

The liberating aspect of love's necessities is, I think, nicely captured in the Kierkegaardian commitment to the idea that self-love seeks its own downfall. That Kierkegaard and Frankfurt are in agreement that loving can both bind us and liberate us is shown by looking at Climacus's account of the "paradox of self-love" in Kierkegaard's *Philosophical Fragments*. Illustrating the way in which paradox is both the "torment" and the "incentive" of the passion of thought, Climacus notes that "the understanding cannot understand it [the paradox], and merely detects that it will likely be its downfall. To that extent, the understanding has strong objections to it; and yet, on the other hand, in its paradoxical passion the understanding does indeed will its own downfall."[22] He turns to the "condition of erotic love [*Elskov*]" as an example of paradoxical passion. He explains: "Self-love lies at the basis of love [*Kjaerlighed*], but at its peak its paradoxical passion wills its own downfall. Erotic love also wills this, and therefore these two forces are in mutual understanding in the moment of passion, and this passion is precisely erotic love. Why, then, should the lover not be able to think this, even though the person who in self-love shrinks from erotic love can neither comprehend it nor dare to venture it, since it is indeed his downfall. So it is with the passion of erotic love. To be sure, self-love has foundered, but nevertheless it is not annihilated but is taken captive and is erotic love's *spolia opima* [spoils of war]."[23]

In other words, self-love moves outward for what is good for us—erotic enjoyment of an other—but finds that in discovering what is good for itself it also thereby discovers that which limits it. The movement of self-love is outward to love of another, but in love of another we find the "torment" of self-love, the subordination to another. Self-love wants yet fears erotic love. At some level—although not as a conscious want, and not as an intention—we want this downfall. To say that passion seeks its own downfall is to say that it is in itself a good to desire; desiring is itself a good even when it leads to its downfall that simultaneously affirms it. Love is free because it desires (or wills) at some level the downfall of being bound, which it does not desire (or will) at another level.

The phenomenon described by Climacus highlights the crucial distinction between levels of willing, contrasting will as foundational with volition as choice. Although Frankfurt explicitly makes the categorical contrast between first-order desires/volitions and second-order desires/volitions in earlier work, this contrast is lacking in *The Reasons of Love*.

Love as need

There is yet another respect in which it is fruitful to consider Kierkegaard and Frankfurt in tandem—namely, the dimension of love as "need." The concept of a "need" is particularly interesting because, on the one hand, it takes the emphasis away from the volitional—we do not choose our needs—and on the other hand, it shows a way of understanding how something not volitional can avoid being construed as heteronomously imposed on us.

Frankfurt writes: "Loving itself is important to us. Quite apart from our particular interest in the various things that we love, we have a more generic and an even more fundamental interest in loving as such" (RL, 51). The need to "*have* final ends" (RL, 58) in order to avoid a pointless and unsatisfying life (RL, 52–53) constitutes "the importance to us of loving" (RL, 59). Thus, two of Frankfurt's explicit commitments—namely, the fact "that we cannot help loving" (RL, 65–66) and the "importance of the activity of caring as such" (IWC, 93)—support the notion of loving as a need.[24]

Kierkegaard is explicit that loving is a need; indeed, I have argued elsewhere that the theme of need pervades *Works of Love* in various ways.[25] In the opening prayer, God is called to witness that "no work can be pleasing unless it is a work of love: sincere in self-renunciation, *a need in love itself*" (my emphasis).[26] It is interesting to note that the word Kierkegaard uses to speak of this "need" is the strong Danish word *Trang*–namely, a kind of passionate craving, a dynamic impulse coming from within and reaching out. The need to love is generated by positive passion, rather than hardship that can be remedied. In other words, in this sense of the need of love it is presence, rather than absence, that is the motivation. Not only are we given love by God, and thus empowered to love, but in addition there is a need in love *to express itself*: Kierkegaard insists that "to be able to be known by its fruits is a need in love" (WL, 10). Thus, in addition to the obvious need humans have to *be loved*,[27] Kierkegaard insists on love's need to express itself—that is, the human need to love, whose heart is doing rather than feeling. In the Preface, Kierkegaard says: "They are *Christian deliberations*, therefore not about *love* but about *works of love*" (WL, 3). Presumably, it is distinctively Christian to be concerned with love in action, expressed in works; moreover, it is about "works of love" that we need to be challenged. As he notes later in a journal comment, "Christ's love was not intense feeling, a full heart, etc.; it was rather the work of love, which is his life."[28] Kierkegaard's tie between "need" and "fruits" connects "need" with the practical ramifications of love in a way that fits nicely with Frankfurt's emphasis.

Kierkegaard compares the need to love to the richness of the poet who has a need to write—"we are saying the utmost when we say of the poet,

'He has a need to write'; of the orator, 'He has a need to speak'; and of the young woman, 'She has a need to love'" (WL, 10). He insists that such a need "signifies the greatest riches!" (WL, 10)—indeed, "the expression of the greatest riches is to have a need; therefore, that it is a need in the free person is indeed the true expression of freedom" (WL, 38). In this way he shows that he assumes (as does Frankfurt) that the demands of love are enriching and liberating. That "love in a human being is a need, is the expression of riches" (WL, 67) and that "the one in whom love is a need certainly feels free in his love" (WL, 38) are commitments that Kierkegaard and Frankfurt share.

The active force of such need is illustrated by Kierkegaard's parallel with a plant's need to express its life; to insist on making love unrecognizable is as much against nature "as if the plant, which sensed the exuberant life and blessing within it, did not dare let it become recognizable and were to keep it to itself as if the blessing were a curse, keep it, alas, as a secret in its inexplicable withering!" (WL, 11). In sum, love needs to express itself or it withers and dies. The analogy with the plant suggests that in all these cases it is love's presence that presses forward, and this is the same message found in his later claim that "love is a need, the deepest need, *in the person in whom there is love* for the neighbor" (WL, 67, my emphasis). In one of his Christian discourses, Kierkegaard implies that the need in love to express itself is a need that is not satisfied in any ordinary way—it does not get filled so that we can stop seeking to love.[29] Interestingly, Frankfurt's claim that "the function of love is not to make people good" (RL, 99) serves to distinguish him from Kierkegaard (insofar as it assumes the irrelevance of the value of the object of love), but it also serves to point to an important locus of agreement—namely, that love is not instrumental.

Finally, Kierkegaard suggests that the real paradoxicality of a commandment to love is found in the fact that "to love people is the only thing worth living for, and without this love you are not really living" (WL, 375). It is paradoxical that we should require a commandment at all, given the strength of our need to love.

The category of "need" is, in the end, double-edged. We do not choose our needs; they orient our fundamental will. But lest nonvolitional seem to entail heteronomy, it is important to note that deep human needs, like the need to love, are liberating even while they are constraining.

III. Conclusion

Put generally, my conclusion is that whereas in other texts Frankfurt concedes that "the fact that someone cares about a certain thing is constituted by a complex set of cognitive, affective, and volitional dispositions and states,"

(IWC, 85), in *The Reasons of Love* he reduces (and thereby misrepresents) that complexity in two ways: by explicitly rejecting the relevance of affective responses and by emphasizing the volitional without making the requisite clarifying distinctions.

More specifically, I have suggested in the preceding that the way Frankfurt posits the possible alternatives in *The Reasons of Love* seems unnecessarily to restrict the possibilities. That is, Frankfurt's dichotomy between affect and volition is a false one: false because he limits "affect" to feeling, and false because "volition" does not represent what is at stake for him. What are lacking are a broader notion of affect, one that includes passion's engagement and interest, and a broader notion of will as engaging. When he equates affect with feeling, Frankfurt excludes the alternative of passionate engagement. On the contrary, Kierkegaard's attention to passion and imagination contribute to elucidating the complex phenomena we experience, viz. captivation and love's necessities, far more than does the language of volition.

In addition, I have argued that with respect to Frankfurt's claim in *The Reasons of Love* that love is "volitional," it is important to distinguish between contexts more clearly than he does. There are *two contexts* in which it does *not* make sense to speak of love as "volitional" because the point is that love is not under our control: namely, the context of the origin of love, out of our control, free, but not necessary; and the context of the entailments of love, love's necessities as out of our control, free but necessary. It is important to note that we cannot speak identically about both contexts since the point about the origin of love is *not* that it is necessary.

There is a *third context* in which it *does* make sense to speak of love as "volitional": namely, the context of the practical expression of love, that is, we are bound to a "doing." This context, in which talk of volitional is relevant, gets confusingly allied by Frankfurt with the context of love's necessities because it is these necessities that get expressed *practically* as opposed to affectively or cognitively; but these are necessities and so not volitional.

There is finally a *fourth context* in which it makes sense to speak of love as volitional if we want to highlight the fact that love's necessities are not heteronomously imposed on us.

In sum, Frankfurt's position is that (1) love is not intellectual or affective in either its source or entailments; (2) rather than being heteronomous, love is free in its entailments; and (3) love is practically constraining—the necessities of love guide our practice. The first is only plausibly seen as a reason for calling love "volitional" if one has an unduly limited choice of options. The third, which might plausibly be seen as a reason for calling love "volitional," is far outweighed by Frankfurt's overwhelming message that love is not under our control. Frankfurt wants to claim that love is a matter of *will* (rather than feeling or cognition) *as nonvolitional* engagement (caring, captivation). He wants to reject the claim that coming to love is a matter of deliberate or self-conscious volition, that is, it is not up to us. He also wants to reject the claim that the expression of love is a matter of deliberate or self-conscious volition, that is, love's necessities bind us.

Kierkegaard would agree that coming to love someone or something is not under our control, as well as that there are constraints on the will that are generated by the character of the will whose formation is not up to us. He is not, however, forced to speak of love as volitional precisely because he has a greater range of options. Kierkegaard would also agree that when we follow love's commands we are not under a heteronomous imposition and that love should be expressed in doing rather than in feelings or judgments— but neither of these truths is best construed under the general rubric of the volitional. The former truth is found in a long tradition of thinkers who distinguish the General Will from the particular will, or Right Reason from particular reason, or *Wille* from *Willkür*, or will from volition. The latter truth is found in the biblical injunction so emphasized by Kierkegaard—that love be recognizable by its fruits.

Notes

1   See M. Jamie Ferreira, *Love's Grateful Striving*, 31–36, 134–35.

2   Frankfurt defends the view that "coming to love oneself is the deepest and most essential—and by no means the most readily attainable— achievement of a serious and successful life" (RL, 68); Kierkegaard speaks compassionately about those who do not love themselves enough: he wants to "teach them to love themselves" (WL, 23).

3   Frankfurt does this when he suggests that "self-indulgence" is not proper self-love, but rather "something else entirely" (RL, 78) and that love is "caring selflessly about the well-being of another" (RL, 61). Kierkegaard distinguishes between "proper self-love" (WL, 18) and "selfish self-love" (WL, 151).

4   Frankfurt asks: "are we not told by an Author whose moral authority compares quite favorably to Kant's that we should love our neighbors as we love ourselves?" (RL, 77) and Kierkegaard writes that the "as yourself" is a "phrase that does not want to teach a person that he is not to love himself but rather wants to teach him proper self-love" (WL, 18).

5   Frankfurt insists that "self-love consists in the purity of a wholehearted will" such that a person is "not at odds with himself" (RL, 96, 97); in Kierkegaard's "Purity of Heart is to Will One Thing," he argued that a "transfigured one" is in "unity with oneself," not "double-minded ... divided in himself" (UDVS, 19, 27).

6   "Appreciating the value of an object is not an essential condition for loving it," although such judgments or perceptions may "arouse love" (RL, 67).

7   There is, of course, more to be said on Frankfurt's behalf because he often refers to the fact that we may love in ways that are harmful to us, so he is not attempting to preclude the relevance of whether something is "suitable or worthy as an ideal or as an object of love" nor to exclude the possibility of "significant criticism" or "principles of discrimination" (IWC, 91).

8   The first Webster's dictionary definition of "volition" is "the act of willing or choosing"; even the *Cambridge Dictionary of Philosophy* defines "volition" as "a mental event involved with the initiation of action."

9   However, he later says that such a "commanding necessity" does not entail "any sense of impotence or restriction" (RL, 64).

10 Loving (or nonloving) is an example of something we "cannot muster the will" to do; the constraint is not imposed on us—we are constrained "by our own will" (RL, 46).

11 He elsewhere says that such necessity is "not a cognitive necessity" that limits "the possibilities of coherent thought"; "someone who is bound by volitional necessity is unable to form a determined and effective intention—regardless of what motives and reasons he may have for doing so—to perform (or to refrain from performing) the action that is at issue" (RL, 45–56).

12 But note that he says that love is not voluntary and the agent is "not free" (NVL, 135).

13 An alternative way of expressing this question is to ask "Under what conditions is a constrained will free?"

14 Robert C. Solomon, *About Love*, 127–29; see also *The Passions*.

15 He notes that "the fact that a person decides to care about something cannot be tantamount to his caring about it" (IWC, 84).

16 The ambiguity is also found in phrases like "love has to do with X more than Y."

17 The language of captivation is also found in "The Importance of What We Care About": the "object captivates him" (IWC, 89).

18 I take up Frankfurt's own term: he refers to the "necessities that love entails" (RL, 63); he insists that "loving entails constraints upon the will" (RL, 80), that "love entails a concern for what the beloved loves" (RL, 88), and that "love entails that the lover has certain volitional attitudes" (NVL, 138).

19 Frankfurt's ambivalence about "passion" is revealed in the way his claim that there may be "ruling passions," including "the passion of love," is followed by the claim that "the passions do not really make any claims upon us at all … [their 'effectiveness'] is entirely a matter of sheer brute force" (NVL, 137).

20 For example, A wants to X (first order) versus A wants to want to X (second order).

21 He contrasts "freedom of action" with "freedom of the will" (IWC, 22).

22 PF, 47.
23 PF, 48.
24 See Frankfurt's essay "Necessity and Desire," for further discussion of "constrained volitional needs" as opposed to desires (IWC, 113).
25 See Ferreira, *Love's Grateful Striving*, 21, 26–28, 39–42.
26 WL, 4; Kierkegaard connects a lack of merit with the need of love to express itself when he continues: "and for that very reason without any claim of meritoriousness!"
27 He refers to a "need to love and be loved by an individual human being" (WL, 155).
28 LP 3 2423 (1849), 44.
29 He writes that "the need brings its nourishment along with it; what is sought is in the seeking that seeks it; faith is in the concern over not having faith; love is in the concern over not loving" (CD, 244).

10

Love as the Ultimate Ground of Practical Reason: Kierkegaard, Frankfurt, and the Conditions of Affective Experience

Rick Anthony Furtak

I

According to both Søren Kierkegaard and Harry Frankfurt, love plays a vital role at the basis of human existence. When Frankfurt argues that love makes it possible for us to engage wholeheartedly in intrinsically meaningful activity, and that it therefore ought to be regarded as "the ultimate ground of practical rationality" (RL, 56), his words echo those of Kierkegaard's treatise *Works of Love*. Here, Kierkegaard identifies love as "the source of everything" and as "the deepest ground of the spiritual life" (WL, 215). This enigmatic, "hidden" influence, as Kierkegaard calls it (WL, 8–10), is the source of certain dizzying mysteries that, Frankfurt observes, must be accounted for by any adequate moral psychology.[1] Furthermore, both Frankfurt and Kierkegaard associate love with belief: it is a "source of reasons," supplying us with grounds for action (RL, 37), and it can also play a decisive role in helping us to overcome skeptical doubt (WL, 5–6, 234). While there are obvious and significant differences between these two authors, the passages I have just cited indicate an unmistakable area of convergence. In explaining love's foundational place in human life, Kierkegaard and Frankfurt articulate a position that may not seem self-evident or even plausible to most readers. Yet, as I will attempt to show, this position is in some respects fundamentally right; and it merits consideration by a larger audience, including those who are not yet familiar with the writings of either of the two thinkers. As I expand upon their provocative suggestions, I will also rely on the work of several other philosophers who have been inspired by Pascal's statement that the heart has its reasons—for example, Max Scheler and Jean-Luc Marion.[2] My aim in the following sections is not merely to report on the views of these thinkers, but to draw upon their most important insights for the sake of defending the following interrelated claims: that love is (a) the condition of possibility for meaningful engagement with the world, (b) the basis of our affective experience, and (c) the ultimate ground of practical reason.

II

Early in *Works of Love*, Kierkegaard presents a series of images having to do with the obscure "origin" at the ground of our existence from which love flows, "along many paths," to illuminate the human world in all of its rich and intricate significance (WL, 8–13). He portrays love as an unseen source of light *and* as an unfathomable wellspring from which water streams forth. The common theme that unites his varying imagery is that love is the hidden ground of a visible reality, and what is implied by this series of metaphors is something like a transcendental argument. By virtue of our experience of "love in its manifestations" (WL, 9), we can justifiably conclude that love must be the "ground of all things" in a more profound sense (WL, 225): that is, even if we cannot empirically verify that love is the ground of life as we know it, we still have good reason to make this inference.[3] That is because love must be posited as a pervasive and foundational influence in order for what *is* apparent to us to be the way it appears. Without this basic affective disposition, we would have only a limited and indirect access to those features of the world that attract our attention and move us to respond emotionally.

Whether I am getting angry at someone who has just stained my favorite shirt, or experiencing prolonged grief after the death of a treasured friend, each of my emotions involves an awareness of someone or something that I value.[4] These valued persons, places, and things define my world of concern: they stand out prominently, while other things recede into the background. When we view the world with the heightened attention and concern that a loving disposition brings, we find that it is charged with meaning or importance. This is because such an outlook disposes us toward taking notice, and appreciating the significance, of things whose reality and value might otherwise have been invisible to us. Because "emotions pick out and focus attention on those things in the … environment that matter for the human being,"[5] an indifferent person to whom nothing matters should not be expected to notice much of what is competing for his or her attention. And is this not consistent with our experience when we are in a state of profound boredom? When we have no interest in our surroundings, we generally find that "our responsiveness to ordinary stimuli flattens," and—within the range of our potential awareness—"differences are not noticed and distinctions are not made" (RL, 54). As Marion says, boredom "renders indifferent every difference" because "that which is, if it does not receive love, is as if it were not."[6] That which we do not distinguish, because it does not matter to us, may as well not exist for us, and in a sense *it does not exist* as far as we are concerned. Now consider what this implies: if it is true that we can hardly take notice of anything that does not seem even minimally valuable or significant, then a comprehensive apathy would amount to a loss of the world, brought about by one's own disinterested withdrawal from it. The stance of "indifferent" knowledge (WL, 228–31) is one from which we may discern some things clearly enough, but there is also much that we fail to see by confining ourselves to such a standpoint. This is why we "cannot dispense with love," even as would-be knowers: as Kierkegaard claims in overtly epistemological language, we will have deceived ourselves into forfeiting everything if we do not follow the imperative to love (WL, 5–7). Just as we can be deceived by believing what is untrue, we can also be deceived by *not* believing what *is* true (WL, 5–6). And what could this mean? That some of what is truly "there to be seen" will be hidden from us if our own state of mind prevents us from taking it in. As an affective disposition, love gives us an enhanced mode of awareness; whereas one who closes himself off from love's influence, perhaps in order to become "absolutely secure against being deceived" (WL, 5), deprives himself of any significant knowledge and lives in an impoverished world of flat, meaningless things.

Most of the time, fortunately, we do not find ourselves in such an emotionally desolate place. Let us turn to the contrapositive of the statement that if we do not feel a sense of X's value then we cannot be aware of X's existence. That is: insofar as we *are* aware of anything, it must be the case that we *do* feel some sense of its value or meaning, for better or worse. Because our attention is directed by our sense of what matters, perceptual awareness is governed by a law of non-indifference. Rightly understood, knowing is based in a conscious mind with an interest in knowing certain things, not in a neutral mind pointed toward matters of indifference: "Were reality absolutely indifferent, consciousness could have no contact with it."[7] And to say that we do not feel indifferent about something is conceptually equivalent to saying that we care about it, at least to some degree. According to Frankfurt's definition, to care about anyone or anything is to view him, her, or it as meaningful or significant: "Insofar as we care about something at all, we regard it as important" (RL, 42). For someone or something to be *loved*, then, is for him, her, or it to be cared about in a specific way, namely as an end in itself. It is in the nature of loving, he adds, "that we regard its objects as having value in themselves" and as existing for their own sakes (RL, 56).[8] What moves us to take an interest in anything even minimally, then, is present in its most intense and emphatic form as unselfish love of another person for his or her own sake. Love "flows in a warm affirmation of the beloved," and "is involved in an invisible but divine task," as Ortega writes. "Think of what it is to love art or your country ... it is like recognizing and confirming at every moment that they are worthy of existence."[9] If we understand love as a mode of care, then we can locate both love and care along a continuum extending from the most slight interest—a state in which we are "not indifferent" about something, or "barely more than nonchalant" about it—all the way to love in its most pronounced forms.[10] This broader sense of the word "love" is what Marion has in mind when he claims that love "makes visible" the things of this world, which are apparent to us only insofar as we are not indifferent to them.[11] If I loved no one and cared about nothing, then the world would be deprived of its axiological salience: as Frankfurt claims, "if we loved nothing, then nothing would possess for us any definitive and inherent worth" (RL, 55). Or, in Kierkegaard's words, love "takes part with us in everything" (JP, 2:1366) such that, if "it were to be absent" even for a moment, then "everything would be confused" (WL, 301). Each of us is aware of the meaning and value of things only because love is already at work behind the scenes, allowing *what is there* to *matter*: without its influence, our experience of the world would not be anything like what it actually is.

III

This idea, extravagant as it might sound, can be situated within a reputable intellectual tradition. As many philosophers since Kant have sought to demonstrate, the nature of the objective world, as it is known by human beings, cannot be established without taking into account the structure of the human subject to whom it is disclosed.[12] Focusing on the realm of affective experience in particular, Merleau-Ponty suggests that if we try to see how any significant reality comes to exist for us through love then "we shall thereby come to understand better how things and beings can exist in general."[13] If love plays a world-disclosing role, it is because it enables us to perceive things as meaningful: by opening us up to an awareness of value, love defines the way the subject views the world.[14] In an edifying discourse called "Love Will Hide a Multitude of Sins," Kierkegaard says that "what one sees depends upon how one sees," adding that "the good" in the world will be apparent from the charitable vantage point of a loving person, whereas an "evil eye" will give us a tainted view of things (EUD, 59–60). The thread that binds together all of these remarks ought to be plain enough: since the truth about the world will vary in accordance with our affective disposition or attunement, it is all important to refine and focus our way of seeing. Things exist *for* us because they matter *to* us, and it may be that our best mode of access to their being is an unselfish love that "wants the object to be nothing other than what it is."[15] Rather than being one element among others within the horizon of human experience, love reveals itself in shaping the way the world unfolds for each of us. As Kierkegaard maintains, "it is generally true that something manifests itself to the one who loves it" (JP, 2:2299), and we are "captivated" by what is other than ourselves only when we are open to "selflessly" caring about what we love (NVL, 135), as Frankfurt says, "for its own sake" (RL, 59). He continues: "the necessity with which love binds the will puts an end to indecisiveness concerning what to care about. In being captivated by our beloved, we are liberated from the impediments to choice and action that consist either in having no final ends or in being drawn inconclusively both in one direction and in another" (RL, 65–66). Our awareness of what we love and care about orients our attention and determines our sense of reality: what is loved is felt to be real, and incontestably significant. Love thus organizes our entire world of experience, allowing what surrounds us to appear as meaningful.

The fact that love makes us aware of the significance of things does not necessarily entail that this significance is projected onto the world by our own minds. It could play the role of the aperture in a camera, opening the eye of the beholder so that what is "out there" can pour in. This would be consistent with Kierkegaard's notion of "an objectivity which takes shape in a corresponding subjectivity" (JP, 6:6360). We need not assume that value must be either totally objective *or else* "merely" subjective, as if only an absolute Good could provide an absolute standard against which we can measure our all-too-human evaluations. On either side of this opposition between a Platonic and a Sartrean view, what is neglected is the "middle term" in the equation (WL, 260)—along with the lover and the beloved, there is something that is neither you nor me that sustains the whole relation.[16] Love is what enables us to apprehend features of reality that are not of our own invention, but that would otherwise be lost on us due to our own blindness. In this way, the perception of value can depend on love, even if love does not involve the *bestowal* of value.

If love is defined as a disinterested concern for the well-being of whomever or whatever is loved, as Frankfurt defines it (see RL, 42–43), then what it means to love my neighbor—I am thinking literally of the person who lives next door—is to take an interest in her life and to value her personal flourishing as an end in itself. It means caring selflessly about her well-being and being "personally affected" by her good or bad fortune as a result (RL, 61). That is, "the lover identifies with his beloved: that is, he takes the interests of his beloved as his own," and "benefits or suffers depending upon whether those interests are or are not adequately served" (RL, 80). In Kierkegaard's work, the same point is made in this way: the "truly loving" person "loves every human being according to his distinctiveness; but 'his distinctiveness' is what for him is *his own*; that is, the loving one … loves what is the other's own" (WL, 269). So, because my neighbor's well-being is defined by *her* interests, my care for her must extend to whatever it is that *she* cares about. Just as Beatrice's love of Dante includes a passionate concern for his literary ambitions,[17] my far more limited love of my neighbor entails caring about her wish to arrive at work on time: this matters to me for no other reason except that it matters to her. Let's imagine that I see her and say hello as I head out for a morning run, and notice that she seems to be flustered: she has just discovered that her car will not start, and now she is almost late for work. Moved by her plight, I offer her a ride, even if this means that I will not have time to go running, and even though I value my morning run more than anything *I* might gain by driving my neighbor to work. In all of this, I have hardly achieved a saint-like extreme of self-denial; and yet I have transcended my own interests and gone out of my way for the sake of my neighbor's good. I care about her, "not as an instance of a type" (RL, 79–80), nor as "an indifferent thoroughfare for impersonal rational activity,"[18] but as a specific person with her own particular set of interests and concerns, and it is in terms of these that her situation makes a claim on me, to which I must now respond. This is how, by virtue of love, a person allows "the subjectivity of another" to become "a reality for himself" or herself.[19] By virtue of this process, my world is both augmented and made more complicated, as I am emotionally affected by all that impinges on the well-being of each person that I love and care about.

IV

My identity as a loving and caring being thus gives rise to "my many-sided interest in the things of this world."[20] Love takes part with us in everything, forming the heart as it flows from the heart (WL, 12), and allowing a meaningful world of concern to come to light for each person who loves. Furthermore, I must acknowledge the "same validity and dignity in every other human being,"[21] insofar as this affective power is active in each of our lives. When I take an interest in the interests of another person, I succeed to some degree in loving what is *their* own in the same way that I love what is *my* own: what I myself care about, or what lies within my world of concern. Frankfurt's use of "self-love" to refer to simply loving what one loves—as is shown by his statement that a person can only love himself "insofar as he loves other things" (RL, 85–86)—is an odd formulation, no doubt. But once we grasp what he means by *loving oneself*, we can see how his account of what it means to love the neighbor "as thyself" (RL, 77) is consistent with Kierkegaard's. Love for one's neighbor means "loving each one individually" (WL, 66–67) and affirming the existence of each human being. As Aquinas says, it means wanting the other person "to be, and to have good things."[22] And the wish for another person's life to be going well makes sense only with reference to what that person loves and cares about. If I love you, then I will be motivated to water your garden while you're away—not necessarily because I am independently convinced of its value or importance, but just because I know how much the garden matters to you, how much you care about it. This is what it means to take an interest in the interests of the other: no matter what religious significance is ascribed to unselfish love, it can be represented and appreciated without any further theological commitment.[23] Some loves transform our existence so profoundly that we can no longer conceive of how our lives might have been without them. Yet love is not operative only in such extreme, overwhelming cases; our discussion also pertains to the common experience of people acting in accordance with "what they love, what deeply matters to them," without "bringing these concerns explicitly into the foreground of deliberation."[24] From our most powerful loves and enthusiasms, to the things we care about to a moderate degree, to that which interests us only slightly, we have a spectrum in which the difference between one extreme and the other is not *whether* something is important to us but *how* significant it is. What I am suggesting is that, in the absence of love, nothing would hold *any* significance for us—there would be no such thing as affective intentionality. This, presumably, is what Frankfurt has in mind when he asserts that loving or caring "is essential to our being creatures of the kind that human beings are" (RL, 17).[25] If we did not love anything even minimally, no part of the universe would stand out and command our attention.

V

There is "a significance in things" which, as Merleau-Ponty says, "I do not constitute," and yet that can be revealed only through the structure of my subjectivity.[26] I am not drastically free to give it whatever meaning I choose, and yet to a dispassionate observer its meaning would not be realized or disclosed. My heightened awareness of those whom I love and care about enables me to appreciate things I would otherwise not have been able to see. A child who has difficulty with language and who therefore struggles in school may have creative gifts that only a loving and perceptive mother could detect, affirm, and encourage. Now, love does not have a magic power to create value that isn't there (no amount of motherly love could bring into being an aptitude or inclination that simply doesn't exist). But the gaze of the loving person who views what *is* there in the most favorable light *does* open up possibilities that had not been apparent to anyone else.[27] Through my emotional disposition, I am able to appreciate things that I would not otherwise have observed. As Kierkegaard notes, Christ did not allocate his love for Peter based on a judgment of how much Peter was "worth loving" (WL, 172–73). He might, like Frankfurt, be open to the charge of neglecting "the importance of objectivity."[28] Yet what Kierkegaard admires is that Christ's love embraced Peter as he was, with all his imperfections, with the thought that this unconditional love might perhaps help Peter to become a better person. Likewise, he claims in *Works of Love* that a true artist is someone who, "by bringing a certain something with him," is able to find *some* beauty anywhere he looks—*not* the one who is so fastidious as to be always looking in vain for "the perfect image of beauty" (WL, 158), or what might be called "in-and-for-itself beauty" (CI, 70).

Of course, what it means to find something valuable is to recognize it "as having value in its own right."[29] Yet a stronger axiological realist than Frankfurt could still maintain that human subjectivity plays a crucial role in the disclosure of value: what is *objective* should, trivially, be at least a *possible* object of knowledge for some imaginable subject. Acknowledging this does not require us to believe that there must exist one singular universal Good, such as the Platonic "in-and-for-itself good" that Kierkegaard targets for critique (CI, 71–72), upon which all of our evaluative standpoints must converge: if it did, then everyone who loves would be rationally obligated to love whatever object is most worth loving. Rather, by virtue of being finite each of us is unable to appreciate the distinctive worth of each and every person, place, activity, or ideal. It is, however, possible to appreciate more of what is good collectively, insofar as our affinities differ: that is, insofar as each of us is attentive to *some* of the many elements and aspects of reality that are worthy of being loved. This is consistent with Kierkegaard's notion of each human being having a unique identity realized in and through loving, and also with the notion that goodness or value is by nature vast and multifaceted, and thus in need of being seen from different points of view. Because the reality of goodness or value is not discredited on such an account, Platonism is not the only form of realism that gives value a solid ontological status.

In speaking of "the significance of things," therefore, we are referring to an aspect of reality that depends on the subject in a way that other features of the world do not.[30] The lovable properties of a person are not like the shape and texture of a solid object, which can be tested and confirmed by many different observers; they are more akin to the color of a rainbow, which is a well-founded phenomenon that does not appear at all from most perspectives. What it means to say that the rainbow is visible and colored is that these appearances are there "to be met with" in the object's "relation to the subject," to borrow a phrase from the *Critique of Pure Reason*.[31] Applying the same idea to the realm of affective experience, we could say that something can be "experienced as meaningful" if it is "met with on the path of care."[32] We are, as Frankfurt states, "creatures to whom things matter" (IWC, 80), and it is not an incidental fact about us that we are loving or caring beings—rather, it is a defining condition of human existence. Loving or caring "is essential to our being creatures of the kind that [we] are" (RL, 17), and our sense of reality is defined by what we love and care about. Because it enables us to perceive what we would have overlooked if our attention had not been not oriented in the same way, love is capable of revealing real features of the world.

VI

Moral agency itself depends upon "the contrast between adequate and delinquent *ways of seeing the other*," and this explains all the attention that is given to "vision" and "perception" in Kierkegaard's moral psychology.[33] By opening our eyes to the significance of other persons and things, love brings to light the axiological dimension of reality and founds our capacity for practical reason. This is what makes it possible for us to have experiences in which things delight and threaten us, alarm and calm us: in short, love is what allows us to experience the world as an emotionally charged environment that moves us in all the various ways that it does. Through this mode of experience, we discern things that dispassionate reason is blind to, "as ears and hearing are blind to colors."[34] This does not mean that what is disclosed to us in such experiences somehow flies in the face of rationality or logic, only that we are relying upon a different faculty when value is perceived. Our emotional responses embody a mode of vision, but what they enable us to see would be invisible to anyone without the necessary sort of affective attunement. Why would any present danger move us to become afraid, if we were entirely lacking in self-love and had no interest in preserving our own life? Because emotions call our attention to those parts of the environment that matter for us, an apathetic or uncaring person will not take notice of much that stands out as salient to someone who is emotionally open, receptive, and engaged. On the other hand, when a person views the world with the heightened attention and concern that a loving disposition brings, he or she finds that it is not neutrally valenced but permeated with tangible significance.

Does this give us any reason to believe that the apparent meaning and value of whatever we love and care about is merely illusory? The question resists any easy resolution, since there are good reasons for answering it in radically different ways. On the one hand, we do not typically experience ourselves as actively endowing the objects of our love with the very attributes we point to when we are describing what we love about them.[35] It would be phenomenologically inaccurate to claim that what I find so moving about the austere beauty of a desert valley, or the gentle rebuke issued by a close friend, is actually emanating from me onto the landscape or the person. When I love someone, it is likely that I am especially aware of her best qualities, because these are amplified in the light of my radiant gaze. This is not tantamount to admiring a falsified image of the person, which obstructs my view of her as she really is. If it were, then it would make no sense to speak of cases in which we "fail to see the individual because we are completely enclosed in a fantasy world" of our own making.[36] Yet we do, rightly, distinguish between delusional images projected by our own souls and the striking things we notice in those whom we love, which we ourselves have not fabricated. Regardless of how "intoxicating" it might be to imagine that "the highest and most perfect kind of love" is one that takes flight from concrete reality, Kierkegaard tells us not to lose sight of the *"actual individual person"* in favor of our own ideal notion of how the person ought to be (WL, 161–64).[37] One good reason for making this distinction, and for believing that love *can* put us in touch with the real world, is that we could not have anticipated much of what we have, in fact, been affected by.[38] In order to give an account of what I love and care about, I must acknowledge that it all depends upon my encounter—or "collision," as Kierkegaard might say—with actual persons, places, and things whose existence is independent of mine.

On the other hand, even if the perceived beauty and value of what we love is not simply bestowed onto it by the beholder, should we not also admit that some contribution is made by our own point of view? When I give an account of what I love and care about, I am revealing something about how *I* view the world; and this is different from an impersonal description of how the world is. William James asks us to contemplate what *that* might be like:

Conceive yourself, if possible, suddenly stripped of all the emotion with which your world now inspires you, and try to imagine it *as it exists*, purely by itself, without your favorable or unfavorable, hopeful or apprehensive comment. It will be almost impossible for you to realize such a condition of negativity and deadness. No one portion of the universe would then have importance beyond another; and the whole collection of things and series of its events would be without significance.[39]

At one point, his thought-experiment almost veers into absurdity, as James invites us to contemplate a world that exists purely in itself. This is precisely what we cannot have any conception of, so it is a rather unfair basis of comparison. Yet his main thesis is well worth taking to heart: insofar as we *can* envision or depict the world as it might appear to an observer totally devoid of emotion, it would seem to be entirely lacking in value or significance. From this insight, however, he draws the wrong conclusion. Immediately after the passage I just cited, he states that the meaning and value that animate "our respective worlds" are "thus pure gifts of the spectator's mind," and he identifies the "passion of love" as "the most familiar and extreme example of this fact."[40] That does not obviously follow.

Without the right kind of affective outlook, we cannot experience the significance of things. But this does not entail that the significance of things is a distortion imposed on them by our own perspective. When Frankfurt says, for example, that what we love "*acquires* value for us *because* we love it" (WL, 39), he makes it sound as though the lover *projects* value onto what is loved, value that the beloved actually does not possess. For this, he has rightly been taken to task, for instance by Troy Jollimore.[41] Yet if we keep in mind that our access to the world is *only* through its effect on sentient beings,[42] then we should not conclude that love gives us a false view of things just because it enables us to see *more* than the cold eye of reason could discern. In some cases, it is evident that, as Scheler claims, "the 'blindness' ... is all on the side of the 'detached observer.'"[43] For instance, recognizing a tone of resentment in the voice of someone we love, which a neutral observer would fail to notice, might lead us to worry about our relationship. And this worry could be founded on very real evidence, providing us with epistemically desirable insight into objective reality. Yet it is our love for this person, our care for the relationship we share with them, that attunes us to take notice of something that others would miss. Contrafactually, if we didn't love this person, we could easily remain cool-headed, impartial, unworried, and thus oblivious to a fact that is transparently evident to anyone who cares enough to perceive it.

VII

Even if there is no standpoint from which our impressions of the world can be compared with the world as it "absolutely" is, we are still right to hold onto the ideal of truthfulness, of being in touch with the world. If we give up on this, as Bernard Williams warns, "we shall certainly lose something, and may very well lose everything."[44] By now, though, we should understand why it would not be obvious that anything *deserves* to be loved, to a detached or indifferent observer. This is a consequence of the fact that a certain affective disposition is needed in order for us to perceive the significance of things. In other words, what we see depends in part on our way of seeing (see WL, 228). Seeing that another person is suffering, for example, requires more than just pointing one's eyes at her while she is located in a well-lit place[45]: it also requires that we view her with the attention and concern that highlight whatever we love and care about. Drawing an analogy between emotional perception and color vision, Kierkegaard points out that it is only "if you yourself have loved" that you know what it is like to experience the world in this light, in the same way that "the blind person cannot know color differences" (CD, 237).[46] The person with normal eyesight, of course, does not generate a world of visible and colorful objects out of his own mind. Rather, he must be constituted in a certain way in order to perceive what is visible—namely, real features of the world that can be detected by those who are suitably disposed or attuned to them. We are creatures for whom the world presents itself as meaningful and significant in ways that compel us to respond emotionally; however, its significance is revealed to us only when it is regarded under favorable conditions and in the appropriate way. Once we reject the incoherent notion of an absolute objectivity viewed "from nowhere," we have no basis for the assumption that there is a value-neutral world "out there" that our emotional responses actually project value *onto*. As Williams asks of the projectivist imagery: "What is the screen?"[47] Indeed, to say that the subject *projects* value onto things makes it sound as if there is an agent already there, prior to and ontologically separate from love: but this is false, if it is love that defines the contours of our involvement in the world. Because each of us becomes "a distinct self by forming bonds of love, or care, with the external world," it follows that "a person's moral identity is defined by love," as I have argued before.[48] This is precisely why love makes it possible "for us to engage wholeheartedly in activity that is meaningful" (RL, 90–96), and also why "the origins of normativity" are "constituted by … the structures of the will through which the specific identity of the individual is most particularly defined" (RL, 48), these being the necessities of love. It is, as Kierkegaard says, a virtue "to be truly in love" (BA, 108); for without love, we could not gain access to the values that orient our existence. Love is "a source of reasons" because "loving something or someone ... *means* or *consists in* ... taking its interests as reasons for acting to serve those interests" (RL, 37). In this sense, love is the ultimate ground of practical reason. Just as colors cannot be seen by a blind person, the significance of things cannot be perceived in the absence of love or care.

This is especially true with respect to the kind of knowledge we gain in becoming acquainted with another person, as they are and as they might potentially become. Rather than simply altering our view of someone who is already quite well-known to us, love is what allows the person to show up and be noticed in the first place. This is why "to love and to know are essentially synonymous," as Kierkegaard proposes in a highly suggestive journal entry (JP, 2:2299). He may be intending something like Scheler's claim that love is knowledge *because* we come to know an "individual personality" only through "the act of loving," which discloses the person in his or her irreplaceable particularity.[49] The "presupposition for loving," and for the sort of knowledge gained through love, is "the distinctiveness of individuality," Kierkegaard contends in another journal passage (JP, 2:2003)—and Frankfurt once again echoes him on this point, noting the "ineluctably particular" significance to the lover of what he or she loves (NVL, 166). Since the "specific particularity" of the beloved other is precisely what one loves about him or her, it would make no sense to settle for a qualitatively similar replacement (NVL, 170).[50] This position is far removed from the Platonic view of the individual beloved as a bearer of properties (such as beauty or goodness) that are more perfectly instantiated elsewhere, not in the individual per se.[51] However, it is fully congruent with the emphasis on distinctive individuality that runs throughout Kierkegaard's corpus,[52] and which even carries a religious significance in some of his writings.

VIII

Continuing with his own deeply Kierkegaardian line of thought, Scheler affirms that love plays a disclosing or unveiling role in the realm of value experience, enhancing our moral awareness and expanding our "range of contact with the universe."[53] Our capacity to love or care enables us to encounter significant aspects of the vast, complex, and multifaceted universe that surrounds us, and which is not value-neutral. We are not talking about how the mind organizes experience in terms of universal categories; instead, what is at issue here is how a significant world takes shape around the vantage point of an individual person. Each of us does this in his or her own way, since a subject or a person *is* above all someone "for whom a world exists,"[54] and love is precisely what allows us to see whatever good is there to be seen. As one of Kierkegaard's pseudonymous authors reminds us, "life is rich enough, if only one understands how to see. One need not travel to Paris and London; besides, this would be of no help if one is unable to see" (CA, 74). Out of all that is worthy of love, each of us only has access to a limited part: this places an outer boundary on what we are emotionally capable of knowing. Opposing Kierkegaard's directive to love *each* person we see, Frankfurt counters with the observation that we simply "cannot afford to love *everything*" (NVL, 173). Finite human beings are condemned to an inevitable partiality with respect to what we love and care about.

The variation between one person's affective sense of the world and that of another has prompted some thinkers to conclude that the virtues of the beloved are "pure gifts," bestowed onto him or her by the one who loves.[55] Yet it is more plausible to link the idea that love enables us to see with a realism about what it brings into view. It is, after all, a realist who will most readily acknowledge that the "thing we think of existed before we thought of it" (just as the virtues of the beloved were there "to be seen" before anyone saw them), and that it "exists even while we think of it in ways that we do not know."[56] There is always more to the object of love, and to the objective world more generally, than what has already been revealed to us. And since each of us can only know so much of what is emotionally knowable, it takes a plurality of loving subjectivities in order to know the whole truth about the world. Our individuality is bound up with our loves and cares, which is why it would be unreasonable for a human being to believe that "anyone who fails to love what he does has somehow gone wrong" (IWC, 90–91). This would be difficult to explain if we were dealing with a universal notion of "the in-and-for-itself good," such as can be found in Plato's dialogues (CI, 71). Only a Stoic, or the "Young Man" in *Stages on Life's Way*, would assume that, if love is rational, then "the lovable" ought to compel universal assent (SLW, 34–40).[57] In being enthusiastic about a person, a place, or even a favorite work of art, we should be cognizant of the fact that what we see in him, her, or it has probably not yet been glimpsed by *everyone* else. And when we love someone or something, we often find ourselves trying to figure out what makes it so captivating, even as we know that this does not exhaust what it has to offer. "As long as love persists," Nehamas comments, the person who loves will always feel that there is more to the beloved that is "still worth coming to know and celebrate."[58] Love points beyond what is immediately present, into a future where much more remains to be discovered. To feel that there is nothing more to be revealed about someone or something is to have ceased loving altogether: as long as we *do* love, what we love presents itself to us as an inexhaustible reality that has many aspects yet to be appreciated and understood. By contrast, when we feel that there's "nothing more to it," this is probably because we just don't care about it anymore.

IX

By making us able to see, love also reveals that there is always more to what we love than has yet been disclosed to us. When I love someone, I am likely to discern whatever good may exist in her: still, in addition to all the adorable characteristics that she has and that I adore, there is always something more. This is another reason for thinking that we will always fall short in attempting to validate our loves and cares in terms of objective merit. Love helps us recognize "less obvious aspects of what is really there," and also to make a charitable interpretation of what is not so obviously worth loving.[59] Although we are not painting the world in false colors through our loves and cares, we *do* need to have the requisite affective comportment in order to apprehend the significance of anything— including the "more beautiful" or "lovable" side of a person *as they are*, rather than as "*we think or could wish that this person should be*" (WL, 158, 164). In loving another person, I take an interest in what he or she loves and cares about; and I cannot possibly know the whole truth about his or her loves and cares prior to loving. This is why love cannot be predicated on any prior evaluation of what is "worth loving," that is, because "our recognition of value comes through love."[60] This also means that I cannot know how my love for this person will influence me and transform my "way of being in the world."[61] If I am open to allowing those whom I love to amend my values and my sense of the good, then I cannot regard myself and my values as unalterably settled in advance of loving, and use my preexisting standards to evaluate a person's loveworthiness. When I hold back and refrain from loving someone because I am in doubt as to whether he or she is *worthy*, the result is that I "do not really see" the person at all (WL, 172–73). Nor would I appreciate all that is there to be seen if I require that the "love of a person or object or activity should be proportional to its value or worthiness to be loved."[62] Not only will this defensive stance close me off from being changed through a responsive engagement with the other, but I am not in a position to know all that is worthy of love in someone or something as long as I stand at a critical distance and judge whether or not he, she, or it is worthy. The standpoint of distrust, on Kierkegaard's account, is directly opposed to that of love (WL, 227–28), and it *could* be nothing more than a resistance to being transformed by seeing another aspect of the multifaceted Good. So the antecedent demand for justification, in terms of objectively love-worthy qualities, is likely to preclude the discovery of exactly what one is supposedly looking for. For both Kierkegaard and Frankfurt, love cannot require any prior assurance that the beloved is "worth loving," due to the way that love allows us to see whatever good *is* objectively there to be seen.

This, I think, is why Marion states that "the project of knowing" another person adequately, "even before loving her," has "no meaning" whatsoever.[63] It is because what we love does not come fully into view, or into the most flattering light, before we love it. This, of course, is because its reality and value are visible only for those with eyes to see. The notion of absolute reality as it is, independent of any observer, is a philosophical myth whose appeal we ought to resist. Taking refuge in Platonic realism about the Good is an understandable reaction against to the misguided claim that value is projected by the will. But we do not have to choose between an absolute "objectivism" and the belief that we are being delusional in finding things significant. Of all people, Kierkegaardians especially ought to be wary of the presumption that something must be *objective* in order to be *real*. Objective being is what Schopenhauer's "will" does *not* have, and yet it is the foundation of everything that does exist as an object. There are many things that we cannot discover *until* we love, which is why a perception of the worth of what one loves is "not at all an indispensable *formative* or *grounding* condition" of love, as Frankfurt insists (RL, 38). He illustrates the point with this example:

> It is not because I have noticed their value . . . that I love my children as I do. Of course, I do perceive them to have value; so far as I am concerned, indeed, their value is beyond measure. That, however, is not the basis of my love. It is really the other way around. (RL, 40)

Clearly, he is in agreement with Kierkegaard's declaration that "it is a sad but all too common inversion to go on talking continually about how the object of love must be so that it can be loveworthy" (WL, 159)—as if that is where the burden of proof ought to be placed. As he says, "if I ask myself whether my children are worthy of my love, my emphatic inclination is to reject the question as misguided," but "not because it goes so clearly without saying that my children *are* worthy" (RL, 39). It is because love must come first, prior to any evaluation of whether or not it deserves to be given. Love cannot always be predicated on a judgment of value because much that is knowable by human beings could not be known by an emotionally neutral observer. There are "no necessities of logic or of rationality that dictate what we are to love" (RL, 47), and nobody is *obligated* to love something just because it is *worthy* of being loved. This, I believe, is what Frankfurt has in mind when he claims that "it is generally not considerations of value" that explain why "a person comes to be selflessly devoted to some ideal or value" rather than another (RL, 40n). He does not mean that what we love or care about is actually devoid of goodness or value. On the contrary, his point is that a loving person, who appreciates maximally the value of the beloved due to the generous attention that he or she directs toward the beloved, cannot begin by making comparative estimates of value and then loving only after finding what is worthiest of being loved. As Kierkegaard points out, the task we face is not to keep a sharp eye out lest we be duped: it is to *find lovable* what we see (WL, 159–62), to see *in such a way* as to discover that what we love and care about *is* worthy. This is why the question, about whether one loves one's children *because* they deserve it, is misguided.

X

The function of love is to make our lives meaningful "and in that way good … to live," Frankfurt claims (RL, 99); and Kierkegaard says that other-directed love is what makes life worth living (WL, 375). They diverge on the question of whether love consistently moves us to become *good*, and in the degree to which they embrace a theistic interpretation of love itself. Yet, more often than not, there are strong parallels between the two thinkers—indeed, even some of the apparent discrepancies in their language turn out to be merely superficial. If Frankfurt occasionally makes statements that come across as excessively projectivist—for instance, "it is by caring about things that we infuse the world with importance" (RL, 23)—we should bear in mind that Scheler, who argues for the existence of "objective values" independent of all beings who are conscious of those values, can also speak in terms of bestowal, as when he writes that "it is the activity and movement of love which embues life with its *highest meaning and value.*"[64] Based on Scheler's realistic account of value, we know that this potentially misleading sentence should not be construed as a defense of antirealism. What he means is that, in light of love, the world "reveals itself" and enters into "*its full existence and value.*"[65] In other words, because it enables us to apprehend what we would miss if we regarded things with a different affective outlook, love is capable of disclosing real features of the world. Similarly, in Frankfurt's case, *letting things become significant* may indeed be closer to what he has in mind than *projecting significance onto things*.[66] The former is more compatible with many of his other statements, such as that it is liberating to be "captivated by our beloved" (RL, 65–66), or to be "seized by the object" of love (IWC, 89). Its value attracts us because it is there *to be met with*, even though it is not there *absolutely*, since a loving subjectivity is a necessary condition of apprehending this particular truth about reality. If I am wrong, and if Frankfurt truly wishes to defend the view that all value is falsely projected onto the beloved by the one who loves, then some of his claims are true for the wrong reasons. On such a reading, he would be right to argue that love is a condition of finding value in the world, but incorrect in holding that this value is a mere illusion.

In order not to overlook the fact that our emotional responses are answerable to a world outside our own minds, whose contours are not of our making, I should reassert that an emphasis on subjectivity is entirely consistent with our legitimate concern for being in touch with reality, and not being deluded. Our interest in having the world accurately revealed to us, however, would be poorly served by binding ourselves to criteria of what is objectively lovable or worth caring about. Love "is not explainable or even justifiable. It is itself the justifier …. If it did not happen to us, we could not imagine it …. It is in the world, but not altogether of it."[67] In love, there is always something gratuitous or unjustified, an excess that we cannot explain—and if this were not the case, then it could not play the role that it does in human life. If love were dependent upon evidence that has already been assessed, then it could not enable us to see or provide a grounding for our moral evaluations. And if our identity and self-understanding were complete prior to loving, then it would not be true that "only the person who loves" knows who he is and what is his "task at every moment" (EO, 2:125; WL, 189–90). If not for the boundless "infinitude of love" (WL, 180–81), then it could not prevail over uncertainty and indecisiveness in the face of all that is *perhaps* worthy of love, binding us decisively to *this* person, *this* ideal, *this* vocation.[68] And, finally, if love needed to be validated by a higher authority—or to pass *through* a purifying medium other than love itself— then it would be idolatrous for Kierkegaard to assert that God is love (WL, 62–63; WL, 121, 301), or that "love" is the only substantive term that can be used to name God (JP, 2:1319 or KJN 2, EE:62).

As it is, love is the power that shapes our ends and grounds our moral life. "If God is love," Frankfurt reflects, then "the universe has no point except simply to be" (RL, 63). This is because love is what discloses the value of being; it moves us to affirm the existence of what we love, unconditionally and for its own sake. It would not make sense to ask whether such a grateful affirmation is worth making because all estimations of worth occur after one has already taken an interest in the world, in this primary and gratuitous way. Love is an "absolute gratuity,"[69] and even if we interpret it as an eternal power then we still must acknowledge that it manifests itself in ways that are invariably entangled with the contingencies of human existence. What I have loved has made an impact on me that has something to do with its distinctive qualities and something to do with its identity as what I encountered at a certain point in my own history. Based upon what I had been until that point, I was able to respond to *this* object in the way that I did; and the fact *that* I did conditions my existence from then on. We are, as Frankfurt concludes, "not free to decide 'at our own liking' what to love or what love requires of us" (NVL, 136). Because love determines what we "cannot help doing" and what we cannot bring ourselves to do, it would be unreasonable for us not "to accept" love's dictates and its "impetus," since we have "no pertinent basis" for resisting its influence (RL, 50–51). If for some reason we did not wish "to accept love as a gift," we would still be indebted to it as the ground of our being (EUD, 157–58). The good news is that this dependency enables us to be wholeheartedly engaged in a life that is worth living; no one who loves is radically in doubt about the meaning of his or her life. From this conception of love it follows both that we regard its objects as valuable in themselves and that we view them as significant in ways that pertain to us. Love, then, is rightly identified as the ultimate ground of moral agency—since it cannot be explained in terms of anything more basic, it ought to serve as a reminder that human life is not an instrumental means to some end outside of itself. Like a musical composition, our life has its own intrinsic significance and serves no purpose other than to be.

Acknowledgments

I am grateful to Karin Nisenbaum and to audiences who responded with helpful comments to earlier drafts of this essay: at the 2008 meeting of the Phenomenology Roundtable in New York and at Colorado College in February 2009. Among those who attended on these two occasions, I should especially thank Kiley Dunlap, Andrew Henscheid, Jonathan Lee, Shahrzad Safavi, and Ella Street. Thanks also to Søren Landkildehus, Vernon Smith, Michael Stocker, John Lippitt, Arne Grøn, Sharon Krishek, Anthony Rudd, and John Davenport, all of whom provided useful feedback during later stages of revision.

Notes

1   See RL, 3–6. "Some Mysteries of Love" is the title of Frankfurt's Lindley
    Lecture (University of Kansas, Lawrence KS, April 2000), which is an early
    draft of part of his book *The Reasons of Love.*

2   Blaise Pascal, *Pensées*, 423: "The heart has its reasons of which reason
    knows nothing: we know this in countless ways." This passage is quoted
    or alluded to approvingly by both Scheler and Marion: See Max Scheler,
    Formalism in Ethics and Non-Formal Ethics of Values, 255; Jean-Luc Marion,
    The Erotic Phenomenon, 217.

3   Cf. WL, 215: here, Kierkegaard identifies love as "the source of everything"
    and as "the deepest ground of the spiritual life." See also RL, 57, where
    Frankfurt claims that the "most fundamental issues of practical reason" can
    be resolved only through "an account of what people love."

4   For an account of emotions as perceptions or apprehensions of significance,
    see my book *Wisdom in Love: Kierkegaard and the Ancient Quest for
    Emotional Integrity.*

5   Jenefer Robinson, *Deeper than Reason*, 42.

6   Jean-Luc Marion, *God without Being*, 123 and 134. See also Pat Bigelow,
    Kierkegaard and the Problem of Writing, 115–16: boredom, as the failure
    "to find anything worthy of interest," renders the world "destitute of
    intelligibility," preventing "truth" or "worldly content" from being disclosed.
    When Frankfurt notes that our wish to avoid boredom is more profound
    than a wish simply to avoid an unpleasant condition (RL, 53–54), he echoes
    Martin Heidegger, *The Fundamental Concepts of Metaphysics*, 159.

7   Michael Weston, *Kierkegaard and Modern Continental Philosophy*, 22. On
    the point he is making, see the discussion of consciousness and interest in
    Kierkegaard's unpublished narrative, *Johannes Climacus* (JC, 170–71).

8   See also RL, 41–43. Frankfurt calls love "an especially notable variant of
    caring," one in which we care about something as an end in itself, and
    which "makes it possible … for us to engage wholeheartedly in activity
    that is meaningful" (RL, 11 and 90). "Loving is a mode of caring," he says
    elsewhere: "among the things we cannot help caring about are those we
    love" (NVL, 165). His occasional tendency to define care simply as a higher-
    order desire (see RL, 16) is not compatible with his more insightful decision
    to distinguish *between* desire and care (RL, 10–14; see also NVL, 155–57)
    rather than defining one in terms of the other.

9   José Ortega y Gasset, *On Love*, 16–17.

10 On "love" and "care" in Kierkegaard, see my essay, Rick Anthony Furtak,
    "Love and the Discipline of Philosophy," 63–65. See also M. Jamie Ferreira,
    Love's Grateful Striving, 43–44. On the near-synonymity of these terms in
    Frankfurt's thought, see Marya Schechtman, "Self-Expression and Self-
    Control," 57–58. A distinction Frankfurt sometimes highlights is that care
    need not involve disinterested concern for the well-being of what one cares

about, whereas love implies this kind of unselfish, other-centered concern for the beloved's well-being: see RL, 42–43.

11 Marion, *The Erotic Phenomenon*, 87–88.

12 Nishida Kitarô, for instance, claims that objective reality "does not come into existence apart from our subjectivity," placing a heavy emphasis on the world-disclosing role played by human beings. See *An Inquiry into the Good*, trans. by M. Abe & C. Ives, 68.

13 Maurice Merleau-Ponty, *The Phenomenology of Perception*, 178. John Drummond defines phenomenology as the systematic endeavor to identify "the conditions that make it possible for objects and a world to be experienced—to disclose themselves—as having the significance they have for us": see "'Cognitive Impenetrability' and the Complex Intentionality of the Emotions," *Journal of Consciousness Studies* 11 (2004): 111.

14 Cf. Scheler, *Formalism in Ethics and Non-Formal Ethics of Values*, 261. The role of love in disclosing a world of value is examined by Peter H. Spader, *Scheler's Ethical Personalism*, 87–95, 229–38.

15 Scheler, "Love and Knowledge," in *On Feeling, Knowing, and Valuing*, edited by Harold J. Bershady, 153.

16 See, for example, WL, 301: "First there is the one who loves, next the one or ones who are the object; but love itself is present as the third."

17 Cf. Martha C. Nussbaum, *Upheavals of Thought*, 572–73. This example demonstrates how "preferential love," when attuned to the person, "can itself generate moral and religious obligations," as George Pattison notes. See his *Kierkegaard's Upbuilding Discourses*, 177.

18 Scheler, *Formalism in Ethics and Non-Formal Ethics of Values*, 371–73.

19 Clare Carlisle, *Kierkegaard's Philosophy of Becoming*, 86. John Lippitt finds it incredible that "the lover's concern for his beloved" might actually be without "any ulterior aim," since all talk of disinterested concern is "self-deception" in his view: see Lippitt, *Kierkegaard and the Problem of Self-Love*, 101–05.

20 Scheler, "Ordo Amoris," in *Selected Philosophical Essays*, 98–99.

21 A. B. Come, "Kierkegaard's Ontology of Love," 91–92.

22 Thomas Aquinas, *Summa Theologica* I–II.28.2–3, quoted by Edward C. Vacek in *Love, Human and Divine*, 295. It is noteworthy that Aquinas is talking about *philia* in this passage, which confounds the attempt either to give *agapē* a unique priority in Christian ethics, or to set it against *eros* in a violent conflict, as Anders Nygren does. I discuss the different forms of love in Kierkegaard's thought, and their underlying unity, in *Wisdom in Love*, 101–05 and 178–82. There is much more to be said on this topic: see, for example, Sharon Krishek, *Kierkegaard on Faith and Love*, 109–37.

23 For Robert C. Roberts, the wish that another person's "true interests be promoted" qualifies as *agapē* only if it's derived from a belief that the person "personifies Jesus Christ and is loved by him." See his *Emotions: An Essay in Aid of Moral Psychology*, 294. This is one way to burden the notion of love

with further theological complications, and to view God not as manifest *in* love but as something extra that needs to be added onto love itself. *Love itself*, according to Kierkegaard in *Works of Love*, *is* God, present as middle term between lover and beloved: "the love-relationship requires threeness: the lover, the beloved, the love – but the love is God" (WL, 121).

24   Theo Van Willigenburg, "Reason and Love," 58.

25   See also Michael Stocker, "Some Considerations about Intellectual Desire and Emotions," 139: "without care, concern, and interest, nothing would be salient, indeed the world would have no categories."

26   See Merleau-Ponty, *The Phenomenology of Perception*, 507–21.

27   As Marion says, the other person "appears only if I gratuitously give him the space in which to appear." See Marion, "What Love Knows," in *Prolegomena to Charity*, trans. by Stephen E. Lewis, 166. For an earlier expression of a similar point, see also William A. Luijpen, *Existential Phenomenology*, 228–30.

28   Susan Wolf, "The True, the Good, and the Lovable," 240.

29   Anthony Rudd, *Self, Value, and Narrative*, 87.

30   On the way that axiological qualities seem to "depend on the subject in a way that the shape or color of a thing arguably does not," see Robert C. Solomon, *True to Our Feelings*, 55. And yet, as Hilary Putnam reminds us, it's been known since the time of Berkeley that "the arguments against the idea that things are colored in the way they seem to be" also undermine any notion "that they are *shaped* in the way they seem to be, *solid* in the way they seem to be, etc."— Putnam, *The Threefold Cord*, 39.

31   Immanuel Kant, *Critique of Pure Reason*, 84–89 [B63-B70]. It makes good sense to distinguish "between the kind of objectivity proper to the hard sciences and that [which is] proper to ethics." See Roger J. Fitterer, *Love and Objectivity in Virtue Ethics*, 4.

32   Martin Heidegger, *Phenomenological Interpretations of Aristotle*, 68–70. The experience of the world in terms of care is what "provides the preconceptual sense" for "all interpretation of objectivity," he adds. Therefore, "it is not the case that objects are first present as bare realities," which only subsequently "receive the garb of a value-character, so they do not have to run around naked." On how reality is founded in care, see also Heidegger, *Being and Time*, trans. by Joan Stambaugh, 195–96 [§43c]. Roberts makes a related claim in *Emotions*, 80: the emotional construal of value is not a matter of "interpretation laid over a neutrally perceived object," but a way of seeing the object itself.

33   Patrick Stokes, "Kierkegaardian Vision and the Concrete Other," 394.

34   Scheler, *Formalism in Ethics and Non-Formal Ethics of Values*, 254–55.

35   An analogous point is made by Rolf Johnson in *Three Faces of Love*, 103–04. Cf. Iain Thomson, "Ontotheology," 106–31.

36   Iris Murdoch, "The Sublime and the Good," in *Existentialists and Mystics*, 215–16. Love, she says, is "the extremely difficult realisation that something

other than oneself is real …. It is the apprehension of something else, something particular, as existing outside us."

37 Kierkegaard's main criticisms of certain views from Plato's *Symposium* are phrased in similar terms: see CI, 41–47. See also Ulrika Carlsson, "Love as a Problem of Knowledge in Kierkegaard's *Either/Or* and Plato's *Symposium*," 41–67.

38 Describing the gift of love, Marion writes: "I did not foresee it, cannot expect it, and will never comprehend it"—*The Erotic Phenomenon*, 103.

39 William James, *The Varieties of Religious Experience*, 140–41.

40 James, *The Varieties of Religious Experience*, 141. See also James, *The Varieties of Religious Experience*, 462: here, he refers to "a mere passion, like love, which views things in a rosier light."

41 Troy Jollimore, *Love's Vision*, 21–22. He concedes that Frankfurt's view "expresses some important truths," and notes that Frankfurt's own examples show his reluctance to embrace an extreme "projectivist" view about the nature of value.

42 John McDowell makes this point, for instance, in *Mind, Value, and Reality*, 114. Regarding the "cold 'eye' of reason" and the perspective of love, see Max Scheler, *The Nature of Sympathy*, 150.

43 Scheler, *The Nature of Sympathy*, 160.

44 Bernard Williams, *Truth and Truthfulness*, 7–17. Evidently, Frankfurt would agree: see OT, 98–101.

45 Cf. Anthony Rudd, *Expressing the World*, 121.

46 The context of this remark is a discussion of what it means to believe in Christ—as Kierkegaard says earlier on the same page, "if you yourself do not believe, then you cannot know whether there is one who has believed in him" (CD, 237). On perceiving the "value-ladenness of the world" and its parallels with color vision, see Patrick Stokes, *Kierkegaard's Mirrors*, 11–12.

47 Bernard Williams, *Ethics and the Limits of Philosophy*, 129.

48 Furtak, *Wisdom in Love*, 98–99.

49 Scheler, *The Nature of Sympathy*, 166–67. As Marion says, "only love opens up knowledge of the other as such"—"What Love Knows," 160. Marion would add, in harmony with Kierkegaard and Frankfurt, that the individuality of the one who loves is also revealed through the act of loving: see *The Erotic Phenomenon*, 107–08 & 195.

50 Frankfurt's claim here is remarkably similar to Eric Santner's: "When one truly loves another person, one loves precisely what is *not* generic about them … in a word, what is irreplaceable." See Eric Santner, *On the Psychotheology of Everyday Life*, 73.

51 See Plato, *Symposium*, 210a–211e. Gregory Vlastos makes a complaint quite similar to Kierkegaard's: namely, that Platonic love is not sufficiently a love of the person "in the uniqueness and integrity of his or her individuality" and as "a valuing subject" in his or her own right. See his classic essay Vlastos, "The Individual as Object of Love in Plato," 31–32. For now, I will

leave aside the question of whether or not the speech of Socrates/Diotima represents views that Plato himself would endorse.

52   On individuality as a condition of truthfulness see, *inter alia*, JP 4:4887, SKP VI B 40:26, and TA 62–63 and 84–88. Kierkegaard remarks that Christianity rests on the principle that "the truth *is* the single individual" (JP 2:2165), and he portrays God as the "origin of all distinctiveness" (WL, 271). On the essential connection between Christian love and the individuality of the person, see also Nussbaum, *Upheavals of Thought*, 559–60.

53   Scheler, "Ordo Amoris," in *Selected Philosophical Essays*, 111, 120.

54   See, for example, Jollimore, *Love's Vision*, 125.

55   "Pure gifts" is a phrase used by William James: see *The Varieties of Religious Experience*, 141.

56   Stephen R. L. Clark, *God's World and the Great Awakening*, 69.

57   On the Stoic position, see Rick Anthony Furtak, *Wisdom in Love*, 103–04.

58   Alexander Nehamas, "Only in the Contemplation of Beauty is Human Life Worth Living," 10. What we come to know about the beloved, Nehamas adds, will perhaps transform us as well. If I love you, then you are not "merely a means to my own ends, which are already established without reference to you, but someone whose own ends can become mine – an end in yourself. I then act on a sense – vague but intense – that there is more to you than I can now see and that it would be better for me to learn what I suspect you can offer." See *Only a Promise of Happiness*, 57–58. Frankfurt also claims that love allows our lives to be quite literally *worth living* (RL, 98–99). Here again, he is in line with Kierkegaard's view: see WL, 375.

59   John Armstrong, *Conditions of Love*, 94–96. See also C. D. C. Reeve, *Love's Confusions*, 21: "love can discover value where nothing else can."

60   This is stated by Anthony Rudd, who nonetheless disagrees with Frankfurt's view that we must simply recognize and accept our deepest loves and cares, as Martin Luther did in taking a stand and saying that he "could do no other" (IWC, 86). For Rudd, love must be explained in terms of justifying reasons, and when those reasons are not apparent *to us* we should "regard [a] lover as foolish and deluded" for loving someone whose "attractive or lovable qualities" he or she has overestimated *as far as we can see*. I rely upon his account as articulated in *Self, Value, and Narrative*, 102–06.

61   Vacek, op. cit., 288. For an articulation of much the same point in a slightly different context, see Armstrong, *Conditions of Love*, 35.

62   Susan Wolf, "The Good, the True, and the Lovable," 229. The narrator of *Repetition* ridiculously doubts the "lovableness" of the woman to whom his young correspondent is devoted (R, 184), while Kierkegaard claims that only "worldly sagacity" would advise us to "take a careful look" before loving (WL, 68). Regarding what follows, see also Karin Nisenbaum, "Understanding the Body's Critique," 57.

63 Marion, *The Erotic Phenomenon*, 79. On why love is prior to knowledge, see also Vacek, *Love, Human and Divine*, 47–48 and Scheler, "Ordo Amoris," 110.

64 Scheler, *Ressentiment*, 83. See also Scheler, *Formalism in Ethics and Non-Formal Ethics of Values*, 266–70.

65 Scheler, "Love and Knowledge," 164. Cf. John H. Nota, *Max Scheler: The Man and His Work*, 65: love "makes visible that which no one suspected was there," although not by "projecting" illusory properties onto whatever is loved.

66 This would make it easier to reconcile the different statements he makes throughout *The Reasons of Love*. On "letting things be significant" (or "relevant"), see Heidegger, *Being and Time*, 324 [§69].

67 Wendell Berry, *Jayber Crow: A Novel*, 249. Cf. Frankfurt's claim: "Love is not a conclusion. It is not an outcome of reasoning, or a consequence of reasons."—TOS, 25. Regarding what follows, see Pierre Hadot, *Plotinus*, trans. by Michael Chase, 50–59.

68 Here, Frankfurt describes how, in "being captivated" by what we love, we put an end to "indifference," "ambivalence," and "indecisiveness concerning what to care about." Kierkegaard first discusses why indifference is not compatible with love, then addresses how love keeps us from being crippled by indecision when we confront an "equilibrium" between two "opposite possibilities" that "cognition" cannot resolve (WL, 233). Kierkegaard, concerned as he is with the issue of what "God wills that I shall do" (JP, 5:5100 or KJN 1, AA:12), would agree in spirit with Frankfurt's quotation from Dante (*Paradiso* 3.85): "In His will is our peace." See RL, 66.

69 Ferreira, *Love's Grateful Striving*, 160. Referring to Montaigne's lines about how, if asked why he loved someone, he could only reply "because it was him; because it was me," Juan-David Nasio says that love is "an impenetrable mystery, that one should not try to explain, but simply acknowledge." See Nasio, *The Book of Love and Pain*, trans. by David Pettigrew & François Raffoul, 28.

11

Kierkegaard's Platonism and the Reasons of Love

Anthony Rudd

Harry Frankfurt's short book, *The Reasons of Love*, is a concise and elegant summary of ideas that he has developed over the past few decades in a series of influential papers. Frankfurt's is one of the most important projects in recent moral psychology. But although his work contains insights of great value, it also, I think, contains mistakes that prevent him from fully developing those insights. A full appreciation of what is of value in Frankfurt's work will force us to go beyond—and indeed oppose—Frankfurt himself on some key issues. And I shall argue that much of what we need to develop this critique can be found in the work of Kierkegaard.[1]

I

In his important early paper, "Freedom of Will and the Concept of a Person,"[2] Frankfurt proposed that what distinguishes persons from sub-personal animals is that persons are capable of "higher-order volitions." That is, we not only have desires, or even thoughts about how to best realize those desires, but we also have the capacity to step back from those desires and consider whether they are the desire we really want to have. We can have desires about our desires (I want a cigarette, but I wish I didn't want it). And, more fundamentally, we can have, not merely higher-order *desires* (as in the example) but higher-order *volitions*, when I firmly identify one of my desires as what I want to be my will. Beings who lack the capacity for such volitions—"wantons," as Frankfurt calls them—are not, or not fully, persons on this account. In *Reasons of Love*, Frankfurt repeats this analysis, arguing that what is essential to us is that we *care* about things (RL, 11, 17); that caring is more than just having a desire (RL, 12); and that it involves making a willing commitment to a desire (RL, 16). I care about

something when I have a higher-order volition endorsing the desire I have
for it. Such caring is crucial for us:

> If there were someone who literally cared about absolutely nothing, then
> nothing would be important to him. He would be uninvolved in his own
> life … of course, he might still have various desires, and some of those
> desires might be stronger than others, but he would have no interest in
> what, from one moment to the next, his desires and preferences would
> be. (RL, 23)

This sounds like a description of one sort of aesthete in Kierkegaard's
sense of the term. (Though there are many different sorts.) And I agree with
both Frankfurt and Kierkegaard that this would be a hopelessly shallow, even
a subhuman, kind of life to live. Our sense of having meaning in life depends
on there being things that we care about.

Frankfurt goes on in Chapter 2 to discuss love. It is a subspecies of care;
the kind in which we care about something for its own sake, rather than as
a means to something else (RL, 42). But, as with other forms of care, love
is an attitude of the will, rather than simply an emotion (RL, 43). It is not,
however, simply under our voluntary control (RL, 44). Love is a constraint
on the will, although it comes from the will itself (RL, 46). At least part of its
importance to us is that love establishes final ends. If I do A for the sake of B,
B for the sake of C, and so forth, then it seems that this chain must terminate
in something that I do simply for its own sake, not as a means to anything
further; otherwise, the whole sequence would be futile and pointless.
"Without final ends, we would find nothing truly important" (RL, 53). And if
that were the case, our lives would be fundamentally boring (RL, 53–55). (It
is significant that Kierkegaard's aesthetic character, "A," who at least professes
to love nothing and to have no final ends, sees the avoidance of boredom as
the central problem of his life.[3]) For Frankfurt it is love that meets our need
for final ends: "Love is the originating source of terminal value" (RL, 55). Our
lives are meaningful to us because we have things (people, countries, causes,
landscapes, stamp collections) that we love; that is, that we care about in a
disinterested way, for their own sake.

In his final chapter, Frankfurt makes the initially surprising claim that the
purest and most fundamental kind of love is self-love. But, it turns out, what
he means by this is that to love the self is to want its aims to be achieved. But
my aims (my final ends) are the flourishing of the things I love. So self-love is
fundamental because it is, or includes my love for everything else I love (RL,
86)—though in its most minimal form it may simply be the "desire of a person
to love" (RL, 90). But, Frankfurt continues, I cannot really love myself unless

I am wholehearted in my loves. This "means having a will that is undivided. The wholehearted person is fully settled as to what he wants, and what he cares about ... He lends himself to his caring and loving unequivocally" (RL, 95). To be divided in my loves means that I cannot fully love myself, for I will hurt either or both of the parts of me that love the incompatible objects; or be paralyzed and unable to really love either. In this sense Frankfurt endorses Kierkegaard's dictum "Purity of Heart Is to Will One Thing," which he glosses as "The pure heart is the heart of someone who is volitionally unified, and who is thus fully intact" (RL, 96).

I think that Frankfurt is importantly right about nearly all of this. To have a meaningful life is to have things that one loves (i.e., cares about for their own sakes). Loving is a disposition of the will that cannot simply be identified with particular emotional states (though I do think Frankfurt excessively downplays the emotions). Love is what directs us to final ends, without which our lives would be literally pointless; and it requires a wholeheartedness, an ability to make commitments and fully endorse them. However, in my summary so far I have taken care to suppress as far as possible those aspects of Frankfurt's arguments that I do not like. In the more critical remainder of my paper, I shall turn to these, and shall try to show that these bad bits actually inhibit or undermine the good bits of Frankfurt's account. So surgery will be needed to separate what is good in Frankfurt's book from the bad elements that threaten to smother it. And to complete the operation we will need to graft on fresh elements that are not present in Frankfurt's own writing—but which are present in Kierkegaard's.

II

I want to start by returning to Frankfurt's early paper on Freedom of Will that I mentioned earlier. An important criticism of that paper was developed by Gary Watson, in his essay "Free Agency," published a few years later.[4] There Watson pursues a project similar in many ways to Frankfurt's. He agrees that freedom, human dignity, and moral responsibility reside in our capacity to step back from our immediate desires, to reflect on ourselves. But he argues that Frankfurt's distinction between higher- and lower-order desires is inadequate to explain what is special about that capacity. For Frankfurt doesn't ask why I identify with or endorse one desire rather than another, nor does he explain why I can't just be a wanton about my second-order desires. Suppose I have conflicting first-order desires to take, and not to take, a drug. Suppose also that I have conflicting desires about which of those desires I want to be my will. Do I need a third-order desire to settle that conflict?

But then what is to stop an infinite regress? Frankfurt was well aware of the problem, even in "Freedom of the Will ..."; there, and in his subsequent "Identification and Wholeheartedness,"[5] he tried to answer it by deploying the notion of wholeheartedness. At some point, he insists, I do just halt the potential regress by choosing to fully identify with one desire rather than the other. But, Watson complains, this, by itself, leaves the decision to identify looking arbitrary.

Watson's own solution is to introduce a distinction between desires (of whatever level) and values. Invoking Plato against Hume, he argues that reason can be a motivating force, apart from desire, by putting me in touch with evaluative principles. What matters is not simply to have desires about desires, but values, on the basis of which I can evaluate my desires. The crucial point here is that values are experienced by the valuer as having an authority for him or her. On Frankfurt's position, that I have this higher-order volition rather than that one, or that I wholeheartedly identify with this one rather than that, must be either a brute contingent fact of my nature and background, or an act of ultimately ungrounded choice. So we have either a deterministic naturalism, or a Sartrean self-creating arbitrariness. (We will see that Frankfurt himself ends up opting for the former.) But there are familiar—and deep—problems with both these options. Similar objections to Frankfurt have been raised by subsequent contributors to the debate he initiated, notably Charles Taylor and Susan Wolf.[6] For Wolf, it is important that our choices (our important ones, at any rate) are made, not just on the basis of our immediate desires, but by what she calls the deep self—the self that can stand back and reflect; do I really want to be governed by these desires? But that deep self must, Wolf adds, be "sane"—in her rather idiosyncratic sense of the word—that is, that self must be in touch with both factual and normative reality, be attuned to the Good and the True.

It isn't clear to me whether Watson's notion of value is meant in a strong ontological sense, implying moral realism, or whether it is intended in a merely psychological sense (I act freely if I act on what I *experience* as authoritative values).[7] And Wolf seems to be rendered uncomfortable by the Platonism of her own terminology (the Good and the True) and tries to downplay the moral realism involved in her theory.[8] I would like to play up that Platonic realism about values. My capacity to stand back and evaluate my desires (which is what defines me as a person, rather than a wanton) can make no sense to me unless I understand myself as evaluating on the basis of principles that I apprehend as authoritative; which means that I cannot consistently think of them as being simply my creations, or even those of my society. But the point is not simply that I must behave *as if* there are objective values, even though there possibly might not be. It is rather that a person, whatever he or she may say in his or her philosophical moments, cannot consistently avoid presupposing the objectivity of values. And, since we are persons, we should think philosophically as persons, for there is no alternative perspective (the view from nowhere) from which we could conceivably come to see that what we must necessarily presuppose is false.[9]

I think then that we are committed to the notion there are authoritative evaluational standards by reference to which we can assess our actions and desires; and if they are to function in this way we cannot think of them simply as our creations, nor as brute contingent facts about what we happen to have evolved to value. Philosophers have argued about how to best make sense of there being such standards and many have, of course, wanted to insist that there are such standards while still resisting the Platonic picture of value as both irreducible and ontologically fundamental. I myself hold the admittedly unfashionable position that if values are real at all then they must be metaphysically fundamental in an at least broadly Platonic sense. I have argued for this elsewhere.[10] However, realism about values is one thing and its metaphysical underpinnings another; and although I will in the remainder of this paper draw on Plato and Kierkegaard to give a realist account of value and love as a contrast to Frankfurt's evaluational antirealism, I think that at least much of what I say could be accepted by someone who is a realist about values, but who wishes to resist my own unabashedly Platonic metaphysics of value.

Frankfurt himself continues to resist the moral realist critique of his work. On his developed account, summed up in *The Reasons of Love*, we don't love things because we see that they have value, we treat them as valuable because we love them. And why do we love them? Because we just do. But we just do because that is the way evolution has happened to set us up. "The things we love ... are determined for us by biological or other natural conditions" (RL, 48). That we love our children and our own lives is, he thinks, a brute result of natural selection (RL, 40, 41). So for Frankfurt, our loves, and our cares more generally, are not responses to values that exist apart from them; on the contrary, values are created by our loves. Phenomenologically, this seems to get things the wrong way round. Taylor notes that "We sense in the very experience of being moved by some higher good that we are moved by what is good in it, rather than that it is valuable because of our reaction ... We experience our love for it as a well-founded love."[11] Frankfurt, in part at least, seems to concede this on the phenomenological level: "the lover does invariably and necessarily perceive the beloved as valuable," but, he continues to insist that "the value he sees it to possess is a value that derives from and that depends on his love" (RL, 39). Elsewhere, Frankfurt sums his subjectivism up in uncompromising terms:

I do not believe that anything is inherently important. In my judgement, normativity is not a feature of a reality that is independent of us. The standards of volitional rationality are grounded, so far as I can see, only in ourselves. More particularly, they are grounded only in what we cannot help caring about and cannot help considering important.[12]

This allows for a sort of quasi-objectivity: "there is indeed an objective normative reality which is not up to us ... However, this reality is not objective in the sense of being entirely outside of our minds. Its objectivity consists in the fact that it is outside the scope of our voluntary control."[13] What we care about, what we love, is ultimately down to the pressures of a deterministic natural world. This is true both on an individual level and a species one. There are some things that humans generally just care about, due to the accidents of our evolutionary history; and others that I just find to be my deepest loves, because of the accidents of my personal history.

Now, it is true that we do not first note, in a dispassionate, rational sort of way, that this, this and this have value; and then decide on the basis of that insight that we should care about or love them. Moreover, I think it is true that we are beings that cannot help loving in some sense. And Frankfurt is right to argue that we can only reflect on what we should care about if we start from already caring about something or other (RL, 26). I think, though, that this is all compatible with the Platonic tradition. According to Socrates' description of the Ascent of Love in Plato's *Symposium*,[14] we are first struck—moved to love by—a particular beautiful person or thing (and this is an intense emotional experience; Plato gives more of a role to the felt emotions than Frankfurt does). And it is important to note that such experiences can overthrow, or at least call into question, the initial beliefs that we might have had about what is good or beautiful. The Platonic idea that love is based on what we perceive to be the value (in this case the beauty) of the beloved does *not* mean that we first work out what it is for anything to have beauty, and then go around looking for objects that will conform to those rigid criteria. It is, on the contrary, only by loving, and perhaps by being disillusioned (think of how we come to develop a mature appreciation of art or music), that we can start to get a sense of the nature of Beauty itself—of that from which, according to Plato, all beautiful things derive the beauty they have, and the knowledge of which gives us the true standard for evaluating the beauty of particular things.

Whatever problems Plato's account of the Ascent may have, it does suggest how (generalizing from beauty to value as a whole) we start from the impulse of love (which is not in our control) for particular objects but then move toward a sense of the standards that define the value more generally. We test our developing (and, much of the time, largely implicit and unarticulated) criteria for what is good and beautiful) against our experiences of being struck and moved by what seem to be instantiations of goodness and beauty. When I do find myself experiencing something as beautiful despite its not fitting my prior criteria, I *might* hold onto those criteria and therefore think: well, I'm delighted by something that is really without value. But then I would be thinking of myself as someone in the grip of an infatuation. To think of my feelings as real love (real aesthetic delight), and not as mere infatuation, *is* to think that what I feel myself loving is actually loveable (beautiful); and by so doing, I would be recognizing the inadequacy of my earlier criteria.[15]

In resisting this realist account of love and value, Frankfurt claims that "Parents do not ordinarily love their children so much, for example, because they perceive that their children possess exceptional value. In fact it is the other way around: the children seem to the parents to be valuable, and they are valuable to the parents, only because the parents love them."[16] Frankfurt here appeals to our quite proper sense that a parent's love for a child shouldn't be conditional on that child's possessing "exceptional value" in the sense of having, say, exceptional intellectual or athletic abilities. But he is wrong to suppose that the realist—even the Platonist—need be committed to denying that. You can love your child for what he or she is, even if that does not include having statistically exceptional talents. Children would not want their parents' love to be conditional on their doing well in maths exams, but they would hardly want parents who assure them that their love is unaffected by the fact that they, the children, actually lack any worth or value in themselves. We want to be loved for who we are; and we want to think there is something actually loveable about who we are. Platonists would hold that we are all valuable, worthy of love, because we all participate in the Form of Humanity and thus, ultimately, in the Form of Good. Christians would hold that we are all loveable because all made in the image of God. (Christian Platonists would not think these need be alternatives.) We are all worthy of love, whether or not we have "exceptional" characteristics.

An objector would respond that we are, on those views, being loved, not for our personal, individual characteristics, but for a universal attribute that we all share. This might justify our being the recipients of a universal *agape*, but what of a personal *eros*? It is, of course, commonly supposed that Plato's account of the Ascent implies that we should eventually rise above our particular loves, so that we cease to have preferential loves for our original beloveds.[17] I think this is a mistaken interpretation,[18] but, setting Plato exegesis aside, I don't think a broadly Platonic realism about values does commit us to this clearly unacceptable conclusion. What is of value about you is not simply your universal humanity, but your unique way of being human and living that humanity.[19] This isn't necessarily a matter of "exceptional" abilities, but of your just being the particular individual you are. Human individuals are not replaceable; not even by those who get similar scores on maths tests and can run about as fast.

But if we are all valuable—and so worthy of love—for our individual characters; why don't we all love everyone? The answer has to do with our finitude (which is not a defect, but, as Kierkegaard insisted, an essential part of who we are[20]). An adequate realist account of love must take account, not only of what is "objectively" valuable about the objects of love, but also of what Wolf has helpfully called the "affinity" that attracts one individual to what is of worth in one person and not another.[21] I love the people I do, not only because of their love-worthy particular characters, but because there is something about those characters that "clicks" with mine—not to mention simply the accidents of our having met and the past history we now share. It is part of our finitude that we cannot *experience* and *appreciate* the value of all persons equally, but we can nonetheless *recognize* that other persons have, objectively, as much value as the ones that we love—and we can hope for them that they will find lovers who will experience and appreciate their value. But even the emotionally limited recognition of the value of those we cannot deeply love ourselves can serve as the basis for a universal morality—in which case morality would turn out to have more connection with issues about particular loves and cares than Frankfurt's rather dismissive remarks about it at the start of his book (RL, 5–9) would suggest. The Platonic Ascent, correctly understood, suggests how my experience of loving another person might enable me to see the value that resides in all persons—without this diluting, or causing me to leave behind, my original particular love.

III

In this section, I will develop the (broadly) Platonic view in a bit more detail as an alternative to the account that Frankfurt gives and I will do so by drawing on aspects of Kierkegaard's work. This might seem an unlikely choice since many of Kierkegaard's commentators, even though they disagree radically among themselves, are united in seeing him as a militant anti-Platonist. This is true of those who interpret Kierkegaard as an "existentialist" in the sense of a proto-Sartrian irrationalist; of theologians, who see Kierkegaard as firmly planted on the right side of a "deep, ugly ditch" separating Biblical and Platonic beliefs; and of postmodernists, who want to see Kierkegaard as pioneering the critique of the "logocentric" metaphysics that they castigate Plato for foisting on us. Certainly there are some fairly critical remarks about

Plato in Kierkegaard's writings, and of course there are large differences between the two thinkers. Nevertheless, Kierkegaard's thought is deeply Platonic, in that, for him, there is an eternal transcendent Good, and it is the right relation to that Good that provides the *telos* for human life.[22] Our need to relate to that Good is something that in some sense we are always aware of; but this awareness is in large measure dim, subconscious, something we need to awaken to. Kierkegaard's account of the movement through the "Stages of Life" can, I think, be most perspicuously understood as a version of the Platonic Ascent. (Not, of course, identical with Plato' own version, but recognizably in the same tradition.) We start with the mindless conformity and/or sensuality of unreflective aestheticism; move to the restlessness of the reflective aesthete; from that to the self-choice that comes with the acceptance of ethical standards; and then to the "religious"—to the recognition of the infinite and the eternal, beyond the realm of social ethics.

To this it might be protested straight away that Kierkegaard makes a point of rejecting Platonic recollection; the idea that we have the truth within us and merely need to recover our knowledge of it. In the *Philosophical Fragments*, his pseudonym Johannes Climacus ironically reinvents Christianity by trying to see what a genuinely and radically "non-Socratic" (i.e., in this context, non-Platonic) hypothesis would have to look like. A central part of this non-Platonic view would be the insistence that we are not merely in a state of ignorance (having forgotten the truth, which is nonetheless still within us); rather, we are in a state of sin, in which we are "outside the truth" are indeed, "untruth."[23] However, Climacus goes on to say that we are not simply apart from the truth, we are actually "polemical against it."[24] But, whether or not this was conscious irony on Kierkegaard's (or Climacus') part, this claim undermines the radically non-Socratic nature of the crypto-Christian hypothesis, for I can't be actively hostile to the Truth (the Good) unless I do in some sense know what it is.[25] Kierkegaard's real claim is, I think, in line with Augustine and a long tradition in Christian theology. Firstly, we do have a deep inward knowledge of God (who is the True and the Good) but, secondly, we have for the most part a very limited and inadequate awareness of that knowledge that we possess; and, thirdly, that this is not because of some accidental forgetfulness that we have suffered from, but is because we are inclined to repress and turn away from that knowledge.

Platonism, of course, agrees with the first and second points. The break with it supposedly comes with the third, the idea that we haven't just forgotten the truth, we are actively repressing it. In *Sickness unto Death*, Kierkegaard again rejects the "Socratic" idea that "sin is ignorance" and insists that "sin is not a matter of a person's not having understood what is right, but of his being unwilling to understand it, of his not willing what is right."[26] But it is actually not clear that Plato's view is that different. In the *Symposium*, after Socrates has recounted Diotima's description of the Ascent, the drunken Alcibiades lurches in and ends up delivering an encomium on Socrates, in the course of which he says that Socrates is the only person who can make him ashamed of his life. Socrates points him to the Good (makes him recollect his existing knowledge of it) and he describes how drawn he is to philosophy. But he cannot bring himself to amend his life. "So," he says, "I refuse to listen to him; I stop my ears and tear myself away from him ... I know perfectly well I can't prove he's wrong when he tells me what I should do; yet, the moment I leave his side I go back to my old ways ..."[27] Whatever the "Socratic" view, Plato, by introducing Alcibiades at this point, couldn't have made much clearer his own recognition that "sin" is more than simply ignorance.[28] Or, to put it another way, if "sin" is ignorance, then that ignorance is not a merely intellectual failing. And the "knowledge" that would be needed to overcome such "ignorance" must be an *erotic* knowledge, more akin to the Biblical sense in which Adam "knew" Eve than it is to a purely intellectual assent to well-justified propositions. To know the Form of the Good is existentially transformative knowledge.

In *Sickness unto Death*, Kierkegaard defines the self as a self-conscious activity of relating "the infinite and the finite ... the temporal and the eternal ... freedom and necessity."[29] In each of these duos, one element stands for our limitation, our rootedness in the specificities of nature, society and history; the other stands for our power of transcendence, our capacity for stepping back from ourselves to evaluate and change who we are. So Kierkegaard would agree with Frankfurt that the capacity for forming higher-order volitions is essential to who we are as persons; and would also agree with him that there are brute facts about our natures and their limitations. What he calls (psychologically) despair and (theologically) sin is the failure to maintain these elements in the creative tension that is selfhood in the full sense. Exaggerating either the aspect of transcendence or what we can call the aspect of immanence thus leads to despair (though not necessarily on the level of consciousness).

Both aspects of selfhood are real whether we like it or not, but that doesn't simply mean we are stuck with them, for the attempt to ignore or repress either can indeed lead to its atrophying. This should not, however, lead us to celebrate our power to re-make ourselves, for we remain creatures who need both aspects, and so the diminishing of either is disastrous for us. So (taking the transcendence side first) we cannot simply become anything that we choose to be or can imagine being; but the attempt to do so, to reject any commitments that might tie us down, or the attempt to ignore our limitations, will lead to the self becoming "volatilized"—lost in fantasy.[30] Correspondingly, we can never simply become sub-personal "wantons," but the withering of the imagination, the sense of possibility, can lead to a life in which a vital part of the personality is simply stifled.[31]

However, Kierkegaard is not just recommending that we stick to a mean, navigating cautiously between extremes; for him the polarities that define the self can only be synthesized if the self, through willing to be itself, comes "to rest transparently in the power that established it."[32] The self only becomes whole through relating itself to God. *The Sickness* is written from an explicitly Christian standpoint, but one can take the point less specifically; the self needs a *telos*, an objective Good beyond itself, in order to avoid despair. This is not to reject or to dismiss as unimportant, Kierkegaard's more specific religious commitments; merely to point out that further argument would be needed to identify the (Platonic) Good with the God of theism, let alone with the God of Christianity. However, in many of his own writings, Kierkegaard remained at the level of what Climacus called "Religiousness A," often invoking 'The Eternal" or "the Good" rather than "God." This is true of the important discourse (sub) titled *Purity of Heart Is to Will One Thing*—a maxim that, as we saw, Frankfurt claims to endorse. However, for Frankfurt, to be "pure of heart" is to be wholehearted in ones loves and cares—even if what one loves is thoroughly evil.

> Being wholehearted is quite compatible not only with being morally somewhat imperfect, but even with being dreadfully and irredeemably wicked ... The function of love is not to make people good. Its function is just to make their lives meaningful, and thus to help make their lives in that way good for them to live. (RL, 98–99)

Here the good is thoroughly subjectivised.[33] Kierkegaard, by contrast, does argue that only the Good can be willed wholeheartedly. This view depends on the deeply Platonic assumption that the Good is our natural *telos*; that we have a need for it which manifests itself in an erotic striving toward it. However much we might, like Alcibiades, wish to stifle that longing, we remain drawn to the Good. Hence, someone who is committed to a life of evil cannot be wholehearted, for s/he cannot entirely suppress that desire for the Good. "a person, despite all his defiance, does not have the power to tear himself away completely from the good ... he also does not even have the power to will it completely."[34] This, it should be noted, is not an empirical claim that could be refuted by empirical examples of really horrible dictators or gangsters; it is a fundamental assumption of the philosophical anthropology that sees humanity as having a constitutive teleological impetus toward the Good. This is not a naïve optimism (not something of which Kierkegaard usually gets accused)—but it does state that to the extent to which we do turn away from the Good (according to Kierkegaard, a considerable extent in all our cases) we are turning against ourselves; something that we cannot do wholeheartedly.

Our capacity for transcendence is what drives us through the Stages of Life; or which imparts a despairing restlessness to us if we don't make that progression. A reflective aesthete like the "A" of *Either/Or* cannot be satisfied with aiming purely at the finite, limited goods of ordinary, conformist social life; nor can he find satisfaction in the equally limited goods of sensuality. There is something in him that can see through and beyond the limitations of such goods, even though they are really good up to a point. But they are not enough for a life based simply around them to have meaning. A is tempted to make an absolute good out of his sheer power of invention and negation (identifying himself purely with his power of transcendence)—but that too would be a mutilation, a repression of part of what he is; it would ignore his finitude, his limits.

Judge William offers a synthesis—the absolute choice of the self "in [its] eternal validity,"[35] on the basis of which one returns to the humdrum but satisfying round of ordinary social life and the duties that go with that. Thus he solves "the great riddle, to live in eternity and yet to hear the cabinet clock strike."[36] But the restlessness of our drive to transcendence cannot be brought off so easily; it is all too easy to take an ironic step back from the conventions of the ninetieth-century Copenhagen bourgeoisie—as it is also from those of the liberal cosmopolitan early twenty-first-century intelligentsia. The human spirit will not be satisfied until it finds something that it cannot step back from, cannot transcend, cannot see through the limitations of—in other words, until it reaches what is absolute, infinite, eternal; wholly, rather than just partially, good. In other words, *The* Good, the Eternal, God.[37]

Of course, Judge William is right that one has to hear the clock strike while living in eternity; we are finite, temporal, and limited by necessity as much as we are oriented to participation in the eternal and the infinite, and open to possibility. Forgetting this leads to the immature religiosity that Kierkegaard condemns as "fantasy" and "intoxication."[38] Plato compares the Good to the sun; but one is not well advised to spend much of one's time gazing raptly into the sun. Rather, it is by the sun's light that one is able to see the particulars around one. Similarly, it is in the light of the Good that one is able to pay a proper and discriminating attention to the messy particularities of one's daily life, and those of the people around one.[39] The "Ascent" needs to be followed by a "Descent," or, to use another of Plato's images, the philosopher must return to the cave in order to apply the universal standard of the Good to the particular situations in which we, as finite beings, live.

"Willing one thing" can't mean willing the Good *instead* of, for example, willing to advance my career or educate my children. Rather, our sense of the Good serves as the standard by which we form our higher-order volitions and thus evaluate and order our particular desires; it doesn't do away with those desires. As Frankfurt very sensibly says, "The degree to which a person's heart is pure is not a function of how many things the person wills. Rather it depends on how they are willed. What counts is the quality of the will ... not the quantity of its objects" (RL, 96). Of course, we will many different things. Purity of Heart, for Kierkegaard, is to will them all in the light of the Good; to have ones higher-order volitions responsive to what is good. This, sadly, is what is missing from Frankfurt's account, which calls only for an internal coherence, a "volitional unification" of the will, no matter what it is directed toward.

IV

Even if we are persuaded that the Kierkegaardian view could be a viable alternative to Frankfurt's, it might seem that we need more in the way of positive reasons why we should adopt it, or why we should prefer it to his. I want therefore to conclude by trying to articulate the discomfort I have with certain aspects of Frankfurt's view, and to indicate why Kierkegaard's seems preferable.

For Kierkegaard, as we saw, the self exists as a self-conscious activity of relating its transcendent and immanent aspects. Frankfurt is well aware of these aspects of the self, but his account fails to maintain them in the creative tension that Kierkegaard rightly sees to be necessary. Frankfurt's original identification of personhood with the capacity for higher-order volition has seemed to some to exaggerate the aspect of transcendence; to identify us with our grimly self-chosen will to endorse some desires and repress others—or at least set them aside as alien. Some of his remarks—especially in his earlier writings—do sound positively Sartrean in their celebration of the literally self-creating power of the will:

> The decision determines what the person really wants by making the desire on which he decides fully his own. To this extent, the person in making a decision by which he identifies with a desire, *constitutes himself* ... These acts of ordering and rejection ... create a self out of the raw materials of inner life.[40]

Against this, Marya Schechtman has argued that we cannot simply make ourselves what we chose to; there is an element of givenness in our natures that needs to be acknowledged.[41] Or, as Kierkegaard would say, to lack finitude or necessity in one's life is a form of despair. But, although I think that Frankfurt does in some ways exaggerate our power of self-shaping transcendence, he also—and at a more fundamental level—exaggerates the opposite pole, that of immanence, limitation, finitude. So, elsewhere Frankfurt insists that a person

> cannot make himself wholehearted just by a psychic movement that is fully under his immediate voluntary control ... A person's will is real only if its character is not absolutely up to him .... It cannot be unconditionally in his power to determine what his will is to be ... Therefore, we cannot be authors of ourselves ... We can be only what nature and life make us, and that is not so readily up to us.[42]

This is clearly the position Frankfurt adopts in *The Reasons of Love*, and in his subsequent Tanner Lectures, *Taking Ourselves Seriously and Getting It Right*. We care about the things we do—identifying with some desires and repudiating others—only because of the brute facts of what our evolutionary history has made us as a species, and the equally brute facts of what our personal histories have made us as individuals. Perhaps the biggest worry I have about this position is that there is something *complacent* about it. That we need to care, and indeed to love, that we need final ends, is, on his view, just a brute fact about us. It is not inexplicable, but the explanation of it will, he assumes, simply be a scientific one; that just happens to be the nature evolution has thrown up for us. This, he thinks, shouldn't bother us; nor should our inability to justify our cares and loves and values in rational terms (RL, 28, 31). I just am a being of this sort, so this is what I take to be important.

Part of the problem with this is that it seems to clash with the intuitions that Frankfurt himself appeals to when he insists on the importance of our being moved, not simply by desires, but by desires that we have reflectively and wholeheartedly endorsed from a higher level. To be persons, we must do more than simply act on the desires we happen to find ourselves feeling; we need to be able to step back and reflect on those desires. But for Frankfurt, although that process can free us from having our deeper cares subverted by short-term desires, in the end it simply involves accepting the brute fact that my cares are these or those. Hence his compatibilism. Freedom for him is being able to act on what I really want; but that is quite compatible with what I really want having been formed by deterministic processes over which I have no control. (Genetics, upbringing, etc.) So Wolf complains that someone so depraved by a terrible upbringing as to have a wholehearted higher-order love of cruelty is, on Frankfurt's account, perfectly free.[43] Wolf takes this as a *reductio*, but Frankfurt seems (though without explicit reference to Wolf) to accept this consequence (RL, 97, 98). Moreover, such a person is, in Frankfurt's sense, able to love himself well; which, Frankfurt says, "may well be the 'highest' or most important thing of all" (RL, 98 fn)—even though it is compatible with being "dreadfully and irredeemably wicked" (RL, 98).

This raises many questions. One of them is whether this shows that Frankfurt has played down the importance of social morality to an excessive degree. But what I want to focus on more is the worry that he has betrayed his own insight that to be a person is to be a self-evaluator. Doesn't he stop too quickly with an "Oh – well, that is what I am then"; too complacent an acceptance of whatever I happen to turn out to be? It's not that I am endorsing Sartrean self-creation, the idea that I can be whatever I choose to be. But isn't there some middle ground here, which avoids the excesses of both deterministic complacency and libertarian megalomania? I don't and can't simply create my values out of nothing by an act of radical choice. But nor do I simply discover that these are my deepest values, while also recognizing that they are ultimately just mine (or ours); that they don't reflect the actual value of things apart from my inclination toward them. In Kierkegaardian terms, one would have to say that Frankfurt's account, which at first seemed to recommend the "despairing" perspective of those who lack necessity and finitude in their lives, ends by giving in to the countervailing despair of those who lack possibility and infinitude.

Both Sartre's and Frankfurt's views are forms of evaluative antirealism; for both of them, we create values rather than discovering them, though for Frankfurt we are constrained in doing so by natural necessity rather than having any choice in what we create. But in this they both end up trivializing the freedom, based on reflective evaluation, which they had initially championed. In Sartre's case this is because a truly radical choice is one based on no reasons; but this makes any choice equally arbitrary. For Frankfurt, we end up caring as we do, not because this is the right thing to do, but because that is just how we are made. For neither of them can the process of stepping back and reflecting on our desires lead to us acting or desiring better since better and worse have no definition apart from our choices. Sartre's view would leave us just as well off flicking a coin each time we needed to choose, while Frankfurt, having initially distinguished persons sharply from mere animal choosers (acting on first-order desires), ends up making the distinction only a relative one (we too are determined by our biology, just in a more complex way).

This brings Frankfurt's position close in some ways to the ethical naturalism recommended by philosophers such as Philippa Foot and Rosalind Hursthouse, according to which there is an objective good for us, but this is not something Platonically absolute and eternal. The good life for a human being is good for us in the same way that the good life for a wolf is good for that wolf; it is a life in which that creature's various potentialities are able to flourish and come to full development.[44] Foot and Hursthouse both take seriously the thought that we are *rational* or cultural animals, so what is good for us is not to be defined in a reductively biological fashion. Nonetheless, I think Kierkegaard would see this position as exaggerating our immanence, finitude, necessity. A wolf has a more or less fixed nature that makes it possible for us to define quite precisely what the good life is for a wolf. Our rationality—or more generally, our capacities for transcendence— does not just add an extra element that needs to be taken into account in deciding what we need to flourish, but throws into question the fixity of our nature.[45] This is why, I think, Frankfurt rejects this view for his antirealism. What is the good for us has to be what we can reflectively endorse as good for us. I can step back from the social or biological givens of my nature and refuse to accept that they define the good for me.[46] But, having resisted ethical naturalism by making this crucial point, Frankfurt, as noted above, collapses back into a kind of biological determinism after all.

But this is more unsettling than Frankfurt seems to realize. I can think—I have these values because I was brought up to have them by my society. But that doesn't mean they are right. And I can also think—I'm a member of a species that evolved to have these values. But that doesn't mean they are right either. Now, this "higher-order" reflection on my first-order moral or evaluative feelings may not stop me having them; maybe I just have to accept that I am unavoidably committed to values that I can see in my reflective moments have no adequate basis. In fact, Frankfurt seems to give us the worst of both worlds; he allows enough of the perspective of transcendence that we can see our biology does not define an intrinsic good for us (hence his antirealism); but then insists that we are fated to act as though it did define an ultimate good anyway. But there is, or should be, something deeply unsettling about this predicament. It would seem to leave us in a version of the "ambivalence" that Frankfurt characterizes as a disease of the will; it would surely make it hard for us to be wholehearted in our commitments.

On the Platonic/Kierkegaardian view, by contrast, I need to appeal to standards outside of me—to the True and the Good—and if I find I am deeply averse to them, then this is not something to be accepted, but to be struggled against. If there is a genuinely authoritative standard, then choices made with reference to that standard are not arbitrary. This can, I think, help us to see the force of Kierkegaard's claim that it is only through being oriented to God that the self is able to hold together the elements of transcendence and immanence in creative tension, and that the loss of that orientation necessarily results in the internal conflict, or self-mutilation that Kierkegaard calls "despair" or "sin." At any rate, we can see why it can seem plausible to claim that the self needs an orientation to the Good to prevent it from despairing in this sense. Frankfurt's crucial insight was that personhood required the capacity for the self-conscious examination and evaluation of one's desires. But evaluation needs a standard by which one is to evaluate; and the standard needs to be one that I can reflectively endorse as being *right*—one that no amount of critical reflection leads me to think of as transcended or gone beyond. Without reference to such an objective Good, the self will be unable to really evaluate and will thus, in Kierkegaardian terms, fall into the despair either of the fatalist/determinist (Frankfurt)[47] or of the defiant character insisting on his power to make himself whatever he wills to be (Sartre).[48]

But if the Platonist or Kierkegaardian avoids the latter (Sartrean) predicament, does she really avoid the former (Frankfurtian) one? If Frankfurt comes to a halt and stops reflecting at the contingencies of our biological nature, doesn't the Platonist come to a similar halt at the ultimately brute given fact of the nature of values, of the Good being what it is? There are two answers to this charge, which I can only indicate briefly here. Firstly, what Frankfurt stops at are, as he clearly recognizes, contingent matters of fact (RL, 48). We might have been different, then we would have valued different things. What the Platonist stops at is inherently normative, and, as such, necessary. It makes no sense to say that the Form of the Good is such as to make justice good, but of course, it might not have been. So for the Platonist reflection comes to an end, not at what just happens to be the case, but at what *should* be the case—which seems, after all, to be where normative reflection ought to terminate.

The second response may help with a worry that is widely held—that the Platonic position is irrational, arrogant, and potentially authoritarian. How can I say, on the basis of some alleged quasi-mystical intuition of the Good, that I can be sure that I have the one true standard for evaluation? I don't think the Platonism I am recommending is subject to this objection, though. For a moral realist, there can be genuine moral mistakes. If the Good is genuinely independent of human thought about it, then it is a standard against which all our moral thinking needs to be measured. And a realistic view of human behavior and thought should make us very aware of how far people may be from grasping the Good—even when they are most convinced that they are doing so. This shouldn't leave us in a skeptical paralysis, but it should leave us always questioning the adequacy of our understanding of the Good, and willing to reflect further on it. What we reach in the Ascent, is not a full, clear, and complete understanding of the Good, but a glimpse of something we are always struggling to articulate fully, and which is always open to further attempts at articulation and clarification. There is nothing more ultimate than the Good; but there is always something further than my current apprehension of it. In that sense, it is anything but a stopping place for reflection.

Notes

1   For a considerably more detailed version of this argument, with connections to other thinkers not discussed here, see Anthony Rudd, *Self, Value, and Narrative.*

2   Originally published in the *Philosophical Review*, 1971; republished in IWC, 11–25.

3   See especially his essay, "Rotation of Crops" in EO 1, 281–300.

4   Gary Watson, "Free Agency," *Philosophical Review*, 1975; reprinted in G. Watson (ed.), *Free Will*, 2nd ed.

5   In IWC, 159–76.

6   Charles Taylor, "Responsibility for Self,"; and Taylor, *Sources of the Self* Part One; Susan Wolf, "Sanity and the Metaphysics of Responsibility," reprinted in G. Watson (ed) *Free Will* 2nd ed.; *Freedom Within Reason*; and Wolf, "The True, the Good and the Lovable; Frankfurt's Avoidance of Objectivity."

7   In a later paper, "The Work of the Will" Watson, while maintaining a "cognitivist" or realist position about morality, claims that his argument would work even on a sophisticated antirealist or projectivist view, such as Blackburn's.

8   See Wolf, *Freedom Within Reason*, 123.

9   For a more detailed development of this argument, see Rudd, *Self, Value, and Narrative*, 92–99, 101–07.

10   See Rudd, *Self, Value, and Narrative*, chapters 5 and 6.

11   Taylor, *Sources of the Self*, 74.

12   TOS, 33.

13   Ibid., 34.

14   See Plato, *Symposium*, 57–60 (210A–212B).

15   Of course, I may find myself torn between my old criteria and my new love, unable to decide about my feelings; but then I would be suffering from what Frankfurt calls a debilitating "ambivalence" in my attitudes.

16   TOS, 25.

17   The classic criticism of the Platonic position for undervaluing the individual in this way is Gregory Vlastos, "The Individual as Object of Love in Plato's Dialogues." A rather more nuanced version of this critique can be found in Martha Nussbaum, *The Fragility of Goodness*, chapter 6.

18 Plato is defended against this line of criticism by, for example, Drew
    Hyland, in his "Philosophy and Tragedy in the Platonic Dialogues," and by
    Frisbee Sheffield in her *Plato's 'Symposium': The Ethics of Desire*, chapter 5.

19 To put the point in terms of the *imago dei* doctrine (whether you take
    this literally or metaphorically): we shouldn't think of the image of God
    in everyone being a universal, identical core underlying our accidental
    differences. Rather, for the infinite to express itself in the finite, it must do
    so in an indefinitely large variety of ways. You image the divine infinity
    in a way that you and only you can do. (This is also connected to the
    Neoplatonic Principle of Plenitude—that the Good diffuses itself as far as it
    possibly can; see the classic discussion by Arthur Lovejoy, who introduces
    the term in his *The Great Chain of Being*, 52 and discusses it throughout
    that book.)

20 See SUD, 30–33.

21 See "The True, The Good and the Loveable," 233.

22 For more detail on this, see my *Self, Value and Narrative*, chapter 2.

23 PF, 13.

24 PF, 15.

25 For a detailed discussion of these difficulties, see, Rudd, "The Moment and
    the Teacher: Problems in Kierkegaard's *Philosophical Fragments*."

26 SUD, 95.

27 *Symposium*, 67 (216 A–B).

28 We should note that Plato and Christianity (and a great many other
    moral, spiritual and political—e.g., Marxism, radical environmentalism—
    traditions) agree in supposing that, as things stand, most of us have
    radically disordered loves. (We are far too concerned with such things
    as power, prestige, etc.) They would therefore agree in rejecting Wolf's
    strikingly upbeat view of the human condition: "I assume, indeed, that
    most of what people love and care about … are well worth loving and
    caring about. And most of the time, most people care to an appropriate
    degree about the various things they care about." ("The True, the Good and
    the Loveable," op. cit., 237).

29 SUD, 13.

30 Ibid., 31–32.

31 See ibid., 41.

32 Ibid., 14.

33 Elsewhere, Frankfurt claims that "immoral lives may be good to live …
    the value to Hitler of living the life he chose would have been damaged by
    the immorality of that life only if morality was something Hitler actually
    cared about …. Unless a person cares about being moral … it will not be
    reasonable for him to do what he is morally obliged to do." ("Reply to Susan
    Wolf," in S. Buss and L. Overton (eds) *Contours of Agency* (op. cit.) 248).

34 UDVS, 33.

35 EO II, 214.

36　Ib, 138.

37　I am deliberately cutting short Kierkegaard's dialectic at this point, short of the move from this generic, platonistic religiousness (Religiousness A) to Christianity. That raises too many issues that would take us beyond what can be handled in this paper. But just as the ethical dethrones rather than abolishing the aesthetic, so Christianity dethrones but does not abolish Religiousness A.

38　SUD, 32.

39　A point well made by Iris Murdoch. (See her *The Sovereignty of Good*.) Platonism as such is not committed to a dualistic, ascetic flight from the world, although aspects of the tradition have (I would say) perverted it in that direction.

40　IW, 170.

41　See Marya Schechtman, "Self-Expression and Self-Control."

42　FP, 100–01.

43　Wolf, "Sanity and the Metaphysics of Responsibility," 379–81.

44　See Philippa Foot, *Natural Goodness* and Rosalind Hursthouse, *On Virtue Ethics*.

45　For a more detailed development of this argument, see Rudd, *Self, Value, and Narrative*, 117–25.

46　This is obvious in such cases as someone who decides not to have children, although leaving offspring is a central part of biological flourishing. But one can also risk or even choose mutilation or death for the sake of ideals.

47　See SUD, 40–41.

48　See ibid., 67–73; a passage that, as Tom Angier has noted, is hard not to read as an anticipatory critique of Nietzsche as well as Sartre. See Tom Angier, *Either Kierkegaard/Or Nietzsche*, 20–22.

List of Contributors

John J. Davenport is professor of philosophy at Fordham University. He is the author of *Narrative Identity, Autonomy and Mortality: From Frankfurt and MacIntyre to Kierkegaard* (Routledge, 2012); *Will as Commitment and Resolve* (Fordham University Press, 2007) and coeditor of *Kierkegaard After MacIntyre* (Open Court, 2001).

M. Jamie Ferreira is Carolyn M. Barbour Professor Emeritus of Religious Studies at the University of Virginia. She is the author of *Kierkegaard: An Introduction* (Blackwell, 2008), *Love's Grateful Striving: A Commentary on Kierkegaard's Works of Love* (Oxford, May 2001), and *Transforming Vision: Imagination and Will in Kierkegaard's Thought* (Oxford, 1991).

Rick Anthony Furtak is associate professor of philosophy at Colorado College. He is the author of *Wisdom in Love: Kierkegaard and the Ancient Quest for Emotional Integrity* (University of Notre Dame Press, 2005) and editor of the *Cambridge Critical Guide to Kierkegaard's Concluding Unscientific Postscript* (Cambridge University Press, 2010).

Troy Jollimore is professor of philosophy at California State University, Chico. He is the author of *Love's Vision* (Princeton University Press, 2011) and *On Loyalty* (Routledge, 2012), as well as three collections of poetry: *At Lake Scugog, Tom Thomson in Purgatory*, and the forthcoming *Syllabus of Errors*.

John Lippitt is professor of ethics and philosophy of religion at the University of Hertfordshire and honorary professor of philosophy at Deakin University. He is the author of *Kierkegaard and the Problem of Self-Love* (Cambridge University Press, 2013), the *Routledge Guidebook to Kierkegaard and Fear and Trembling* (2003, second edition forthcoming), and *Humour and Irony in Kierkegaard's Thought* (Palgrave, 2000). He is coeditor of the *Oxford Handbook of Kierkegaard* (Oxford University Press, 2013) and *Narrative, Identity and the Kierkegaardian Self* (Edinburgh University Press, 2015).

Marilyn G. Piety is associate professor of philosophy at Drexel University. She is the author of *Ways of Knowing: Kierkegaard's Pluralist Epistemology* (Baylor University Press, 2010) and translator of Kierkegaard's *Repetition* and *Philosophical Crumbs* (Oxford University Press, 2009). She has published articles on Kierkegaard in various books and scholarly journals and maintains two blogs *Piety on Kierkegaard* and *The Life of the Mind* (the latter on her website mgpiety.org).

Anthony Rudd is an associate professor of philosophy at St. Olaf College. He is the author of *Self, Value and Narrative: a Kierkegaardian Approach* (Oxford University Press, 2012), *Expressing the World: Skepticism, Wittgenstein and Heidegger* (Open Court, 2003), and *Kierkegaard and the Limits of the Ethical* (Oxford University Press, 1993). He is coeditor of *Kierkegaard After MacIntyre* (Open Court, 2001).

Alan Soble has been teaching and writing about the philosophy of love for 40 years. Among his publications are *The Philosophy of Sex and Love*, 2nd ed. (Paragon House, 2008), *Eros, Agape, and Philia* (Paragon House, 1998), and *The Structure of Love* (Yale University Press, 1990). He is currently an adjunct professor at Drexel University.

Charles Taliaferro is professor of philosophy at St. Olaf College. He is the author of several books, including *The Golden Cord; a Short Book on the Sacred and the Secular* (University of Notre Dame Press, 2012), *Contemporary Philosophy of Religion* (Blackwell, 1998), and *Consciousness and the Mind of God* (Cambridge University Press, 1994). He is also the coauthor of *The Image in Mind: Theism, Naturalism and the Imagination* (Continuum, 2010) and *A Brief History of the Soul* (Blackwell, 2012) and coeditor of *The Routledge Companion to Theism (2012).*

Annemarie van Stee is a PhD candidate in philosophy at the University of Leiden, completing a dissertation on the relation of philosophical anthropology (including the work of Kierkegaard) to contemporary cognitive neuroscience. She spent the spring semester of 2014 as a visiting researcher at the Centre for Subjectivity Research in Copenhagen.

Sylvia Walsh is scholar in residence at Stetson University. She is the author of *Kierkegaard: Thinking Christianly in an Existential Mode* (Oxford University Press, 2009), *Living Christianly: Kierkegaard's Dialectic of Christian Existence* (Penn State, 2005), and *Living Poetically: Kierkegaard's Existential Aesthetics* (Penn State, 1994). She is also translator of Kierkegaard's *Discourses at the Communion on Fridays* (Indiana University Press, 2011); translator and coeditor of *Fear and Trembling* (Cambridge University Press, 2006) and coeditor of *Feminist Interpretations of Kierkegaard* (Penn State, 1997).

Bibliography

Note to Readers: For source information on most Kierkegaard works cited in this book, and for most of Frankfurt's essays, please see the information given with the list of abbreviations in the frontmatter. Editions of Kierkegaard works other than the Princeton editions are included here. For edited collections, when multiple essays from a single collection are cited, we include a separate entry for the edited collection below, and short entries for each essay. When only a single essay from a collection is cited, all the information for that collection is included in the entry below for the single essay. Information for cited films and works quoted within primary sources is included in the chapter notes, but not in this bibliography.

Andic, Martin. "Love's Redoubling and the Eternal Like for Like." In *International Kierkegaard Commentary: Works of Love*, edited by Perkins, 9–38.

Angier, Tom. *Either Kierkegaard/Or Nietzsche: Moral Philosophy in a New Key*. London: Ashgate, 2006.

Anscombe, G.E.M. *Intention*, 2nd edition. Ithaca, NY: Cornell University Press, 1963.

Aristotle. *Nicomachean Ethics*. Translated by T. Irwin. Indianapolis, IN: Hackett, 1985.

Armstrong, John. *Conditions of Love*. New York: W. W. Norton, 2003.

Augustine. *Confessions*. Translated by R. S. Pine-Coffin. New York: Penguin, 1961.

Badhwar, Neera. "Friends as Ends in Themselves." *Philosophy and Phenomenological Research* 48, no. 1 (Sept. 1987), 1–23.

Baier, Annette. "Trust." *The Tanner Lectures on Human Values* 13 (1992), 109–74.

Baier, Annette. "Trust and anti-trust." *Ethics* 96, no. 2 (1986), 231–60.

Baier, Annette. "Caring about Caring: A Reply to Frankfurt." *Synthese* 53, no. 2 (1982), 273–90.

Bernstein, Mark. "Love, Particularity, and Selfhood." *Southern Journal of Philosophy* 23 (1986), 287–93.

Berry, Wendell. *Jayber Crow: A Novel*. New York: Counterpoint, 2000.

Bigelow, Pat. *Kierkegaard and the Problem of Writing*. Tallahassee: Florida State University Press, 1987.

Biviano, Erin Lothes. *The Paradox of Christian Sacrifice: the Loss of Self, the Gift of Self*. New York: Crossroad, 2007.

Blustein, Jeffrey. *Care and Commitment*. New York: Oxford University Press, 1991.

Borges, Jorge Luis. "Kafka and his Precursors." In Borges' *Labyrinths*, Harmondsworth: Penguin, (1985), 234–36.

Bovens, Luc. "The value of hope." *Philosophy and Phenomenological Research* 59 (1999), 667–81.

Brentlinger, John. "The Nature of Love." In *Plato's Symposium*, Translated by Suzy Groden, edited by John Brentlinger, 113–29. Amherst, MA: University of Massachusetts Press, 1970. Reprinted in *Eros, Agape, and Philia*, edited by A. Soble, 136–48. New York: Paragon House, 1989.

Brown, Robert. *Analyzing Love*. Cambridge: Cambridge University Press, 1987.

Burgess, Andrew. "Kierkegaard's Concept of Redoubling and Luther's *Simul Justus*." In *International Kierkegaard Commentary: Works of Love*, edited by Perkins, 39–55.

Buss, Sarah and Lee Overton, eds. *Contours of Agency: Essays on Themes from Harry Frankfurt*. Cambridge, MA: MIT Press, 2002.

Calhoun, Cheshire. "Standing for Something." *The Journal of Philosophy* 92, no.5 (May 1995), 235–60.

Cappelørn, Niels Jørgen and Hermann Deuser, eds. *Kierkegaard Studies Yearbook 1998*. Berlin: Walter de Gruyter, 1998.

Capps, Donald. *The Depleted Self*. Minneapolis, MN: Fortress Press, 1993.

Carlisle, Clare. *Kierkegaard's Philosophy of Becoming*. Albany, NY: SUNY Press, 2005.

Carlsson, Ulrika. "Love as a Problem of Knowledge in Kierkegaard's *Either/Or* and Plato's *Symposium*." *Inquiry* 53, (2010), 41–67.

Chisholm, Roderick. *Theory of Knowledge*. 3rd edition. Englewood Cliffs: Prentice Hall, 1989.

Clark, Stephen R.L. *God's World and the Great Awakening*. Oxford: Oxford University Press, 1991.

Cohen, G.A. "Deeper into Bullshit." In *Contours of Agency*, edited by Buss and Overton, 321–39.

Come, Arnold B. "Kierkegaard's Ontology of Love." In *International Kierkegaard Commentary: Works of Love*, edited by Perkins, 79–119.

Compact Oxford English Dictionary of Current English, 3rd edition. Oxford: Oxford University Press, 2003.

Crosby, John. "Personal Individuality: Dietrich von Hildebrand in Debate with Harry Frankfurt." In *Personalist Papers*, 19–31. Washington, DC: Catholic University of America Press, 2004.

Davenport, John J. "Earnestness." In *Kierkegaard's Concepts*, Tome II, edited by Jon Stewart and William MacDonald, 221–27. Volume 15 in the series *Kierkegaard Research: Sources, Reception and Resources*. Berlin: De Gruyter, 2014.

Davenport, John J. "Selfhood and 'Spirit'." In *Oxford Handbook of Kierkegaard*, edited by John Lippitt and George Pattison, 230–51. Oxford: Oxford University Press, 2013.

Davenport, John J. *Narrative Identity, Autonomy, and Mortality: From Frankfurt and MacIntyre to Kierkegaard*. Abingdon: Routledge, 2012.

Davenport, John J. "Norm-Guided Formation of Cares without Volitional Necessities." In *Autonomy and the Self*, edited by Michael Kühler and Nadja Jelinek, 47–75. Dordrecht: Springer, 2012.

Davenport, John J. "Life-narrative and death as the end of freedom: Kierkegaard on anticipatory resoluteness." In *Kierkegaard and Death*, edited by Patrick Stokes and Adam Buben, 160–83. Bloomington: Indiana University Press, 2011.

Davenport, John J. *Will as Commitment and Resolve: An Existential Account of Creativity, Love, Virtue, and Happiness*. New York: Fordham University Press, 2007.

Davenport, John J. "The Binding Value of Earnest Emotional Valuation." *International Journal of Decision Ethics* 2, no.1 (Fall 2006), 107–23.

Davenport, John J. "Entangled Freedom: Ethical Authority, Original Sin, and Choice in Kierkegaard's Concept of Anxiety." *Kierkegaardiana* 21 (2001), 131–51.

Davenport, John J. "The Meaning of Kierkegaard's Choice Between the Aesthetic and the Ethical." In *Kierkegaard After MacIntyre: Essays on Freedom, Narrative, and Virtue*, edited by Davenport and Rudd, 75–112.

Davenport, John J. "Towards an Existential Virtue Ethics: Kierkegaard and MacIntyre." In *Kierkegaard After MacIntyre*, edited by Davenport and Rudd, 265–324.

Davenport, John J. and Anthony Rudd, eds. *Kierkegaard After MacIntyre: Essays on Freedom, Narrative, and Virtue*. Chicago, IL: Open Court Publishing Co., 2001.

de Sousa, Ronald. "The Rationality of Emotions." In *Explaining Emotions*, edited by Amléie O. Rorty, 127–52. Berkeley, CA: University of California Press, 1980.

de Sousa, Ronald. *The Rationality of Emotions*. Cambridge, MA: MIT Press, 1987, pb. 1990.

Delaney, Neil. "Romantic Love and Loving Commitment: Articulating a Modern Ideal." *American Philosophical Quarterly* 333, no. 4 (1996), 339–56.

Dillon, Robin S. "Self-forgiveness and self-respect." *Ethics* 112, no. 1 (2001), 53–83.

Drummond, John. "'Cognitive Impenetrability' and the Complex Intentionality of the Emotions." *Journal of Consciousness Studies* 11 (2004), 109–26.

Ebels-Duggan, Kyla. "Against Beneficence: A Normative Account of Love." In *Ethics* 119, no. 1 (2008), 142–70.

Edidin, Peter. "Between Truth and Lies, An Unprintable Ubiquity." *The New York Times*, Feb. 14, 2005. http://www.nytimes.com/2005/02/14/books/14bull.html.

Enoch, David. *Taking Morality Seriously: A Defense of Robust Realism*. New York: Oxford University Press, 2011.

Evans, C. Stephen. *Kierkegaard's Ethic of Love: Divine Commands and Moral Obligations*. Oxford: Oxford University Press, 2004.

Ferguson, Harvey. "Modulation: A Typology of the Present Age." In *Immediacy and Reflection in Kierkegaard's Thought*, edited by Paul Cruysberghs, John Taels, and Karl Vertstrynge, 121–41. Leuven: Leuven University Press, 2003.

Ferreira, M. Jamie. "The Problematic Agapeistic Ideal—Again." In *Ethics, Love, and Faith in Kierkegaard*, edited by Mooney, 93–110.

Ferreira, M. Jamie. *Love's Grateful Striving: A Commentary on Kierkegaard's Works of Love*. Oxford: Oxford University Press, 2001.

Firestone, Chris L. and Nathan Jacobs, *In Defense of Kant's "Religion."* Bloomington: Indiana University Press, 2008.

Fisher, Mark. *Personal Love*. London: Duckworth, 1990.

Fitterer, Roger J. *Love and Objectivity in Virtue Ethics*. Toronto: University of Toronto Press, 2008.

Foot, Philippa. *Natural Goodness*. Oxford: Clarendon Press, 2001.

Fossum, Merle A. and Marilyn J. Mason. *Facing Shame*. New York: W. W. Norton, 1989.

Frankfurt, Harry. *Taking Ourselves Seriously – Getting It Right*. Stanford, CA: Stanford University Press, 2006.

Frankfurt, Harry. *On Bullshit*, Princeton, NJ: Princeton University Press, 2005.

Frankfurt, Harry. *The Reasons of Love*. Princeton, NJ: Princeton University Press, 2004.

Frankfurt, Harry. *Necessity, Volition, and Love*. New York: Cambridge University Press, 1999.

Frankfurt, Harry. *The Importance of What We Care About*. New York: Cambridge University Press, 1988.

Frankl, Viktor E. *Man's Search for Meaning*. New York: Random House, 2004.

Furtak, Rick Anthony. *Wisdom in Love: Kierkegaard and the Ancient Quest for Emotional Integrity*. Notre Dame: University of Notre Dame Press, 2005.

Furtak, Rick Anthony. "The Virtues of Authenticity: A Kierkegaardian Essay in Moral Psychology." *International Philosophical Quarterly* 43, no.4 (December 2003), 423–38.

Furtak, Rick Anthony. "Love and the Discipline of Philosophy." In *Ethics, Faith, and Love in Kierkegaard*, edited by Edward F. Mooney, 59–71. Bloomington: Indiana University Press, 2008.

Garrard, Eve and David McNaughton. *Forgiveness*. Durham: Acumen, 2010.

Govier, Trudy and Wilhelm Verwoerd. "Forgiveness: The Victim's Prerogative." *South African Journal of Philosophy* 21, no. 2 (2002), 97–111.

Green, Ronald M. "Kant on Christian Love." In *The Love Commandments: Essays in Christian Ethics and Moral Philosophy*, edited by Edmund N. Santurri and William Werpehowski, 261–80. Washington, DC: Georgetown University Press, 1992.

Green, Ronald M. *Kierkegaard and Kant: The Hidden Debt*. Albany: State University of New York Press, 1992.

Griswold, Charles. *Forgiveness*. Cambridge: Cambridge University Press, 2007.

Groenhout, Ruth. "Kenosis and feminist theory." In *Exploring Kenotic Christology*, edited by C. Stephen Evans, 291–312. Oxford: Oxford University Press, 2006.

Hadot, Pierre. *Plotinus; or, The Simplicity of Vision*. Translated by Michael Chase. Chicago: University of Chicago Press, 1993.

Halwani, Raja. *Virtuous Liasons: Care, Love, Sex, and Virtue Ethics*. Chicago, IL: Open Court/Carus Publishing Co. 2003.

Hannay, Alastair. *Kierkegaard*. London: Routledge, 1982.

Hannay, Alastair. "Kierkegaard on Natural and Commanded Love." In *Ethics, Love, and Faith in Kierkegaard*, edited by Mooney, 111–18.

Hardcastle, Gary and George Reisch, eds. *Bullshit and Philosophy*. Chicago: Open Court, 2006.

Hare, John E. *The Moral Gap: Kantian Ethics, Human Limits, and God's Assistance*. Oxford: Clarendon Press, 1996.

Hegel, G.W.F. "On Love." In *On Christianity: Early Theological Writings*, Translated by T. Knox, 302–8. New York: Harper and Bros, 1948.

Heidegger, Martin. *Being and Time*. Translated by Joan Stambaugh. Albany, NY: SUNY Press, 1996.

Heidegger, Martin. *Being and Time*. Translated by John Macquarrie and Edward Robinson. New York: Harper and Row, 1962.

Heidegger, Martin. *Phenomenological Interpretations of Aristotle*. Translated by Richard Rojcewicz. Bloomington: Indiana University Press, 2001.

Heidegger, Martin. *The Fundamental Concepts of Metaphysics*. Translated by William McNeill and Nicholas Walker. Bloomington: Indiana University Press, 1995.

Hirschman, Albert O. "Against parsimony: three easy ways of complicating some categories of economic discourse." *American Economic Review Proceedings* 74 (1984), 88–96.

Huemer, Michael. *Ethical Intuitionism*. London: Palgrave Macmillan, 2006.

Hume, David. *A Treatise of Human Nature*, edited by L.A. Selby-Bigge. Oxford: Clarendon Press, 1968.

Hume, David. *An Enquiry Concerning the Principles of Morals*, edited by L.A. Selby-Bigge and revised by P. H. Nidditch. Oxford: Clarendon Press, 1975.

Hunter, J.F.M. *Thinking about Sex and Love*. New York: St. Martin's Press, 1980.

Hursthouse, Rosalind. *On Virtue Ethics* Oxford: Oxford University Press, 1999.

Hyland, Drew. "Philosophy and Tragedy in the Platonic Dialogues." In *Tragedy and Philosophy*, edited by N. Georgopoulos, New York: Macmillan/St. Martin's Press, 1993.

James, William. *The Varieties of Religious Experience*. New York: Vintage Books, 1990.

Johnson, Rolf M. *Three Faces of Love*. DeKalb, IL: Northern Illinois University Press, 2001.

Jollimore, Troy. *Love's Vision*. Princeton, NJ: Princeton University Press, 2011.

Kant, Immanuel. *Religion within the Boundaries of Mere Reason*. Translated and edited by Alan Wood and George di Giovanni. Cambridge: Cambridge University Press, 1998.

Kant, Immanuel. *Groundwork of the Metaphysics of Morals*, 1st edition. Translated and edited by Mary Gregor. Cambridge: Cambridge University Press, 1998.

Kant, Immanuel. *Lectures on Ethics*. Translated by P. Heath. Cambridge: Cambridge University Press, 1997.

Kant, Immanuel. *The Metaphysics of Morals*. Translated by Mary Gregor. Cambridge: Cambridge University Press, 1996.

Kant, Immanuel. *Critique of Practical Reason*, 3rd edition. Translated by Lewis White Beck. New York: Macmillan/Library of Liberal Arts, 1993.

Kant, Immanuel. *Critique of Pure Reason*. Translated by Norman Kemp Smith. New York: St. Martin's Press, 1965.

Keeley, Louise Carroll. "Loving 'No One,' Loving Everyone: The Work of Love in Recollecting One Dead in Kierkegaard's *Works of Love*." In *International Kierkegaard Commentary: Works of Love*, edited by Perkins, 233–4.

Kirmmse, Bruce. "Affectation, or the Invention of the Self: A Modern Disorder." In *Ethics, Love, and Faith in Kierkegaard*, edited by Mooney, 24–38.

Knappe, Ulrich. *Theory and Practice in Kant and Kierkegaard*. Berlin: Walter de Gruyter, 2004.

Korsgaard, Christine M. *Sources of Normativity*. Cambridge: Cambridge University Press, 1996.

Korsgaard, Christine. "Morality and the Logic of Caring." In *Taking Ourselves Seriously and Getting It Right*, edited by Debra Satz, 55–76. Stanford, CA: Stanford University Press, 2006.

Kraut, Robert. "Love *De Re*." *Midwest Studies in Philosophy* 10 (1986), 413–30.

Krishek, Sharon. *Kierkegaard on Faith and Love*. Cambridge: Cambridge University Press, 2009.

Kupperman, Joel. *Character*. New York: Oxford University Press, 1991.

Lamb, Roger E. "Love and Rationality." In *Love Analyzed*, edited by Lamb, 23–47.

Lamb, Roger E., ed. *Love Analyzed*. Boulder, CO: Westview, 1997.

Larkin, Philip. "This Be The Verse." In *The Norton Anthology of Modern and Contemporary Poetry*, edited by Jahan Ramazani, vol. 2. New York: W. W. Norton and Company, 2003.

Larmore, Charles. *The Practices of the Self*. Translated by Sharon Bowman. Chicago: University of Chicago Press, 2010.

Lear, Jonathan. "Whatever." *The New Republic*, March 21, 2005, 23–25.

Lewis, C.S. *The Four Loves*. New York: Harcourt, Brace, 1960.

Lewis, H.D. *The Elusive Self*. Philadelphia, PA: Westminster Press, 1982.

Lillegaard, Norman. "Thinking with Kierkegaard and MacIntyre about Virtue." In *Kierkegaard After MacIntyre*, edited by John J. Davenport and Anthony Rudd, 211–32.

Lippitt, John. "Learning to hope: the role of hope in *Fear and Trembling*." In *Kierkegaard's Fear and Trembling: A Critical Guide*, edited by Daniel W. Conway, 122–41. Cambridge: Cambridge University Press, 2015.

Lippitt, John. *Kierkegaard and the Problem of Self-Love*. Cambridge: Cambridge University Press, 2013.

Lovejoy, Arthur. *The Great Chain of Being* Cambridge, MA: Harvard University Press, 1957.

Luijpen, William A. *Existential Phenomenology*. Pittsburgh, PA: Duquesne University Press, 1960.

Marion, Jean-Luc. *The Erotic Phenomenon*. Translated by Stephen E. Lewis. Chicago, IL: University of Chicago Press, 2007.

Marion, Jean-Luc. *Prolegomena to Charity*. Translated by Stephen E. Lewis. New York: Fordham University Press, 2002.

Marion, Jean-Luc. *God without Being*. Translated by Thomas A. Carlson. Chicago, IL: University of Chicago Press, 1991.

Martens, Paul. "'You Shall Love': Kant, Kierkegaard, and the Interpretation of Matthew 22:39." In *International Kierkegaard Commentary: Works of Love*, edited by Perkins, 57–78.

McDowell, John. *Mind, Value, and Reality* Cambridge, MA: Harvard University Press, 1998.

Merleau-Ponty, Maurice. *The Phenomenology of Perception*. Translated by C. Smith. London: Routledge Classics, 2002.

Metz, Thaddeus. "Recent Work on the Meaning of Life." *Ethics* 112 (July 2002), 781–814.

Michalson, Gordon E. Jr., *Fallen Freedom: Kant on Radical Evil and Moral Regeneration*. Cambridge: Cambridge University Press, 1990.

Mill, J.S. *Utilitarianism: With Critical Essays*, edited by S. Gorovitz. Indianapolis, IN: Bobbs-Merrill, 1971.

Mill, J.S. *On Liberty and other writings*. Edited by Stefan Collini. Cambridge: Cambridge University Press, 1989.

Millgram, Elijah. "On Being Bored out of Your Mind." *Proceedings of the Aristotelian Society* 104, no. 2 (2004), 163–84.

Mitchell, Leslie. *Bulwer Lytton: The Rise and Fall of a Man of Letters*. London: Hambledon and London, 2003.

Montaigne, Michel. "On Affectionate Relationships" ["On Friendship"]. In *The Essays of Michel de Montaigne*, edited and translated by M. A. Screech, 211–15. London: Penguin, 1991.

Mooney, Edward F. "On Authenticity." In *Excursions with Kierkegaard*, edited by Edward F. Mooney, 151–72. New York: Bloomsbury, 2013.

Mooney, Edward F. *Selves in Discord and Resolve: Kierkegaard's moral-religious psychology from Either/or to Sickness unto Death*. New York: Routledge, 1996.

Mooney, Edward F. *Knights of Faith and Resignation*. Albany, NY: SUNY Press, 1991.

Mooney, Edward F., ed. *Ethics, Love, and Faith in Kierkegaard*. Bloomington: Indiana University Press, 2008.

Murdoch, Iris. *Existentialists and Mystics*. New York: Penguin Books, 1998.

Murdoch, Iris. *The Sovereignty of Good*. London: Routledge, 1970.

Nasio, Juan-David. *The Book of Love and Pain*. Translated by David Pettigrew and François Raffoul. Albany, NY: SUNY Press, 2004.

Nehamas, Alexander. "Only in the Contemplation of Beauty is Human Life Worth Living." *European Journal of Philosophy* 15 (2007), 1–18.

Nehamas, Alexander. *Only a Promise of Happiness*. Princeton, NJ: Princeton University Press, 2007.

Nisenbaum, Karin. "Understanding the Body's Critique." *Perspectives: An International Postgraduate Journal of Philosophy* 1 (2008), 51–63.

Nishida Kitarô. *An Inquiry into the Good*. Translated by M. Abe and C. Ives. New Haven: Yale University Press, 1990.

Nota, John H. *Max Scheler: The Man and His Work*. Chicago, IL: Franciscan Herald Press, 1983.

Nozick, Robert. "Love's Bond." In *The Examined Life*, 68–86. New York: Simon and Schuster, 1989.

Nussbaum, Martha. *Upheavals of Thought: The Intelligence of Emotions*. Cambridge: Cambridge University Press, 2001.

Nussbaum, Martha. *The Fragility of Goodness: luck and ethics in Greek tragedy and philosophy*. Revised ed. Cambridge: Cambridge University Press, 2001.

Nussbaum, Martha. *Love's Knowledge: Essays on Philosophy and Literature*. New York: Oxford University Press, 1990.

Nussbaum, Martha. "The Speech of Alcibiades." In *The Fragility of Goodness*, 165–99. Cambridge: Cambridge University Press, 1986.

Nygren, Anders. *Agape and Eros*. Translated by Philip S. Watson. New York: Harper and Row, 1969.

Nygren, Anders. *Den kristna kärlekstanken genom tiderna*. Agape and Eros. England: S.P.C.K. House, 1932, 1938. Philadelphia, PA: Westminster Press, 1953 and translated by P. S. Watson. Chicago: University of Chicago Press, 1982.

O'Donovan, Oliver. *The Problem of Self-love in St. Augustine*. Eugene: Wipf and Stock, 2006.

Ortega y Gasset, José. *On Love: Aspects of a Single Theme*. Translated by Tony Talbot. New York: Meridian Books, 1957.

Outka, Gene. *Agape: An Ethical Analysis*. New Haven: Yale University Press, 1972.

Pangle, Lorraine Smith. *Aristotle and the Philosophy of Friendship*. Cambridge: Cambridge University Press, 2002.

Parfit, Derek. *On What Matters*. Vol. 1. edited by Samuel Scheffler. Oxford: Oxford University Press, 2011.

Pascal, Blaise. *Pensées*. Translated by A. J. Krailsheimer. London: Penguin Books, 1995.

Pattison, George. *Kierkegaard's Upbuilding Discourses*. London: Routledge, 2002.

Pattison, Stephen. *Shame: Theory, Therapy, Theology*. Cambridge: Cambridge University Press, 2000.

Perkins, Robert L., ed. *International Kierkegaard Commentary: Works of Love*, Vol. 16. Macon, GA: Mercer University Press, 1999.

Phillips, D.Z. and Timothy Tessin, eds. *Kant and Kierkegaard on Religion*. London: Macmillan Press Ltd., 2000, and New York: St. Martin's Press, Inc., 2000.

Piety, M.G. "Kierkegaard on Rationality." In *Kierkegaard After MacIntyre*, edited by Davenport and Rudd, 59–74.

Plato. *Euthyphro*. In *The Last Days of Socrates*, Translated by H. Tredennick. New York: Penguin, 1969.

Plato. *Symposium*. Translated by Alexander Nehemas and Paul Woodruff. Indianapolis, IN: Hackett Publishing Co., 1989.

Plato. *Symposium*. Translated by R. Waterfield. Oxford: Oxford University Press, 1994.

Price, A.W. *Love and Friendship in Plato and Aristotle*. Oxford: Clarendon Press, 1989.

Pugmire, David. *Sound Sentiments: Integrity in the Emotions*. Oxford: Oxford University Press, 2005.

Putnam, Hilary. *The Threefold Cord: Mind, Body, and World*. New York: Columbia University Press, 1999.

Pyper, Hugh S. "Forgiving the Unforgivable: Kierkegaard, Derrida and the Scandal of Forgiveness." *Kierkegaardiana* 22 (2002), 7–23.

Radzik, Linda. *Making Amends: Atonement in Morality, Law and Politics*. Oxford: Oxford University Press, 2009.

Reeve, C.D.C. *Love's Confusions*. Cambridge, MA: Harvard University Press, 2005.

Ricoeur, Paul. *Oneself as Another*. Translated by Kathleen Blamey. Chicago, IL: University of Chicago Press, 1992.

Roberts, Robert C. "The virtue of hope in *Eighteen Upbuilding Discourses*." In *International Kierkegaard Commentary: Eighteen Upbuilding Discourses*, edited by Robert L. Perkins, 181–203. Macon, GA: Mercer University Press, 2003.

Roberts, Robert C. *Emotions: An Essay in Aid of Moral Psychology*. Cambridge: Cambridge University Press, 2003.

Robinson, Jenefer. *Deeper than Reason: Emotion and Its Role in Literature, Music, and Art*. Oxford: Oxford University Press, 2005.

Rorty, Amélie. "The Historicity of Psychological Attitudes: Love Is Not Love Which Alters Not When It Alteration Finds." *Midwest Studies in Philosophy* 10 (1986), 399–412.

Rousseau, Jean-Jacques. "Discourse on Origin and Foundations of Inequality Among Men." In *The Basic Political Writings*, edited and translated by Donald Cress, 25–82. Indianapolis, IN: Hackett Publishing, 1987.

Rudd, Anthony. *Self, Value, and Narrative: A Kierkegaardian Approach.* Oxford: Oxford University Press, 2012.

Rudd, Anthony. *Expressing the World.* Chicago: Open Court, 2003.

Rudd, Anthony. "The Moment and the Teacher: Problems in Kierkegaard's *Philosophical Fragments.*" *Kierkegaardiana* 21 (2000), 92–115.

Rudd, Anthony. *Kierkegaard and the Limits of the Ethical.* Oxford: Clarendon Press, 1993.

Santner, Eric. *On the Psychotheology of Everyday Life.* Chicago, IL: University of Chicago Press, 2001.

Schechtman, Marya. "Self-Expression and Self-Control." In *The Self,* edited by Galen Strawson, 45–62. Oxford: Blackwell, 1995.

Schechtman, Marya. "Self-Expression and Self-Control." *Ratio* 17, no. 4 (2004), 409–27.

Scheler, Max. *Ressentiment.* Translated by L. B. Coser and W. W. Holdheim. Milwaukee, WI: Marquette University Press, 1994.

Scheler, Max. *Formalism in Ethics and Non-Formal Ethics of Values.* Translated by M. F. Frings and R. L. Funk. Evanston, IL: Northwestern University Press, 1973.

Scheler, Max. *On Feeling, Knowing, and Valuing,* edited by Harold J. Bershady. Chicago: University of Chicago Press, 1992.

Scheler, Max. *Selected Philosophical Essays.* Translated by D. R. Lachterman. Evanston, IL: Northwestern University Press, 1973.

Scheler, Max. *The Nature of Sympathy.* Translated by Peter Heath. London: Routledge and Kegan Paul, 1970.

Scruton, Roger. *Sexual Desire: A Moral Philosophy of the Erotic.* New York: Free Press, 1986.

Shafer-Landau, Russ. *Moral Realism: A Defense.* New York: Oxford University Press, 2003.

Sheffield, Frisbee. *Plato's "Symposium": The Ethics of Desire.* Oxford: Oxford University Press, 2006.

Simpson, Brent and Rob Willer. "Altruism and Indirect Reciprocity: The Interaction of Persons and Situations in Prosocial Behavior." *Social Psychology Quarterly* 71, no. 1 (2008), 37–52.

Singer, Irving. *The Nature of Love, vol. 1: Plato to Luther,* 2nd edition. Chicago, IL: University of Chicago Press, 1984.

Singer, Irving. *The Nature of Love, vol. 2: Courtly and Romantic.* Chicago, IL: University of Chicago Press, 1984.

Singer, Irving. *The Nature of Love, vol. 3: The Modern World.* Chicago, IL: University of Chicago Press, 1987.

Soble, Alan, ed. *Eros, Agape, and Philia: Readings in the Philosophy of Love.* New York: Paragon House, 1989.

Soble, Alan. "Concerning Self-Love: Analytic Problems in Frankfurt's Account of Love." *Essays in Philosophy* 12, no. 1 (2011), 55–67. http://commons.pacificu.edu/eip/vol12/iss1/5.

Soble, Alan. "Review of *The Reasons of Love*." *Essays in Philosophy* 6 no. 1 (2005). http://commons.pacificu.edu/eip/vol6/iss1/30.

Soble, Alan. "Irreplaceability." In *Sex, Love, and Friendship*, edited by A. Soble, 355–57. Amsterdam: Rodopi, 1997.

Soble, Alan. "Union, Autonomy, and Concern." In *Love Analyzed*, edited by Lamb, 65–92.

Soble, Alan. *The Structure of Love*. New Haven, CT: Yale University Press, 1990.

Sokal, Alan. "Transgressing the Boundaries: Towards a Transformative Hermeneutics of Quantum Gravity." *Social Text* 46/47 (spring/summer 1996), 217–52.

Solomon, Robert C. *True to Our Feelings*. Oxford: Oxford University Press, 2007.

Solomon, Robert C. *About Love: Reinventing Romance for Our Times*. New York: Simon and Schuster, 1988.

Solomon, Robert C. *The Passions*. Notre Dame, IN: University of Notre Dame Press, 1983.

Solzhenitsyn, Alexander. *Nobel Prize Lecture*. Translated by Nicholas Bethel. London: Stenvalley Press, 1973.

Spader, Peter H. *Scheler's Ethical Personalism*. New York: Fordham University Press, 2002.

Stafford, J. Martin. "Hume, David." In *Sex from Plato to Paglia: A Philosophical Encyclopedia*, vol. 1, edited by A. Soble, 476–79. Westport, CT: Greenwood Press, 2006.

Stocker, Michael. "Some Considerations about Intellectual Desire and Emotions." In *Thinking about Feeling*, edited by Robert C. Solomon, 135–48. Oxford: Oxford University Press, 2004.

Stokes, Patrick. *Kierkegaard's Mirrors: Interest, Self and Moral Vision*. Basingstoke: Palgrave, 2010.

Stokes, Patrick. "Kierkegaardian Vision and the Concrete Other." *Continental Philosophy Review* 39 (2006), 393–413.

Taliaferro, Charles and Alison J. Tepley, eds. *Cambridge Platonist Spirituality*. New York: Pavlist Press, 2005.

Taliaferro, Charles. *Evidence and Faith; Philosophy and Religion since the Seventeenth Century*. Cambridge: Cambridge University Press, 2005.

Taliaferro, Charles. "A God's Eye View." In *Faith and Analysis*, edited by H.A. Harris and C.I. Insole. Hampshire: Ashgate, 2005.

Taliaferro, Charles. "Relativizing the Ideal Observer Theory." *Philosophy and Phenomenological Research* 49, no. 1 (1988), 123–38.

Taylor, Charles. *Sources of the Self*. Cambridge: Cambridge University Press, 1989.

Taylor, Charles. "Responsibility for Self." In *The Identities of Persons*, edited by Amelie Rorty, 281–300. Berkeley: University of California Press, 1976.

Taylor, Gabriele. *Deadly Vices*. Oxford: Oxford University Press, 2006.

Taylor, Gabriele. "Deadly Vices?" In *How Should One Live? Essays on the Virtues*, edited by Roger Crisp, 157–72. New York: Oxford University Press, 1998.

Thomson, Iain D. "Ontotheology." In *Interpreting Heidegger: New Essays*, edited by Daniel O. Dahlstrom, 106–31. Cambridge: Cambridge University Press, 2010.

Vacek, Edward C. *Love, Human and Divine: The Heart of Christian Ethics*. Washington, DC: Georgetown University Press, 1994.

Valéry, Paul, Preface on Stendhal. In Stendhal, *Oeuvres complètes* (Gallimard/Pléiade, 1957 vol. I; reprinted as "Stendhal," in Valéry, *Masters and Friends*, Translated by Martin Turnell. Princeton, NJ: Princeton University Press, 1968: 176–212).

Van Hooft, Stan. *Hope*. Durham: Acumen, 2011.

Van Willigenburg, Theo. "Reason and Love." *Ethical Theory and Moral Practice* 8 (2005), 45–62.

Velleman, David. "Beyond Price." *Ethics* 118 (2008), 191–212.

Vlastos, Gregory. "The Individual as an Object of Love in Plato." In *Platonic Studies*, 3–34. Princeton, NJ: Princeton University Press, 1973. Reprinted in *Eros, Agape, and Philia*, edited by A. Soble, 96–124. New York: Paragon House, 1989.

Vlastos, Gregory. "The Individual as Object of Love in Plato's Dialogues." In *Platonic Studies*, 2nd edition, 3–34. Princeton, NJ: Princeton University Press, 1981.

von Hildebrand, Dietrich. *The Nature of Love*. Translated by John F. Crosby. South Bend: St. Augustine's Press, 2009.

Walsh, Sylvia. *Kierkegaard: Thinking Christianly in an Existential Mode*. Oxford: Oxford University Press, 2009.

Walsh, Sylvia. *Living Christianly: Kierkegaard's Dialectic of Christian Existence*. University Park: The Pennsylvania State University Press, 2005.

Walsh, Sylvia. Review of *Love's Grateful Striving* by M. Jamie Ferreira. *International Journal of Philosophy of Religion* 53, no. 2 (2003), 115–17.

Watson, Gary, ed. *Free Will*. 2nd edition. Oxford: Oxford University Press, 2003.

Watson, Gary. "Free Agency." In *Free Will*, 2nd ed., edited by Watson, 337–51.

Watson, Gary. "The Work of the Will." In *Weakness of Will and Practical Irrationality*, edited by Sarah Stroud and Christine Tappolet, 172–200. Oxford: Clarendon Press, 2003.

Wenisch, Fritz. Review of *The Nature of Love, Faith and Philosophy* by Dietrich von Hildebrand, *Faith and Philosophy*, Vol. 29, no. 1 (January 2012), 118–122.

Weston, Michael. *Kierkegaard and Modern Continental Philosophy*. London: Routledge, 1994.

Westphal, Merold. "Commanded Love and Moral Autonomy: The Kierkegaard-Habermas Debate." In *Kierkegaard Studies Yearbook 1998*, edited by Cappelørn and Deuser, 1–22.

White, Richard. *Love's Philosophy*. Lanham, MA: Roman and Littlefield, 2001.

Williams, Bernard. *Truth and Truthfulness*. Princeton, NJ: Princeton University Press, 2002.

Williams, Bernard. *Ethics and the Limits of Philosophy*. Cambridge, MA: Harvard University Press, 1985.

Williams, Bernard. "Persons, Character, and Morality." In *Moral Luck*, 20–39. Cambridge: Cambridge University Press, 1981, pb 1985.

Williams, Bernard. "A Critique of Utilitarianism." In *Utilitarianism: For and Against*, edited by J.J.C. Smart and Bernard Williams, 77–150. Cambridge: Cambridge University Press, 1973.

Williams, Charles. *All Hallows Eve*. New York: Pellegrini and Cudahy, 1948. Reprint, Grand Rapids: Eerdmans, 1981.

Wolf, Susan. "The True, the Good, and the Lovable: Frankfurt's Avoidance of Objectivity." In *Contours of Agency*, edited by Buss and Overton, 227–44.

Wolf, Susan. "Happiness and Meaning: Two Aspects of a Good Life." *Social Philosophy and Policy* 14 (1997), 207–25.

Wolf, Susan. "Sanity and the Metaphysics of Responsibility." In *Free Will*, 2nd edition, edited by Watson, 372–87.

Wolf, Susan. *Freedom Within Reason*. Oxford: Oxford University Press, 1990.

Yeats, William Butler. "For Anne Gregory." In *Eros, Agape, and Philia*, edited by A. Soble, 293. New York: Paragon House, 1989.

Index

Note: The letter "n" following locators refers to notes and locators with "f" and "ff" refer to following folios.